℘ROFILES of FAITH

THE RELIGIOUS BELIEFS OF EMINENT AMERICANS

C. BERNARD RUFFIN

✠ LIGUORI/TRIUMPH
Liguori, Missouri

LP796   206

Published by Liguori/Triumph
An Imprint of Liguori Publications
Liguori, Missouri

Library of Congress Cataloging-in-Publication Data

Ruffin, C. Bernard.
    Profiles of faith : the religious beliefs of eminent Americans / C. Bernard
Ruffin.
        p.   cm.
    Includes bibliographical references.
    ISBN 0-7648-0106-6
    1. Celebrities—United States—Religious life. 2. United States—Religion.
I. Title.
BL2525.R84   1997
200'.92'273—dc21   97-15972

Printed in the United States of America
01 00 99 98 97   5 4 3 2 1
First Edition

This book is dedicated to the glory of God and in pious and loving memory of my mother and of her sisters and niece—my aunts—the "Jones Sisters of Chambersburg," nearly all teachers and writers, who all provided instruction, encouragement, and assistance during the years of their earthly pilgrimage.

Blondine Jones Bruce (1898–1981)
Mary Jones Nightengale Carter (1902–1994)
Amy Jones Atkinson (1906–1981)
Carrie Elizabeth Jones (1908–1925)
    (whom I know only through her writings)
Lillian Jones Ruffin (1915–1963) My Mother
Eldora Jones White (1917–1994)
Louise Jones Hubbard (1919–1996)

Contents

Introduction

What did he believe? What were her religious beliefs? Trying to discover details from the available literature about the religious life of historical figures is usually much more difficult than discovering details about their political or material accomplishments, their personal idiosyncrasies, and, in recent years, their sex life. This book is written to remedy that situation by telling something of the religious convictions of some of the best-known players on the stage of American history.

It is perhaps best to begin by stating what this book is *not*. It is *not* about the men and women who have made the greatest spiritual impact on Western civilization. It is not about the persons judged to have been the greatest religious leaders in American history. The subjects of this book are, with very few exceptions, people whose chief contribution was in a field other than religion. It deals with politicians, scientists, businesspeople, actors, athletes, musicians, writers, and educators, and addresses the questions: What did they believe? What was their attitude toward religion? I have therefore set out to document what is known of the religious beliefs and spiritual values of eminent American celebrities of the past.

I am in no way attempting to designate these individuals as "the most religiously significant men and women of United States history." Some of these people, as will be readily evident, were not very religious at all. The criteria for selection are these: (1) the subjects are reasonably well known; (2) they were all American citizens or long-time residents; (3) they are dead; (4) there is sufficient material in existence about them to build a sketch that illuminates their religious principles.

With three or four exceptions, perhaps, I have carefully avoided clergy and religious, as well as people who wrote extensively on religion. The reader will therefore look in vain for sketches of such persons as Jonathan Edwards (who, since he died before American independence, was technically British anyway), Lyman and Henry Ward Beecher, Charles Grandison Finney, Harry Emerson Fosdick, Thomas Merton, Martin

Luther King, Jr., Malcolm X, and cardinals, bishops, and other church leaders. Many individuals of this sort have been the subject of massive volumes, the product of a lifetime of study, and to attempt to treat them here with the brevity that such sketches require would constitute a grave injustice to the work of these biographers. Some would question the inclusion of Dwight Lyman Moody, the nineteenth-century evangelist. He was included because (1) he was a layman, not a religious; and (2) he was, by his own vigorous insistence, not a theologian, and his message was deliberately very simple and straightforward and only minimally liable to interpretation.

Not included are those whose religious ideas are not clear. For example, some time was spent with biographies of a certain poet and the conclusion was reached that if scholars who have pored over the papers of this man for years could not agree as to what his religious beliefs were, I was certainly in no position to discern them.

An important factor determining inclusion in this book is the availability of source material, which tends to be more abundant the further back in time one goes. This is true, first, because of the fact that the longer one has been dead, the more time historians have had to collect, organize, and publish one's papers, and, second, because eighteenth- and nineteenth-century people tended to communicate their innermost thoughts in letters and diaries more often than people from the twentieth century, who tend to communicate such feelings, if they do at all, by telephone or e-mail. Because of this, the sketches of the earlier subjects tend to be substantial. Therefore, the reader should understand that the brevity of the sketches of most of the more recent subjects reflects, not haste nor disinterest, but the availability of material. For some of the recently deceased, however, it has been possible to locate and contact, through telephone or correspondence, individuals who actually knew the person concerned, who have been able to provide valuable insights not available through any printed source.

The sketches in this volume are arranged in strict chronological order, according to the year and month of birth, even if it means that husbands and wives (such as Abraham and Mary Lincoln) and groups of people normally considered together (such as Civil War leaders) may be separated. Some married couples are treated individually (for example, Franklin Roosevelt and Eleanor Roosevelt), and others are treated as a unit (for example, Andrew and Rachel Jackson). The sketches deal with the career of the subject only to the extent that it affected his or her religious beliefs, and thus the sketches presented here are not minibiographies, but, rather, portraits in faith.

Profile 1

Benjamin Franklin

Born: Boston, Massachusetts, January 17, 1706
Died: Philadelphia, Pennsylvania, April 17, 1790

B enjamin Franklin, journalist, scientist, inventor, and statesman, was easily the best-known American in Europe at the time of the American Revolution. A couple of decades after his death, his younger contemporary John Adams complained that Franklin and Washington were the only two fathers of independence whose names could still be recalled by the majority of the rising generation of schoolchildren.

The son of an English-born candlemaker and his second wife, Franklin was the fifteenth of seventeen children. He was baptized shortly after his birth in Boston's Old South Church, where his parents were active members. Although the elder Franklins raised Ben "piously," Franklin recalled in later years that he did not enjoy going to church, and, during family prayers at home, he taught himself geography by studying the maps on the wall while other family members were deep in devotion. When he was fifteen, Franklin began to "doubt of revelation itself,"[1] and, so began to proclaim himself a Deist.

Growing up in colonial Boston in the first quarter of the eighteenth century, young Franklin had, probably, only two meaningful religious options, Puritanism or Deism. These categories are not the names of denominations, but of religious philosophies. The Old South Church, like most other churches in Boston, was Congregationalist, founded by men who believed that society should be governed by practicing Christians who were members of congregations that chose their own ministers and were not subject to the control of king, bishop, or pope. Until about two decades before Franklin's birth, all political power in Massachusetts had been in the hands of the "saints" who were members of these congregations.

It was not easy to become a church member. In order to be accepted into membership, a candidate had to demonstrate that he had undergone an experience of divine illumination and that his life overflowed with a supernatural grace that translated itself not only into a personal knowledge of God but into good works. Prospective members had to undergo long periods of probation to test their sincerity. The elder Franklin, for example, had undergone a nine-year period of probation before he was invited to join the Old South Church.

Puritans, whose religious philosophy derived from the teaching of the sixteenth-century French reformer John Calvin, believed that human beings were born "totally depraved," incapable of any good, until baptism *and* conversion and enlightenment. Furthermore, Puritans usually taught that men and women could do nothing to bring about their salvation. Divine enlightenment was entirely the prerogative of God, who apparently did not will the salvation of all people, but rather predestined a goodly portion of his creation to the fires of hell.

In reaction to what they considered a grim doctrine, many of the younger generation in the early eighteenth century—especially intellectuals—embraced what came to be known as Deism. Deism took many forms. Some Deists believed that God created the universe and governed it; others held that God was an impersonal intelligence who set in motion the activity that resulted in the world and its creatures, and took no personal interest in individual men and women. Although some Deists believed in an afterlife and some did not, most rejected the idea that Jesus was God and almost all believed that knowledge about God was to be obtained through common sense—through reason, rather than revelation (that is, the authoritative word of Scripture or church).

The teenaged Franklin concluded that "revelation had indeed no weight with me." He concluded that various actions were "good" because they were beneficial to humankind, and others "bad" because they were harmful—not because they had been commanded or forbidden by some higher power. He also concluded that "truth, sincerity, and integrity in dealings with men were of the utmost importance to the felicity of life."[2]

At this point, Franklin stopped going to church. He rejected some Puritan doctrines, such as predestination to hell, but continued to believe in the existence of a "deity" who "made the world and governed it by his Providence." He never doubted that "our souls are immortal" or that "all crime will be punished and virtue rewarded, either here or hereafter." He held that "the most acceptable service of God was...doing good to man."[3]

At seventeen, Franklin moved from Boston to Philadelphia, where he established himself first as a printer, then as a scientist of international renown, and then as a political leader. There was far more religious diversity in Philadelphia than in Boston, and, in his twenties, Franklin concluded that the religious principles in which he believed were to be found in nearly all religions. He came to respect all faiths, although "with different degrees of respect." The trouble, he thought, with the various religious denominations was that they were all contaminated with human doctrines that obscured the essence of divine truth, and, while failing to "promote or confirm morality," these doctrines tended, instead, to "make us unfriendly to one another."[4]

Yet he wrote as a young man, "Since men are endued with reason superior to all other animals that we are in our world acquainted with, therefore I think it seems required of me, and my duty, as a man, to pay divine regards to something."[5] He started to attend a Presbyterian church. But he was dissatisfied with the minister, whose sermons were "either political arguments, or explications of the peculiar doctrines of our sect." They seemed to aim "to make us Presbyterians" rather than "good citizens."[6] And, so, after a time, Franklin stopped going to church altogether and devoted his Sundays to study.

Though he evidently rejected the divinity of Christ, Franklin nonetheless continued to believe in the resurrection of the body. This is evident in the epitaph he wrote for himself in 1728:

> The body of B. Franklin Printer (Like the cover of an old book its contents torn out and stript of its lettering & gilding) lies here, food for worms. But the work shall not be lost; for it will (as he believed) appear once more, in a new and more elegant edition revised and corrected, by the Author.[7]

However, Franklin's religion, at this time, largely consisted of an attempt to achieve moral perfection through his own effort. He drew up a chart of thirteen virtues that he considered necessary: temperance, silence, order, resolution, frugality, industry, sincerity, justice, moderation, cleanliness, tranquillity, chastity, and humility. His definition of chastity was not indulging in sexual activity except for health or offspring, and his idea of humility was to "imitate Jesus and Socrates,"[8] both of whom he evidently placed on the same level.

Franklin conceded that "on the whole," he never "arrived at the perfection" he had "been so ambitious of obtaining," and, indeed, "fell far short of it." Yet he felt that the effort made him "a better and happier man than I otherwise should have been."[9]

Late in 1745, the British sent troops to capture the strategic French fort of Louisburg in Nova Scotia. One of Franklin's brothers was a part of the expedition that was dispatched from Boston. In a letter to him the following year, Franklin expressed his doubts concerning the efficacy of prayer: "You have a fast and prayer day [to ensure victory] in which I compute five hundred thousand petitions were offered up to the same effect in New England...which, set against the prayers of a few priests in the garrison, to the Virgin Mary, give a vast balance in your favor. If you do not succeed, I fear I shall have but an indifferent opinion of Presbyterian prayers, in such cases, as long as I live."[10] Incidentally, the British did capture Louisburg.

By this time Franklin had become acquainted with George Whitefield, the young Church of England minister who had come to America several years before to begin preaching to crowds "in the open air."[11] Until his death at fifty-six in 1770, Whitefield crossed the Atlantic seven times and traveled the length and breadth of the British colonies in America, often preaching forty to sixty times a week, usually out-of-doors, sometimes to crowds of as many as fifty thousand people.

Like Franklin, he was concerned about the deadness of American churches. However, instead of Franklin's philosophy of reason and good works, Whitefield urged his hearers toward that experience of rebirth that the Puritan leaders of the Boston of Franklin's youth had deemed essential. So many people throughout the colonies experienced religious conversions that the revivals led by Whitefield and other preachers have come to be known as the Great Awakening.

Franklin first met the twenty-five-year-old Whitefield in 1739. The Deist was curious as to why people were attracted to Whitefield, since he believed that he "abused them" by convincing them that "they were naturally half beasts and half devils." But Franklin was amazed at the effect of Whitefield's preaching: "From being thoughtless or indifferent about religion, it seemed as if all the world were growing religious, so that one could not walk through the town in an evening without hearing psalms sung in different families of every street."[12]

Franklin attended several of Whitefield's meetings. The clergyman was soliciting donations for an orphanage in Georgia. Franklin later wrote, "I silently resolved he should get nothing from me." Franklin had in his pocket a number of copper coins, three or four silver dollars, and five gold pieces. As Whitefield preached, Franklin found, to his amazement, that his resolution was beginning to soften. He "concluded to give the coppers." Then, "another stroke of his oratory made me ashamed of that, and determined me to give the silver; and he finished so admirably, that I emptied my pocket wholly into the collector's dish, gold and all."[13]

Franklin came to respect Whitefield. At least once, the preacher stayed in the Franklin home. Although he did not then accept everything that he proclaimed, Franklin was convinced that Whitefield was "perfectly honest," and even offered to print his sermons and tracts. However, Franklin later wrote, "He used, indeed, sometimes to pray for my conversion, but never had the satisfaction of believing that his prayers were heard."[14]

Whether because of the effect of Whitefield or owing to other influences, Franklin seems to have moved closer to orthodox Christianity as he became older. When he was eighty-one, he was a delegate to the Constitutional Convention. After several days of acrimonious debate, he moved that the convention open its sessions with prayer. Forty years earlier, he had made light of the power of prayer. Now he told his quarreling colleagues that the disappointing progress they had achieved to date was "proof of the imperfection of the human understanding." He noted how the delegates had "gone back to ancient history for models of government" and had "viewed modern states all around Europe" without finding any "suitable to our circumstances." Addressing the chairman, George Washington, Franklin asked, "How has it happened, Sir, that we have not hither to once thought of hum-

bly applying to the Father of Lights to illuminate our understandings?"
He went on to say:

> I have lived, Sir, a long time, and the longer I live, the more
> convincing proofs I see of this truth: that God governs in
> the affairs of men. And if a sparrow cannot fall to the ground
> without his notice, is it probable that an empire can rise
> without his aid?...I...believe that without his concurring
> aid we shall succeed in this political building no better than
> the builders of Babel.[15]

Only three or four members were in favor of getting a local minister to
pray, and the motion was never voted on.

Almost three years later, Franklin replied to Ezra Stiles, president of
Yale, who asked to know something about his religion. He wrote:

> Here is my creed. I believe in one God, creator of the Uni-
> verse. That he governs it by his Providence. That he ought
> to be worshiped. That the most acceptable service we
> render to him is in doing good to his other children. That
> the soul of man is immortal, and will be treated with justice
> in another life respecting its conduct in this. These I take to
> be the fundamental principles of all sound religion, and I
> regard them as you do in whatever sect I meet with them....[16]

As he grew older, Franklin came to the belief that the affairs of men
and nations are governed by the hand of an almighty God. He looked
forward to heaven and wrote a friend, "We shall never suffer from the
gout there nor from our nerves....Ambition, envy, pretensions, jealousy, prejudices...will vanish at the sound of the trumpet. Every day
we shall love one another in order that we may love another still more
the day after; in a word, we shall be completely happy."[17] Franklin
seems never to have resolved his questions concerning the divinity of
Christ. In his letter to Stiles, he said: "As to Jesus of Nazareth, my opinion of whom you particularly desire, I think the system of morals and
his religion, as he left them to us, the best the world ever saw or is
likely to see, but I apprehend it has received various corrupting changes,
and I have...some doubts as to his divinity; though it is a question I do

not dogmatize upon, having never studied it, and I think it needless to busy myself with it now, when I expect soon an opportunity of knowing the truth with less trouble."[18] Still unable to make up his mind concerning Jesus, Franklin, who was then on his deathbed, trusted in the mercies of a good and wise God to bring him to the knowledge of the truth, whatever it was.

During his last illness, Franklin kept a picture of the Last Judgment at the foot of his bed, instructing his family to keep the picture where it was always in his view. On April 17, at the age of eighty-four, he died. For many months he had suffered great pain, but, just before the end, remarked, "These pains will soon be over. They are for my good. What are the pains of a moment compared with the pleasures of eternity?"

～

Profile 2

George Washington

Born: Westmoreland Co., Virginia, February 22, 1732
Died: Mount Vernon, Virginia, December 14, 1799

Ever since the Father of his Country breathed his last, oceans of ink have been expended on the subject of his religious beliefs. Over the years, some have insisted that Washington was an evangelical, born-again Christian; others have described him as a Deist who believed in an impersonal god and rejected the divinity of Christ; one tradition even holds that he was secretly a Roman Catholic.[1]

Washington's religious beliefs might be clearer if the letters that he exchanged with his wife had survived. It has been assumed that General and Lady Washington had a mutual agreement that, when one of them died, the survivor would burn all their correspondence. Unlike John, Abigail, and John Quincy Adams, and Thomas Jefferson, who expressed their ideas on religious subjects in letters that they copied and saved, Washington seems to have been a much more private person who felt that his personal affairs—including his religious beliefs—were of no concern to the world.

We do know something about Washington's religious practices from surviving documents. Like most substantial Virginians, he was baptized into the Church of England. He would remain until his death affiliated with that denomination, which, after independence, became the Protestant Episcopal Church. For more than twenty years, from the time Washington was thirty-one until he was fifty-two, he served as a vestryman in the Truro Parish in northern Virginia. In those days, the vestry was responsible for such things as imposing parish taxes, relief to the needy, determining the physical boundaries of the parish, supervising the construction and repair of churches, and hiring and paying clergy. Before the Revolution, Washington worshiped at the Pohick Church, some seven miles from Mount Vernon, where, in keeping with the custom of the day, he bought a pew. During the early 1780s, he does not seem to have attended church regularly. In 1785, he joined Christ Church in what is now downtown Alexandria.

While he was president, he attended church regularly. The first year of his administration (1789–1790), when the federal capital was in New York City, Washington attended St. Paul's Chapel and Trinity Church. After the government moved to Philadelphia, the president worshiped either at Christ Church or St. Peter's. All four churches were Episcopalian.

Although he was an Episcopalian, Washington's diaries reveal that, in the course of the years, he occasionally worshiped at churches of other denominations. For instance, in October 1774, just before the Revolution, while in Philadelphia, he "went to the Presbyterian meeting in the forenoon and the Romish [Roman Catholic] Church in the afternoon."[2] The diary also mentions occasional attendance at Congregational and German Reformed churches. Washington's wife's grandson, George Washington Parke Custis, recalled that the general was "always a strict and decorous observer of the Sabbath," who invariably "attended divine service once a day when within reach of a place of worship."[3] However, after retiring to Mount Vernon, Washington, in the last two years of his life, stopped going to church regularly. About once a month he went to Christ Church, but claimed that since the church was nine miles away, it was not practical to attend, and spent most Sundays reading and answering mail.[4]

Washington's step-granddaughter, Eleanor Parke Custis, recalled that "no one in church attended to the services with more reverential respect."[5] In keeping with eighteenth-century custom, the general rarely, if ever, took Communion, even though his wife received the sacrament whenever it was offered.[6]

Mrs. Custis also recalled that "during the devotional parts of the service," while most parishioners knelt, Washington stood. Whether this was due to theological considerations or to the fact that the general, who was in his sixties when Custis remembered him, found kneeling painful is not clear.

Certainly there exist numerous anecdotes that show that Washington knelt in prayer earlier in life. Mason Locke Weems, one of Washington's earliest biographers, a writer who is not generally renowned for his care in separating fact from gossip, recounted the story of a Quaker, Isaac Potts, with whom Washington was staying, who, during the winter encampment at Valley Forge in 1777–1778, stumbled, one wintry day, upon Washington, who was kneeling in prayer in the snow. On July 4, 1859, a ninety-nine-year-old Revolutionary War veteran named Anthony Sherman told a reporter for the *National Tribune* that during the war Washington often went "into the thicket" to pray and "he used often to pray in secret for aid and comfort from God."[7] A Mrs. Watkins, who claimed that Washington lodged with her family for a time during the Revolution, recalled that she and her sister used to eavesdrop on Washington as he prayed aloud in his room, until their father caught them and made them stop.[8] An unnamed cousin of Washington, interviewed, like the other witnesses quoted here, years after Washington's death, insisted that he knelt alone in prayer in his room between nine and ten each night. The informant knew this because one evening he looked through the keyhole and saw the general kneeling on the floor with an open Bible in front of him.[9]

Washington said grace before and after meals. A former slave, identified only as Juba, interviewed years after his master's death, insisted that the Washingtons made the sign of the cross when they blessed the table.[10]

That religion was important to Washington is evident by his order (no doubt written by an aide but approved by him) directing the appointment of paid chaplains. This order was issued on July 9, 1776, and in it, he insisted that "all inferior officers and soldiers pay them a suitable respect." The chaplains were to see to it that the men "attend carefully upon religious exercises." Washington insisted, "The blessing and protection of Heaven are at all times necessary, but especially so in times of public distress and danger."[11]

Not only did Washington order his men to attend religious services, he, from time to time, ordered days of fasting, humiliation, and prayer after defeats, and issued proclamations of thanksgiving after victories. After the surrender of British general John Burgoyne, Washington issued this order: "Let every face brighten and every heart expand with grateful joy and praise to the Supreme disposer of all events, who has granted us this signal success. The chaplains of the army are to prepare short discourses, suited to the joyful occasion, to deliver to their several corps and brigades at 5 o'clock this afternoon."[12] When word reached him that the alliance with France had been approved, Washington issued the following order: "It having pleased the Almighty ruler of the Universe propitiously to defend the cause of the United American States and finally by raising up a powerful friend among the princes of the earth [Louis XVI of France] to establish our liberty and independence upon lasting foundations, it becomes us to set apart a day for gratefully acknowledging the Divine Goodness and celebrating the important event which we owe to his benign interposition."[13] Again, after American independence was made all but certain with the surrender of Charles Cornwallis at Yorktown, the commander in chief proclaimed on October 20, 1781: "Divine Service is to be performed tomorrow in the several brigades or divisions. The commander in chief earnestly recommends that the troops not on duty should universally attend with that seriousness of deportment and gratitude of heart which the recognition of such reiterated and astounding interpositions of Providence demand of us."[14]

Washington also forbade his soldiers to use foul language. Denouncing the "foolish and wicked practice of profane cursing and swearing," in an order dated August 3, 1776, Washington directed his soldiers to reflect that they had few grounds to hope for "the blessing of Heaven on our arms, if we insult it by our impiety and folly."[15]

When Washington assumed the office of president on April 30, 1789, in his inaugural address he called on the help of God. "It would be peculiarly improper to omit in this first official act," he said, "my fervent supplications to that Almighty Being who rules over the universe, who presides in the councils of nations, and whose providential aids can supply every human defect, that his benediction may consecrate to the liberties and happiness of the people of the United States a Government instituted by themselves for these essential purposes, and may enable every instrument employed in its administration to execute with success the functions allotted to his charge." Continuing to speak of "the Great Author of every public and private good," the president declared that people of the United States were especially bound to be grateful to "the Invisible Hand which conducts the affairs of men." Every step by which the United States took shape was "distinguished by some token" of divine intervention, not the least, the peaceful adoption of the new Constitution, which had been ratified not without substantial opposition.[16] Going on, Washington insisted that "the propitious smiles of Heaven can never be expected on a nation that disregards the eternal rules of order and right which Heaven itself has ordained." Concluding, he declared, "I shall take my present leave; but not without resorting once more to the benign Parent of the Human Race in humble supplication that, since he has been pleased to favor the American people with opportunities for deliberating in perfect tranquillity...so his divine blessing may be equally conspicuous in the enlarged views, the temperate consultations, and the wise measures on which the success of this Government must depend."[17]

There was no annual thanksgiving holiday in Washington's time, but the president twice proclaimed days of thanksgiving, on which all Americans were enjoined to give thanks to God for a particular grace. The first thanksgiving day was proclaimed on October 3, 1789, to commemorate the adoption of the Constitution. Washington decreed: "Whereas it is the duty of all nations to acknowledge the providence of Almighty God, to obey his will and to be grateful for his benefits, and humbly to implore his protection and favor...[n]ow therefore I do recommend and assign Thursday the 26th day of November next to be devoted by the people of these states to the service of that great and glorious Being, who is the beneficent Author of all good that was, that is, or that will be."[18]

In 1794, riots broke out on the western frontier over taxes recently imposed on whiskey, disorders that challenged the authority of the new government. When, through a show of military force, the rebellion was ended bloodlessly, Washington proclaimed a second thanksgiving day to celebrate the end of the insurrection and also America's successful preservation of neutrality during the war between France and Britain.

In his *Farewell Address* (written by Alexander Hamilton, but corrected and approved by the president), Washington declared that America could not enjoy political prosperity without the "indispensable supports" of "religion and morality," which were necessary for "private and public felicity." Moreover, he maintained, morality cannot be maintained without religion. The "national morality," he contended, could not "prevail in exclusion of religious principle."[19]

Washington was tolerant of expressions of religious faith that were different from his own. He believed that Christians had the right to choose the form of worship most suitable to their individual tastes and sensibilities. Writing to his friend, the Marquis de Lafayette, he explained, "Being no bigot myself to any mode of worship, I am disposed to indulge the Professors of Christianity in the church that road to heaven which seems to them the most direct, plainest, easiest, and least liable to exception."[20] During his presidency, Washington wrote to one Sir Edward Newenhem on October 20, 1792, expressing his horror of sectarian conflict: "Of all the animosities which have existed among mankind, those which are caused by a difference of sentiments in religion appear to be the most inveterate and distressing, and ought most to be deprecated. I was in hopes that the enlightened and liberal policy which has marked the present age would at least have reconciled Christians of every denomination so far, that we should never again see their religious disputes carried to such a pitch as to endanger the peace of society."[21]

Shortly after his appointment as commander in chief of the Continental Army, Washington issued an order, November 5, 1775, forbidding his men to celebrate Guy Fawkes Day, or "Pope's Night," by burning a dummy of the pope. This holiday celebrated the thwarting of plans by Roman Catholic extremists in the early 1600s to blow up the British Parliament. In his order, Washington deplored "that ridiculous and childish custom of burning the effigy of the pope." Since the colonists were then seeking the cooperation of the people of Canada, who were then mostly Roman Catholic, Washington insisted that "to be insulting to their religion is so monstrous as not to be suffered or excused...."[22] While the commander's decision may have been at least partially motivated by political considerations, the beautiful blessing Washington later bestowed on the Hebrew Congregation of Savannah, Georgia, was evidently prompted only by a spirit of tolerance: "May the same wonder-working Deity, who long since delivering the Hebrews from their Egyptian oppressors planted them in the promised land...still continue to water them with the dews of Heaven and to make the inhabitants of every denomination participate in the temporal and spiritual blessings of that people whose God is Jehovah."[23]

Some have pointed out that Washington's religious statements are usually vague, and that he almost never mentions Jesus in his formal declarations, or even in his surviving correspondence. Most of those who knew Washington well and left written recollections agree that, in conversation, the general seldom talked about his religious beliefs or referred much to Christ.

Bishop William White, who was rector of Christ Church in Philadelphia and who served as chaplain to Congress during the time Washington was president (and Philadelphia was the capital), recounted: "I do not believe that any degree of recollection will bring to my mind any fact which would prove General Washington to have been a believer in the Christian revelations further than as may be hoped from his constant attendance on Christian worship."[24]

Likewise, Dr. James Abercrombie, who also served as pastor of Christ Church in Philadelphia, expressed reservations about Washington's faith because of his failure to take Communion: "That Washington was a professing Christian is evident from his regular attendance in our church; but...I cannot consider any man as a real Christian who uniformly disregards an ordinance so solemnly enjoined by the divine Author of our holy religion, and considered as a channel of divine grace."[25] Washington's grandchildren recalled that on Sacrament Sunday the general would go home and then send the carriage back for Lady Washington, who would remain to commune.

James Madison, who served with Washington as a delegate at the Constitutional Convention and who was a congressman from Virginia during Washington's tenure as president, recalled in later years that Washington was not well-read in theology and apparently accepted the tenets of his church without questioning them. He had never studied "the arguments for Christianity" or "the different systems of religion," and therefore Madison doubted that Washington "had formed definite opinions on the subject," so "he took these things as he found them existing, and was constant in his observance of worship according to the received forms of the Episcopal Church in which he was brought up."[26]

Washington seldom referred to God as "God," and almost never as "the Lord." He liked to use expressions such as "the Beneficent Author of All Good," "the Supreme Disposer of All Events," or "the Great Author of Every Public and Private Good." Some regard this as an indication that Washington did not believe in a personal God. Washington's inclinations to use what might be called euphemisms for God may well have resulted from a sense of awe and a reluctance to speak with familiarity of the "Almighty Being" before whom even presidents, generals, and masters of plantations are but as specks of dust.

There is, in fact, evidence that Washington did believe in the divinity of Christ. In a circular letter to America's thirteen governors, written from his headquarters in Newburgh, New York, in June 1783, Washington mentions "the Divine Author of our blessed religion," declaring that, without "an humble imitation" of his example, "we can never hope to be a happy Nation."[27] Again, a few years earlier, on May 12, 1779, he exhorted a delegation of Delaware Indians: "You will do well to wish to learn our way of life, and, above all, the religion of Jesus Christ. These will make you a greater and happier people than you are."[28]

A letter written to his brother, John Augustine, on the death of the latter's son in 1783, expressed Washington's need to submit at all times to the will of God. "It is a loss I sincerely regret," he wrote, "but it is the will of Heaven, whose decrees are always just and wise; I submit to it without a murmur." He spoke further of how the will of heaven "is not to be controverted or scrutinized by the children of this world" and how it "becomes the Creatures of it to submit with patience and resignation to the will of the creator, whether it be to prolong or to shorten the number of days."[29]

Although there is no indication whether Washington believed in hell, it seems clear that he did believe in heaven. In a couple of letters, written late in life, he refers to his imminent departure to "the land of the spirits" and "the world of the spirits." When his mother died in 1789, he wrote to his sister of his "hope that she is translated to a happier place."[30] In April 1790, he wrote to the General Assembly of Virginia that he was thinking of "that awful moment, when I must bid adieu to "Sublunary [i.e., earthly] scenes" and mentioned his desire for happiness "hereafter in a brighter world."[31]

George Washington bade adieu to sublunary scenes on the night of December 14, 1799. According to adulatory biographer Mason "Parson" Weems, the dying statesman told his weeping physician, "O no! Don't! Don't! I am dying, gentlemen, but thank God, I am not afraid to die." The last thing he said was, "Father of mercies! Take me to thyself."[32] Weems' account of Washington's deathbed conversation is not supported by the journal of Tobias Lear, the general's secretary, whose description of Washington's passing is considered definitive by nearly all biographers.

According to Lear, Washington said nothing during the last day of his life to indicate that he was thinking of religion. In fact, he seemed to be concerned about business matters. To Lear he said, "I find I am going. My breath cannot continue long, I believed from the first attack it would be fatal. Do you arrange and record all my late military letters and papers—arrange my accounts and settle my books, as you know more about them than anyone else, and let Mr. Rawlins finish recording my other letters, which he has begun."[33] Then he told Lear, "I am just going. Have me decently buried, and do not let my body be put into the vault in less than three days after I am dead."[34]

What is interesting about Washington's passing is that there is no indication that any clergyman was summoned. When Lady Washington died two years later, a pastor was present to administer Holy Communion. Perhaps the absence of a clergyman at Washington's bedside reflects nothing more than the nature of his death, which happened very suddenly, less than thirty-six hours after he complained of being ill. By the time the critical nature of his condition was apparent, it may have been too late for a minister to reach his bedside.

There are some, however, who believe that Washington became disaffected with his church in later years. Even though he was not ill, he seldom attended after he left the presidency. He last attended on November 17, 1799 (a month before he died), but had not been present before that time since May. It is said that Washington had become angry with the rector for preaching a sermon decrying his failure to take Communion.[35]

It is believed by some that Washington failed to send for an Episcopal clergyman because he had secretly become a Roman Catholic. This was an idea popular among a number of Roman Catholic journalists in the nineteenth century. They pointed to the fact that once he contributed fifty dollars—a very large sum in those days—to a Roman Catholic church in Philadelphia and to the fact that he apparently gave to other charities associated with the church.[36] They pointed to a tradition that the Washingtons kept above the head of their bed in Mount Vernon a painting of the Immaculate Conception of Our Lady and took it with them wherever they went.[37] They pointed to the fact that one or more former slaves expressed the opinion that the general was Roman Catholic,[38] and to the tradition that one Father Leonard Neale visited Washington four hours before he died and then sent a "secret packet" to Rome.[39]

Most of these claims cannot be substantiated. Washington did have some Roman Catholic friends. He attended Roman Catholic services at least twice during his life, including a High Mass. He may have occasionally contributed generously to Roman Catholic churches and charities. He also banned, as we have seen, the desecration of the image of the pope on Guy Fawkes Day, but evidently this was as much for practical considerations as it was out of sympathy for the Church of Rome. According to the inventory of his estate, he did own a painting of the Virgin Mary, as well as one of Saint John. There is no indication that the painting was of the Immaculate Conception. In fact, the doctrine was not formally proclaimed until years after Washington's death. There is no documentation to indicate where in Mount Vernon the painting of Mary was displayed. Some former slaves may have believed that Washington was Roman Catholic, but there is no reason to believe that these people, deprived entirely of education, were in a position to distinguish Roman Catholicism from other liturgical expressions of the Christian faith. Washington's surviving diaries fail to mention anyone by the name of Leonard Neale. Of course, Washington would not have made an entry the day of his death, but it would seem unlikely that, on his dying bed, he would have sent for a stranger. Neither Lear nor anyone else who claimed to be at or near Washington's deathbed spoke or wrote of Neale or any other clergyman. Moreover, no secret packet relative to Washington's conversion has ever been located in the Vatican Archives or elsewhere.

Washington's familiarity with Roman Catholic ritual would not likely have come from his association with the Episcopal church. Since the nineteenth century, there have been numerous "high Episcopalians" or "Anglo-Catholics" in America, who have many ritual and liturgical practices in common with Roman Catholics. But the Episcopalians of eighteenth-century Virginia are believed to have been "low"; their services were relatively simple and "protestant" in form. Washington's religious beliefs, however, are likely to have been influenced by his association with the Freemasons, in which he had been active since the age of twenty. As in the case of his religious beliefs, there is little in Washington's surviving writings to indicate how he felt about being a Mason. In Newport, Rhode Island, in 1789, he spoke to King David's Lodge and said that he was "persuaded that a just application for the principals on which the Masonic fraternity is founded, must be promotive of private virtue and public prosperity."[40] He said about Freemasonry virtually the same thing he said about religion and its effect on the public good.

It is also recorded that on December 27, 1778, Washington, then commander in chief of the Continental Army, attended a Masonic ceremonial at Christ Church in Philadelphia for "the anniversary of St. John the Evangelist."[41] (Perhaps the painting he had of St. John had something to do with Freemasonry.) It is known that Washington also took pride in a Masonic apron made for him by Roman Catholic nuns in Nantes, France.[42] These two insignificant scraps of information suggest that Washington's apparent affinity for Roman Catholicism might actually have been related to his association with the Masonic Order. One of the reasons why the Roman Catholic Church condemned Freemasonry was because the Lodge preserved elements of traditional worship without subscribing to the Church's specific doctrines. Familiarity with these rituals may have made Washington more knowledgeable of and sympathetic to Roman Catholicism than many of his contemporaries. Because the Masonic Order is a "secret society," it is probably impossible to know the extent to which Washington was influenced by Masonic beliefs. If his familiarity with Roman Catholic rites and rituals was not a result of his association with Freemasonry, his religious tolerance may well have been.

Washington was certainly not an evangelical Christian in the modern sense of the word. Although an aged Revolutionary War veteran insisted that Washington had a vision of the Virgin Mary at Valley Forge, there is no solid evidence of any "intimacy" with God. He was not, however, a Deist in any meaningful sense, inasmuch as he seems to have believed in the divinity of Christ and the revelation of God's will through the Bible. He nowhere speaks of his faith as being defined by "reason." Although he seems to have adhered to most of those points on which all Christians agree, he seems to have taken pains to avoid those which divided.

George Washington might best be described as a minimalist Christian, a basic Christian, who belonged to the Episcopal Church, but who was not averse to worshiping in churches of other denominations; who believed strongly in prayer, in the active intervention of a just and merciful God in the lives of men, women, and nations; who insisted on the necessity of submitting to the will of God and living by the Bible's moral code; but who shied away from all theological and denominational specificities.

～

Profile 3

John Adams

Born: Braintree, Massachusetts, October 30, 1735
Died: Quincy, Massachusetts, July 4, 1826

The acerbic and outspoken Massachusetts attorney, who helped prepare the Declaration of Independence, who served as a negotiator of the Treaty of Paris of 1783 which secured the recognition of American independence, and who became his country's second president, once wrote his wife, "I never write or talk upon divinity. I have had more than I could do of humanity."[1] In making this statement, he was not accurate. Happily, for subsequent generations, he and his wife, Abigail, preserved nearly all the letters they received and copied nearly every one they sent. Adams's correspondence reveals that he, in fact, said and wrote a great deal about divinity.

Like many of his contemporaries, Adams was a Deist who believed that reason, rather than Scriptures or church tradition, was the primary key to understanding God. In a letter to Thomas Jefferson on September 14, 1813, he made this clear: "The human understanding is a revelation from its Maker which can never be disputed or doubted. There can be no skepticism...incredulity or infidelity here. No prophecies, no miracles are necessary to prove this celestial communication. This revelation has made it certain that two and one make three; and that one is not three; nor can three be one. We can never be so certain of prophecy, or the fulfillment of any prophecy; or of a miracle.... Miracles or prophecies might frighten us out of our wits; might scare us to death; might induce us to lie; to say that we believed that 2 and 2 make 5. But we should not believe it. We should know the contrary."[2]

What convinced Adams of the existence of God was "the amazing harmony of our solar system...the stupendous plan of operation" designed by God.[3] "What now can preserve this prodigious variety of species and this inflexible uniformity among the individuals," he wrote, "but the continual and vigilant providence of God?"[4]

Reason impelled Adams to reject the Athanasian Creed, which was

19

the basis of nearly all Christian denominations and which formulated the doctrine of the Trinity. No miracle, no revelation, he claimed, could ever convince him to go against common sense to accept a doctrine which stated that three is one and one is three.

Reason also compelled Adams to reject the idea of hell. In a letter to Jefferson, Adams exclaimed: "Can prophecies or miracles convince you or me that divine benevolence, wisdom, and power created and preserves, for a time, innumerable millions to make them miserable forever, for his own Glory?"[5]

Likewise he dismissed the idea of a devil. He claimed that the notion of Satan came from a misinterpretation of the second epistle of Peter and the epistle of Jude. Writing to Jefferson in 1814, he said: "That there is such a person as the devil is not part of my faith, nor that of many other Christians; nor am I sure it was the belief of any of the [New Testament] writers. Neither do I believe the doctrine of demoniacal possessions, whether it was believed by the sacred writers or not; and yet my unbelief in these articles does not affect my faith in the great facts of which the Evangelists were eye and ear witnesses. They might not be competent judges in the one case, though perfectly so with respect to the other."[6] It was, of course, through reason that Adams could determine when the New Testament was trustworthy and when it was not.

Adams also rejected belief in the divinity of Jesus, declaring in a letter to his son John Quincy: "An incarnate God!! An eternal, self-existent, omnipotent, omniscient author of a stupendous universe, suffering on a cross!!! My soul starts with horror at the idea, and it has stupefied the Christian world. It has been the source of almost all the corruptions of Christianity."[7]

Despite these denials, John Adams nonetheless insisted that he was a Christian. Lashing out against Calvinists and Athanasians (believers in the Trinity), he exclaimed to Jefferson: "Howl, snarl, bite, ye Calvinistic, ye Athanasian divines, if you will. Ye will say I am not a Christian. I say ye are no Christians, and there the account is balanced."[8]

Adams believed that the great cultures of the world should share their religious traditions. He hoped that his grandchildren would study the sacred writings of the Hindus, the Persians, and the Chinese, and that eventually people all over the world, familiar with each tradition, would "compare notes and hold fast to all that is good."[9]

Yet he wrote to his friend and fellow signer of the Declaration of Independence, Benjamin Rush: "The Christian religion, as I understand it is the brightness of the glory and the express portrait of the eternal, self-existent, independent, benevolent, all-powerful and all-merciful creator, preserver, and father of the universe....It will last as long as the world....Ask me not whether I am Catholic or Protestant, Calvinist, or Armenian. As far as they are Christian, I wish to be a fellow disciple with them all."[10] On another occasion, Adams wrote: "The Christian religion is above all the religions that ever prevailed or existed in ancient and modern times, the religion of wisdom, virtue, equity, and humanity....[I]t is resignation to God, it is goodness itself to man."[11] He told Jefferson that "the fundamental principal of...all Christianity is, 'Rejoice always in all things. Be thankful at all times for all good and all that we call evil.'"[12] Christianity, he maintained, brought "the great principle of the law of nature and nations—love your neighbor as yourself, and do to others as you would have that others do to you."[13]

Adams said very little about Jesus in his writings, but seems to have held that he was the greatest philosopher of all time. While earlier sages had been unable to overcome "[p]rejudice, custom, passion, and bigotry," Jesus had "awakened mankind to truth."[14]

For John Adams, as for Thomas Jefferson (as we shall shortly see), Christianity was a philosophy, a system of ethics. When Jefferson compiled a biography of Jesus by blending the Gospels and throwing out everything that smacked of the supernatural, Adams approved.[15] When, however, Thomas Paine, in his *The Age of Reason,* not only rejected the divinity of Christ and the inerrancy of Scripture, but scrapped the entire Bible, Adams was aghast and referred to the pamphleteer as a "blackguard." Adams wanted to interpret the Scriptures in light of reason, but he did not want to reject them. He wanted to reverence Jesus as a wise man, but not as God incarnate. Writing to Benjamin Rush on February 2, 1807, Adams explained: "The Bible contains the most profound philosophy, the most perfect morality, and the most refined policy that was ever conceived upon the earth. It is the most republican book in the world, and therefore I revere it."[16]

When at home in Quincy, Massachusetts, Adams spent morning and afternoon Sundays in the First Congregational Church, of which he was a member, and spent the rest of the Sabbath reading and reflecting on the Christian faith, at least as he understood it. When he was vice president, in New York and then in Philadelphia, and when he was president, he generally attended an Episcopal church. The seat of government was moved to Washington, D.C., only during the last months of his term as president, and there is no indication where or whether he worshiped publicly. Adams found the Episcopal service "more cheerful and comfortable" than the Congregational and Presbyterian rites. The ritual, which in those days was simple, or "low," was "very humane and benevolent, and sometimes pathetic and affecting."[17] He hated elaborate ritual, and after visiting a "Romish [Roman Catholic] chapel," he expressed his dislike at what he saw: "Poor wretches fingering their beads" and "chanting Latin, not a word of which they understood." He was surprised, however, by the power of the Mass. He found the sermon "sensible" and was carried away by the "exquisitely soft and sweet" music, and mused, "I am amazed that Luther and Calvin were ever able to break the charm and dissolve the spell."[18]

Hierarchies and formal creeds drew Adams's utter contempt. He wrote Jefferson: "The question before the human race is whether the God of nature shall govern the world by his own laws, or whether priests and kings shall rule it by fictitious miracles. Or, in other words, whether authority is originally in the people, or whether it has descended for 1800 years in a succession of popes and bishops, or brought down from heaven by the Holy Ghost in the form of a dove in a phial of holy oil."[19]

Adams felt that one of the greatest virtues of Christianity was that it was accessible to everyone and that matters of morality could be interpreted by children, servants, women, and men.[19] Accordingly, he held professional theologians in indignant contempt for obfuscating the simple moral teachings of Jesus. Christianity, he said, was intended not to make people "good riddle-solvers, or good mystery-mongers, but good men, good magistrates, and good subjects, good husbands and good wives, good parents and good children, good masters and good servants."[20]

Adams had a strong antipathy for the Roman Catholic Church in general and for the Jesuit Order in particular, of which he wrote, "This society has been a greater calamity to mankind than the French Revolution or Napoleon's despotism" because it obstructed the "improvement of the human mind."[21] In later years, he was obsessed by the fear that the Jesuits were going to take advantage of America's religious liberty to infiltrate and ultimately take over the country. In an almost paranoical mood, he wrote his son John Quincy in May 1816: "We shall have Jesuits in all shapes in America...as Federalists and Republicans, in the shape of monarchists and democrats. We shall have Jesuits as Calvinists and Arminians, as Unitarians and Athanasians, as philosophers and men of letters, as editors of newspapers and printers...."[22] He wrote Jefferson that Jesuits in the United States were "more numerous than anybody knows."[23]

Adams, in fact, seemed to distrust all Christian denominations. In a letter to Jefferson on May 18, 1817, Adams, who was in his early eighties, raged, "Do you know that the Church of England is employing more means and more art, to propagate their demipopery among us than ever? Quakers, Anabaptists, Moravians, Swedenborgians, Methodists, Unitarians, Nothingarians in all Europe are employing underhand means to propagate their sectarian system in these states." Even though one might argue that "the multitude and diversity" of these sects constituted America's protection from them, Adams feared that men like George Whitefield, Ignatius Loyola, or Muhammad might arise, unite most Americans, and destroy religious freedom by persecuting dissenting minorities.[24] Not only did he fear that orthodox Christians would persecute the Deists, but given the opportunity, the Deists would "persecute the Christians, and atheists would persecute Deists with as unrelenting cruelty as any Christians would persecute them or one another."[25]

Throughout his life, Adams speculated about the origins of the universe. Ultimately, he concluded that "there is now, never will be, and never was but one being who can understand the universe [that is, God] and that "it is not only vain but wicked for insects to pretend to comprehend it."[26] He believed that "God has infinite wisdom, goodness, and power. He created the universe. His duration is eternal....His presence is as extensive as space."[27] The universe, Adams held, contained millions of planets with intelligent life, and he speculated that humans could not argue about the relationship of such beings to God until "it is proven at least probable that all these species of rational beings have revolted from their rightful sovereign."[28] He also believed that God could easily suspend the laws that he had created and thus Adams had no objections to the miracles of Jesus, even though he denied his divinity and seemed to reject most of the miracles recorded in the Scriptures."[29]

Adams admitted that God's actions are not always comprehensible. Writing to Rush on July 23, 1806, he said: "God throws empires and kingdoms as he does rains, plagues, earthquakes, storms, sunshine, good and evil, in a manner that we cannot comprehend, and, as far as we can see, very often without that regard to [the] morality which we think should govern the world. But, although we see not as he sees, we have reason enough to establish a rational belief that all these things are disposed by an unerring wisdom, justice, and benevolence."[30]

God put man on earth to do his best to "amend and improve others and in every way ameliorate the lot of humanity; invent new medicines, write new books, build better houses and ships, institute better governments, discountenance false religions, propagate the only true one, diminish the vices, and increase the virtues of all men and women wherever we can."[31]

Despite his lack of orthodoxy, Adams was convinced that civilization could not exist without "religion." "Without religion this world would become something not fit to be mentioned in polite society, I mean hell," he wrote Jefferson. Even though he dismissed the idea that human beings were capable of perfection as "mischievous nonsense," he also rejected outright the notion that humankind was born totally corrupt. "So far from believing in the total and universal depravity of human nature," he wrote, "I believe there is no individual totally depraved. The most abandoned scoundrel that ever existed never yet wholly extinguished his conscience, and while conscience remains, there is some religion."[32]

Moreover, he felt that American civilization could not flourish without Christian morality, and the key to this was the chastity of American women. He wrote to Rush on February 2, 1807: "I say that the national morality never was and never can be preserved without the utmost purity and chastity in women, and without national morality, a republican government cannot be maintained. Therefore, my dear citizens of America, you must ask leave of your wives and daughters to preserve your republic."[33] He said he would write a book about this before he died, but he never did. Adams believed that chastity and fidelity was essential for men as well as women. He wrote his wife, "I have no confidence in any man who is not exact in his morals."[34] In an autobiographical memoir written for his children, he wrote that from the age of ten or eleven he was of "an amorous disposition," and though he was fond of girls, all his girlfriends were "modest and virtuous" and "always maintained this character through life." Furthermore, "no virgin or matron ever had cause to blush at the sight of me, or to regret her acquaintance with me."[35]

Consequently, he was appalled by reports of extramarital activities by other politicians. He deplored Alexander Hamilton's "fornications, adulteries, and his incests" [Adams believed the rumor that Hamilton was sleeping with his wife's sister],[36] and seemed to believe the accusations against Jefferson that the Virginian had fathered children by one or more of his slaves at Monticello, describing this behavior as the "unavoidable consequence of that foul contagion in the human character—Negro slavery."[37]

Adams believed strongly in an afterlife, basing this belief, characteristically, not on the revealed word of the Bible or pronouncement of a church, but upon reason. Shortly after the death of his wife, Abigail, Adams wrote Jefferson: "I know not how to prove physically that we shall meet and know each other in a future state; nor does revelation, as I can find, give us any positive assurance of such a felicity, my reasons for believing it, as I do most undoubtingly, are all moral and divine." He went on to say that "I believe in God and in his wisdom and benevolence and I cannot conceive that such a being could make such a species as the human merely to live and die on this earth. If I did not believe a future state, I should believe in no God. This universe, this all…would appear with all its swelling pomp a boyish firework. And if there be a future state, why should the Almighty dissolve forever all the tender ties which unite us so delightfully in this world and forbid us to see each other in the next?"[38]

On January 14, 1826, Adams wrote to Jefferson: "I am certainly very near the end of my life. I am far from trifling with the idea of Death, which is a great and solemn event." He regarded it, however, "without terror or dismay" because it was either a transformation or the end. Although he could not believe that death was the end of existence, if it was, "then there is an end of all, but I shall never know it, and why should I dread it?" If death was, as he actually believed, a transition, "I shall be under the same constitution and administration of government in the universe and I am not afraid to trust and confide in it."[39]

On June 17, 1826, Adams was visited in his home in Quincy by Daniel Webster, the young and influential Massachusetts senator, who found the ex-president lying on a sofa, being fanned by a servant. When Webster offered, "I hope the President is well today," Adams replied, "No, I don't know, Mr. Webster. I have lived in this old and frail tenement a great many years; it is very much dilapidated; and, from all that I can learn, my landlord doesn't intend to repair it."[40]

The end of John Adams's earthly life came on July 4, 1826, the fiftieth anniversary of the signing of the Declaration of Independence. Told that it was the Fourth of July, he replied, "It is a great day. It is a good day." Those were his last coherent words. Later he murmured something that someone interpreted as "Thomas Jefferson survives," but, according to his son, these words were "indistinctly and imperfectly uttered,"[41] and memorable because it turned out that Jefferson had in fact died around the same time that Adams was talking about him.

John Adams was characterized by a biographer as a man who "thought independently and often." He was well read in everything from the Greek and Roman poets and philosophers to Pascal and Goethe and Voltaire to the lives of the saints. He believed fervently that reason was God's way of revealing himself and rejected any belief, creed, any tradition that did not make sense to him. Although he rejected the divinity of Christ and many other traditional Christian teachings, he believed strongly in an all-powerful Creator-God, who actively governed the universe and directed the lives of human beings for the best. He felt that no nation could be successful unless it followed the ethical code that God inspired in Jesus of Nazareth, which, if followed, would lead to peace, harmony, and universal brotherhood. Adams's religious belief is perhaps most succinctly condensed in a letter written to Jefferson in 1813: "The love of God and his creation; delight, joy, triumph, exultation in my own existence, tho' but an atom, a molecule organic in the universe, are my religion."[42]

∼

Profile 4
Thomas Paine

Born: Thetford, Norfolk, England, January 29, 1737
Died: New York City, New York, June 8, 1809

The British-born political writer, whose pamphlet, *Common Sense*, written shortly after his arrival in America, played an important role in influencing public opinion in the colonies toward a demand for complete independence from Great Britain in 1776, left America in 1787 and went to France. There he supported the French Revolution, became a French citizen, and was elected to the National Convention. When France went to war with Britain, Paine was imprisoned as a citizen of a nation at war with France. After about a year, he was released when American Minister James Monroe convinced authorities that Paine was in fact a United States citizen. While in prison, Paine began a work called *The Age of Reason*, which alienated many of his former friends because of its unveiled hostility toward Christianity. This work led Theodore Roosevelt many years later to characterize him as a "dirty little atheist."

Paine was not, in fact, an atheist, for he claimed that he wrote *The Age of Reason* to combat the spread of atheism in France. Paine proclaimed himself a Deist, but his Deism was different from that of Franklin or Adams. Their argument was that the teachings of Jesus had been distorted by ignorant followers, and that the use of "reason" enabled the intelligent reader of the Bible to distinguish between Jesus' actual words and later inventions. Paine, however, utterly rejected Christianity and indignantly rejected the Bible almost completely.

Paine was a native of England. His father, a corset-maker, was a Quaker, and his mother belonged to the Church of England. Paine was apparently baptized in his mother's church, but attended Quaker meetings when he was a boy. Although he never became a member, the Society of Friends was the only religious organization (except for the one he would organize himself) for which he retained any respect.

When he was seven or eight, young Paine heard a relative read a sermon *Redemption by the Death of the Son of God* and was revolted because it seemed to show that God acted "like a passionate man that killed his son when he could not revenge himself any other way." He thought to himself, "As I was sure a man would be hanged that did such a thing, I could not see for what purpose they preached such sermons."[1] Despite his early alienation from traditional religion, when he was twenty-one, he heard John Wesley preach, and underwent an apparent religious conversion, and for a while acted as a sort of lay preacher, delivering sermons to a congregation in Dover.[2] This conversion proved to be quite temporary, and for the rest of his life, Paine evidently never again attended any organized church.

For most of his life, however, Paine said little about his ideas concerning religion. John Adams noted that, when he first met Paine in 1776, he was startled when, in conversation, Paine expressed a contempt for the Old Testament, "and indeed of the Bible at large."[3] It was not until his fifties, when he began his two-part essay, that Paine put his ideas on paper, only to become the object of controversy and outrage.

In his essay, Paine stated, "I believe in one God, and no more; and I hope for happiness beyond this life." He declared, "I believe in the equality of man, and I believe that religious duties consist in doing justice, loving mercy, and endeavoring to make our fellow creatures happy."[4]

He went on to say that creation was the only source of revelation. By meditating on the created order, people could know God. Like many of his contemporaries, Paine saw an orderly and harmonious universe. Of the Creator, Paine wrote: "Do we want to contemplate his power?

We see it in the unchangeable order by which the incomprehensible whole is governed. Do we want to contemplate his munificence? We see it in the abundance with which he fills the earth. Do we want to contemplate his mercy? We see it in his not withholding that abundance even from the unthankful."[5]

Paine argued for the existence of a "first cause...of all things" from the fact that nothing can make itself.[6] He insisted that creation is the only word of God: "It is only in the Creation that all our ideas and conceptions of a Word of God can unite. The Creation speaks a universal language, independently of human speech or human language, multiplied and various as they can be. It is an ever-existing original, which every man can read."[7]

In his belief that God could be best understood through understanding the natural world, Paine differed little from many intellectuals of his day, who could not bring themselves to accept the received testimony of other human beings as the revealed and authoritative word of God. Paine's belief was that he could not believe anything he had not himself experienced: "When Moses told the children of Israel that he received the two tablets of the commandments from the hands of God, they were not obliged to believe him, because they had no other authority for it other than his telling them so; and I have no other authority for it than some historian telling me so."[8] Paine's argument here is not very different from the one Adams made in his letter to Jefferson in which he said that if he had been on Sinai with Moses, he might have been awed and intimidated into giving his assent to an illogical proposition, but he could never have believed it.

Many of those who agreed with Paine's views were put off by the anger and hostility of Paine's bitter attacks on the Church, the Bible, and Christianity itself. Although in *The Age of Reason* he admitted that he did not own a Bible, Paine dismissed "the stupid Bible of the Church" as a collection of "groveling tales and doctrines" which were "fit only to excite contempt," a mass of "imposition and forgeries"[9] that formed the basis for "stupid sermons."[10] The Old Testament Paine condemned as a mishmash of "obscene stories," permeated by an "unrelenting vindictiveness."[11]

Paine was, if possible, even more unrelenting in his attack on the

New Testament, as a collection of morbid reveries on "a man dying in agony on a cross," which was "better suited to the gloomy genius of a monk in a cell, by whom it is not impossible they were written, than to any one breathing the open air of Creation."[12] He charged: "Putting aside everything that might excite laughter by its absurdity, or detestation by its profaneness, and confining ourselves merely to an examination of its parts, it is impossible to conceive a story more derogatory to the Almighty, more inconsistent with his wisdom, more contradictory to his power"[13] than the New Testament.

The Gospels, Paine averred, were but "detached anecdotes," and not a biography of Jesus.[14] He questioned whether Paul actually wrote the epistles bearing his name and condemned the writings attributed to him as the work of a "manufacturer of quibbles."[15]

Although he did not directly attack Jesus, Paine declared that the doctrine of the redemption was "fabricated."[16] Paine was convinced that if Jesus had wanted to found a new religion "he would undoubtedly have written the system himself, or procured it to be written in his lifetime."[17]

In an essay called *Modern Infidelity*, which Paine wrote in 1805 after he had returned to America from France, he maintained that if Jesus were "a God," he could not die, and if he were a man "he could not redeem." He went on to argue that the death of Jesus would make no difference. "Did God thirst for blood?" he asked. "If so, would it not have been better to have crucified Adam upon the forbidden tree, and made a new man?"[18]

Paine even went so far as to suggest that Christians should make Judas and Pontius Pilate saints, "for they were the persons who accomplished the act of salvation."[19]

Christianity Paine rejected as little more than "a species of atheism—a sort of religious denial of God," which "professes to believe in man rather than in God." For him, it "is as near to Atheism as twilight is to darkness."[20] He had nothing but contempt for nearly all organized religions. In *The Age of Reason* he insisted: "All national institutions of churches, whether Jewish, Christian, or [Islamic], appear to me no other than human inventions, set up to terrify and enslave mankind and monopolize power and profit."[21]

After Paine was released from his French prison, a reasonably moderate government, called the Directory, took power, and even considered restoring the Roman Catholic Church, which had been abolished during the radical phase of the French Revolution. Paine vehemently objected to any "talk of priests and bells whilst so many infants are perishing in hospitals, and aged and infirm poor in the streets." In fact, he objected to the very idea of a professional clergy: "No man ought to make a living by religion. It is dishonest to do so. Religion is not an act that can be performed by proxy. One person cannot act religion for another. Every person must perform it for himself; and all that a priest can do is to take it from him."[22]

Yet for all his cynicism and for all his contempt for revealed and organized religion, Paine seemed to believe in an afterlife. In *The Age of Reason* he said he hoped for "happiness beyond this life." In an unpublished essay, written in his last years, entitled "My Private Thoughts of a Future State," he contended, "I do not believe, because a man and woman make a child, that it imposes on the Creator the unavoidable obligation of keeping the being so made in eternal existence hereafter. It is in his power to do so, or not to do so, and it is not in our power to decide which he will do."[23]

Paine actually believed that the human race was divided into three categories: those whose lives "have been spent in doing good, and endeavoring to make their fellow mortals happy," who will be happy in the afterlife; the "very wicked," who "will meet with some punishment"; and those who are "so very insignificant, both in character and conduct, as not to be worth the trouble of damning or saving, or of raising from the dead."[24]

Paine became a founder of a new religion in France, the Theophilanthropists. The aim of this organization was, first, to perform humanitarian services; second, to "render theology the most entertaining of all studies"; and, finally, to "give scientific instruction to those who could not otherwise obtain it."[25]

The Theophilanthropists met on Sundays, with as many as forty people attending the meetings. They read odes in unison and sang "theistic and humanitarian" hymns. There were "ethical readings" from the New Testament, the Koran, and from the Hindu, Greek, and Chinese philosophers. They observed four holidays: the birthdays of

George Washington, Jean Jacques Rousseau (the French philosopher), the Greek philosopher Socrates, and Vincent de Paul (a French priest who devoted his life to the poor—one of the few Christians Paine evidently respected). The meeting place had a small, plain altar, decorated with flowers which symbolized all races and creeds.[26]

Paine returned to America in 1802 and died in New York in 1809. In his later years, he was furiously resistant to the efforts of friends to convert him, and was known to fly into rages when the subject of religion was raised.[27] Shortly before the end, he was visited by an old lady, whom he had never met, who declared, "I come from Almighty God to tell you that if you do not repent of your sins and believe in our blessed Savior Jesus Christ, you will be damned!" This prompted the response: "You were not sent with any such impertinent message.... Pshaw! He would not send such a foolish, ugly old woman as you about with his message. Go away!"[28]

A few days before he died, Paine, who had been gravely and painfully ill for months, was visited by two ministers, who urged him to put his faith in Jesus Christ. Raising himself in bed on his elbow, the dying man snapped, "Let me have none of your popish stuff! Get away with you!"[29]

A day or so before the end, his doctor asked, "Do you wish to believe that Jesus Christ is the Son of God?" Paine was silent for several minutes, as if deep in thought. Then he said, firmly and deliberately, "I have no wish to believe on that subject."[30]

∼

Profile 5
Charles Carroll of Carrollton

Born: Annapolis, Maryland, September 19, 1737
Died: Baltimore, Maryland, November 14, 1832

The planter and businessman who served as senator from his native Maryland during the First Congress of the United States is best known as the last surviving signer of the Declaration of Independence. He was one of the few early American statesmen who was a Roman Catholic.

The Carrolls were English, of Irish descent, and settled, in the late 1600s, in the colony of Maryland, which had been founded by Cecilius Calvert, Lord Baltimore, the scion of another English Catholic family of substance. Shortly after the arrival of the Carroll family in Maryland, Britain's unpopular Catholic king, James II, was overthrown, and in the reaction that followed, the Calverts were stripped of their proprietorship of Maryland, which was then administered directly by the crown until the Revolution. The Church of England became the established church in Maryland. Under the old charter, everyone who believed in Jesus Christ had full civil liberties. Now, not only were all residents required to pay taxes to support the established church, members of other denominations lost all their legal rights. By the time Charles Carroll was born in 1737, Roman Catholics could neither vote nor hold public office in the colony they had founded. They could not even worship in public, although wealthy people like the Carrolls had their own private chapels, staffed by their private chaplains.

Charles Carroll was sent to Europe to study when he was eleven and did not return to Maryland until he was twenty-eight. At that time, his father gave him an estate, Carrollton Manor, in Frederick County, and thereafter he was known as Charles Carroll of Carrollton. When the Revolutionary War broke out, the prohibition against Roman Catholics holding office was no longer in effect, and Charles Carroll was elected to the Continental Congress, in which capacity he was serving when he signed the Declaration of Independence. He also helped to draw up the constitution of the state of Maryland. After serving in the U.S. Senate for three years, he retired in 1792 to spend his time developing his property, which included more then seventy thousand acres in Maryland, Pennsylvania, and New York. Late in life, he helped to found the Baltimore and Ohio Railroad.

Carroll, though a devout Roman Catholic, was tolerant of other expressions of Christianity. A few years before his death he declared, "When I signed the Declaration of Independence I had in view not only our independence from England, but the toleration of all sects professing the Christian Religion and communicating to them all great rights."[1] Although he believed that the Church of Rome was the true church, he once told a friend, "I execrate the intolerating spirit of the Church of Rome."[2] Even though Carroll had been educated by the Jesuits and revered their "virtue," their "learning," and their "apostolic labors," he was uncomfortable about the "extensive privileges" that the popes had conferred on the Jesuits and was critical of their meddling in politics, as well as the rule by which they were bound to their superior through what he considered blind obedience. "Reason," Carroll wrote, "was not given to man merely to restrain his passions or merely to regulate his actions, but to weigh and examine whether the actions he is solicited or commanded by others to perform are such as can stand the scrutiny and sentence of an unerring, if unprejudiced, Judge."[3]

While reason led Adams and Franklin and Jefferson to reject many aspects of orthodox, organized Christianity, Carroll's reason led him to adhere to the doctrines of the church of his fathers. Once, early in his career, when friends encouraged him to become a Protestant because it was politically and socially advantageous to do so, Carroll refused. There were three reasons why he refused to give up Roman Catholicism. First, it would break his father's heart. Second, he did not believe in making decisions merely "to humor the prejudices of fools." Third, he was truly convinced of the truth of his religious faith.[4]

Though totally committed to his church, Carroll never tried to force Roman Catholicism on others, nor did he consider Protestants hellbound. "I feel no ill will or illiberal prejudices against the sectarians which have abandoned that faith," he wrote of non-Catholics. "If their lives be conformable to the duties and morals prescribed by the Gospel, I hope and believe they will be rewarded with eternal happiness."[5]

Carroll believed that only a virtuous life lived in expectation of eternity could bring satisfaction. Human desires, he wrote, are "insatiable" when not "fixed on the only object capable of satisfying man, and intended to satisfy him, by rendering him completely happy—infinitude—and to the enjoyment of this, virtue only can entitle us."[6]

For many years, Carroll carried on a correspondence with his son, who seems to have been indifferent or hostile to religion. In January 1801, he wrote: "Without virtue there can be no happiness, and without religion, no virtue. Consider yourself as always in the presence of the Almighty. If this sentiment be strong and vivid, you will never sin or commit any action you would be ashamed to commit before men."[7]

As the years progressed, Carroll became more urgent. In 1815, he wrote: "At the hour of your death, ah! my son, you will feel the emptiness of all sublunary things; and that hour may be nearer then you expect. Think on your eternal welfare."[8] Six years later, Carroll wrote again to call to his son's attention "the shortness of life and the certainty of death and the dreadful judgment we must all undergo, and on the decision of which a happy or a miserable eternity depends." Carroll urged his son to reflect on the future life and to "merit heaven" by a virtuous life. If the letter induced the younger Carroll to make a religious commitment, "it will comfort me and import to you that peace of mind which the world cannot give, and which I am sure you have long ceased to enjoy."[9] It is not clear whether Carroll's son, who died before his father, ever made this commitment.

Although Carroll, in his letters and writings, made several statements that indicate a belief that men and women are saved by means of virtue, he believed, in fact, that salvation came through faith in Christ. He made this clear at the age of eighty-nine when he wrote: "On the mercy of my Redeemer I rely for salvation, and on his merits, not on the works I have done in obedience to his precepts, for even these, I fear, a mixture of alloy will render unavailing and cause to be rejected."[10]

Around the same time Carroll wrote a friend in Philadelphia about his thoughts about eternity: "I am fast approaching the last scene, which will put an end to all earthly cares and concerns. I am looking to that state from which all care, all solicitude, and all passions which agitate mankind are excluded. Revelation instructs us that eternal happiness or eternal misery will be the destiny of man in the life to come. The most pious, the most exemplary have trembled at the thought of the dreadful alternative. Oh! what will be the fate of those who little think of it, or, thinking, square not their actions accordingly."[11]

Carroll remained healthy and active, physically and mentally, until few weeks before his death at ninety-five. Not long before the end, Carroll told a priest, "I have lived to my ninety-sixth year. I have enjoyed continued health. I have been blessed with great wealth [he was reputed to be the richest man in America], prosperity, and most of the good things which the world can bestow—public approbation, esteem, applause; but what I now look back on with the greatest satisfaction to myself is that I have practiced the duties of my religion."[12]

The last day of his life was a cold November day. Carroll, suffering from a failing heart, sat propped up in an armchair in front of the fire in his room. In front of him was a table with blessed candles, a crucifix, and a silver bowl full of holy water. Carroll's two daughters knelt on either side of their father, accompanied by their children. Behind the armchair knelt three or four elderly slaves. The Rev. John E. Chaunce, president of St. Mary's College, dressed in his rich vestments, administered the last rites. Carroll kept his eyes closed, but, according to one of the doctors in attendance "he was so familiar with the forms of this solemn ceremony that he responded and acted as if he saw everything....At the moment of offering the Host he leaned forward without opening his eyes, yet responsive to the word of the administration of the holy offering. It was done with so much intelligence and grace that no one could doubt for a moment how fully his soul was alive to the act."[13]

The sick man had been fasting in preparation for the sacrament, but when he had received Communion and was urged to eat, he refused, telling his physician, "Thank you, Doctor, not just now. This ceremony is so deeply interesting to the Christian that it supplies all the wants of nature. I feel no desire for food." A few minutes later the doctor and a granddaughter lifted Carroll from his chair and put him in bed. "Thank you. That is nicely done," said the old man, who, still refusing to eat, soon fell asleep. When the doctor shifted his position in bed to make him more comfortable, Carroll opened his eyes and said, "Thank you, Doctor." A few hours later Carroll died in "a gentle sleep."[14]

∼

Profile 6
Thomas Jefferson

Born: Shadwell, Virginia, April 13, 1743
Died: Monticello, Virginia, July 4, 1826

On a note, found in his desk after his death, Thomas Jefferson left instructions for his tombstone, which was to record his three greatest achievements. He wished to be remembered as "author of the Declaration of American Independence, of the Statute of Virginia for Religious Freedom, and father of the University of Virginia." That he also served as third president of the United States, he evidently regarded as of lesser importance.

In a letter written to John Adams, Thomas Jefferson, then in his mid seventies, wrote, "Say nothing of my religion. It is known to my God and myself alone. Its evidence before the world is to be sought in my life. If that has been honest and dutiful to society, the religion which has regulated it cannot be a bad one."[1]

Although Jefferson sometimes said that he did not like to talk about religion, in reality he said a great deal about it. He considered himself a religious man and described himself as a Deist, as well as a Christian. To him, these were one and the same, for his religion was based not on assent to revealed doctrine, but on reason, common sense, and constructive and benevolent actions.

In another letter to Adams, he responded to his friend and former political rival, "If the moral precepts, innate in man and made a part of his physical constitution, as necessary for a social being, if the sublime doctrines of philanthropism and Deism taught by Jesus of Nazareth in which all agree, constitute true religion, then without it, this would be, as you again say, 'something not fit to be named, even indeed a hell.'"[2]

Repeatedly, in his voluminous writings, Jefferson argued in this way. True religion was the moral system taught by Jesus of Nazareth, the greatest of all philosophers—to the extent that the immature pronouncements of this young sage, who lost his life before he was able to develop his ideas fully, could be deduced from the garbled writings of his ignorant followers. Jefferson held Jesus in high regard, but had the lowest contempt for nearly all institutional churches, which he believed were organized for the personal gain of professional clergy, who deliberately distorted the simple teachings of the philosopher from Nazareth, so that ordinary people could not understand, and would be forced to rely upon the representatives of the church, psychologically, politically, and financially.

Jefferson expended much ink on the subject of Jesus. In a letter written when he was seventy-nine to one Benjamin Waterhouse, the statesman and philosopher attempted to summarize the teaching of Jesus in three general tenets: (1) "There is only one God, and he is all perfect"; (2) "There is a future state of rewards and punishments"; (3) "To love God with all thy heart and thy neighbor as thyself is the sum of religion."[3]

In his *Syllabus of an Estimate of the Merit of the Doctrines of Jesus, Compared with Those of Others*, written two decades earlier while he was president, Jefferson went into greater detail. One of his cardinal beliefs was that Jesus was simply a reformer of Judaism. The Jews, he believed, entertained ideas about God that were "degrading and injurious," and taught a system of ethics which was "not only imperfect, but often irreconcilable with the sound dictates of reason."[4] It was "into this state of things among the Jews," Jefferson explained, "that Jesus appeared. His parentage was obscure; his condition poor; his education null; his natural endowments great; his life correct and innocent; he was meek, benevolent, patient, firm, disinterested, and of the sublimest eloquence."[5] Later, Jefferson would write to Adams: "Abstracting what is really his from the rubbish in which it is buried...we have the outlines of a system of the most sublime morality which has ever fallen from the lips of man."[6]

Believing that Jesus' true teachings were easily distinguishable from the "dross," Jefferson, during his presidency, put together a collection of those quotes attributed in the Bible to Jesus which he himself thought authentic, a work sometimes referred to as "Jefferson Bible." He called it *The Life and Morals of Jesus Christ* and said he first intended it for the instruction of American Indians in what he considered the essentials of the Christian faith. Making a "harmony" of the Gospels—

mainly Matthew, Mark, and Luke—he constructed a continuous narrative, eliminating all the supernatural elements and ending with the burial of Jesus. The "Jefferson Bible," in its first edition, was forty-six pages long.

In his *Syllabus,* Jefferson described Jesus' teachings as "more pure and perfect" than those of any other philosopher, and the man of Nazareth went beyond both Jew and Greek in applying his "universal philosophy" not just to "neighbors and countrymen," but to all humankind, "gathering all into one family, under the bonds of love, charity, peace, common wants, and common aids." Not only did Jesus' teachings involve action, "he pushed his scrutinies into the heart of man" and "erected his tribunal in the region of [humankind's] thoughts and purified the waters at the fountainhead." In addition, Jefferson found that Jesus "emphatically" taught "the doctrine of a future state."[7]

The man whom Jefferson characterized as a "benevolent moralist" did not "live to fill up" the outlines of his "system of...sublime morality."[8] Jesus' fate was "the ordinary fate of those who attempt to enlighten and reform mankind." He fell victim "to the jealousy and combination of the altar and throne."[9]

While Jefferson apparently regarded the Gospels as the bungling, but sincere attempt of unlearned followers to reproduce in writing the teachings they remembered, he seems to have had little respect for the epistles of Paul or any other part of the Bible that attributed supernatural characteristics to Jesus. He complained about the disfigurement of the teachings of Jesus by followers who "engrafted on them the mysticisms" of Plato, "frittering them into subtleties and obscuring them with jargon."[10]

Jefferson believed that the key to understanding God was reason. The Bible, as he wrote one of his nephews, had to be read as you would read the Roman historians. He advised: "The facts which are within the ordinary course of nature, you will believe on the authority of the writer...but those facts in the Bible which contradict the laws of nature must be examined with more care, and under a variety of faces. Here you must recur to the pretensions of the writer to inspiration from God. Examine upon what evidence his pretensions are founded and whether the evidence is so strong as that its falsehood would be more improbable than a change in the laws of nature." If a biblical account does not square with the laws of nature or with common sense, it is to be dismissed, and classed with those accounts related by ancient historians that involve "showers of blood, speaking of statues, beasts, etc."[11]

On reading the New Testament, Jefferson advised that one must note "it is the history of a personage called Jesus"—a sublime philosopher who eventually convinced himself that he was divine through self-deception. "Keep in your eye the opposite pretensions," Jefferson warned, "(1) of those who say he was begotten of God, born of a virgin, suspended and reversed the laws of nature at will, and ascended bodily into heaven, and, (2) of those who say he was a man of illegitimate birth, of a benevolent heart, enthusiastic mind, who set out without pretensions to divinity, ended in believing them, and was punished capitally for sedition, by being gibbeted, according to the Roman law...."[12]

Jefferson had no use for any part of the Bible that did not accord with his idea of reason. The year before he died, responding to one General Alexander Smith, who had written a commentary on the Apocalypse and wanted the ex-president's opinion, Jefferson dismissed the Book of Revelation as "the ravings of a maniac, no more worthy of explanation than the incoherencies of our nightly dreams....There is no coherence enough in them to countenance any suite of rational ideas."[13]

Jefferson, in a late letter to Adams, made a list of the traditional Christian doctrines which he rejected: the virgin birth, the "deification" of Jesus, the creation of the world by Jesus, Jesus' miraculous powers, the Resurrection and Ascension, the Trinity, original sin, predestination, and the "corporeal presence of the Eucharist."[14]

It is interesting that Jefferson nonetheless chose to believe in heaven. When Abigail Adams died in the fall of 1818, Jefferson wrote her widower John, whose beliefs were similar to his own: "It is of some comfort to us both that the term is not very distant at which we are to deposit our sorrows and suffering bodies, and to ascend in essence to an ecstatic meeting with friends we have loved and lost and whom we shall love and never lose again."[15]

Theology, Jefferson was convinced, was Platonistic nonsense, invented by clergy who stood to gain profit and privilege by obscuring the teachings of Jesus. He wrote Adams: "The Christian priesthood, finding the doctrines of Christ leveled to every understanding, and too plain to need explanation, saw, in the mysticisms of Plato, materials with which they might build up an artificial system which might, from its indistinctness, admit everlasting controversy, give employment for their order, and introduce to it profit, power, and preeminence. The doctrines which flowed from the lips of Jesus himself are within the comprehension of a child: but thousands of volumes have not yet explained the Platonism engrafted on them: and for this obvious reason that nonsense can never be explained."[16]

Jefferson nurtured an especial contempt for Athanasius, the fourth-century bishop of Alexandria, Egypt, whom he blamed for introducing the idea of the Trinity, and for John Calvin, the sixteenth-century French reformer whose writings helped to form the basis of the Puritanism he despised, with its doctrine of election and predestination. Of the doctrine of the Trinity, Jefferson wrote Adams: "It is too late in the day for men of sincerity to pretend they believe in the Platonic mysticisms that three are one and one is three; and yet the one is not three and the three are not one."[17] To Waterhouse, he ridiculed the Calvinistic beliefs: "(1) that there are three gods; (2) that good works or the love of our neighbor are nothing; (3) that faith is everything, and the more incomprehensible the proposition, the more merit in its faith; (4) that reason in religion is of unlawful use; (5) that God from the beginning elected certain individuals to be saved, and certain others to be damned, and that no crimes of the former can damn them, no virtues of the latter save."[18] Both Athanasius and Calvin, Jefferson excoriated as "impious dogmatists" and "false shepherds" who were "mere usurpers of the Christian name, teaching a counter-religion made up of the deliria of crazy imaginations."[19]

Jefferson seemed to harbor only hatred and revulsion toward Christian clergy. He wrote a Mrs. Samuel Harrison Smith in 1816: "My opinion is that there would never have been an [unbeliever] if there had never been a priest."[20] It is not completely clear why Jefferson harbored such animosity toward Christian clergy of all sects. He was baptized into the Church of England, the established church of most of the colonies, of which nearly all prominent families were a member. The Anglican clergy of Virginia, during Jefferson's youth, had a reputation for cynicism, materialism, and immorality. Even Patrick Henry, who was much more conventionally religious than Jefferson, characterized the typical clergyman as "rapacious as a harpie" and ready to "snatch from the hearth of every honest farmer his last hoe-cake."[21]

As a boy Jefferson studied under clergymen, first, at a Latin school run by William Douglas, rector of St. James Parish, then, at a school run by James Maury of the Fredericksburg Parish. Jefferson seems to have disliked both men. He seems to have been especially repelled by Maury. This minister, married and the father of a huge family, was neither lazy nor immoral, but seems to have been grim, sour, cheerless, embittered, and harshly intolerant of other Christian denominations, whose clergy he dismissed contemptuously as "dupes, deceivers, and madmen."[22]

Whether it was because most of the clergy he knew in his formative years he found unworthy of his respect, or whether there were other reasons as well, Jefferson, as an adult, thought that Christian ministers were quite unnecessary. He wrote Adams: "We should all...like Quakers, live without an order of priests, moralise for ourselves, follow the oracle of conscience, and say nothing about what no man can understand, nor therefore believe."[23]

Understandably, Jefferson worked fervently to end the tax-supported church in Virginia. As a member of the Virginia Assembly in 1776, he wrote and sponsored an Act for Establishing Religious Freedom. Up to that time, at least on paper, one could still be put to death for "heresy" in Virginia and jailed for denying the Trinity or the divine authority of the Scriptures. In his bill, Jefferson proposed that "no man shall be compelled to frequent or support any religious worship, place, or ministry whatsoever, nor shall [he] be enforced, restrained, molested or burdened in his body or goods, or shall [he] otherwise suffer, on account of his religious opinions or belief; but that all men shall be free to profess, and by argument to maintain, their opinions in matters of religion, and that the same shall in no wise diminish, enlarge, or effect their civil capacities."[24] When the bill finally passed, almost a decade after it was introduced, Jefferson, as we have seen, considered it one of his greatest achievements.

Despite his negative feelings toward organized churches and ministers, Jefferson did not want to suppress religion. He did not feel that people had to be protected from religion. He seemed to feel that the greater the diversity of religious practice and opinion, the more likely men and women were, through exercise of reason, to arrive at the knowledge of the truth. He seemed to envision a society of many religious practices, subject to no restrictions or limitations. His ideas on this matter were addressed in his book, *Notes on Virginia*, which he wrote during the 1780s. In it, he argued that people are answerable to God alone in matters of conscience. The legitimate powers of government extended "to such acts only as are [physically] injurious to others. But it does me no injury for my neighbor to say there are twenty gods or no god. It neither picks my pocket nor breaks my leg....Constraint may make him worse by making him a hypocrite, but it will never make him a truer man. It may fix him obstinately in his errors, but it will not cure them. Reason and free inquiry are the only effectual agents against error. Give a loose to them, they will support the true religion by bringing every false one to their tribunals, to the test of their investigation. They are the natural enemies of error, and of error only."[25]

Addressing the eighteenth-century assumption that religious uniformity was necessary for the health of the state, Jefferson argued: "Millions of innocent men, women, and children, since the introduction of Christianity, have been burnt, tortured, fined, imprisoned; yet we have not advanced one inch towards uniformity. What has been the effect of coercion? To make one-half of the world fools, and the other half hypocrites."[26]

One gets the impression that, in the religiously free society that Jefferson envisioned, the multiplicity of churches would be short-lived. Intelligent people enjoying free inquiry would soon adopt the beliefs held by Jefferson. In later years, Jefferson liked to refer to himself as "unitarian." (He was never a member, however, of the Unitarian Church.) In 1822, he expressed his opinion that within another generation, nearly everyone would come to hold beliefs similar to his own: he wrote Waterhouse that he believed that there was not a young person then living in the United States who would not die a Unitarian![27]

Throughout his life, Jefferson was an advocate for the abolition of the old "established" or tax-supported churches, which all the states had at the time of independence. Although the Constitution states that Congress may not establish a national church, it was still legal for states to have their own established churches, and some of them continued to have them well into the nineteenth century. When Connecticut disestablished the Congregational Church, Jefferson was jubilant, and in a letter to Adams, rejoiced in "the resurrection of Connecticut to light and liberality."[28]

Despite his extreme beliefs, Jefferson did attend church during his presidency. He went to Christ Episcopal Church, which met just south of the Capitol, at New Jersey Avenue and B Street Southeast. Later, when Sunday services came to be offered on a weekly basis at the House of Representatives, Jefferson went there where the worship was of the ecumenical sort that the president liked. Every denomination of Christians was, from time to time, represented—including the Roman Catholics and the Quakers. Occasionally, there were women speakers. Music was supplied by the Marine Band.[29] Sometimes the content of the preaching was largely secular. It is not known what Jefferson thought of the services at the House, but, years after he left Washington, he criticized ministers who preached about things other than religion—especially politics. Whenever preachers discoursed on the science of government or "the character or conduct of those administering it," it was, he argued, "a breach of contract."[30]

In his later years, Jefferson contributed money to Episcopal, Baptist, and Presbyterian churches in Charlottesville (where he lived on his estate, Monticello) and even drew up architectural designs for an Episcopal church.[31] He was concerned about the lack of religious instruction at the newly founded University of Virginia. In 1822, he wrote that "the relations which exist between man and his Maker, and the duties resulting from those relations, are the most interesting and important to every human being, and the most incumbent on his study and investigation. The want of instruction in the various creeds of religious faith existing among our citizens presents, therefore, a chasm in a general institution of the useful sciences."[32]

Unwilling to have the University of Virginia impose its own version of religion on the students, he wanted "pious individuals" to establish religious schools on the grounds of the university. These schools would be independent of the university and of each other, but the students would be allowed to take classes at the university. This would enable students of the ministry to have access to a first-class secular education, and it would also allow students at the university to study under and worship with professors of their own denomination.[33]

Despite his rejection of most of the traditional doctrines of Christianity and his hostility to the very concept of the ministry, Jefferson was religious in his own way. He believed that the universe was governed, not by "blind fatality" but by "the creator and benevolent Governor of the world," who could suspend the operations of natural law whenever it suited him.[34] Jefferson also rejected the concept of evolution. He believed that humankind, along with all of nature, had been created spontaneously and remained in the same form as when created.[35] He also believed that God punished people and nations for their crimes. "We are not in a world ungoverned by the laws and powers of a superior agent," he wrote. "Our efforts are in his hand, and directed by it; and he will give them their effect in his own time."[36]

Jefferson believed that slavery was wrong and that God would punish societies that permitted slavery. Speaking of Virginia in his *Notes on Virginia*, he wrote, "I tremble for my country when I reflect that God is just."[37] Despite this observation, Jefferson (who seemed to believe that blacks were inferior and should be resettled in Africa) owned many slaves. Whereas Washington freed all his slaves through his will, Jefferson's will manumitted only five of his slaves.

Throughout his life, Jefferson seems to have been consistent in his religious views. Speaking of his last illness, he told a grandson, "Do not imagine for a moment that I feel the smallest solicitude about the result; I am like an old watch, with a pinion worn out here, and a wheel there, until it can go no longer."[38] His last visitor, Henry Lee, recalled that the sick man referred to his impending death "as a man would to the prospect of being caught in a shower—an event not to be desired but not to be feared."[39] To his oldest and only surviving child, Martha Jefferson Randolph, he gave an ornate box, containing a poem he had written for her, expressing his hope for eternal life.[40]

He retained to the end his dislike of priests. Just before he died he dreamt that a clergyman who lived nearby had come in his room. He said that he was willing to see him as a friend, but not as a priest: "I have no objection to see him as a kind and good neighbor."[41]

A legend was circulated that, just before Jefferson breathed his last, on July 4, 1826, he suddenly sat up in bed and prayed in Latin: "Lord, now lettest Thou Thy servant depart in peace, according to Thy word; for mine eyes have seen Thy salvation, which Thou hast prepared before the face of all people; a light to lighten the Gentiles, and the glory of Thy people Israel." But Robley Dunglison, the physician in attendance, denied this, insisting that Jefferson had said nothing of the sort. In fact, he had been in a coma for twenty-four hours before his death.

～

Profile 7
Abigail Smith Adams

Born: Weymouth, Massachusetts, November 22, 1744
Died: Quincy, Massachusetts, October 28, 1818

After he and Abigail Adams had celebrated their golden anniversary, John Adams, with "gratitude to the giver of every good and perfect gift," told his son John Quincy what his wife meant to him: "In all the vicissitudes of my fortunes, through all the good report of the world, in all my struggles and in all my sorrows, the affectionate participation and cheering encouragement of your mother has been my never-failing support, without which I am sure I should never have lived through them."[1] The second First Lady and the first mistress of the White House (after the seat of the federal government was moved to Washington just before the end of John Adams's single term as president) was the daughter of William Smith, pastor of the First (Congregational) Church of Weymouth, Massachusetts. At the age of fourteen, she was received into her father's church, and for the rest of her life she was a devoted adherent to her childhood faith. The many letters preserved from her pen make it clear that her faith in God motivated everything that she did and was reflected in her reactions to the events in her life. The fact that she was frequently separated from her husband and children occasioned the writing of an immense volume of letters, which shed an excellent light on her thought and personality.

The Congregationalists among whom Abigail Smith Adams formed her ideas were not the textbook Puritans of popular imagination. Far from emphasizing the severe justice of an angry God who predestines men and women to heaven or hell before their birth, Abigail's father and many religious people of that time and place stressed the goodness of an all-powerful God who controlled all events, both those which mortals call good and those which they call evil. They emphasized submission to the will of God and the responsibility of human beings to change the world for the better, while not strongly developing the ideas of the Trinity or the divinity of Christ.

Abigail Adams's reliance upon God is evident in the letter that she wrote to her husband, then a member of the Continental Congress, after the Battle of Bunker Hill, near Boston in 1775, in which an American force, after repelling two British attacks, was forced into retreat after running low on ammunition. "The race is not to the swift, nor the battle to the strong," she wrote John, "but the God of Israel is he that giveth strength and power unto his people. Trust in him at all times; ye people, pour out your hearts before him. God is a refuge for us."[2]

Bible verses were also prominent in her letter to John reporting the death of her mother, Elizabeth Quincy Smith, who died of dysentery in 1775: "Have pity upon me, have pity upon me, O thou my beloved, for the hand of God presseth me sore. Yet will I be dumb and silent, and not open my mouth, because thou, O lord, hast done it." After quoting Job 19:21 and Psalm 39:9, Abigail cried out: "How can I tell you (oh, my bursting heart!) that my dear mother has left me this day, about five o'clock, she has left this world for an infinitely better [one].... Blessed spirit! Where art thou? At times I am almost ready to faint under this severe and heavy stroke, separated from thee, who used to be a comforter to me in affliction; but, blessed be God, his ear is not heavy that he cannot hear, but he has bid us call upon him in time of trouble."[3]

During one of John's long absences overseas, when she had not heard from him for some time and was uncertain where he was, she wrote: "Hitherto my wandering ideas have roved, like the son of Ulysses, from sea to sea and from shore to shore, not knowing where to find you; sometimes I fancied you upon the mighty waters, sometimes at your desired haven, sometimes upon the ungrateful and hostile shore of Britain, but at all times and in all places under the protective care and guardianship of that Being who not only clothes the lilies of the fields and hears the young ravens when they cry, but hath said, 'Of how much more worth are ye than many sparrows,' and this confidence, which the world cannot deprive me of, is my food by day and my rest by night and was all my consolation under the horrid ideas of assassination—the only event of which I had not thought, and in some measure, prepared my mind."[4]

To her oldest son, John Quincy, in Europe with his father, she wrote after he told her how he had narrowly escaped a shipwreck: "You have seen how inadequate the aid of man would have been if the winds and the seas had not been under the particular government of that being who 'stretched out the heavens as a span,' who 'holdeth the ocean in the hollow of his hand.'"

Continuing, she declared: "The only sure and permanent foundation of virtue is religion. Let this important truth be engraven upon your heart. And, also, that the foundation of religion is the belief of the one only God, a just sense of his attributes, as a Being infinite, wise, just, and good, to whom you owe the highest reverence, gratitude, and adoration."[5]

When John was elected president in 1797, in her letter to him she quoted the prayer that Solomon rendered for divine assistance upon his succession to the throne of Israel: "'And now, O Lord my God, thou hast made thy servant ruler over the people. Give unto him an understanding heart, that he may know how to go out and come in before this great people; that he may discern between good and bad. For who is able to judge this, thy so great a people?' were the words of a royal sovereign; and not less applicable to him who is invested with the Chief Magistracy of a nation, though he wears not the crown nor robes of royalty."[6]

When twenty-five-year-old Maria Jefferson Eppes died in 1804,

Abigail Adams wrote her father, Thomas Jefferson, who, by then had been bereft of five of his six children, "I have tasted of the bitter cup [she had lost three of her six] and bow with reverence and submission before the Great Dispenser of it, without whose permission and over-ruling providence not a sparrow falls to the ground. That you may derive comfort and consolation in this day of your sorrow and afflic-tion from that only source calculated to heal the wounded heart, a firm belief in the being, perfections, and attributes of God, is the sin-cere and ardent wish of her who once took pleasure in subscribing herself your friend."[7]

When her daughter Abigail died of breast cancer during the sum-mer of 1813, a few weeks after surviving a three-hundred-mile trip from her home in New York State to be with her parents in Quincy, Massachusetts, Abigail wrote to her son John Quincy, then American minister to Russia, describing his sister's death. "I cannot but consider it as the Benignant hand of Providence which supported her through a journey of such length and gave us the opportunity to witness her even resignation, her patient sufferings, and her peaceful death. Whilst my heart bleeds and the recollection deepens my sorrow, I bow submissive to the heavenly mandate, and ask for you, my son, that consolation you need, under this additional stroke [he had lost an infant daughter less than a year before] of providence."[8]

Although, in her letters, Abigail Adams complained about discrimi-nation against girls in education and argued for women's political rights, she was not a feminist in the modern sense, for she believed that women's place is in the home. Like her husband, she believed that Christian women should be paragons of moral purity and "delicacy."[9] As a Christian, she opposed racial discrimination. For example, just before her husband became president in 1797, one of her black (hired) servants expressed a desire to go to evening school. She was horrified when the parents of two white boys complained about the presence of the Negro child. Mrs. Adams defended the principle of "equality of rights" to the complainers, insisting, "The boy is a freeman as much as any of the young [white] men, and merely because his face is black, is he to be denied instruction? How is he to be qualified to procure a livelihood?...I have not thought it any disgrace to myself to take him into my parlour and teach him both to read and write."[10] The complaints were silenced.

Like her husband and her son, Abigail Adams distrusted formal creeds and denominational polity and politics. Late in life, she wrote John Quincy's wife, Louisa: "When will mankind be convinced that true religion is from the heart, between man and his creator, and not the imposition of men or creeds or tests?"[11] Living according to the teachings of Jesus was for her far more important then the embrace of formal creeds or denominational alignment.

Like John, Abigail suffered from a strong aversion to Roman Catholicism. They were repelled by their experiences in France in the 1780s, where they lived while John was negotiating treaties of commerce in Paris. The laxity of morals they observed among the French appalled them, and Abigail blamed the "religion of the country." She held the sacrament of penance especially at fault. She called it "The Ceremony of the Closet."[12]

Abigail Adams's religious background and upbringing was such that the doctrine of the Trinity and of the divinity of Christ was beyond her comprehension. She was uneasy about the growth of Trinitarian, or Athanasian, Christianity, in her day, regretting "to see a narrow, selfish, exclusive system gaining ground instead of that liberal spirit of Christianity recommended by St. Paul."[13]

She, like her husband and Jefferson, appropriated the word "unitarian," only recently in common use, to describe her theological stance. "There is not any reasoning which can convince me, contrary to my senses, that three is one and one three," she affirmed. She cited the first commandment, which "forbids the worship of but one God," and pointed to various passages in the New Testament that seemed to her to indicate that Jesus was subordinate to God the Father. Among them was his statement in Mark 10:18, in which he declared, "Why do you call me good? No one is good but God alone. A second was his declaration, "The Son can do nothing on his own, but only what he sees the Father doing" (John 5:19). A third was Jesus' prayer to his Father, "If it is possible, let this cup pass from me" (Matthew 26:39). A fourth was his prayer on the cross, "My God, my God, why have you forsaken me?" (Matthew 27:46).[14]

Abigail affirmed that "Jesus Christ derived his being and all his power and honors from the Father."[15] She said, from reading the Scriptures, "I am led to believe in the unity of the Supreme Being, and that Jesus Christ was divinely inspired and specially delegated to communicate the will of God to man, and that, after having fulfilled his mission upon earth, he ascended into heaven from whence we are assured he shall come to judge the world in righteousness, all power given to him by the Father."[16]

Abigail Adams was more orthodox in her beliefs about Jesus than her husband. She never rejected the idea that Jesus was the savior of humankind. She did not believe that he was the equal of God; rather she felt that he was divinely inspired of God and given his supernatural powers by God. John seems to have thought of Jesus chiefly as an example.

Abigail believed that men and women attained salvation through a sincere attempt to live according to the teachings of Christ, for which God would reward them with eternal life. "The Scriptures fully testify," she wrote, "that a conformity to his precepts and example, as far as human nature is capable of it, will be rewarded by future happiness in the world to come."[17] She further said: "We are assured that those who fear God and work righteousness shall be accepted of him—and that, I presume, of whatever sect or persuasion, after all our inquiries we are permitted to see through a glass dimly."[18]

In a sense, Abigail Adams believed in salvation by works. A man or women is saved by living according to the teachings of Christ. However, she expected that the All-Merciful, through his love, would accept all those who acted out of sincerity, realizing that on earth mortals "see through a glass dimly," and that individual inquiries after truth lead to differences of "sect or persuasion," which will be overlooked by the All-Just. Her theology of salvation presumed on the infinite mercy and love of God to forgive human limitations of understanding and behavior.[19]

When Abigail Adams died after a brief illness on October 28, 1818, at the age of nearly seventy-four, her son John Quincy, when he received the news, exclaimed "Oh, God, may I die the death of the righteous and my last end be like hers!"[20] He said of her, "Never have I known another human being the perpetual object of whose life was so unremittingly to do good. It was a necessity of her nature. Yet so unostentatious, so unconscious even, of her own excellence, that even the objects of her kindness often knew not whence it came."[21] He characterized her as "an angel upon earth. She was a minister of blessing to all human beings within her sphere of action. Her heart was the abode of heavenly purity. She had no feelings but of kindness and beneficence—yet her mind was as firm as her temper was mild and gentle. She had known sorrow, but her sorrow was silent. She was acquainted with grief, but it was deposited in her own bosom—she was the real personification of female virtue—of piety, of charity, of ever active and never intermitting benevolence. Oh God! Could she not have been spared yet a little longer? My lot in life has almost always cast at a distance from her. I have enjoyed but for short seasons and at long intervals the happiness of her society, yet she has been to me more than a mother. She has been a spirit from above, watching over me for good, and contributing by mere consciousness of her existence, to the comfort of my life."[22]

∼

Profile 8

James Madison

Born: Port Conway, Virginia, March 16, 1751
Died: Montpelier, Virginia, June 28, 1836

The Virginia lawyer, planter, and legislator came to be known as the Father of the Constitution because of the active role he played in the Constitutional Convention of 1787. Along with Alexander Hamilton and John Jay, he contributed to the writing of *The Federalist Papers*, a series of eighty-five essays which supported the Constitution and which played an important role in persuading the states—especially New York—to ratify the Constitution. As a congressman from Virginia, he wrote the first ten amendments to the Constitution, which comprise the Bill of Rights. Later, he became the fourth president of the United States.

Though Madison was raised in the Church of England, most of his contemporaries were convinced that he was never a very religious man. While studying at what is now Princeton University, Madison briefly "partook of the spirit" of a religious revival that broke out among the students. Madison, accordingly to one writer, even considered entering the ministry. Many of Madison's family and friends, however, agreed with a cousin who later insisted that Madison's religious commitment and his desire to enter the ministry "died a quick death."[1]

Throughout his long life, Madison was fiercely committed to the idea of separation of church and state and hostile, like his friend Jefferson, to the idea of an established church. When he was in his twenties, he learned that some Baptist preachers had been jailed in Virginia's Culpeper County for preaching without a license which the Church of England had been unwilling to grant, he wrote heatedly: "That diabolical hell-conceived principle of persecution rages among some....There are at this time in the adjacent county not less then 5 or 6 well-meaning men in close gaol for publishing their religious sentiments, which, in the main, are very orthodox. I have neither patience to hear talk or think of anything relative to this matter, for I have squabbled and scolded, abused and ridiculed so long about it, to so little purpose that I am without common patience."[2]

In 1777, the Tithe Law had been abolished in Virginia, effectually disestablishing the Church of England in Virginia since there was no longer a tax for its support. Seven years later, Revolutionary leader Patrick Henry, a member of the Assembly, was convinced that disestablishment had led to a decay in morale and an indifference to the Christian faith, and proposed a resolution that citizens "pay a moderate tax or contribution annually for the support of the Christian religion."[3] Madison, who was also a member of the Assembly, hotly opposed Henry, insisting that his bill constituted another establishment of religion.

Establishment, historically, he said, had always undermined the vitality of the Christian faith, which tended, on the other hand, to be most fervent in time of persecution. He offered that "war and bad laws" were the real causes of the conditions that disturbed Henry, and argued that "laws to cherish virtue, a better administration of justice, personal example, the education of youth...were the true remedies for declining morale and religion."[4] Moreover, Madison declared, Henry's proposal would ensure that Christianity would inevitably be subject to definition by the courts, which could end up penalizing religious persuasions not of their liking.

Madison was still not satisfied when the delegates amended Henry's proposal to include all religions, not just Christianity. As a result, he drew up a "Memorial and Remonstrance Against Religious Assessments," in which he insisted that religion was not within the jurisdiction of civil authority, contending that, throughout history, religious establishments tended to "erect a spiritual tyranny," which, in turn, served to foster "political tyranny."[5]

As a result of Madison's eloquent protest—and Henry's election as governor of Virginia (which removed him from the Assembly)—the proposal for a tax assessment for "teachers of religion" did not pass. Madison also resurrected Jefferson's Statute for Religious Liberty and secured its passage, abolishing heresy as a crime as well as religious tests for civil office.[6]

A few years later, when Madison, as a member of the First United States Congress, wrote the Bill of Rights, his very first amendment began: "Congress shall make no law respecting an establishment of religion, or prohibiting the free exercise thereof." The fact that Madison chose to address this matter first indicates how strongly he felt about religious freedom. Some years later, he wrote that the separation between government and religion comprises "the great barrier against usurpations on the rights of conscience. As long as it is respected, and no longer, these will be safe. Every provision for them short of this principle will be found to leave crevices at least through which bigotry may introduce persecution; a monster that, feeding and thriving on its own venom, gradually swells to a size and strength overwhelming all laws divine and human."[7]

During Madison's two terms as president he and his wife, Dolley, frequently attended St. John's Episcopal Church, across from the White House. In line with his passion for separation of church and government, he tried unsuccessfully to block the appointment of a chaplain for Congress on the grounds that such an office and appointment was unconstitutional. He also vetoed a bill that would have incorporated an Episcopal congregation in the District of Columbia, objecting that this was a law "respecting the establishment of religion" and that the government had no jurisdiction in this matter.[8]

In 1812, he bowed to congressional pressure from the west and south and involved the United States in a war with Great Britain. When Congress requested him to recommend to the nation a day set aside for prayers for victory and peace, Madison responded with a proclamation that "all who shall be piously disposed" were invited to give thanks and "offer supplications to the Great Parent and Sovereign of the Universe." Continuing, the president listed the divine blessings for which the American people could be thankful, such as the bounty of the land, the extension of arts and manufacturers, and a political Constitution founded on the will of the whole people. He then suggested that the "Almighty Power that helped to make the states an independent and sovereign people" should be invoked to bless the nation's military activities and to inspire the enemy with a spirit of justice and accommodation, so that "we may be enabled to beat our swords into plowshares and enjoy in peace" the rewards of industry and enterprise."[9]

Unlike Jefferson and the Adamses, Madison seldom addressed religious topics in his correspondence. William Meade, an Episcopal bishop who knew him late in life, wrote that he had the impression that Madison's "creed was not strictly regulated by the Bible." However, despite whatever his private sentiments may have been, "he was never known to declare any hostility to [Christianity]. He always treated it with respect, attended public worship in his neighborhood, invited ministers of religion to his house, had family prayers on such occasions—though he did not kneel himself at prayers. Episcopal ministers often went [to his home] to see his aged and pious mother and administer Holy Communion to her."[10] George Ticknor of Boston recalled a dinner with Madison in which the latter "pretty distinctly intimated" to him that he preferred unitarian doctrines and rejected the Athanasian Creed.[11]

In many respects, therefore, Madison's beliefs seem to have been similar to those of Jefferson and John Adams. Along with a rejection of the Athanasian Creed, he also seems to have believed that God and his attributes were best understood from the contemplation of nature rather than through the Bible. In 1826, he wrote a friend that he believed that there was a "road from nature up to Nature's God."[12] He also wrote that "belief in an all-wise, all-powerful God is essential to the moral order of the world and the happiness of men," and that, confronted with the idea of infinity, it was easier for the human mind to assent "to the self-existence of an invisible cause possessing infinite power, wisdom, and goodness than to the self-existence of the universe, visibly destitute of those attributes."[13]

Despite the perception of some that Madison did not believe in the literal inspiration of the Bible, he told the English writer Harriet Martineau in 1831, "The whole Bible is against Negro slavery; but...the clergy do not preach this and the people do not see it."[14] Nonetheless, like Jefferson and Washington and others who deplored the institution of slavery, Madison continued to own slaves to the day of his death.

Although Madison was somewhat infirm during his last years, he did not welcome death. "Afflictions of every kind are the onerous conditions charged on the tenure of life," he wrote toward the end, "and it is a silencing, if not a satisfactory, vindication of the ways of Heaven to man that there are but few who do not prefer acquiescence to them to a surrender of the tenure itself."[15]

However, in his last illness, when his physicians offered to prolong his life so that he could die on the Fourth of July, like Adams and Jefferson, he refused, and departed the world on June 28, 1836. It was said that on the last day of his life, the ex-president spoke "with great calmness and self-possessions of his religious sentiments,"[16] but the informant failed to record what he said. A little later, when his niece asked what the matter was, Madison replied, "Nothing more than a change of mind, my dear," and slumped dead in his chair.[17]

~

$\mathcal{P}rofile\,9$
Alexander Hamilton

Born: Nevis, British West Indies, January 11, 1755 (or 1757)
Died: New York, New York, July 12, 1804

orn out of wedlock on the island of Nevis in the British West
Indies, Alexander Hamilton arrived in New York as a teenager,
studied at King's College (now Columbia University), served as an
aide to Washington during the Revolutionary War, then returned to
New York to study and practice law. A delegate to the Constitutional
Convention in 1787, he favored a strong central government with a
powerful chief executive and weak states. Despite the fact that the
finished product was not entirely satisfactory to him, he joined James
Madison and John Jay in writing a series of essays defending the new
constitution. As America's first secretary of the treasury, he did a great
deal to establish a sound economy. He was also the founder of the
Federalist Party.

During his first year in America, Hamilton lived in the home of
Elias Boudinot, a devout Presbyterian layman. Of Boudinot it was
said, "No one could have lived for a year without kneeling regularly
in prayer or becoming a confirmed atheist."[1] The young student seems
to have been favorably influenced by his landlord, for his roommate,
Robert Troup, later wrote that during this time Hamilton was "atten-
tive to public worship and in the habit of praying upon his knees both
night and morning."[2] "A zealous believer in the fundamental doctrines
of Christianity," Hamilton argued with Troup and worked to confirm
his roommate's faith in "revealed religion."[3]

After leaving King's College, Hamilton did not impress his friends
and colleagues as a particularly religious man. Although he married
Eliza Schuyler, an Episcopalian so pious that she was called the Little
Saint.[4] Hamilton never joined any church. For many years he seemed
to embrace the Deism popular among eighteenth-century intellectuals, holding to a belief in "natural law from which all human laws
derived their validity. He believed that "the sacred rights of mankind"

were "written, as with a sunbeam, in the whole volume of human nature, by the hand of the divinity itself."[5] Like many of his contemporaries, Hamilton believed that human beings could arrive at such convictions, not by the authority of Bible or clergy, but through reason and common sense.

When, at the Constitutional Convention, Benjamin Franklin moved that each session be opened with prayer, Hamilton objected, insisting, "I see no need for calling in foreign aid."[6] Later, when a Presbyterian minister asked him why there was no mention of God in the Constitution, Hamilton answered flippantly, "Indeed, Doctor, we forgot it."[7]

The horror of the French Revolution seemed to have a profound effect on Hamilton, especially the attempt on the part of the revolutionary government to promote atheism. Anticipating war with France, he wrote an acquaintance in April 1797, that, in making preparations for war, Congress should mobilize "the religious ideas of Americans." If hostilities actually came, a day of humiliation and prayer would be in order, to impress the minds of Americans that they were fighting for religion against atheism."[8] The following year Hamilton again deplored in writing the "terrible design" of the French reformers to "destroy all religious opinion and to pervert a whole people to Atheism."[9] In April 1802, he proposed a "Christian Constitutional Society" for the twin objects of "the support of the Christian religion" and "the support of the Constitution of the United States" by employing "all lawful means" to "promote the election of fit men."[10]

By this time, Hamilton believed that religion was indispensable to civilization. He was experiencing also a deepening of his religious faith from broad, general principles to a specific faith in Christ. One of his sons wrote that it was reason that led his father to the Bible through the contemplation of creation: "His religious feelings grew with his growing intimacy with the marvelous works of nature, all pointing in the process and their results to a great pervading, ever active Cause. Thus his mind rose from the visible to the invisible; and he found intensest pleasure in studies higher and deeper than all speculation. His Bible exhibits on its margin the care with which he perused it....With these readings [of the Bible and commentaries] he now united the habit of daily prayer, in which exercise of faith and love the Lord's

Prayer was always a part. The renewing influences of early pious instruction and habit appear to have returned in all their force on his truest sensibilities."[11]

Hamilton's remarks in a letter to his friend Benjamin Rush in 1801, a few months after Hamilton's oldest son lost his life in a duel, reveals how close he had drawn to orthodox Christian belief: "Why should I repine? It was the will of heaven, and he is now out of the reach of the world of folly, fully of vice, full of danger…. I firmly trust also, that he has safely reached the haven of eternal repose and felicity.[12]

Two years later Hamilton himself accepted a challenge to a duel by Aaron Burr, vice president of the United States, who claimed that Hamilton's opposition had cost him election as New York's governor. A letter Hamilton wrote to his wife (whom he did not inform of his intentions) seems to indicate that he had resolved not to shoot at Burr, for, he said, "The scruples of a Christian have determined me to expose my own life to any extent, rather than subject myself to the guilt of taking the life of another…. [I would] rather…die innocent than live guilty."[13]

If he were a Christian, why would Hamilton agree to participate in a duel in the first place? In another letter he wrote his wife before the duel (these were not to be delivered until after his anticipated death or wounding), he said that avoiding, the "interview" would render him "unworthy of your esteem."[14] To many men of Hamilton's generation whatever their religious persuasions or lack thereof, nothing—not even love of family, and seemingly even love of God—was as important as honor.

In the two letters to the Little Saint, Hamilton expressed a hope for "a happy immortality" through "redeeming grace and divine mercy," by which he cherished "the sweet hope of meeting you in a better world."[15]

On July 11, 1804, mortally wounded in his duel with Burr, Hamilton, having been brought to the home of a friend, sent for the Right Rev. Benjamin Moore, Episcopal bishop of New York and rector of Trinity Church. Although he had not joined, in recent years Hamilton had been attending Trinity Church regularly with his family. When the bishop arrived, Hamilton, in agonizing pain, gasped, "It is my desire to receive Communion at your hands. I hope you will not conceive there is any impropriety in my request. It has been for some time past the wish of my heart, and it was my intention to take an early opportunity of uniting myself to the church, by reception of that holy ordinance."[16] Bishop Moore, however, refused to administer Communion, since, by participating in a duel, Hamilton had committed a grave sin.

Desperate for the Eucharist, Hamilton then sent for Dr. John M. Mason, a Presbyterian minister, who also refused to administer it to him. Mason explained that Presbyterian policy forbade the administration of the Lord's Supper "privately, to any person under any circumstances." Mason tried to comfort Hamilton by telling him that the Eucharist was merely "an exhibition and pledge" of the mercies of Christ. Faith in Christ made this mercy possible without the pledge. Before Mason left, Hamilton, clasping his bands toward heaven, told him, "I have a tender reliance on the mercy of the Almighty, through the mercy of the lord Jesus Christ."[17]

Later that same day, the dying man tried to console his hysterical wife, reminding her, "Remember, my Eliza, you are a Christian."[18] These were his last articulate words, but when Bishop Moore returned the next day, he asked Hamilton to make an appropriate response to his questions. He asked if Hamilton had intended to hurt Burr. The dying man shook his head. He asked him if he forgave Burr, and Hamilton nodded. Thereupon, Moore finally administered Communion, which Hamilton, speechless, but conscious, received "with great devotion." After that he seemed "perfectly at rest," and, within an hour, he quietly died.[19] Though Hamilton (whom many found arrogant and overbearing and who admitted to at least one instance of marital infidelity) could hardly be called a saintly man, it seems clear that by the time he died, even though he never joined a church, he experienced, in the words of a friend, a "conviction of the truths of the Christian religion,"[20] and sought sincerely and strenuously in his last hours, to make peace with his Savior.

∼

Profile 10

John Marshall

Born: Prince William County, Virginia, September 24, 1755
Died: Philadelphia, Pennsylvania, July 6, 1835

The Virginia lawyer, statesman, and diplomat served as secretary of state under John Adams before his appointment as chief justice of the United States Supreme Court, a position he held until his death thirty-four years later. During this time, he dramatically strengthened the power of the court and of the federal government.

Like many men of the eighteenth and nineteenth century, Marshall, who presumably was baptized in the Church of England, never joined it or any other church. Like many of his contemporaries, he was disgusted with the materialism and lack of spirituality in what became the Episcopal Church. One historian characterized the spiritual life of the Virginia churches as "low and hopeless," disgraced by lazy and immoral clergy who spent much of their time drinking, gambling, and carousing.[1] Indeed, Marshall is said once to have remarked, when asked to contribute to a fund for a theological seminary, that it was almost unkind to encourage young men to enter the Episcopal ministry, because the Church was too far gone ever to be revived.[2]

When the Church of England was disestablished in Virginia after American independence, many were convinced that this aggravated the spiritual indifference of the people of Virginia. We have seen how, in the 1780s, Patrick Henry introduced a bill into the Virginia legislature to require a tax for support of the Christian ministry, with the revenues distributed among clergymen of all denominations. Marshall, then a twenty-nine-year-old delegate, was one of those who supported this unsuccessful measure.[3]

Marshall was always vaguely religious and regularly attended Episcopal services with his wife, Mary Ambler, who was a member, and their six children. When the Monument Church was built near his Richmond home in 1814, the chief justice was a leading fundraiser and a major contributor to the building fund. He put down $390 (a huge sum in those days) for a pew there, and sat there nearly every Sunday he was in town, although it was so cramped that he, an extremely tall man, had to sit next to the door of the pew, open it, and rest his legs in the aisle.[4]

Marshall said and wrote little about religion. Bishop William Meade, a younger contemporary who knew him for many years, characterized Marshall as "unitarian in belief," but a "sincere friend of religion," who went to church with his family, not out of personal conviction, but "to set an example."[5] He seems to have been tolerant of other religions. He certainly lacked the anti-Roman Catholic bias of the Adamses, as he is known to have backed a practicing Catholic for appointment to the North Carolina Supreme Court. He certainly believed in God, as is clear from an incident that happened in a hotel in Winchester, Virginia, when a group of men were ridiculing the idea of God's existence in Marshall's presence and asked him what he thought. Marshall conceded that he had not thought much about the matter, but said he believed that "creation must have a creator," and that the creator also must have been all-powerful "to have filled unlimited space with worlds." The creator must have been all-wise "to have produced universal harmony" and be "all goodness" in that he "provided the means of happiness for all his creatures."[6]

Late in life, Marshall seems to have moved beyond a vague Deism toward traditional Christianity. A daughter recalled, after his death, that her father was "converted" late in life to a belief in the divinity of Christ by reading a book called *Keith on Prophecy*. She claimed that he decided to join the Episcopal Church and receive Communion, but died before he had the opportunity.[7] When Marshall died in Philadelphia at the age of nearly eighty, the chief justice was still unchurched. There are no accounts of his last days or any indication that he summoned a clergyman.

∼

Profile 11
Andrew Jackson

Born: Waxhaw, South Carolina, March 15, 1767
Died: Nashville, Tennessee, June 8, 1845

and

Rachel Donelson Robards Jackson

Born: Pittsylvania Co., Virginia, June 15, 1767
Died: Nashville, Tennessee, December 22, 1828

T he election of the seventh president of the United States was said to herald a coming of the Age of the Common Man. Andrew Jackson was the first chief executive of his nation who was not born to the upper class, and he was the first to represent a state west of the eastern seaboard. Although he was born in poverty to immigrants from Northern Ireland—his father had died shortly before his birth—Jackson, who moved from his native Carolinas to Tennessee as a young man, had quickly become a wealthy planter, and over the years before his election had attained national prominence as a soldier and politician—and notoriety as a touchy, hard-nosed man who "regarded neither God nor man."[1]

Although his mother reportedly wanted him to become a Presbyterian minister, Jackson was a violent bully as a child who, according to one biographer, when crossed, "swore a blue-streak—fine, bloodcurdling oaths that could frighten people half to death."[2] As a young man, living in Salisbury, North Carolina, he was characterized as "the most roaring, rollicking, game-cocking, horse-racing, card-playing, mischievous fellow that ever lived in Salisbury."[3] A "street brawler, duelist [and] gambler" (in the words of a biographer), he was known for a "mean, vicious temper that frequently exploded into ugly language and acts."[4] Not surprisingly, he seldom attended church as a young man.

Around 1790, when he was twenty-three, he became the husband of Rachel Donelson Robards. A few years later, after it was learned that her divorce was not official at the time of their original marriage, the Jacksons went through another wedding ceremony. After that, lively and fun-loving Rachel gradually settled down to become devoutly religious. She joined a Presbyterian church near the Hermitage, the Jackson estate near Nashville, which she managed and made prosperous. Andrew was devoted to her. During their marriage, it is said that their only source of tension was his desire to hold public office and her wish that he live the settled life of a country gentleman. Although she was never able to put a damper on his worldly ambition, Rachel gradually made her influence felt in her husband's spiritual life.

Despite his success, Jackson continued to be, in his thirties and forties, not only an intelligent and able legislator and soldier, but a coarse, belligerent, and sometimes violent man. He fought several duels, in one of which he killed a man who cast aspersion on Rachel's honor. An often cruel slave master, in September 1804, he took out an advertisement in the *Nashville Tennessee Gazette*, in which he offered a reward of fifty dollars for the capture of a runaway slave, as well as "ten dollars extra for every hundred lashes any person will give him."[5]

Yet Rachel's influence was sometimes evident even then. For instance, after she joined a church, she insisted that he offer grace at table at every meal, and he complied. One day the Jacksons had a group of dinner guests whom Andrew was regaling with war stories, seasoned "with a profusion of expletives." Uncomfortable with his vulgar language, Rachel interrupted, "Mr. Jackson, will you ask a blessing?" Immediately and obediently Andrew broke off his narrative and pronounced a "reverential" blessing, but immediately resumed his salty stories.[6]

Jackson was never an atheist and he was never, like John Adams and Thomas Jefferson, critical of organized religion. In 1796, he was a member of the convention that prepared Tennessee's constitution, and opposed a measure that would have banned religious leaders from holding state offices. He also supported an unsuccessful bill that would have prohibited anyone from holding public office who denied "the being of God and future rewards and punishments."[7]

During the War of 1812, Jackson frequently wrote to his wife of his belief that God was protecting him. After he wrote Rachel expressing such sentiments, she answered: "How often I have thanked the Supreme Governor that rules and directs the just and virtuous. You say his overruling power is more conspicuous in the field of battle than in our peaceful dwellings. Surely that is correct. It's Christian-like. I can almost say thou art a Christian."[8] Even though Rachel was pleased that Andrew was writing like a Christian, it seems clear that she did not believe that he was one!

After the Battle of New Orleans in January 1815, Jackson asked the Roman Catholic authorities of that city to proclaim a day of thanksgiving "to be performed in the Cathedral in token at once of the great assistance we have [received] from the ruler of all events and of our humble sense of it."[9] Yet, in that same period of his life, Jackson fought a bloody campaign to shatter the Indian nations who lived in what is now the southeastern United States. In the course of the fighting, he ordered the destruction of the village of Tallushatchee. His troops surrounded the town, and, according to a witness, shot the inhabitants "like dogs."[10] Jackson's men found a ten-month-old infant in the arms of his dead mother. Urged to kill the child with the others, Jackson refused and actually sent the baby, whom he named Lyncoya, to the Hermitage, where Rachel raised him as a son. When the lad died of tuberculosis at sixteen, both Rachel and Andrew mourned him "as a favorite son."[11]

Peter Cartwright, a Methodist minister who knew Jackson in midlife, characterized him as "a very wicked man," yet one who "always showed great respect for the Christian religion and the feelings of religious people."[12] Cartwright was once a guest minister in Nashville and was warned by the host pastor that Jackson was in the audience and so he needed to be careful what he said. Jackson was by now a national hero. It was widely known with what genocidal ferocity he dealt with the Indian nations. It was also common knowledge that he had no scruples about killing rebellious soldiers in his own army. It was well-known that he hanged two British subjects who dared to aid the Indians whom he was liquidating. Cartwright had good reason to fear offending the general, but he indignantly blurted out to the other minister, loud enough to be heard throughout the congregation, "Who is General Jackson? If he don't get his soul converted, God will damn him as quick as he would a Guinea negro." The horrified host minister warned, "General Jackson will chastise you for your insolence before you leave the city."

It so happened that the next day Cartwright and Jackson met by chance in front of an inn. The young minister was stunned when the general, far from angry or vindictive, told him, "Mr. Cartwright, you are a man after my own heart." Praising his courage, he continued, "A minister of Jesus Christ ought to love everybody and fear no mortal man."[13]

When Jackson became governor of Florida in 1821, he was joined by his wife. "When pious Rachel saw New Orleans, where they stopped en route, she complained in a letter to her sister, "Oh, the wickedness, the idolatry of the place! Unspeakable riches and splendor. I know I never was so tried before, tempted, proved in all things....Pray for your sister in a heathen land, far from my people and church."[14] The city of Pensacola, Florida, was no better than New Orleans. She complained about "the Sabbath profanely kept, a great deal of noise and swearing in the streets; shops kept open; trade going on...."[15] She successfully prevailed upon her husband to issue an order to authorize the mayor and city council to close all businesses on Sunday.

In 1823, Jackson, serving as senator from Tennessee, wrote Rachel, who did not accompany him to Washington, to assure her that he was attending church: "Every Sunday we spend at church. The family [where he was lodging] belong to the Methodist society. On last Sunday...I went with Mrs. Watson to her church. She belongs to the Presbyterians. Today I went to hear a Baptist whose church is near us, and was edified by a good, concise discourse. So, my dear, you see that, notwithstanding I am in the midst of intrigue, gaiety, and bustle, I spend my Sundays and leisure hours agreeably, and I hope, profitably."[16] Jackson's friend, John Eaton, assured Mrs. Jackson in writing, "Every Sunday he takes himself to some one of the churches...."[17]

That same year he built a church on three acres of the Hermitage estate for Rachel, who became one of the first charter members. The church, first called the Ephesus Church, and later the Hermitage Church, was intended as nondenominational, but it was always staffed by Presbyterian pastors. It served primarily the people who lived on the Hermitage estate: the Jacksons and their relatives and servants. Rachel very much wanted Andrew to join the church, but he demurred, believing that, in light of his past conduct, his request to join a church at this stage of his life would be interpreted as a political move. Just before he began his 1828 campaign for the presidency, he told her "My dear, if I were to do that now, it would be said, all over the country, that I had done so for the sake of political effect. My enemies would all say so. I cannot do it now, but I promise you that when I am clear of politics I will join the church."[18] Jackson also seemed to feel that as a politician he simply could not live in conformity to the teachings of a Christian church. When the daughter of a friend joined a church, he wrote the friend, "It is what we all ought to do, but men in public business [have] too much on their minds to conform to the rules of the church."[19]

When Jackson was running for president on the Democratic ticket in 1828 against John Quincy Adams, the sitting chief executive, Adams's handlers unearthed the fact that the Jacksons lived together as a married couple before Rachel was legally free of her first husband, and suggested that Mrs. Jackson was an immoral woman. One of Jacksons' friends admitted, "The General and Mrs. Jackson both perhaps acted imprudently, but no one believes they acted criminally—the whole course of their lives contradicts such an idea."[20] The attacks on her character broke Rachel's heart, figuratively and literally.

After the election, Rachel Jackson reluctantly made preparations to accompany Andrew to Washington. While shopping in Nashville, she saw a pamphlet that contained especially foul insinuations against her character and she became hysterical. Shortly after her return to the Hermitage, she suffered a heart attack. Three days later she died in the arms of her maid, shortly after confiding, "I had rather be a doorkeeper in the house of God than live in that palace."[21] Ever afterwards, Jackson placed her picture in his bedroom, so that it would be the first thing he saw when he opened his eyes and the last to meet his gaze when he closed them to go to sleep.[22]

As president, Jackson attended church regularly, but not with the same congregation. During his first term, he rented one pew at the Second Presbyterian Church and another at "Mr. Post's Church," whatever that was.[23] Later, he rented pews at St. John's Episcopal Church and First Presbyterian. Each day he read the Bible, but still refused to apply for church membership anywhere.

After he retired to the Hermitage, Jackson attended the Hermitage Church each Sunday. He also conducted family prayers every day, first reading aloud a chapter of the Bible, then leading in the singing of a hymn, before praying aloud, often with tears coursing down his cheeks. Then, in 1838, at the age of seventy-one, he made good his promise to Rachel. He informed James Smith, pastor of the Hermitage Church, that he identified with the Presbyterian denomination more then he did with any other, but that he could not accept the doctrine of predestination. "I believe that every man has a chance for his own salvation," he insisted.[24]

After John Todd Edgar, pastor of First Presbyterian Church of Nashville, preached at the Hermitage Church, the former president spent the rest of the day in prayer. That evening, along with his daughter-in-law, Sarah, who was also not a church member, he prayed. After Sarah retired, Jackson prayed all night, until, at dawn, "a great peace" fell on him.[25] The next day, he informed Edgar that he wanted to be admitted to the church. When the pastor asked him if he could freely forgive all his enemies, Jackson told him that, in all honesty, he could not. When Edgar told him that he could not join the church without an act of will forgiving all those who had ever offended him, Jackson thought for a long time, then agreed to forgive his enemies unconditionally. And so both Jackson and his daughter-in-law were received into full membership in the Hermitage Church on July 15. Jackson took his first Communion with tears trickling down his face. Thus culminated a pilgrimage in search of God that had taken nearly forty years.

Andrew Jackson's religious beliefs are evident in the letters he wrote during the latter part of his life, and from records of his conversations. "True religion is calculated to make us not only happy in this, but in the next and...better world," he wrote. "It is in religion alone that we can find consolation for such bereavements as the loss of our dear friends.... It is religion alone that can give peace to us here, and happiness beyond the grave. It is religion alone that can support us in our declining years, when our relish is lost for all sublunary enjoyments, and all things are seen in their true light, as mere vanity and vexation of spirit."[26]

As for the Bible, he wrote to a relative: "Withdraw from the busy cares of this world and put your house in order for the next by laying hold 'of the one thing needful.' Go read the scriptures. The joyful promises it contains will be balsam to all your troubles, and create for you a kind of heaven."[27]

Unlike the Adamses and Jefferson and Madison, Jackson believed explicitly in the divinity of Christ. Shortly before he died, he wrote a friend that he hoped for a blessed immortality "in our Glorious Redeemer, who died for us that we might live." It was through Christ's atonement that Jackson had hope for eternal life.[28]

One of Jackson's most fervent beliefs was in "a providence who holds our existence here in the hollow of his hand."[29] God, he believed, was in control of the life of each man and each woman. God had a purpose and a plan for everyone. As early as 1823 Jackson wrote a friend: "We are traveling our journey through life. When our time is fulfilled here below, we will rest. Providence will continue with us here until we fulfill those purposes that his goodness has designed, and we ought always to say, 'The Lord's will be done.'"[30]

Submission to God's will was very important to Jackson. "Rely on our dear Savior," he wrote, and "always be ready to say 'May the Lord's will be done!'" Suffering, he believed, was designed by the heavenly father to purify mortals for heaven. Therefore one must resign oneself to "present suffering and chastisement."[31]

We have seen how Jackson, when in Washington as senator and later as president, attended churches of various denominations. Although he preferred the Presbyterian Church, his views were quite ecumenical. He wrote a friend, "I do not believe that any who shall be so fortunate as to be received to heaven through the atonement of the blessed Savior will be asked whether they belonged to the Presbyterian, the Methodist, the Episcopalian, Baptist, or Roman Catholic [church]."[32] To a woman who relayed to him in writing her grandmother's accusation that he was a Roman Catholic he replied, "We ought therefore to consider all good Christians, whose walks correspond to their professions, be [they] Presbyterian, Episcopalian, Baptist, Methodist, or Roman Catholic."[33] To a clergyman, he declared "All true Christians love each other, and while here below, ought to harmonize; for all must unite in the realms above. I have thought one evidence of true religion is when all those who believe in the atonement of our crucified Savior are found in harmony and friendship together."[34]

Even though Jackson's spiritual life deepened, he seemed to have no qualms about owning slaves. By the time he died, he had 150. He held a low opinion of their intelligence and ability. When his mansion burned, before declaring the catastrophe to be the will of God, he groused about "the cursed negroes…[so] confused that nothing could be done until some white one came to their relief."[35] (In light of Jackson's treatment of his slaves early in his life, there would seem to be no reason why his servants would be particularly interested in salvaging his property). When he was close to death, he thought he was being kind by assuring his slaves, not that they would be freed, but that they would have good masters. He also supported the deportation of the surviving Indians of the Southeast to lands beyond the Mississippi. He felt that the Indians were so inferior and lacking in intelligence that they would be completely exterminated if they were not removed out of the way of whites.[36]

Although Jackson held views about non-white people that are considered reprehensible in the late twentieth century, his attitude, at least in old age, changed somewhat. By the 1830s, he notified his overseers that be would not permit his slaves "to be treated with cruelty."[37] In 1839, there was a fight among the black patrons of a dancehall, in which a man was killed. Four of Jackson's slaves were arrested and charged with homicide. Their master, because over one hundred people had been involved in the incident and he was sure that no one had a clear idea of what actually had happened, resolved to win the acquittal of the men, even though it was his own nephew who obtained the warrant against them. Jackson declared that it was "a constitutional guarantee that all men [are] by law presumed to be innocent until guilt [is] proven." For Jackson, "all men" (at least at this stage of his life) included slaves. He went on to spend $1,000, much of which he had to borrow, for the successful defense of the four men.[38] Of course, these slaves were valuable property. By the time he died, however, it seems clear that his slaves genuinely loved him. One of them recalled that, just before he died, Jackson told her, "Christ has no respect to color."[39]

Jackson wrote that people should be "prepared freely to resign this troublesome earthly tabernacle for an eternity of bliss."[40] He explained: "Knowing that we have to die, we ought to live prepared to die well, and then let death come when it may. We will meet it without alarm and be ready to say, 'The Lord's will be done.' "[41] All life was a preparation for heaven, where, clothed in a "heavenly body promised to all who believe in our glorious Redeemer," the faithful would be united with loved ones in the presence of Christ.[42]

Andrew Jackson's religious faith was apparent throughout the lingering and agonizing illness that led to his death. By late 1844, Jackson was confined to his home. A lifelong smoker, he could scarcely breathe, and suffered from fits of suffocation. By the New Year, he could not lie down without suffocating. By spring his entire body was swollen and he was racked by excruciating pain. During his last days, he told his daughter-in-law, "Do not weep. My sufferings are less than those of Christ upon the cross."[43] He told friends, "I feel my time is approaching, but I am prepared to die. When the angel of death comes I shall say with pleasure, 'March on. I'll follow.' "[44] In great agony, he told a visitor, "I am in the hands of a merciful God. I have full confidence in his goodness and mercy....The Bible is true....I have tried to conform to its spirit as near as possible. Upon that sacred volume I rest my hope for eternal salvation, through the merits and blood of our blessed Lord and Savior, Jesus Christ."[45] To his foster son, he said, "I am greatly afflicted, suffer much.... How far my God may think proper to bear me up under my weight of affliction, he only knows."[46]

During his last week, he said little. He spent most of his time in silent prayer, as was apparent from the way he moved his lips and hands. On the morning of Sunday, June 8, 1845, he opened his eyes and thanked his daughter-in-law for her kindness during his long illness. Then he bade farewell to all the members of his family. Although he and Rachel had no biological children, they had an adopted son, Andrew, Jr., as well as foster children, who now had spouses and children and in-laws. One by one, he took them by the hand and kissed and blessed them. He told the children that they had good parents and that they must be obedient children. "Keep holy the Sabbath day and read the New Testament."

In the words of his physician, he then delivered "one of the most impressive lectures on the subject of religion that I have ever heard. He spoke for half an hour on his faith in Christ, the hope of salvation, and his anxiety that they should "all look to Christ as their only Savior." Then he addressed his slaves, many of whom were outside, looking in the window. "You must do your duty," he told them. "As much is expected of you according to your opportunities as from whites. You must try to meet me in heaven."[47] He declared, "God will take care of you for me. I am my God's. I belong to him. I go but a short time before you and I want to meet you all in heaven, both white and black."[48] Jackson told his beloved servant Hannah, "I want all to prepare to meet me in Heaven; I have a right to the Tree of Life. My conversation is for all you. Christ has no respect to color. I am in God and God is in me. He dwelleth in me and I in him."[49] Then to the slaves who stood outside weeping, he called out, "Oh, do not cry. Be good children and we shall all meet in heaven."[50] A half an hour later, he died.

∽

Profile 12
John Quincy Adams

Born: Braintree, Massachusetts, July 11, 1767
Died: Washington, D.C., February 23, 1848

The oldest son of John and Abigail Adams had an illustrious career as a lawyer, educator, senator, diplomat, and, finally, as secretary of state, before becoming the only son of an American president to be elected as his nation's chief executive. Many believe that Adams's greatest contributions came during the last seventeen years of his life, when he served as a representative of his native Massachusetts in Congress, where he proved a formidable opponent of slavery.

Many found John Quincy Adams cold, outspoken, and abrasive, but few doubted his sincerity or his religious devotion. All those who knew him agreed that his private life was one of "unsullied purity,"[1] and one of his early biographers declared that "in all his public acts, he seemed animated by the thought that he stood in the presence of God" and that few politicians ever acted "with a more continued and obvious reference to religion as a motive, as a guide, as a comfort."[2]

John Quincy Adams's spiritual portrait emerges clearly in the diary he kept for more than fifty years, in which he frequently went into great detail concerning his religious reflections. So extensive are his diary entries that one wonders how Adams had time during the day for anything other than writing in it!

A careful and methodical man, Adams strove to make the best use of every moment of the day. When he was president, he got out of bed usually around five a.m. After making a fire (in cold weather), he wrote until breakfast at nine. From ten to eleven he read newspapers. Then he saw visitors, attended to official business, and answered mail until half past three in the afternoon, when he went riding or walking for an hour or so. At five, he and his wife Louisa had dinner and talked until seven or eight, then Adams went to his room and wrote until eleven or twelve.[3] Every morning and every evening he read several chapters from the Bible. Sometimes his study consisted of translating the New Testament passage he was reading from the original Greek, or paraphrasing a Psalm in verse of his own composition.

When he was seventy-three, Adams wrote that "the duties of man to God are worship, reverence, gratitude, submission, and resignation," duties which translate to "prayer and praise in action." For him "the only acceptable obedience to God" was treating others in a spirit of "justice, charity, and mercy."[4]

Around this time in his life, Adams wrote down his personal creed: "I have at all times been a sincere believer in the existence of a Supreme Creator of the world, of an immortal principle within myself, responsible to that creator for my conduct upon earth, and of the divine mission of the crucified Savior, proclaiming immortal life and preaching peace on earth, good will to men, the natural equality of all mankind, and the law, 'Thou shalt love thy neighbor as thyself.'" Adams admitted that he was assailed by "involuntary and agonizing doubts" on all of these articles of faith. Because he felt that he was "a frequent sinner before God" and needed to be "admonished of it and exhorted to virtue," he felt it necessary to attend worship services in any church of any denomination that he felt appropriate.[5]

Never sure of his salvation, at the age of sixty-nine he wrote: "I know that I have been, and am, a sinner—perhaps by the depravity of the human heart, an unreclaimable sinner; but I cannot, if I would, divest myself of the belief that my Maker is a being whose tender mercies are over all his works; that, having the power to make me both will and do, however he may chastise, he will not cruelly punish thoughts which his pleasure may control, or deeds which, however wrongful or improper, his power can turn to good. We are passive instruments in his hands. He will not suffer us to do evil, and then sentence us severely for what he has suffered us to do."[6]

Adams had no use for formal creeds and doctrines, because he believed that "thinking men" cannot control what they believe. He felt that all creeds are "bundles of absurdities," and that people could not be held responsible for beliefs which they could not "command [their] judgment to be satisfied with."[7] He reflected, "Rational conclusions of mind rest upon their own foundations and need no buttress [such as formal creeds] to support their foundations; and whenever a man repeats a formulary of his belief, it must be taken as an act, not of his judgment, but of his will."[8] Although willing to admit that some Christians consciously made an act of will to believe what reason might cause them to doubt, Adams felt that this was insincere.

A Christian's beliefs, Adams was convinced, should be based on a study of the Scriptures. Like his parents and like Jefferson, he had little use for professional theologians. He urged one of his sons to read the Bible for himself in order to "avoid entanglement with the controversies of theologians and avoid being a partisan between Roman, Greek, and Protestant churches."[9]

John Quincy Adams believed that the Bible was divinely inspired, and that the reading of it would lead to habitual meditation "upon subjects of the highest interest to the welfare of the individual in this world, as well as prepare him for that hereafter to which we are all destined."[10] After hearing a minister preach about the Bible's promises about the world to come, he wrote in his diary, "These promises of the

Scriptures, these transcendently sublime prophecies of the Old Covenant, and these practicable means and irresistible tendencies to their fulfillment in the New, are the most precious pledges of my faith. If I did not believe them I should be compelled to reject the whole book. I do most faithfully believe them."[11] Although he believed the Scriptures to be divinely inspired, he interpreted many passages symbolically. For example, he expressed amazement that anyone could understand the narrative of the Fall from paradise in a literal sense.

He reacted angrily to the ultraliberal theologian, philosopher, and poet Ralph Waldo Emerson, who declared "the old revelations superannuated and worn out, and [announced] the approach of new revelations and prophecies."[12] He also deplored the modern theologians whose interpretation of the Bible favored social justice in such a way as to promote drastic changes in "the foundations of human society" and favored the poor over the rich. People who taught this "fraudulent philosophy" sapped and undermined religion, instigating "the laboring classes...to hatred and violence against the proprietors."[13]

During a public lecture in Boston in November 1840, in which the congressman held his audience "transfixed," Adams, speaking of the Scriptures, declared, "Worldly theory is but a cobweb of the brain, compared to the truths of the Bible. If there never had been revelation, what would man know of his true position in this life or of his duty here in relation to a hereafter?"[14]

Adams agonized over his convictions concerning the person and work of Jesus. Like his parents, he rejected the idea of the Trinity. When a preacher at St. John's Episcopal Church in Washington tried to justify the doctrine and threatened with damnation anyone who did not subscribe to it, Adams reflected, "I have tried very hard and very sincerely to believe in the doctrine of the Trinity, because there are passages in the New Testament which I cannot deny give countenance to it; but when a dogmatist gives me a text which to my naked reason furnishes an argument against it which I find it difficult to answer, and then threatens me with eternal damnation for not believing him—my spirit revolts against the yoke."[15]

Likewise, Adams frequently wrestled with doubts about the Atonement. After attending a Presbyterian service in April 1831, he wrote:

"That the execution as a malefactor of one person, the creator of all worlds, eighteen hundred years ago, should have redeemed me, born nearly eighteen centuries after his death, from eternal damnation, is not only too shocking for my belief, but I ask myself what there can be above the level of beasts which perish in the animated being that can believe it."[16] The idea that Christ was God and suffered to save the human race Adams attributed to the misreading of the Gospel of John and the Epistles of Paul. Adams believed that doctrines such as the divinity of Christ were perverse. "That He should suffer by his own decree to save me, his own creature, from the penalty of his own law, is as inconceivable to me as that He should be his own son."[17]

At seventy Adams insisted that "the mission of Christ is to teach all mankind the way to salvation." He believed that people could save themselves through proper living and that Jesus died for mankind in the sense that his "ignominious death was necessary to the universal spread of his doctrine."[18] Jesus, he decided, came to earth to proclaim immortal life and to teach peace, goodwill, and the natural equality of mankind. He was our Savior in that he was sent by God to reveal the type of behavior pleasing to God, by which mortals could merit salvation, earning God's favor through their conduct. Christ was thus a teacher and example rather than a redeemer.

As a young man, Adams did not attend church regularly. He blamed "the tumult of the world, false shame, a distrust of my own worthiness to partake of Communion," as well as his frequent changes of residence.[19] After his father died, Adams, now president, resolved to join the church where his parents had been members, and on October 1, 1826, at the age of fifty-nine, he took his first Communion at the First Congregational Church of Quincy, Massachusetts.

After that he attended church nearly every Sunday, sometimes twice in the day. He wrote a friend: "There is no denomination of Christians with whose devotions I cannot cheerfully associate, and none to whose peculiar doctrines I can conscientiously subscribe."[20] When at home in Quincy, he usually attended the church of which he was a member. In Washington, he occasionally attended the First Unitarian Church of Washington, located at 6th and D Streets, Northwest. Most of the time, he attended either St. John's Episcopal Church, across from the

White House, or Second Presbyterian Church (the ancestor of the New York Avenue Presbyterian Church, which Lincoln would later attend). He rented pews in both of them. When he was serving in the House, he often attended the religious services that had been held there since the time of Jefferson. He felt that, as a representative of the people, it was his duty to attend.[21]

What did Adams hope to find in church? While president he wrote the answer in his diary: "Hope in the goodness of God, reliance upon his mercy in affliction, trust in him to bring light out of darkness and good out of evil."[22] Through attendance at church, Adams received "a vague and indefinite confidence of...passing unhurt through the furnace that awaits me."[23]

Adams liked to listen to sermons, even if he disagreed with them. His diary is full of criticisms. For instance, on April 4, 1830, after worshiping at a Presbyterian church in Washington, he wrote, "It is the general character of Presbyterian preaching to testify rather then to allure....Believing in the goodness and mercy of the Creator, I disbelieve those who represent him as existing only to hurl thunder— nothing but thunder. Nor do I think the moral character is improved by tempering the mind to action under the perpetual terror of the scourge....Listen with pleasure to the exposition of the mercy and goodness of God....Exhortations to righteousness and truth, brotherly kindness and charity, have more prevailment over me then unceasing denunciations of vengeance and punishment."[24] Yet he continued to attend Presbyterian services, perhaps because the messages with which he disagreed gave him something to think about.

Adams became concerned because American church attendance seemed to be declining. At seventy-one, after attending St. John's Episcopal Church, he complained to his diary: "The neglect of public worship in this city is an increasing evil, and the indifference to all religion throughout the whole country portends no good."[25] He partly attributed this to the "time-serving, cringing, subservient morality" of America's "counterfeit" clergy, as evidenced in the weak stand most Protestant denominations were taking on the issue of slavery.[26]

Adams's stand on slavery was uncompromising. He was infuriated that some ministers tried to justify slavery by citing such biblical slaveholders as Abraham, Isaac, and Jacob, and by citing the example of Saint Paul, who sent the slave Onesimus back to Philemon. "These preachers," Adams complained, "might just as well call our extermination of the Indians an obedience to Divine commands, because Jehovah commanded the children of Israel to exterminate the Canaanitish nations."[27] He was angry that the rector of St. John's Episcopal Church never criticized slavery. He groused, "No minister of the word of God, south of Mason and Dixon line, ventures to preach one word against slavery."[28] For John Quincy Adams, slavery was "a sin before the sight of God,"[29] and for this reason he vigorously opposed the annexation of Texas, which eventually entered the Union as a slave state. A few years before his death, he wrote to a group of supporters from Bangor, Maine, that "the extinction of slavery from the face of the earth" was "nothing more or less than the consummation of the Christian religion."[30]

Adams also opposed, as we have seen, the policy of his government toward the Indians. When he was president, he alienated some of his supporters by his refusal to support a measure that would have uprooted Indians in the east from their ancestral homes and deport them beyond the Mississippi, a measure that would become reality under his successors in the White House.

Adams's religious views influenced his other public positions, such as his opposition to capital punishment. "A religious principle that man has no right to take the life of man," he wrote in 1840, "will soon accomplish the abolition of all capital punishments."[31]

As might be expected, Adams favored a style of worship that was distinctly "low church." He disliked the display of the cross and the veneration of the Virgin Mary, and considered the ordination of clergy by bishops "insupportable and blasphemous," because it involved the "pretension" of the bishop to be able to confer the Holy Spirit and to be able to pardon or retain sins at his discretion.[32] Yet he deplored the custom of American Protestant churches of his day, which did not celebrate Christmas or Easter, supporting the Roman Catholic and Eastern Orthodox practices of solemnizing the two festivals "with the most animated devotion."[33] He also believed in infant baptism,[34] and not only believed in angels, but was "almost tempted to address them in prayer."[35]

Adams sought a personal relationship with his God, whom he trusted, to whose will he submitted, into whose hands he committed his destiny. After he was defeated in his bid for reelection, he wrote in December 1828: "My only trust is in the Divine Disposer; and of him all that I can presume is to stay the hand of his wrath, to grant me fortitude to endure, and, in disposing of me as to him shall seem wise and good, to extend to my wife and children an abundant portion of his mercies and consolations."[36] A few days later, he recorded: "I began the year in prayer, and then, turning to my Bible, read the first Psalm. It affirms what the righteous man is, and promises that he shall be blessed. This is comfort and consolation, and points in general terms to the path of duty. May the light of this lamp never forsake me." In a similar vein, he wrote on his seventy-fourth birthday, in 1841: "May I supplicate the Father of Spirits for the will and power to improve my last days in conformity to his will, for the good of my own family and the family of man, and in preparing to appear before his presence to plead for mercy; and for his protecting arm to shield and sustain the helpless whom I leave behind."[37]

Adams's faith sustained him through the many trials of his life, including such domestic catastrophes as the apparent suicide of his son George, just a month after Adams had left the White House.

In his diary he described how George—who had been a passenger on a ship—got up in the night and talked to two or three passengers "in a manner indicating a wandering mind," then disappeared from the upper deck of the ship. Thus, mused Adams, "it pleased the Discloser of all events to take him to himself." He poured out his anguish to his God, agonizing: "Blessed God! forgive the repining of mortal flesh at this most difficult dispensation of thy will! Forgive the wanderings of my own mind under its excruciating torture!" He begged God to have compassion on his wife, "and bear her up with thine everlasting arms. Deep have been her afflictions heretofore. But this! Oh this! Stay thy hand, God of mercy. Let her not say, My God! My God! why hast thou forsaken me? Teach her and me to bear thy holy will and to bless thy name."[38]

"This world," Adams declared in a lecture, "is but a great firma-
ment of moral and intellectual light which should serve to point us
toward eternal glory in the life to come."[39] To attain heaven was for
Adams the primary goal of earthly existence. Like everything else he
believed, he questioned this mystery when he reflected on it. For instance, he wrote in his diary on May 29, 1842: "The resurrection of
the body is the profoundest mystery of the Christian religion and the
most difficult article of the Christian faith. The perishable or corrupt-
ible property of matter seems to be so inseparable from it that imper-
ishable or immortal matter is an incredible confusion of words."[40]

When John, the second of his three children, died in the fall of 1834,
after a three-year illness, the father confided in his diary: "May God in
his infinite mercy receive him to the joys of heaven."[41] The next day he
wrote: "Oh, let me not murmur at the will of God—let me cast myself
and him upon the mercies of an omnipotent creator and preserver; let
me believe that for suffering upon Earth there is compensation in
Heaven and that there the tears of sorrow are wiped away, and that
every virtue shall be blessed with its reward—my child, my child—in
the bosom of your God may never-ending joys—joys unspeakable and
full of glory—cancel all the sufferings of which your portion was so
great here below, and may it one day be the blessed destiny of your
parents to enjoy them with you."[42]

At seventy-nine, Adams seemed aware that the sands of life were
running out, when, on October 31, 1846, he confided to his diary: "I
have not improved the scanty portion of his gifts as I might and ought
to have done. May I never cease to be grateful for the numberless
blessings received through life at his hands, never repine at what he
has denied, never murmur at the dispensations of Providence, and
implore his forgiveness for all the errors and delinquencies of my life!"[43]
Three weeks later, in Boston, he suffered a stroke, after which he said,
"I...consider myself for every useful purpose to myself or to my fellow
creatures, dead."[44] Even so, he returned to Congress, and it was there,
on the floor of the House, on February 21, 1848, he suffered a second
massive stroke. Twelve hours before he had been reading to his wife
from a new book of sermons by the rector of Washington's St. John's
Episcopal Church. Carried into the office of the Speaker of the House,

and laid on a sofa, just before lapsing into a coma from which he never awoke, he murmured, "This is the last of earth. I am content." Two days later there passed from the earthly scene a man of whom a later historian, Theodore Parker, wrote: "If there was an American who loved the praise of God more than the praise of men, I believe Mr. Adams was one...[He] looked beyond time, beyond men; looked to the eternal God, and, fearing him, forgot all other fear."[45]

∼

Profile 13
Elizabeth Ann Bayley Seton

Born: New York, New York, August 28, 1774
Died: Emmitsburg, Maryland, January 4, 1821

Mother Seton founded the first American order of nuns and, in 1975, became the first native-born American to be proclaimed a saint in the Roman Catholic Church. She has also been hailed as the founder of the parochial school system of America.

Elizabeth Bayley was born into a prominent New York family. Her father, Richard Bayley, was an eminent physician who taught medicine at what is now Columbia University and served as city health officer, and her maternal grandfather, Richard Carleton, was the rector of St. Andrew's Episcopal Church. Young Elizabeth, or Betty, who lost her mother when she was three, was part of a large family that included an older full sister and a number of younger half-siblings. Like nearly all the leading citizens of colonial times, the Bayleys were members of the Church of England. When Betty was a little girl and the United States became independent, this became the Episcopal Church.

Betty was sincerely religious, even as a child. As she grew older, she became an avid reader of the Bible, and, at the age of fifteen, was favored with a deep spiritual experience. One day in May she climbed into a wagon with a servant who was driving to the woods to cut some brush, and while he was cutting, she wandered into a beautiful meadow, where, surrounded by the sights and sounds and smells of nature, she lay on the ground and found her heart "filled even with enthusiastic love of God and admiration of his works." She wrote: "God was my father, my all. I prayed, sang hymns, cried, laughed, talking to myself of how far he could place me above all sorrow. Then I laid still to enjoy the heavenly peace that came over my soul; and, I am sure, in the two hours so enjoyed, grew ten years in the spiritual life."[1]

Her spiritual development did not diminish after she became, at nineteen, the wife of merchant William Magee (Willie) Seton and, over a period of years, the mother of their five children. Her inner life is chronicled in the letters she wrote to family and friends and by the entries in her diary, typical of which is one for May 23, 1802, in which she declared: "My soul was first sensibly convinced of the blessing and practicability of an entire surrender of itself and all its faculties to God. It has been the Lord's Day indeed to me, though many temptations to forget my heavenly possession in his constant presence have pressed upon me. In this last hour of his day I am at rest within his fold...."[2]

Betty Seton's faith was not all inward prayer and meditation. When she was twenty-three, with some of her friends, she founded a society to assist impoverished, widowed mothers, and served as treasurer of that organization for several years.[3]

As a young woman she regularly attended Trinity Episcopal Church, where, after 1800, one of the pastors was the charismatic John Henry Hobart, who later became Episcopal bishop of New York. Hobart and his wife become close friends of Willie and Betty Seton, and, for a time Betty's spiritual guide, her "blessed teacher."

At thirty, Elizabeth Seton was a devoutly religious woman whose faith extended from private devotions to social action. She had recently persuaded her husband, Willie, to commit his life to Christ. A member of the Episcopal Church, she had what would later be called an "ecumenical outlook." She did not consider one branch of Christianity superior to another. Her faith was based on the Scriptures and on private devotion, and, as far as she was concerned, if anyone truly loved Jesus Christ and made a faith commitment to him, the religious affiliation was unimportant. She believed that "everybody would be saved who meant well."[4] Around her neck she wore a crucifix, which was a custom practiced chiefly by Roman Catholics at that time; she admired "the life of the cloister"; she loved Methodist hymns; and she felt that there was much that was attractive in the way of the Quakers.[5] This would soon change.

Late in 1804, Willie Seton was bankrupt and, suffering from tuberculosis, he and Betty decided to take a trip to Italy, where he also had business associations, in hopes that this would improve his health. This did not happen, especially since, because of reports of yellow fever in New York, the Setons and other passengers were quarantined for a month in a cold, damp room in a public hospital upon their arrival in Italy. Soon afterward, William Seton died, and Betty was befriended by his business associates, Antonio and Filippo Filicchi, and their wives (one of whom was American). Three months after Seton's death, Antonio, who had business in America, accompanied Seton's widow and oldest daughter (the other children had stayed behind with relatives) back to New York. In the meantime, the four Filicchis had been pressing Betty Seton to convert to Roman Catholicism.

Later, Seton's friends would say that she had always been a "natural Catholic." Not only was she impressed by the beauty and solemnity of the churches of Italy, she was struck by the fact that Roman Catholics could partake of holy Communion every day. New York's Episcopal churches at that time were what would later be termed "low." In other words, the services were simple. Moreover, holy Communion was celebrated only on Sacrament Sunday, which occurred no more then once a month—often just three or four times a year. Communion, or the Eucharist, had always meant a great deal to Mrs. Seton. On Sacrament Sunday, she often went to different churches in New York that had their services at different times, so that she could partake of the Lord's Supper as frequently as she could. When she received, according to one biographer, "her teeth chattered against the cup of wine in an ecstasy of trembling awe."[6]

The Episcopalians of Seton's time and place believed that the sacrament of holy Communion was symbolic. Seton's encounter with the churches of Italy was her first exposure to the concept of the "real presence"—held by Roman Catholics, Eastern Orthodox and "high church" Episcopalians and Lutherans—that Jesus is present physically as well as spiritually in the sacrament.

The Filicchis insisted that theirs was the only valid church and faith. "If there is but one faith and nobody pleases God without it," Seton asked Filippo Filicchi, "where are all the good people who die out of it?"

"I don't know," he answered. "That depends on what light of faith they had received. But I know where people go who can know the right faith if they pray for it and inquire for it, and yet do neither."

"You want me to pray and inquire and be of your faith?"

"Pray and inquire," urged Filicchi. "That is all I ask you."[7]

When Seton returned to America, many of Seton's friends were horrified when they learned that she was considering affiliation with Catholicism. Some of them objected because they found the insistence by the Roman Catholic Church that it was the only true Church offensive; more objected because they found Roman Catholicism socially unacceptable. It was a poor man's religion, associated with immigrants. A conversation Seton had with her sister, Mary Magdalene Bayley Post, is illustrative. When Elizabeth argued that the Roman Church was "the first church...the old church the apostles began," Mary and her husband objected, "Church of the Apostles? Why, is not every church from the Apostles?"[8]

While Seton's Episcopalian friends, including Hobart, her pastor, frantically tried to talk her out of it, her Roman Catholic friends, especially Antonio Filicchi and his associates tried to push her in.[9] Seton was emotionally drained by this tug of war until, in January 1805, she decided to go to St. George's Episcopal Church on Sacrament Sunday. In her journal, Seton wrote: "The wants and necessities of my soul were so pressing that I looked straight to God, and told him, 'Since I cannot see the way to please you, whom alone I wish to please, everything is indifferent to me, and until you do show me the way you mean me to walk in, I will trudge on in the path you suffered me to be born in, and go even to the very sacrament where I once used to find you.'"

However, she decided that she "left the house a Protestant" and "returned to it a Catholic," determined that she would never again go to a Protestant church. At St. George's, after the public confession, when the bishop gave his absolution, Seton decided, "I had not the least faith in his prayer." When the Eucharist was celebrated and she remembered that her prayer book stated that it was to be received only "spiritually," she was thrown into emotional turmoil which was resolved only when she decided, "I will go *peaceably and firmly* to the Catholic Church—for if faith is so important to our salvation I will seek it where true faith first began, seek it among those who received it from God himself."

She continued, "The controversies on it I am quite incapable of deciding, and as the strictest Protestant allows salvation to a good Catholic, to the Catholics I will go and try to be a good one. May God accept my intention and pity me.[10]

Hobart, her Episcopal pastor, had tried to convince her that the Roman Catholic Church was the church of the Antichrist. Seton decided, "As to supposing the word of Our Lord has failed, and that he suffered his first foundation to be built on by Antichrist, I cannot stop on that without stopping on every other word of Our Lord and being tempted to be no Christian at all, for if the first Church became Antichrist, and the second holds her rights from it, then I should be afraid both might be Antichrist, and I make my way to the bottomless pit by following either."[11]

And so, on March 25, 1805, Elizabeth Bayley Seton was received into the Roman Catholic Church, much to the dismay of many of her family and friends. Seton's godmother disinherited her and some of her acquaintances shunned her. Others continued to love her and encouraged her in the work she later undertook, even though they disagreed with some of her religious positions. One such person was Seton's sister, Mary Post, who dearly loved her, but could never accept the idea that there was "any true church or false church, right faith or wrong faith." She insisted that anyone who believed in Jesus Christ as Lord and Savior was safe.[12]

Whereas Seton's contemporaries, Charles Carroll and Roger Taney, both born into Roman Catholic families, seemed to take a much more tolerant view of Protestants, Seton, the convert, for the rest of her life, took seriously and literally the teaching of her Church, that outside the Church there is no salvation. Later she wrote: "O my God! My heart trembles and faints before him...while I ask him, 'How am I here?—I taken, they left.'"[13] Referring to the passage about the Last Judgment (Luke 17:34) in which Jesus foretells that there will be two people in a bed, and one will be taken and the other left, she implied that, in his mysterious purpose, God chose her for salvation, but left behind many of her family and friends. She described the Roman Catholic Church as "the only ark in the world," and insisted that "all the heathens, savages, sects, etc." were in her heart "for prayer," but "never in my brain for what became of them." She simply relied in faith on God's wisdom and mercy.[14]

Her attitude toward Protestants seems to have been one of pity. Only Roman Catholics enjoyed the fullness of faith, and it was with "sorrow and anguish of heart" that she thought about "the naked, unsubstantial, comfortless worship they partake who know not the treasure of our faith—theirs founded on words of which they take the shadow while we enjoy the adored substance in the center of our souls."[15]

Seton tried to set up a school in New York, but she was unable to raise sufficient funds or acquire many students because of objections to her religious persuasion. In 1808, she was urged to go to Baltimore, which had a substantial Catholic population and where more support would be available. There she organized the Sisters of Charity of St. Joseph and took her first vows in March 1809. Shortly afterward she moved to rural Emmitsburg, Maryland, where she set up St. Joseph's School, which later became St. Joseph's College. This provided an education for wealthy girls, but she was able to use the tuition she received from these students to set up a free school for poor girls, and it was for this reason that she was later called the "foundress of the parochial school system in the United States."[16] Within a few years, she opened up communities in Philadelphia and New York.

Even those who disagreed with her religious positions recognized Mother Seton as a kind, sincere, and devout woman who performed a great work. One of her most prominent characteristics was her confidence in God. "All in our God, whether cloudy or clear, that is our comfort. The world or anything in it can neither give nor take."[17] When, toward the end of her life, she was faced with a shortage of financial support because of an economic depression, she wrote, "The black clouds I foresee may pass by harmless, or if in the Providence of grace they fall on me, Providence has an immense [umbrella] to hinder or break the force of the storms—what a comfort."[18]

Indeed, she delighted in the will of God. Throughout her life she endured many hardships. She lost her mother when she was three. Her father died when she was in her twenties while trying to combat an epidemic of yellow fever. She, her husband, and seemingly, most of their family suffered from tuberculosis, and at Emmitsburg, she buried two of her daughters as well as two young sisters-in-law. Yet she did not question the purpose of the Almighty. "I am the happiest of creatures in the thought that not the least thing can happen but by his will or permission; and all for the best," she wrote.[19] Another time she declared, "Our misery is not to conform ourselves to the intentions of God as to the manner in which he will be glorified. What pleases him does not please us. He wills us to enter in the way of suffering, and we desire to enter in action. We desire to give—rather than receive—and do not purely seek his will."[20]

The key to knowing and performing God's will was faith and prayer. "Prayer is all my comfort; without it I should be of little service to him," she wrote while still an Episcopalian, while her husband was dying.[21] After she became a Roman Catholic, her attitude toward prayer remained the same, although she prayed the rosary and asked the intercession of the Blessed Virgin Mary. Her definition of "faith" was the gift of believing in the teachings of the Roman Catholic Church. "I see faith as a gift of God to be diligently sought and earnestly desired, and groan to him for it in silence—since our Savior says, 'I cannot come to him unless the Father draws me.' "[22] She believed that "good reading, prayer, the sacraments, good resolutions often renewed, the remembrance of our last ends" all tended to secure "our predestination."[23] In other words, God gives human beings the gift to believe in the teachings of the Roman Catholic Church, which secured salvation. She believed that godly actions, in cooperation with this divine gift, were necessary to produce "perseverance," which "alone obtains the crown."[24]

Although she utterly rejected the Calvinism of her early spiritual mentor, John Hobart, the possibility always remained for her that, despite her faith and good works, she might still be sent to hell. Shortly before she died, she wrote a friend, "Oh, if all goes well for me [and she is saved], what will I not do for you [from heaven]. You will see. But, alas, yet if I am not one of his elect...when going down I must still lift the hands to the very last look in praise and gratitude for what he has done to save me," for in such a case, "it is only I to be blamed." This was a common belief at the time among many Protestants in the Calvinistic tradition, the idea that one must be willing to be "damned for the glory of God."[25]

Mother Seton was painfully ill during the last year or two of her life with tuberculosis and with what was diagnosed as an abscess of the breast. She considered sufferings "steps to heaven." She declared: "Tribulation is my element. If it only carries me home at last, never mind the present."[26] She looked forward to heaven, even if she did not regard her salvation as a certainty. After one of her daughters died, she wrote, "If we think of such trifles in the company of God and the choirs of the blessed—what will we think of the trials and cares, pains, and sorrows we had once upon Earth? Oh, what a mere nothing.... Eternity!—to love and serve him only—who is to be loved and eternally served and praised in heaven."[27]

Two years before she died she wrote a friend: "Mind not my health. Death grins broader in the pot every morning, and I grin at him and I show him his master....I see nothing in this world but blue sky and our altars. All the rest is so plainly not to be looked at, but all left to him, with tears only for sin. We talk now all day long of my death and how it will be just like the rest of the housework. What is it else? What came in the world for? Why in it so long? But this last great eternal end—it seems to me so simple; when I look up at the crucifix, simpler still."[28] Shortly before the end, referring to the abscess in her breast, she wrote: "If this be the way of death, nothing can be more peaceful and happy; and if I am to recover, still how sweet to rest in the arms of Our Lord! I have never felt more sensibly the presence of Our Dearest than since I have been sick. It seems as if Our Lord stood continuously by me in a corporeal form, to comfort, cheer, and encourage me in the different weary and tedious hours of pain."[29]

When one of her nuns, seeing her in pain, told her that she was praying that her sufferings would make it unnecessary for her to experience purgatory, Seton told her, "My blessed God, how far from that thought I am, of going straight to heaven, such a miserable creature as I am!"[30] She refused to drink a potion to ease her pain, declaring: "Never mind the drink. One Communion more—and then eternity!"[31] "I am thankful, Sisters," she said to the members of the community who gathered around her bed, "for your kindness to be present at this trial. Be children of the Church. Oh, thankful!"[32] Her very last words were the prayer, "May the most just, the most high and the most amiable will of God be in all things fulfilled, praised, and exalted above all forever!"[33]

~

Profile 14

Roger Brooke Taney

Born: Calvert County, Maryland, March 17, 1777
Died: Washington, D.C., October 12, 1864

The American lawyer and statesman, appointed chief justice of the United States Supreme Court by Andrew Jackson, served nearly three decades and was famous for upholding the rights of the states and the interests of the South. He was one of a very few Roman Catholics in public life at the time, but few influential people, however, seemed threatened by his religious affiliation. Daniel Webster, the powerful senator from Massachusetts, voiced the opinion of most of their contemporaries when he commented in 1850 that "a Roman Catholic is chief justice and no man imagines that the administration of public justice is less respectable or less secure."[1]

Taney (whose name was pronounced *tawny*) was born to the landed aristocracy in Calvert County, in southern Maryland. He was of English ancestry and his ancestors were Roman Catholics when they immigrated to America well over a century before his birth. Roger studied under private tutors until he entered Dickinson College, in

Carlisle, Pennsylvania, from which he graduated at twenty. As a boy he was taught to read from the Bible by his tutor, who was Episcopalian.[2]

As a young man, he moved to Frederick in northern Maryland, where he practiced law for two decades. In January 1806, he married Anne Key, the sister of Francis Scott Key, the attorney best-known for writing the words to "The Star-Spangled Banner." Anne was an Episcopalian and, although she and Roger were married by a Roman Catholic priest, they both refused to agree to raise their children as Roman Catholics. Instead, the Taneys had a prenuptial agreement that all their sons would be reared Roman Catholic and all their daughters Episcopalians. Of their seven children, only one was a boy, and he died shortly after birth. So all six Taney girls were raised Episcopalian, with their father's full consent.[3] Although they frequently attended evening services with their father, they attended morning services with their mother. One of the girls, as an adult, did become a Roman Catholic. Once, on a visit to the Taney home, Roger's pastor tried to convert the girls, and drew a mild rebuke from their father, who told him that "such matters are not debated in our family."[4]

Friends agreed that "no man was more happily married than Roger Taney." It was said that "The Chief Justice and Mrs. Taney seemed made for each other. The two made their home all but perfect in parental love and filial piety."[5] Both were described by those who knew them as exemplary Christians.[6] On their forty-sixth wedding anniversary in 1852, Roger wrote Anne, "Although I am sensible that, in that long period, I have done many things that I ought not to have done, and have left undone many things which I ought to have done, yet in constant affection to you I have never wavered—never being insensible how much I owe to you—and now I pledge you again a love as true and sincere as that I offered you on the 7th of January 1806."[7] Both husband and wife were active in their respective churches, both considered the other a true Christian, and both believed that they would meet in heaven.

Although Taney never tried to force his religious beliefs on anyone,[8] he was an actively practicing Roman Catholic throughout his long life. Late in life he wrote a relative, "Most thankful I am that reading, reflection, studies, and experiences of a long life have strengthened and confirmed my faith in the Catholic Church, which has never ceased to teach her children how they should live and how they should die."[9] He insisted that "religion was the moving principle of his life."[10] Each day, before he began his duties, he knelt in prayer "to seek divine guidance." He and Anne closed each day with family prayers, which included their black servants.[11]

Taney regularly made his confession. He was frequently seen waiting his turn in a line of black penitents outside the confessional box. Once, when a priest tried to accommodate him promptly, he rejected the preferential treatment, and remained in his place in line.[12]

In 1855, Anne Taney died, after forty-nine years of marriage. Their daughter Alice died in the same year. Taney, then eighty, told his priest, "The truth is, Father, that I have resolved that my first visit should be to the cathedral, to invoke strength and grace from God, to be resigned to his holy will, by approaching the altar and receiving holy Communion—preceded, of course, by confession."[13] Around the same time, he wrote a cousin, "It has pleased God mercifully to support me through his visitation, and to recall my bewildered thoughts and enable me to feel the chastisement comes from him and that it is my duty to submit to it with calmness and resignation."[14]

The witness of this man, acknowledged by all who knew him to be a sincere Christian, was gravely marred two years later when he wrote the majority opinion in the Supreme Court case known as *Scott v. Sandford*, better known as the Dred Scott Decision. Dred Scott, a slave of about sixty, had sued his master for his freedom on the grounds that he had resided for some time in free territory. He contended that if a slaveholder took his slaves into a state or territory where slavery was illegal, the slaves were legally free. Taney and his court disagreed, because, they insisted, the Constitution protects the rights of U.S. citizens to their property—and slaves are property. Taney further declared that slavery was legal in every section of the country and that no state or territory had the right to forbid or restrict it.

Worse, Taney went out of his way to insist that the Negro was not a citizen and had no rights. Taney declared, "The Negroes are not included, and were not intended by the Constitution to be included in 'the people'; but were considered a subordinate and inferior race of beings, who had been subjugated by the dominant race, and whether emancipated or not, yet remained subject to their authority, and had no rights or privileges, but such as those who held the power and government might choose to grant them." He insisted that for more than a century before the Declaration of Independence, African Americans had "been regarded as beings of an inferior race, and altogether unfit to associate with the white race, either in social or political relations, and, so far inferior that they had no rights which the white man was bound to respect, and that the Negro might, justly and lawfully, be reduced to slavery for his benefit."[15]

The Dred Scott Decision was the occasion of horror and revulsion in the North. One member of the Congress spoke for many when he wondered how "a humane Christian man could assert publicly such a monstrous theory."[16] One of Taney's biographers regretted the "false and inhuman" sentiment expressed by an otherwise "humane and truthful man."[17]

Although Reverdy Johnson, a prominent politician who was a close friend of Taney, claimed, after Taney's death, that Taney had asserted the idea of black inferiority, not to justify it, "but to deplore it," most believed that Taney, at that point in his life at least, believed strongly in what he had written.[18]

Yet the first eight decades of Taney's life seem to belie his reputation as a racist and Negrophobe that he built for himself through the Scott decision. Early in his career, he often defended the legal rights of blacks. Once he helped a free black man purchase his wife.[19] In 1818, while defending Jacob Gruber, a white Methodist minister charged with inciting slaves to revolt during a sermon in Hagerstown, Maryland, Taney decried the "reptiles, who live by trading in human flesh, and enrich themselves by tearing the husband from the wife—the infant from the bosom of the mother." He called slavery an "evil" and a "blot on our national character." He said that every real lover of freedom hoped that slavery would be—gradually—wiped away.[20]

Throughout his life, he opposed segregation—at least in seating—in Roman Catholic churches. Even after the Dred Scott Decision, he confided to a friend, "Thank God that at least in one place all men are equal—in the Church of God."[21]

Thirty years before the Dred Scott Decision, Taney freed all of his slaves, except two who were too old and feeble to function on their own. "These two I supported in comfort, as long as they lived," Taney insisted. He went on to say that "none of those whom I manumitted disappointed my expectations, but have shown, by their conduct, that they were worthy of freedom and knew how to use it."[22] When he freed his slaves, he gave each of them a wallet. Once a month, the freedmen were to come to him to have the wallet filled with small change.[23] He gave them only small sums because he did not believe that blacks were competent to handle larger amounts of money.

Taney held no personal animosity toward blacks. He was opposed to slavery, but favored a process of gradual emancipation and a resettling of the Negroes in Africa. But he held a low opinion of the intellectual capacity of the African American. He genuinely felt that the black person was not capable of functioning successfully in white society. He wrote to one of his critics that his experience showed that emancipation was often a disaster to the freedman. He insisted that, in many cases, slavery actually "promoted [the] happiness" of the black man. He contended that the legal protection of the slave from maltreatment by his master had to be offered only in such a way that it did not impair "that degree of authority which is essential to the interest and well-being" of both master and slave. He felt that if the slaves received more privileges, "they would probably be told that they were wrung from their master by their Northern friends and be taught to regard them as the first step to a speedy and universal emancipation, placing them on a perfect equality with the white race."[24]

Taney, therefore, did not believe that his stand in the Dred Scott Decision was inconsistent with his identity as a Christian, because he seemed genuinely to believe that Negroes were incapable of exercising their rights as citizens and were better off under the control of whites, although preferably not as slaves. However, even though he personally opposed slavery, he insisted that the Constitution permitted it. Thus, he never regretted the decision and felt persecuted by those who charged him with hypocrisy.

Taney remained chief justice until his death at eighty-seven. He was constantly in conflict with Abraham Lincoln. During Taney's last year, it was rumored that he planned to declare the Emancipation Proclamation unconstitutional, but death intervened in October 1864. Taney had been ill for some time with a painful intestinal complaint. The day he died he told one of his daughters, "My little girl, my race is run. I have no desire to stay in this valley of sorrows, but for my poor little ones. My end is near. Please call the priest, for I wish to prepare myself to see God with all the precious aids and blessings our Holy Mother Church can give."[25] Just before he died, his pains ceased. He raised his head, and with his eyes "clear and bright," he prayed, "Lord Jesus, receive my spirit!" An hour later, with "a sweet, peaceful face,"[26] he died at his home, 23 Blagden's Row, near Indiana Avenue in Washington, D.C.

～

Profile 15
Henry Clay

Born: Hanover County, Virginia, April 12, 1777
Died: Washington, D.C., June 29, 1852

A lthough he failed in his three attempts to capture the presidency, Henry Clay, first representative and then senator from Kentucky, was one of the most influential statesmen of his time. As Speaker of the House, he was a major factor in America's entry into the conflict known as the War of 1812. Later, as the Great Pacificator, over a period of thirty years, he was able to engineer three important compromises in Congress to mollify radicals from the Northern and Southern factions sufficiently to postpone civil war. Clay was known as a great orator, and people often walked thirty miles to hear him speak.

Like so many of his contemporaries, Clay was unchurched for most of his life. His father, a Baptist minister, died when he was four, and Clay never showed any interest in that denomination. His wife of more than fifty years, Lucretia Hart, was a devout Episcopalian, and Clay frequently attended church with her, but he entered his seventh decade without even being baptized.

Clay was by no means an atheist or agnostic. Although he had a reputation as a gambler and a heavy drinker, he believed, at least on paper, in Christian morality. He belonged to the Baltimore Sabbath Association, about which he wrote, "I share with them in sentiments of profound reverence for the Sabbath, as a religious institution, and...I fervently hope that all laudable endeavors to inculcate the proper observance of it may be crowned with success."[1]

Throughout his life he believed in a God who controlled human destiny. Speaking to the House of Representatives concerning a proposal he was endorsing, he said, "I would invoke the aid of the Most High. I would anxiously and fervently implore his Divine assistance, that he would be graciously pleased to shower on my country his richest blessings; that he would sustain...the humble individual that stands before him, and lend him the power, moral and physical, to perform the solemn duties which now belong to his public station."[2] Another time, he commented that he believed that God would "settle all things as they should be, and that whatever wrong or injustice I might experience at the hands of men, he, to whom all hearts are open and fully known, [will], in the end, by the inscrutable dispensations of his providence, rectify all error, redress all wrong, and cause ample justice to be done."[3]

Clay stood for toleration of all religions. He corresponded with Mormon founder Joseph Smith and told him that he sympathized with the Latter Day Saints in their "sufferings under injustice." He believed that Smith and his followers should "enjoy the security and protection of the Constitution and the laws."[4] Clay worked to secure the appointment of Charles C. Pise, a Roman Catholic priest, as chaplain to the Senate.[5] When one of his granddaughters expressed her intention to become a nun, Clay urged her to do whatever would make her happy, and insisted that he had no prejudice against Roman Catholics who were "as sure of eternal happiness in another world as the most pious Protestants."[6]

As Clay grew older, he felt the need for a deeper commitment. He wrote, "I am a member of no religious sect. I am not a professor of religion. I regret that I am not. I wish that I was, and I trust that I shall be. But I have, and always have had, a profound respect for Christianity, the religion of my fathers, and for its rites, its usages, and its observances."[7]

Not only was Clay frustrated by his failure to be elected as president, he endured much suffering in his private life. He and his wife were the parents of eleven children. None of his six daughters lived to be thirty, and all of them predeceased their parents. Two of his sons suffered from psychiatric problems, and another was an alcoholic. When his last surviving daughter, Anne, developed life-threatening complications after childbirth, Clay, for the first time in his life, began to pray regularly. When he learned of her death, he fainted, falling to the ground as if he had been shot. When he regained consciousness he could not stop crying, and sobbed, "I have prayed for this dear child, night and morning have I fervently prayed for her; but oh! My prayers have not been heard."[8] He wrote his wife, "Alas!...The Great Destroyer has come, and taken from us our dear, dear only daughter....If the thunderbolt of Heaven had fallen on me—unprepared as I fear I am—I would have submitted...to a thousand deaths to have saved this dear child....Ah! How inscrutable the ways of providence! I feel that one of the strongest ties that bound me to the Earth is broken—forever broken. My heart will bleed as long as it palpitates."[9] A few weeks later, when he tried to introduce a bill in the Senate, he broke down and admitted that he was devastated by the most severe affliction with which providence could have visited him.

In his grief, Clay did not curse God nor question his existence. He admitted that his pious wife Lucretia possessed "a resource" in her grief that he did not have.[10] As Clay grew older, grief and disappointment tended to draw him closer to God. Like many people of his day, his reaction to suffering was a feeling of the need to submit to God's will. In 1842, he wrote a minister friend, "My mind has been often seriously impressed by grave consideration of preparation for a future state; but like the crowd in the active bustle of life and its varied occupations, I have perhaps too much neglected so weighty a matter."[11] In October 1844, he wrote another minister, "Although I am not a member of any Christian church, I have a profound sense of the inexpressible value of our religion, which has increased and strengthened as I have advanced in years; and I sincerely hope that I may yet be inspired with that confidence in the enjoyment of the blessings, in another state of existence, which it promises, that disarms death of all its terrors."[12] A month later, after his final defeat for the presidency, he spoke of the Bible to a group of supporters, "I do not know of anything but that book that can reconcile us to such events."[13]

Now in his late sixties and still unbaptized, many believed that Clay hesitated to request the sacrament because he had never had a clear-cut experience of conversation. Then in February 1847, his son, Henry Clay, Jr., serving in the Mexican War—a conflict his father had strenuously opposed—died in the Battle of Buena Vista—bayoneted to death. The death of the young man in "this most unnecessary and horrible war with Mexico" completely devastated Clay. He wrote, "There are some wounds so deep and so excruciatingly painful that only he can heal them by whose inscrutable dispensations they have been inflicted. And the death of my beloved son is one of them....Oh, God! How inscrutable are thy dispensations!"[14]

Clay now decided to take the step. He commented that perhaps his sufferings were intended to "detach us altogether from this world" and "prepare us for another and a better world."[15] On June 22, 1847, at the age of seventy, Henry Clay was baptized in his mansion in Lexington, Kentucky, along with one of his daughters-in-law and four of his grandchildren. The next month he joined the Episcopal Church, making his first Communion in the chapel of nearby Transylvania University. Andrew Jackson had once commented that Henry Clay would either die a drunkard or join the church.[16]

The Great Pacificator, suffering from tuberculosis, was now nearing the end of his life. He confided to a friend that he was "not certain of having experienced that change of heart which divines call the new birth," but declared that for years he had prayed every night and was "depending on Jesus for my hope of immortality."[17] Just before he died he told another friend, "I hope that I have done some good during the time I have lived, and I trust that the attention I have given of late respecting my future state will entitle me to a happy home in another and better world. There is something within me that tells me of a future state. This frail and failing body of mine tells me that this is not my home, for, while the body fails, the mind grows stronger, and points us to that place where we shall forever rest free from all troubles."[18] On June 28, 1852, after months of terrible suffering, which he bore with "the fortitude of a Christian hero,"[19] Clay died in the National Hotel in Washington (across from the present site of the National Gallery of Art). His friend and colleague, John Crittenden, senator from Kentucky, said that in his final illness, Clay's patience, meekness, and gentleness "shone around him like a mild celestial light, breaking upon him from another world."[20]

∼

Profile 16
Daniel Webster

Born: Salisbury, New Hampshire, January 18, 1782
Died: Marshfield, Massachusetts, October 24, 1852

Daniel Webster, senator from Massachusetts for more than twenty years and U.S. secretary of state in the early 1840s, was one of the most influential political leaders of his time. He is perhaps best remembered today as a speaker whose oratorical powers were said to be "unequaled in America and unexcelled in the wide world,"[1] who, at a time when some politicians fought for the rights of states, supported the authority of the central government and argued for the indivisibility of the Union. A nation in which individual states could defy the will of the central government (as some tried to do over the issues of slavery and import taxes) was no nation; such a union, he said, was but a "rope of sand." The freedoms to which Americans were accustomed could be maintained only by a strong union, as he affirmed when he concluded a famous speech in the Senate with the words, "Liberty and Union, now and forever, one and inseparable."[2]

Webster was born in New Hampshire, one of eight children of a farming family. Both of his parents were members of the local Congregational Church and were very religious. Daniel's mother gave him a

Bible when he was a small child, and later he claimed that he could never "recollect a time when I could not read the Bible."[3] Every evening the family had devotions, during which Daniel's father would read Scripture to the family. Daniel began to memorize the Bible, and, when, as a boy he worked in a tavern, he recited passages of Scripture for the teamsters as he watered their horses.[4] Throughout his life, he read a portion of the Bible each day, and, in mature years, he made it a point to read through the entirety of the Scriptures during the course of a year.[5] "The Gospel leaves the individual sinner alone with himself and his God," he declared.[6] He believed that the Bible was "the will and word of God" that could be understood "in the plain and obvious meaning of its passages." It was infallible. "It fits man for life," he said. "It prepares him for death."[7]

While he was a student at Dartmouth College, Webster faithfully attended the chapel services mornings, evenings, and Sundays. When he taught school briefly at Fryeburg, Maine, he opened and closed each school day with prayer,[8] and, throughout his life, he believed that children should be taught religion in school, insisting that education was useless unless there was "a fragrance of Christianity about it."[9] He made his position very clear when, late in life, he served as attorney for the heirs of one Stephen Girard. They were trying—unsuccessfully, as it turned out—to overturn the will of the Philadelphia businessman who left several million dollars to set up a school for orphan boys with the condition that no clergyman or priest or missionary be allowed on the premises, so that the minds of the boys could be protected until they were old enough to make their own decisions about religion.[10] Webster argued that the existence of such a school would undermine the foundation of the American nation by spreading unbelief in what had been founded as a Christian nation.[11] He argued that Christianity was the law of the land—a "general, tolerant Christianity, independent of sects and parties," a Christianity inclusive of "the massive cathedral of the Catholic; the Episcopalian church, with its lofty spire pointing heavenward; the plain temple of the Quaker; [and] the log church of the hardy pioneer of the wilderness."[12] On another occasion Webster insisted that civilization could, indeed, not flourish without Christianity.[13]

In 1807, just before his marriage to Grace Fletcher, the daughter of a Congregational minister, Webster joined the Congregational Church of Salisbury, New Hampshire, where he was then living. Around this time he composed a personal "Confession of Faith," which he affirmed for the rest of his life and which declared Webster's belief in the existence of God and the Trinity, freewill, resurrection of the dead, predestination, salvation through the merits of Jesus Christ as the Son of God, plus other traditional Congregationalist beliefs. He concluded his confession of faith with these words: "Finally, I believe that Christ has imposed on all his disciples a life of active benevolence, that he who refrains only from what he thinks to be sinful, has performed but a part, and a small part, of his duty; that he is bound to do good and communicate, to love his neighbors, to give food and drink to his enemy, and to endeavor, so far as in him lies, to promote peace, truth, piety, and happiness in a wicked and forlorn world, believing that in the great day which is to come, there will be no other standard of merit, no other criterion of character, than that which is already established, 'By their fruits ye shall know them.'"[14]

Webster remained a Congregationalist all his life. When he moved to Boston in 1816, he joined the fashionable Brattle Street Church, where one of his friends was pastor. Although it had the reputation for being liberal, Webster never modified his own personal creed. When at his estate at Marshfield, he attended a nearby Congregational church, but in Washington be usually worshiped at an Episcopal church, where be enjoyed the formal liturgy.[15]

Like many Northerners, Webster believed that slavery was incompatible with the spirit of Christianity, but he was not an abolitionist, and felt that it was better to rely on "moral suasion," to convince his Southern countrymen that slavery was wrong, than to impose an end to the institution. He felt that the kindness, love, and justice that were the teachings of Christ would slowly, but surely and peacefully, eradicate slavery.[16]

Some of Webster's contemporaries were not impressed by Webster's professions of piety. He projected the image of the crafty and sometimes devious politician for whom pragmatism often seemed more important than principle—what would work was more important than what was right. He was accused of heavy drinking, of extravagant living, and of mismanagement of his finances. Webster's critics pointed to moral flaws which they believed to be symptoms of a feeble religious commitment,[17] of shallow faith and superficial religion. An editorial written shortly after Webster's death described him as a man with "a great deal of religiosity in his nature, but...not what is commonly termed a religious man." A later writer claimed that for Webster, religion was "a sentiment, not a conviction."[18]

Webster's friends felt that despite his apparent arrogance, religion meant more to him than showed outwardly. Although there is no evidence that he ever had anything like a religious conversion or even that he ever agonized over his sins or his relationship with God, some of Webster's writings and statements indicate that his religious faith was important to him, especially during times of personal trial. For instance, after his wife and two of his brothers died within a short time of one another, Webster wrote to a friend in January 1832, "For that anguish of the heart which the death of beloved objects creates, there is no solace but Christian resignation; no balm but in the soft effusions of that spirit which can say, 'Not as I wilt, but as thou wilt!' " He believed that afflictions "strengthen religious feelings" as did "that devout trust which teaches us that all is in his hand, and assures us that the end will be all right."[19]

Webster's religious faith was quite in evidence during his last illness. Dying of liver disease at his estate, Marshfield, after signing his will, he went on to declare to his lawyer, "My general wish on earth has been to do my Maker's will. I thank him now for all the mercies that surround me. I thank him for the means he has given me of doing some little good; for my children, those beloved objects; for my nature and associations. I thank him that I am to die, if I am, under so many circumstances of love and affection. I thank him for all his care."

He went on to say, "No man who is not a brute can say that he is not afraid of death." Of Christ he said, "The Christ mystery is Jesus Christ—the Gospel. What would be the condition of any of us if we had not the hope of immortality? What ground is there to rest upon but the Gospel?...But, thank God, the Gospel of Jesus Christ brought life and immortality to light—rescued it—brought it to *light*."[20]

Under the influence of painkillers, Webster fell asleep, but roused himself to begin, in a weak and faltering voice, the Our Father. After he was propped up on pillows, he continued clearly and distinctly, to the end. When his pastor read him the Twenty-Third Psalm, Webster responded enigmatically, "Yes, thy rod, thy staff, but the fact, the fact I want!" A few hours later, while his son read to him from his favorite poem, Thomas Gray's "Elegy Written in a Country Churchyard," Webster smiled and died.[21]

∼

Profile 17

John Caldwell Calhoun

Born: Abbeville, South Carolina, March 18, 1782
Died: Washington, D.C., March 31, 1850

Senator from South Carolina for many years, John C. Calhoun, who also served as vice president and as secretary of state, and who, along with Daniel Webster and Henry Clay, was a part of the great triumvirate of leaders who dominated the United States Congress for more than thirty years. A defender of the interests of the South and of States' Rights, he wrote the *South Carolina Exposition and Protest*, which argued that states have the right to "nullify or refuse to enforce, legislation from the United States Congress which they judge to be unconstitutional.

Born into a Presbyterian family, Calhoun, at twenty, left his native South Carolina to enroll in the junior class of Yale College in New Haven, Connecticut. Yale was then in the midst of a revival led by its dynamic and devout president, Timothy Dwight. Two years earlier, there was only one student at Yale, which was still run by Congregational ministers, who regularly partook of holy Communion in the chapel. By 1802, when Calhoun arrived, half of the student body had been admitted to the Lord's Supper after professing a personal commitment to Jesus Christ. Dwight minced no words. He denounced dancing, called the theater gross and immoral, and even described Shakespeare as "the language of vice."[1] Above all, Dwight called on the young men to commit their lives to Christ in an act of faith. The revival continued during Calhoun's stay at Yale, but the South Carolinian was not converted. Although he accepted much of what Dwight had to say about morality, he rejected what the college president taught about faith. He always insisted that he could not accept any doctrines or creeds unless he could "imagine them in practical operation and foresee their results."[2] This he claimed he was unable to do with traditional Christianity.

Calhoun was a rather cold, severe man, who never joked or engaged in small talk and was noted for self-discipline and self-reliance. He did not smoke, and drank only wine, and this in moderation. He did not play cards, nor, for that matter, take any recreation. He was faithful to his wife, Floride, and devoted to their ten children.

The master of, at one time, nearly one hundred slaves, he believed that Negroes were inferior, but was concerned that his servants were happy, well-fed, and content.[3] One of his sons had a plantation in an unhealthy area of Alabama, and, to preserve the health of the slaves, Calhoun and the son rotated the work force between South Carolina and Alabama in six-month shifts. One could argue that this practice resulted from concern over financial investment, but it was also a fact that Calhoun was reluctant, under any circumstances, to separate slave families.

In his own way, Calhoun was a religious man. He was an avid reader of the Bible and believed that many of its prophecies applied to his own time. He was especially obsessed with a prophecy from the eleventh chapter of Daniel which read: "With a great army...the king of the north shall come, and throw up siege-works, and take a well-fortified city. And the forces of the south shall not stand."[4] This passage, he feared, referred to a civil war that would break out in America and which the South would lose. A minister who discussed religion with Calhoun was "astonished to find him better informed than himself on [the] very points where he had expected to give him information.[5] Calhoun's wife, Floride, belonged to an Episcopal church, and he attended regularly with her. At worship, he was disturbed when anybody in the congregation showed signs of inattention. Each night he held family prayers, and became indignant when guests refused to participate in them. Once, when one visitor declined to pray, Calhoun ordered a slave to saddle the man's horse and put him out.[6]

Calhoun, who from an early age, admired Jefferson, shared many of the Virginian's religious ideas. The South Carolinian believed that the existence of Providence, as he usually called God, was evident through the observation of an orderly universe, which operated "according to discoverable laws."[7] When he was in his late fifties, although increasingly troubled by the growing power of the North and of the central government, he wrote to a friend, "I look with perfect composure on the advance of time, knowing that [whatever happens] is the order of Providence and that it is our highest duty to acquiesce to his decrees. My confidence in his wisdom and goodness is without limits and has been the support which has sustained me through all the vicissitudes of life."[8]

One of Calhoun's objections to traditional Christianity was that it taught that human beings were, without the grace of God, hopeless sinners. As a man of blameless moral life, he found himself unable to confess his "personal unfitness."[9] And so he never joined any church until June 1822, when, at forty, he became a charter member of the First Unitarian Church of Washington, D.C., which opened at 6th and D Streets, NW. This was the same church that John Quincy Adams occasionally attended. Like Jefferson, Calhoun believed that "Unitarianism is the only true faith and will ultimately prevail over the world."[10]

Like many other early proponents of Unitarianism, Calhoun believed in heaven. When one of his daughters died, he told his wife, for example, that Providence would assure that the child would be "far more happy than she could be with us."[11] He also believed that Providence governed the affairs of the world and of all human beings.

There is no indication that Calhoun ever accepted the divinity of Christ. Once, when a friend urged him to "seek God in Christ," Calhoun was silent.[12] When he was dying in Washington in March 1850, he refused to see a minister. When the chaplain of the Senate visited him and, apparently, urged him to accept Christ as his Savior, Calhoun dismissed him, retorting angrily, "I won't be told what to

think! This is a subject that I have thought about all my life!"[13] Later
he told his doctor, "I have an unshaken reliance upon the providence
of God."[14] Later the same day, after insisting, "I am perfectly comfortable," he died quietly, serenely, and confidently.

∼

Profile 18
James Knox Polk

Born: Pineville, North Carolina, November 2, 1795
Died: Nashville, Tennessee, June 14, 1849

and

Sarah Childress Polk

Born: Murfreesboro, Tennessee, September 4, 1803
Died: Nashville, Tennessee, August 14, 1891

The statesman from Tennessee served as Speaker of the House of
Representatives and then as governor of his state before his election as president. Although he served but one term, the Democrat was
one of America's strongest and most successful chief executives. He
had only four goals when he attained the presidency: to lower import
duties, to establish what was called an independent treasury, and to
acquire Oregon and California. He achieved all these goals.

Described by those who knew him as rigid, humorless, obstinate,
pompous, suspicious, and secretive,[1] he did not impress most people
as particularly religious. His mother was a devout Presbyterian, but
his father never went to church. Young Polk was not baptized because
the policy of his mother's pastor was to christen only children from a
union in which both parents were church members. The boy was, however, exposed to traditional Christian teaching and practice through
his mother. When he attended the University of North Carolina, it was
run by Presbyterian clergy, and students were required to attend chapel

each day at 6:15 in the morning, as well as Sunday services. They also had to pass exams on biblical doctrine.[2]

Polk evidently felt that spiritual convictions were not an appropriate subject for conversation or correspondence. One of his friends recalled that Polk believed that "religion [was] the very best possession in the world, and the last to be spoken of," and felt that it should "dwell quietly in the heart and rule the life."[3]

After his wife joined the Presbyterian church, Polk attended regularly with her, but made no move to join. He confided to friends that he preferred the Methodist church, and that if he were ever to unite with any denomination, it would be with the Methodists.[4]

When the Polks entered the White House in 1845, they began to attend the First Presbyterian Church, located near the Capitol. They went nearly every Sunday, except when Sarah Polk was sick. On those occasions, the President worshiped at Foundry Methodist Church, at 14th and G Streets, a few blocks from the White House, or at the services in the Senate chamber, where his friend, Henry Slicer, a Methodist minister, was chaplain.

Polk kept a diary of his White House years, but, unlike John Quincy Adams, seldom commented on religious matters. The diary records Polk's angry reaction to a Presbyterian minister who publicly criticized him for appointing two Roman Catholic priests as army chaplains: "I have met with no man during my administration among the numerous office seekers who have beset me for whom I have so profound contempt. To attempt to connect me with religious feuds between sects...proves him to be a man destitute of both religion and principle."[5] The only time Polk expressed in his diary (or anywhere else) his private feelings on religious matters occurred early in his presidency, after be heard a sermon on the Day of Judgment and wrote: "I thought of the vanity of this world's honors, how little they would profit me a half century hence, and that it was time for me to be putting my house in order."[6]

Polk survived his presidential term by only three months, dying in Nashville of an intestinal disorder. Unwilling to die unbaptized, he sent for his wife's minister, Dr. John T. Edgar, pastor of the First Presbyterian Church of Nashville and a friend of the late Andrew Jackson.

"Sir, if I had suspected twenty years ago that I should come to my deathbed unprepared," Polk explained, "it would have made me a wretched man. Yet I am about to die and have made no preparation. Tell me, sir, can there be grounds for a man thus situated to hope?"[7] Edgar returned the next day and Polk explained that sixteen years before he had told his friend, John B. McFerrin, a Methodist minister, that if he were ever to be baptized, McFerrin would be the man to do it. Polk went on to explain to the Presbyterian pastor that, although his wife and mother were Presbyterians, his own beliefs were more in line with the Methodists.[8]

And so it was decided that both Edgar and McFerrin would preside in a private service in the ex-president's sickroom, but that it would be McFerrin who would baptize the dying man and administer holy Communion. And so it happened. After receiving the Eucharist, Polk turned to his brother William and murmured, "I had intended to do this for a long time, but, in the hurry and business of life and the political affairs of the country, I postponed it till now."[9] The next day, Polk died.

Sarah Childress Polk survived her husband for more than thirty years; they had no children. She seems to have been the spiritual leader in the marriage. In 1833, when she was thirty, she joined the Presbyterian Church of Columbia, Tennessee, and, when she and her husband moved to Nashville, she united with the First Presbyterian Church there, where she remained active into her eighth decade.

"I am only an atom in the hands of God," she once said.[10] After her death, one of her pastors characterized her as a woman with a "sunny temper" and "cheerful disposition," whose life was grounded in "absolute submission to the Lord's will," and who believed that "everything sent to her in the way of sorrow was a means of discipline."[11]

Sarah Polk once told her pastor, "In view of what Jesus suffered for me, I esteem no suffering too great to be borne for him."[12] She was in the habit of offering up her sufferings to God in the belief that he would accept them for the benefit of those for whom she prayed, that they would shower down as blessings for them.

According to her pastor, she was always thankful to God and received anything that happened to her in life "as from God's hand."[13] She saw God's hand in everything and was always praising him for his goodness to her. "God is good to me beyond my deservings," she once said.[14]

As First Lady she served as her husband's secretary and was in the habit of kneeling in prayer before any important appointment or engagement. The Spanish Madonna, as she was called because of her dark beauty and pious bearing, banned the serving of hard liquor in the White House and proscribed dancing as undignified. She also disapproved of playing cards and of going to the theater or even concerts. She laid down the law that no state business of any kind was to be conducted in the White House on Sunday.[15]

A continual reader of the Bible, Sarah Polk also believed in the power of prayer. At the age of eighty-five, when asked if she believed that prayer would cure the sick, she replied: "Let the ladies pray, and if they think any sickness they have may be cured by prayer, it is a beautiful faith. I have often prayed for such things, and whenever I have failed to get the desired answer, my faith was only strengthened, because I considered that my prayer might not have been made in the right spirit or the right time, and that another time my desire might be granted."[16]

Toward the end of her life, failing health made it impossible for the former First Lady to attend church, but, during the time that services were held, she was observed at the window, gazing longingly in the direction of her beloved congregation. In the summer of 1891, she was told that the hyacinths were beginning to fade, and said: "I have rejoiced, just as the flowers do, in a free and fragrant life. But now it is time to fade and disappear."[17] When she was told that death was close at hand, she exclaimed: "Praise God from whom all blessings flow! I am ready and willing to go."

As all her relatives and many friends gathered at her bedside, Sarah Polk spoke about her faith in Christ, repeating her favorite Bible verses and portions of her favorite hymn, "I Would Not Live Always, I Ask Not To Stay." She then placed her hands, in turn, on the heads of all ten people in the room, saying to each: "The Lord bless thee and keep thee and give thee happiness and love and everlasting peace!"

For a time, she lay silently. When one of her nieces started to weep hysterically and cry, "Aunt Sarah, do you love me?" she opened her eyes and protested: "I do! I do!" A few minutes later she whispered: "Ice." When a niece tried to administer the ice with a spoon, the old lady snatched the ice in her hand and placed it in her mouth, insisting, "I am *not* a baby, my dear!" Two minutes later she gave "two gentle sighs" and died "with an expression of serenity and peace."[18]

∼

Profile 19
Sojourner Truth

Born: Hurley, Ulster County, New York, c1797
Died: Battle Creek, Michigan, November 26, 1883

The eccentric and colorful reformer was celebrated for her home-spun speeches on behalf of the great causes of her day, such as the abolition of slavery, women's rights, and temperance. A tall, black-skinned former slave from upstate New York, whose childhood language was Low Dutch, she spoke, in private conversation, "correct and beautiful English," but in most of her speeches and interviews affected black dialect.[1] Nevertheless, her effect was usually described as electrifying.

Slavery was legal in the state of New York until the late 1820s. Isabella Baumfree (or Bomefree) was born a slave of Johannes Hardenburgh in Hurley, Ulster County. Her parents, James and Elizabeth, were the parents of several children, of whom Isabella was the next to the youngest, but all of them were eventually sold. Isabella was nine when she was sold away from her parents, and, in the first three decades of her life, knew four different masters, was frequently mistreated, and grew up illiterate, and, in her own words, "ignorant as a horse."[2] However, through her mother, whom she called "Mau-Mau-Bett," she received the rudiments of religious instruction. Elizabeth, who spoke only Dutch, taught her daughter to be honest, to obey her master, and to pray the Our Father. She taught her that God lives in the sky and can see everything that happens on earth. "When you are beaten…or fall into any trouble, you must ask help of him, and he will always hear and help you."[3]

As a young girl, Isabella often went to a little island in a nearby stream. There, in its cover of willow shrubbery, she prayed to God. She remembered her mother's instructions, and prayed the Our Father, conversing with God as if he were another person. She had the curious idea that God could not hear her unless she spoke aloud, and so she prayed at the top of her voice. She demanded "with little expenditure of reverence or fear, a supply of all of her more pressing wants." Sometimes "her demands approached very near to commands," for she "felt as if God was under obligation to her, much more than she was to him." She would bargain with God, promising to be good if he helped her out of her difficulties.[4]

When she was twenty-nine, she walked away from her master, John Dumont, of New Paltz, New York, and found employment with Isaac Van Wagenen of Wagondale, who legally purchased her from Dumont, but treated her as a free woman. There she was so comfortable that she stopped praying to God. Around Pentecost, 1827, somewhat bored, she resolved to return to the Dumonts, so she could celebrate the holiday, singing, drinking, smoking, and dancing with her slave friends,[5] when, suddenly, just as she was about to leave the Van Wagenens, she had a vision. Talking about her experience in the third person, she recounted years later, "God revealed himself to her, with all the suddenness of a flash of lightning, showing her in the twinkling of an eye that he was all over, and that there was no place where God was not."[6]

She was acutely conscious of her sinfulness. She had an overwhelming sense of her own "vileness" and a sense of God's "holiness and all-pervading presence, which filled immensity."[7] Then "all her unfulfilled promises arose before her, like a vexed sea whose waves run mountains high; and her soul, which seemed but one mass of lies…and [so] she would now fain have hidden herself in the bowels of the earth, to have escaped his dread presence. But she plainly saw there was no place, not even in hell, where he was not; and where could she flee?"[8]

With a sense of dread, she prayed aloud, "O God, I did not know you were so big."[9] Going back into the house, she tried to resume her work, but could not. She tried to pray, but she could not because she felt too vile to talk to God. She felt that she could not approach God directly anymore. She felt that someone was needed to address the Deity on her behalf. Then a space seemed to open between her and God, and "at length a friend appeared to stand between herself and an insulted Deity; and she felt as sensibly refreshed as when, on a hot day, an umbrella had been interposed between her, scorching heat, and a burning sun."[10] But who was the "friend"?

The vision "moved restlessly about, like agitated waters," as Isabella continued to ask, "Who are you?...I don't know you." She prayed until "breath and strength seemed to be failing," and then the "friend" said "distinctly" that "It is Jesus."[11]

Up to that time, she had heard of Jesus, but had thought of him merely as "an eminent man," like Washington or Lafayette. But "now he appeared to her delighted mental vision as so mild, so good, and so every way lovely, and he loved her so much. Ah, how strange that he had always loved her, and she had never known it!"[12]

She never thought of Jesus as God, and, years later, when someone, reading the Bible to her, explained that Christ was divine, she was incredulous. Later in life she explained: "I only know what I saw. I did not see him as God; else, how could he stand between me and God? I saw him as a friend, standing between me and God, through whom love flowed as from a fountain."[13]

After her conversion, she started to preach. One of the Van Wagenen family later recalled that Isabella was "going through all the kitchen, preaching as she went," and "kept preaching all day," making something of a nuisance of herself.[14] She also began to attend Methodist meetings in a private home. She liked the spontaneity of the services and the emphasis on a personal religious experience. Shortly after that she joined a Methodist church in Kingston, New York. She began to pray with her five children (she had been married to and separated from a man named Thomas Dumont) and take them to church. She also began to give testimonies, and it soon was apparent that she was an effective public speaker.

Moving to New York City at thirty-two, she joined the predominantly white John Street Methodist Church, which she left to join Zion Methodist, which was all black. Methodists encouraged preaching by laypeople, and Isabella preached in various churches, as well as on the streets, where she tried to evangelize prostitutes. Her only text was, "When I found Jesus."[15] Her preaching was electrifying, and, according to a Methodist official who knew her, "The influence of her speaking was miraculous."[16]

Then, in her mid thirties, she became involved with a cult headed by a man named Robert Matthias, who led a group he called The Kingdom. Although he was a Gentile, Matthias called himself a Jewish teacher, as well as a prophet of the Lord and "the Spirit of Jesus." Moreover, he claimed to have the power to heal the sick, forgive sins, and punish the wicked. He taught a belief in reincarnation.[17] After Matthias was discredited, Isabella resumed her street preaching, and took up the life of a traveling evangelist. Now she asked God for a new name. As she told an interviewer: "When I left the house of bondage, I left everything behind. I wasn't going to keep nothing of Egypt on me, and so I went to the Lord and asked him to give me a new name. And the Lord gave me Sojourner, because I was traveling up and down the land, showing the people their sins and being a sign unto them. Afterward, I told the Lord I wanted another name, because everybody else had two names; and the Lord gave me Truth, because I was to declare the truth to the people."[18]

Around this time, groups of men and women were withdrawing from society to communes, or "utopian communities," where they tried to build a perfect society. In her forties, Truth belonged to such a group in Massachusetts, known as the Northampton Association. This community had no particular religious creed, but believed in freedom of religion, thought, and speech. After this group broke up, Truth became involved with the spiritualists. Such groups, organized in an attempt to contact the dead, were also popular then. Eventually, she settled in a spiritualist community near Battle Creek, Michigan, called Harmonia. Although she took an active role in seances,[19] was a friend of the famous medium Leah Fox Underhill, and was once, at the age of seventy-one, an elected delegate from Michigan to the spiritualist convention in Rochester, New York, she denied that she was a spiritualist.[20] For one thing, unlike most of her associates, who claimed to receive messages from the other world through a "control" in the form of the spirit of a dead person, Truth's "control" was God, from whom she claimed to receive direct revelations.[21]

The group to which Sojourner Truth became most happily associated was the Progressive Friends, a group of liberal Quakers, many of whom were involved in most of the reform movements of the day as well as in spiritualism. Although she never formally joined any Friends' meetings, Truth frequently dressed in the style of the Quakers of the time, and was quite comfortable with the doctrine of the "inner light" by which each person was directed by an individualistic experience of God.

Sojourner Truth's beliefs are difficult to describe, because they were not always consistent. Without education and, apparently severely dyslexic, she was never able to learn to read, and had to rely on others to read the Bible to her. Because adults frequently interpreted, she preferred her readers to be children. The keystone of her creed was her insistence: "I talk to God and God talks to me."[22] When she spoke, she claimed, "The Lord just puts the words in my mouth, and I go to hear myself as much as anyone else comes to hear me."[23] Since her faith was the result of direct revelation, she did not have to worry about consistency.

For example, during the 1850s, she seemed to be a pacifist, and opposed the use of violence in ending slavery. Yet when civil war broke out, she enthusiastically supported the Union side, declaring that if she were younger, she would be "the Joan of Arc of the Army of the Lord."[24]

Throughout her life, she felt that God was easily accessible, at least to her. "God is a great ocean of love," she affirmed, "and we live and move in him as the fishes in the sea."[25] She most emphatically believed in the efficacy of prayer. "Let others say what they will....I believe in it, and I shall pray. Thank God, yes, I shall always pray."[26]

Yet she held a number of views not consistent with orthodox Christianity. For one, since she believed that her own experience with God was her Bible, she did not believe that the Scriptures were inerrant. She compared the words of Holy Writ with "the witness within her," believing "that the spirit of truth spoke in those records, but that the recorders of those truths had intermingled with them ideas and suppositions of their own."[27] Two years before she died, she was quoted as saying that she wished someone would "write a new Bible" that would discard the Mosaic "eye for an eye" laws and substitute them with "new spiritual doctrines to keep pace with the wonderful inventions of our time."[28]

Although she said, "God's brightness…is hot enough to scorch all the sinners in the world,"[29] she denied the existence of hell. She once said that she believed in hell when she was young, but when she got older, "I found out there wasn't no such thing as hell."[30] She felt that the concept of eternal punishment was the conception of "narrow minds."[31]

She also did not believe that the Lord would return to destroy the wicked. She once told an assembly of Seventh Day Adventists: "You seem to be expecting to go to some parlor away up somewhere, and when the wicked have been burnt, you are coming back to walk in triumph over their ashes—this is to be your New Jerusalem! Now, I can't see anything so nice in that, coming back to such a muss as that will be, a world covered with the ashes of the wicked!"[32]

She frequently had hard things to say about clergymen. She once complained of ministers who "went away into Egypt among the bones of dead Pharaohs and mummies, and talked about what happened thousands of years ago."[33] Likewise, she railed against "big, Greek-crammed mouthing men" in the pulpit.[34] She had hard words even for the celebrated evangelists Moody and Sankey, who were precipitating many conversions during the latter years of her life. "What do you expect?" she complained. "That those two men are going to tote all you women to heaven?…I tell you, it's the doers of the word, not the hearers, God wants."[35]

Another cornerstone of Sojourner Truth's creed was that the Christian was to be a doer of God's word. The experience of God does not draw a person out of the world, it impels him or her to be actively involved in the world, to serve the needs of humankind. She was appalled by large, expensively outfitted urban churches which were surrounded by poverty. She felt that these were "big, lumbering things, covering up costly space and doing good to no one."[36] Christians, she felt, needed to be involved in the struggle against slavery, for equal rights for women and minorities, against the death penalty, and against the use of alcohol and tobacco. Christ would bring his kingdom to earth through the efforts of men and women. "He ain't a-coming flying in the air," she said, "but he's coming in the spirit, bless the Lord."[37] People should not wait for the Lord to come to "clean up the world," but men and women should "take hold" and clean it up themselves, conscious that "He is with you all the time."[38] Thus she seemed to feel that Christians would create, through their efforts, the new world promised by Jesus—through the help of God. If men and women are in union with God, they would live in such a way that war, poverty, disease, and other evils would be defeated. She had no use for solitary mystical contemplation if it did not lead to concrete actions to change the world. God, she believed, filled his children with the passion to help others. People, she felt, would "never get to heaven by lifting themselves up in a basket, but they must lift those up below them, and then they will all go up together."[39]

Sojourner Truth's religious faith was therefore very individualistic. A dynamic, personal relationship with God was its center. God, for her, was active and accessible, and empowered those who prayed to him to express his love in concrete actions to benefit others. Although she disliked otherworldly Christianity, she believed in heaven. She compared death to stepping out of one room into another. "Stepping out into the light," she exclaimed, "oh, won't that be glorious?"[40] According to tradition, just before she died at the age of eighty-six, she cried out, "Oh, I'm not going to die! I'm just going home like a shooting star!"

~

Profile 20
Nathaniel Hawthorne

Born: Salem, Massachusetts, July 4, 1804
Died: Plymouth, New Hampshire, May 19, 1864

The author of novels and short stories with strong religious themes was never a church member. His son wrote of him: "He had deep and reverent religious faith, though of what precise purport I am unable to say."[1] Likewise, looking back on his childhood, he recalled that his parents were "religious, but I never knew what denomination."[2]

Hawthorne was born into an old Massachusetts family which had fallen on hard times, financially. Family members traditionally blamed the decline of the once-wealthy family on a seventeenth-century ancestor, Judge John Hathorne who took part in the infamous Salem witch trials and was allegedly cursed by an innocent woman whose condemnation he helped to secure. Some have believed that Hawthorne himself took the story seriously and was at times burdened by a sense of shame concerning the misdeeds of his ancestor. Certainly, the theme of the curse inspired the novel, *The House of the Seven Gables*.

The future author was baptized at the age of two at the First Congregational Church of Salem. By the beginning of the nineteenth century, many of New England's Congregational churches, founded by Puritans, had embraced a Unitarian theology, often denying the divinity of Christ and the authority of Scripture. Hawthorne's mother identified herself as a Unitarian, but the author never joined any church, and, after going away to study at Bowdoin College in Brunswick, Maine, seldom attended worship services, although after his children were born, he led family devotions, and, while living in England in the 1850s, sometimes attended a Unitarian church in Liverpool.

As a young man, Hawthorne lived for a time at Brook Farm, a utopian commune organized by Transcendentalists. Transcendentalists, whose best-known exponent was Ralph Waldo Emerson, a lecturer and writer who left the pulpit of a Unitarian church because he concluded that Unitarianism was too conservative, believed in a vague and scarcely definable philosophy that asserted that human beings were naturally good and that God was to be experienced in nature.

Hawthorne has sometimes been associated with the Transcendentalists, but he dismissed the ideas of what he called "the dreamy brethren" as unreal, and once described his friend Emerson as "stretching his hand out of cloudland in vain search of something real."[3] In his short story, "The Celestial Railroad," he represented the Transcendentalist as a giant who "makes it his business to seize upon honest travelers and fatten them for his table with plentiful meals of smoke, mist, moonshine, raw potatoes, and sawdust."[4]

Like many people of his time, Hawthorne was interested in spiritualism. He claimed, at times, to see ghosts in his home. For instance, he once wrote, "Our ghost used to heave deep sighs in a particular corner of the parlor, and sometimes rustled paper, as if he were turning over a sermon."[5] Another time, he commented that it was possible that humans shared the planet with other beings "of whose existence and whereabouts we could have no perception, nor they of ours, because we are endowed with different sets of senses."[6] But he took a dim view of the spirits allegedly conjured up in seances by mediums. If they were genuine, then these spirits had become idiotic after leaving the body: "To hold intercourse with spirits of this order, we must stoop and grovel in some element more vile than earthly dust. These goblins, if they exist at all, are but the shadows of past mortality."[7] After attending a series of seances, he concluded definitively: "I cannot consent to let Heaven and Earth, this world and the next, be beaten up together, like the white and yolk of an egg."[8]

Hawthorne disliked formal theology and had little respect for Protestant clergy. Though he was not a churchgoer, he regularly read the Bible and sometimes prayed, although he commented, "I thank God (whenever I happen to think of it)."[9] Son-in-law George P. Lathrop characterized Hawthorne and his wife, Sophia, as "full of reverence for Christ, little differing in devoutness from that paid to him as the Son of God, one with the Trinity."[11] He spoke of Christmas as "the holiest of the holy days—the day that brought ransom to all other sinners." As to the exact nature of Christ, Hawthorne was somewhat foggy. He wondered why the evangelists did not record what the risen Christ told his disciples about himself—"whether God or Man, or both, or something in between."[12]

He believed in the life of the world to come. When his mother died he wrote that a belief in a just and loving God necessitated a belief in eternity: "Oh, what a mockery if what I saw were all. Let the interval, between extreme youth and dying age be filled up with what happiness it might! But God would not have made the close so dark and wretched, if there were nothing beyond; for then it would have been a fiend that created us, and measured out our existence, and not God. It would be something beyond wrong; it would be an insult to be thrust out of life into annihilation in this miserable way."[13] When his brother-in-law died, he wrote his wife: "He is already in the Celestial City, more at home than ever he was in his mother's house."[14] Because of his belief in life after death be disliked the idea of burial and cemeteries. "Our thoughts should follow the celestial soul," he declared, "and not the earthly corpse."[15]

Although he believed deeply in the reality of sin and the possibility of spiritual self-destruction, he trusted in the mercy of God and was uncomfortable with those who were quick to consign the erring to the everlasting flames. When, in his youth, he attended a funeral in which a strict Baptist preacher publicly expressed doubts concerning the salvation of the man who was being buried, Hawthorne commented to a friend that "God's mercy endureth forever."[16] Likewise, when he visited the Sistine Chapel he was repelled by Michelangelo's painting of Christ as the Last Judgment. As he looked at the masterpiece, he found himself taking the part of the wicked, "and asking for at least a little pity, and not such a denunciatory spirit on the part of him who had thought us worth dying for."[17]

Despite his lack of interest in formal worship, Hawthorne respected the concept of church. In his last novel, *The Marble Faun,* he commented: "Christian faith is a grand cathedral with divinely pictured windows. Standing without, you see no glory, nor can possibly imagine any; standing within, every ray of light reveals a harmony of unspeakable splendors."[18]

While he considered the Protestantism of his experience lifeless[19] and "formless,"[20] in later life he became fascinated with Roman Catholicism. "The popish religion," he wrote, "certainly does apply itself most closely and comfortably to human occasions; and I cannot but think that a great many people find their spiritual advantage in it....You cannot think it all a farce when you see peasant, citizen, and soldier coming into church, each on his own hook, and kneeling for moments or hours, directing his silent devotions to some particular shrine; too humble to approach his God directly, and therefore seeking the mediation of some saint who stands beside the Infinite Presence."[21] He particularly admired the institution of the confessional. Although one of his daughters, in midlife, became a Roman Catholic and eventually founded a Dominican congregation with a ministry to destitute cancer patients, Hawthorne, although some called him an "unconscious Catholic,"[22] never joined the Church of Rome—or any other church.

Nathaniel Hawthorne was a religious man who believed in God, in Christ as Savior, in the divine inspiration of Scripture, and the necessity of moral rectitude, but his beliefs were theologically nonspecific, and he apparently thought it was better that way. He trusted in the mercy of God, as he put it in one of his stories, to lead the "night wanderers" who "bear the lamp of Faith, enkindled at a celestial fire" to "that heaven whence its radiance was borrowed."[23]

~

Profile 21
Robert Edward Lee

Born: Stratford, Virginia, January 19, 1807
Died: Lexington, Virginia, October 12, 1870

Franklin Delano Roosevelt characterized Robert E. Lee as "one of our greatest American Christians and one of our greatest American gentlemen."[1] A historian once declared: "Robert Lee was one of the small company of great men in whom there is no inconsistency to be explained, no enigma to be solved. What he seemed, he was—a wholly human gentleman, the essential elements of whose positive character were...simplicity and spirituality."[2] It is recounted that during the war, when some of Lee's soldiers were discussing the theory of evolution, all nodded in assent when one of their number insisted, "Well, boys, the rest of us may have developed from monkeys, but I tell you none less than God could have made such a man as Marse Robert."[3]

One of several children of a Revolutionary War general who fell on hard times, and then died, Lee was raised by his mother in relative poverty before he entered West Point. Shortly after his graduation, he married the daughter of George Washington's adopted son, George

Washington Parke Custis. Although he was not a member of any church for most of his life, he was known as an ideal army officer who did not swear or tell bawdy jokes and who was entirely devoted to his wife, from whom he was separated by various military assignments for long periods of time. He was also known as a prayerful man who attended church services whenever possible, and who routinely expressed himself as he did to his wife, whom he wrote during his service in the war with Mexico: "I endeavored to give thanks to our Heavenly Father for all his mercies to me, for his preservation of me through all the dangers I have passed, and [for] all the blessings which he has bestowed upon me...."[4]

On July 17, 1853, at the age of forty-six, Lee, along with two of his daughters, was confirmed at Christ Church, in Alexandria, Virginia. Episcopal Bishop John Johns, who confirmed him, told him, "Colonel Lee, if you make as valiant a soldier for Christ as you have made for your country, the Church will be as proud of you as your country now is."[5] Lee evidently did his best, in the tumultuous years remaining to him, to make the bishop's words a reality.

By the time that Lee became a member of the Episcopal Church, many congregations were adopting a style of worship and theology that was similar to Roman Catholicism. Lee, however, was definitely not an Anglo-Catholic, but a "low church man" who preferred a simple style of worship. He tried to steer clear of theological controversy. For instance, although holy Communion was very important to him, when asked if he believed that Christ was physically present in the sacrament, he said that he did not know.[6] Of the observance of Lent, he once said, "The best way for most of us is to fast from our sins and eat what is good for us."[7]

Edward Clifford Gordon, who was one of Lee's aides, recounted that the General had a violent temper and was fond of war. In fact, he wrote that Lee was "fond of elegance of every sort; fine houses, furniture, plate, clothing, ornaments, horses, equipage." He loved "excitement" and "grandeur," but "all these appetites and powers were brought under the control of his judgment and made subservient to his Christian faith."[8] Because self-control and humility were so much a part of Lee's personality, most people who knew him casually never saw the side of him that Gordon described. T. A. Ashby, a physician whose undergraduate work was at Washington College when Lee was its president, described him as a remarkably impassive man who spoke in a "soft, gentle voice" which was "seldom raised above a whisper," who tended to conceal his feelings and who was "less emotional than any human being I ever saw."[9] So important was self-control to him that, in later years, when a mother held out her baby to be blessed by him, the General told her, "Teach him he must deny himself."[10]

When told that people were praying for him, Lee said, "I am nothing but a poor sinner, trusting Christ alone for salvation, and need all the prayers they can offer for me."[11] He believed in the divinity of Christ and the necessity of each man and woman to trust him for salvation. He always carried a Bible with him, even in the field in the midst of military campaigns. Shortly after the war, he wrote a relative: "I prefer the Bible to any other book. There is enough in it to...open the way to true wisdom; and to teach the only road to salvation and eternal happiness. It is not above human comprehension, and is sufficient to satisfy all its desires."[12] Another time he wrote: "There are things in the old Book which I may never be able to explain, but I accept it as the infallible word of God, and receive its teaching as inspired by the Holy Spirit."[13]

When the Southern states began to secede in 1860, Lee was deeply troubled, and it was with great anguish of mind that he turned down the offer of the Lincoln government to head the Union army and ultimately decided to take up arms in defense of his state. He believed that secession was wrong, but he also believed that the federal government had no right to use force to coerce the seceding states back into the Union. As the states were seceding, he wrote to one of his sons: "The country seems to be in a lamentable condition and may have been plunged into civil war. May God rescue us from the folly of our own acts, save us from selfishness, and teach us to love our neighbors as ourselves."[14] At the very start of the war, he wrote to a Northern admirer who wrote for his photograph: "It is painful to think how many friends will be separated and estranged by our unhappy disunion. May God reunite our severed bonds of friendship, and turn our hearts to peace! I can say in sincerity that I bear animosity against no one. Wher-

ever the blame may be, the fact is that we are in the midst of a fratri-
cidal war. I must side either with or against my birthplace, my home,
my children. I should like, above all things, that our difficulties might
be peaceably arranged, and still trust that a merciful God, whom I
know will not unnecessarily afflict us, may yet allay the fury for war.
Whatever may be the result of the contest, I foresee that the country
will have to pass through a terrible ordeal, a necessary expiation, perhaps of our national sins. May God direct all for our good and shield
and preserve you and yours."[15]

Lee had no doubt that the years of devastating carnage was God's
will or that the outcome would be directed by the hand of the Almighty. He, for one, could only take the course which, after prayerful
consideration, he believed best and leave the rest in the hands of the
All-Wise. "I know he will order all things for our good, and we must
be content."[16] At the war's beginning, he told a minister, "I am not
concerned with results. God's will ought to be our aim, and I am quite
contented that his designs should be accomplished and not mine."[17]
The outcome of individual battles, like that of the war, was up to God.
Of course, it was his duty to use his expertise to plan and direct the
battles, but, ultimately, victory or defeat was ordered by the All-Just.
Even the effects of weather on the outcome of battle showed the hand
of the Lord. After a defeat, he wrote his wife, "If the river had not
unexpectedly risen, all would have been well with us; but God, in his
all-wise providence, ruled otherwise, and our communications have
been interrupted, and almost cut off."[18]

He always prayed for the enemy. After the war, he insisted, "I have
fought against the people of the North because I believed they were
seeking to wrest from the South its dearest rights. But I have never
cherished toward them bitter or vindictive feelings, and I have never
seen the day when I did not pray for them."[19]

The general seemed never to question the morality of warfare itself
and seemed never to doubt that when he ordered thousands of young
men into the monstrous bloodbath, that he was acting in consistency
with the will of God. To defend one's family and one's homeland was
for Lee honorable, virtuous, godly. Nevertheless he was still appalled
by the horrific carnage. Just as in World War II, British General Ber-

nard Montgomery, on his deathbed, lamented, "I've got to meet God—and explain all those men I killed...."[20] Lee, to the end of his days, was tormented by the horror of the war's hideous slaughter. It is said that many nights he paced the floor in sleepless anguish, unable to keep from his mind the scenes of the gory battlefield. The torment of his mind was eased by his conviction that he had acted out of honorable motives after actively seeking the will and guidance of God. The outcome had been God's business. The business of human beings was to seek his will and submit to it when it was evident.

Lee encouraged his soldiers to believe as he did. He did everything he could to promote the religious revivals that broke out among his men during the war, and attended some of the preaching meetings. When Confederate President Jefferson Davis, a month after the devastating defeat at Gettysburg, declared August 21, 1863, as a day of "fasting, humiliation, and prayer," Lee issued an order to his men in which he declared: "Soldiers! God is our only refuge and our strength. Let us humble ourselves before him. Let us confess our many sins, and beseech him to give us a higher courage, a purer patriotism, and a more determined will; that he will convert the hearts of our enemies; that he will hasten the time when war, with its sorrows and sufferings, shall cease, and that he will give us a name and place among the nations of the earth."[21] Of course, after more than a half million men had perished, it was evident that the Almighty was unwilling to give the Confederate States a name and place among the nations of the earth.

From the beginning of the war, Lee suspected that the bloodbath was God's punishment for "national sin." Lincoln, too, was convinced that the war was divine punishment, but was certain that the national sin was slavery. Lee, however, denied that the war was over slavery, and became angry when he was accused of fighting for the right of men to own other human beings. Lee, who went to war to protect the people of the South from invasion and gain independence for the Confederacy much as his father had fought for independence from the British Empire, thought that slavery was wicked. After the war he insisted: "So far from engaging in a war to perpetuate slavery, I am rejoiced that slavery is abolished. I believe it will be greatly for the interests of the South."[22]

Lee was certainly not an abolitionist, and before the war favored a gradual and voluntary emancipation, which he felt would accelerate as more and more Southerners were enlightened through the adoption of an active Christian faith. Several years before the war he conceded that the effect of the "mild and melting influence of Christianity" would be very slow. Christians should pray for the end of slavery and use "all justifiable means in our power to end it."[23]

Lee himself never owned more than a half-dozen slaves at a time, and offered to send those who were willing to go to Liberia.[24] This was a solution proposed by many of Lee's contemporaries, both North and South, white and black. Liberia was at the time generally considered a sort of American colony, and those persons of color who chose to immigrate there were thought of as "colonists." Lee and many other people believed that African Americans were better off as slaves in America than they were in traditional African societies. The people who held this opinion were not all white. Chaney Mack, a former slave, in an interview, after telling how her father and uncle were lured onto a slave ship, spoke of Africa in highly negative terms: her father's people were hunters and gatherers; they ate wild animals raw; they had no conception of God or heaven; they practiced cannibalism.[25] Another former slave, Mary Johnson, also affirmed that the natives of Africa she knew were wild and cannibalistic, without knowledge of God or religion before white preachers were brought to convert them.[26] Proponents of colonization expected that the freedmen who settled in Liberia would set up an American-style democracy that would eventually prove a model to the entire continent. Most important, they would serve to Christianize the natives. Lee said that his former slaves in Africa wrote "most affectionate letters" to him, some of which he received through the Union lines during the war.[27]

Lee's home was Arlington, an estate across the river from Washington, which originally belonged to his wife's parents, George Washington and Mary Fitzhugh Custis, who owned dozens of "people," as they called their unpaid servants. The Custises were considered kind masters, who taught some of their slaves to read and write, instructed them in religion, and arranged, at least for some, a sacramental marriage. Lee was the executor of George Custis's will, which provided that his slaves would be manumitted within five years of his death. When this time came—in 1862—Lee, in the midst of his wartime duties, made sure that the "people" of Arlington obtained their freedom papers.

Lee said and wrote things that have led some to conclude that he was a racist. He was certainly appalled by Reconstruction, as it was carried out in Virginia and in other parts of the South. He was unhappy that the traditional ruling class—the people he considered most fit to govern—were deprived of power. He was also dismayed that political power was placed in the hands of former slaves, who were now able to vote and hold public office. This empowering of the freedmen Lee (and most of his peers) considered a cynical act of a vindictive federal government which wanted to punish the South by turning freedmen against their former masters.

When called upon to testify before the Joint Congressional Committee on Reconstruction in 1866, he made uncomplimentary remarks about Negroes: "They are an amiable, social race. They like their ease and comfort, and, I think, look more to the present-time than to the future." He also said that he did not think the Negro "as capable of acquiring knowledge as the white man is."[28] On another occasion, he expressed the opinion that Virginia would be better off if it could stop relying on its black labor force.

Although Lee, at least from the scanty documentation that exists, seemed unimpressed by the intellectual capacities of the Negro, there is no evidence of hostility. One reason for his opposition to slavery is that he felt that a free white work force was preferable. He never advocated violence against blacks. He simply felt that they were not ready for social or political equality. When he signed a letter opposing black voting rights, he declared: "This opposition springs from no feeling of enmity, but from a deep-seated conviction that, at present, the Negroes have neither the intelligence nor the other qualifications which are necessary to make them safe depositories of political power."[29] He was, however, a Virginia aristocrat and never questioned that his social class as well as his "race" was best suited to rule. As a Christian, he believed that he had to be kind to all people, but this kindness did not necessitate the conferral of what he considered an ill-timed political equality on people not prepared for it and in such a way as to risk, if not ensure, disaster for everybody concerned.

There are two incidents which illustrate that Lee's actions in racial matters were not inconsistent with his Christian profession. In 1868, a student at Washington College was shot and wounded by a Negro. This was the heyday of the Ku Klux Klan, and the assailant was in grave danger of lynching. There were, in fact, rumors that the accused man would be lynched. President Lee stated that there would be no lynching and that such a thing would be "an outrage against law and order."[30] The campus remained calm and the accused, whatever his ultimate fate, did not meet it at the hands of a lynch mob.

On another occasion, the congregation of the fashionable St. Paul's Episcopal Church in Richmond was stunned when, after the rector, Dr. Charles Minnigerode, invited the people to partake of holy Communion, the first person to reach the rail was a man, tall, well-dressed, and black. The custom had been (and would for many years remain) for blacks in the congregation to take Communion separately, and only after the whites had received the sacrament. The whites in the church seethed with anger, convinced that the man of color was trying to "offend and humiliate them" and to inaugurate a "new regime." Moments passed, as not a soul got up to join the black man at the Communion rail. Then Lee arose and calmly walked to the altar rail and knelt down near the black communicant. The effect, as one observer wrote, was like "magic." The congregation immediately proceeded to the rail and took Communion with Lee and their unwanted guest.[31]

As president of Washington College, Lee envisioned it as "a classical college with a Christian atmosphere."[32] One of his goals was to lead all of his students to Christ. "If I could only know that all the young men in the college were good Christians, I should have nothing more to desire," he declared. "I dread the thought of any student going away from the college without becoming a sincere Christian."[33] He made sure that all of his students who boarded in town lived with Christian families. He did not require his young men to attend chapel services, which were offered each morning, but he attended each day to set and example.

Even before the war's end, Lee was suffering from heart disease, and, during his years at Lexington, his health steadily declined. As might be expected, he was in no fear of death. For years his writings and his conversations demonstrated an expectation of a joyous eternity. For example, when the child of one of his friends died, he wrote: "I believe that it is far better for the child to be called by its heavenly Creator into his presence in its purity and innocence, unpolluted by sin, and uncontaminated by the vices of the world."[34] When, during the war, his only daughter-in-law died, he wrote his wife: "She, I trust, will enjoy peace and happiness forever, while we must patiently struggle on under all the ills that may be in store for us. What a glorious thought it is that she has joined her little cherubs [her dead infants] and our angel Annie [one of the Lees' daughters, who had recently died at twenty-three] in heaven."[35]

Lee served on the vestry of Grace Episcopal Church of Lexington, where he was a faithful worshiper. On Sunday, September 28, 1870, after sitting through a long meeting dealing with fund-raising, he suffered a stroke at home. During the next two weeks, he was unable to say more then a few words. When his doctor told him to hurry and get well, since his horse, Traveller, needed exercise, Lee simply shook his head. When a son spoke to him about recovery, he shook his head and pointed toward heaven. When a daughter tried to get him to take his medication, he refused, insisting, "It is of no use."[36] After that, he seemed to be delirious, and in his delirium, his wife heard him relive the horrible scenes of the battlefield. Finally, he called out, "Strike the tent!" On October 12, after receiving the last rites of the Episcopal Church, Robert Edward Lee left this earthly life.

Shortly before his stroke, Lee had confided to his wife, "I wish I felt sure of my acceptance." When she assured him that everyone who loved and trusted the Savior had no cause to fear, he did not answer. She thought about their conversation after he died and concluded, "A more upright and conscientious Christian never lived."[37] Among the general's papers was found scribbled a note which seemed to express his overall attitude to life. It read: "God disposes. This ought to satisfy us."[38]

Profile 22
Henry Wadsworth Longfellow

Born: Portland, Maine, February 27, 1807
Died: Cambridge, Massachusetts, March 24, 1882

Probably the most popular poet of his time, the aristocratic New Englander wrote verse that was attractive to the ordinary reader because it could be easily understood and frequently told a story or provided a clear moral lesson. While some critics have found his verse shallow, everybody who knew him personally seemed to like Longfellow and respect him as a gentle, compassionate man of unimpeachable character.

One critic wrote: "I know of no poet who has written so little that is professedly Christian, and whose poetry is notwithstanding so shot through with Christian spirit. It seems as if the same Savior who had cleansed him had also bidden him, 'See that thou tell no man!' "[1]

Longfellow's daughter, Alice, told an interviewer that her father "was born a Unitarian and remained one all his life."[2] As a boy he attended the First Parish Meeting House in Portland with his family. Like many New England churches of that time, it had been started by Puritans, but, by the late 1700s, had become what Longfellow's brother Samuel (himself a Unitarian minister) called "early Unitarian."[3] Although they rejected many of the severe doctrines of John Calvin and played down, if not denied, the doctrine of the Trinity, the people of First Parish were as devoutly churchgoing as their Puritan ancestors. The Longfellows attended two church services on Sunday; their mother read the Bible to her numerous children in the afternoon, and, in the evening the family sang hymns.

When Longfellow was a student at Bowdoin College, he wrote a friend a letter in which he set forth his religious beliefs in the greatest detail that is to be found in any of his extant writings. The thrust of his argument was that human creeds and doctrines have distorted the comforting teachings of Christ into a harsh and depressing system, and made it difficult for laypeople to "walk in the light and liberty of religion." He insisted that "human systems have done much to deaden the true spirit of devotion and to render religion merely speculative." He continued, asking, "Would it not be better for mankind if we should consider it as a cheerful and social companion, given us to go through life with us from childhood to the grave, and to make us happier here as well as hereafter; and not as a stern and chiding task-master to whom we must cling at last through mere despair."[4]

Longfellow's brother Samuel wrote: "His nature was at heart devout....He did not care to talk much on theological points." He recounted that the poet's views of life and death and the hereafter were "essentially cheerful, hopeful, optimistic."[5] Longfellow once told a friend who was brooding about death and the world to come that he was in general "pretty quiet and calm in regard to these matters."[6]

He felt that "all sects of Christians" were acceptable, and was hurt by the "narrowness" of those people who did not consider Unitarians Christians. When his daughter Edith became an Episcopalian and ex-pressed concern about his reaction, he wrote: "Do not trouble your-self with the thought that you have given me pain. You have only gone from one chapel to another in the same church. The many-mansioned house of Christianity is ample enough for all creeds....The danger is that sects are apt to be exclusive, instead of being inclusive. This is a great pity, and a great mistake. Life is the thing, and not the creed."[7] Because of his belief that the unpardonable sin was sectarian strife, he hated Calvinism, which he associated with intolerance.

Many of Longfellow's friends wondered if be believed in Christ as Savior. Indeed, toward the end of his life, he referred frequently to Jesus as "Our Savior."[8] His son-in-law wrote that in his final years Longfellow did in fact believe in the "divine inspiration of Christ and his Resurrection, and held him as his master and example."[9]

Religious observance was as important to Longfellow in his adult life as it had been in his family home. When he was a professor at Harvard, all students and faculty were required to attend morning and evening chapel services on the campus of what was then a Unitar-ian institution. Students who belonged to other denominations were usually given the dispensation to attend services in the churches of their particular sect. Because they lived far enough from campus, the

Longfellow family was excused from the requirement of attending the evening services. But the poet and his wife, Frances, observed "the old Puritan Sunday." According to his son, Ernest: "We were not allowed to read the same books as on weekdays, and had special Sunday clothes, which were especially uncomfortable."[10] There was no Sunday school connected to the college chapel, so Frances Longfellow gave "religious instructions" to her five children at home Sunday afternoons.[11]

Longfellow's Unitarianism was evident in his support, common among men of his denomination, of the liberal causes of the day. Although not an activist nor heavily involved in politics, the poet opposed slavery all his life, and, after the war, supported his great friend, Charles Sumner, senator from Massachusetts, in his attempt to bring about racial equality. Some of his letters make it clear that, unlike many of his contemporaries, Longfellow believed that the Negro should be accepted into society as the equal of the white. He was always sympathetic to the Indian, whom he celebrated in his epic *Hiawatha*, and he supported the rights of labor. He was also opposed to capital punishment and hoped that Christian love would sweep it from the earth.

Although he was a Unitarian, in later life Longfellow appears to have been somewhat attracted to Roman Catholicism. On his first trip to Italy, when he was twenty-one, he wrote disapprovingly of the Church of Rome to his sisters,[12] but his attitude changed over the years. He translated Dante's *Divine Comedy* into English and wrote a number of poems in middle and later life that show great respect for Roman Catholic spirituality. He once said that to renounce Roman Catholicism was almost like "repudiating Western civilization itself," and he came to find devotion to the Virgin Mary one of the "most attractive features" of Catholicism.[13]

Conversely, in some respects he seemed to hold liberal Protestantism in low regard late in life, and apparently held Martin Luther at fault. "What began with Luther ended with Voltaire," he complained. He once referred to Protestant denominations as "wildcat sects." He was appalled at those who "seem disposed to throw Christianity aside, like worn-out machinery, which has done its work, and must now give place to something better! Oh, man of glorious intellect! What has Christ done to thee, that thou shouldst deny him!"[14] Nonetheless,

Longfellow never changed his affiliation, and remained a Unitarian with increasingly conservative, increasingly orthodox religious views. Patient suffering and submission to the will of God were a frequent theme in both his public and private writings. In his early forties he wrote a poem, "Resignation," after the death of a baby daughter, in which he said that these afflictions are "celestial benedictions in dark disguise."[15]

Patient resignation to the will of God was evident even earlier in the poet's life when his first wife, Mary Potter, died of complications of pregnancy while they were living in Holland. When he realized that Mary's life was in danger, Henry wrote his father, "God grant that she may recover—but if this is not his will may we all be resigned to whatever he may ordain."[16] When she died he wrote his father-in-law about Mary's own resignation, and he reflected, "When I think, however, upon the goodness and purity of her life, and the holy and peaceful death she died, I feel great consolation in my bereavement, and can say, 'Father, Thy will be done.'"[17]

Resignation was difficult after the death of his second wife, Frances Appleton, who after eighteen years of marriage, died of burns sustained in an accident in their home in Cambridge. Shortly after this disaster, he wrote a friend: "I am at least patient, if not resigned; and thank God hourly—as I have from the beginning—for the beautiful life we led together, and that I loved her more and more to the end....My heart aches and bleeds sorely for the poor children. To lose such a mother and all the divine influences of her character and care! They do not know how great their loss is, but I do! God will provide. His will be done."[18] There was no questioning of God. There was no doubt that the catastrophe was permitted by God.

For Longfellow, the sufferings of life were bearable because of the promise of eternal life. He wrote a bereaved friend in 1866: "These are terrible experiences, but, as a friend once said to me, 'In God's photography...this life is only the negative, and the next life the positive, and what looks dark here will look light hereafter.'"[19] In one of his poems one of the characters declares: "The grave itself is but a covered bridge, leading from light to light, through a brief darkness."[20]

Sometimes Longfellow had to struggle with temptations against faith. We have seen that, as a young man, he admitted that occasionally "a horrible doubt cut into the cool, still surface" of his soul, as a skate into ice. William Dean Howells, eminent author and critic, many years the poet's junior, recalled that once, when discussing the future life with Longfellow, the older man said something "to the effect that he wished he could be sure, with the sigh that often clothed the expression of a misgiving within him."[21]

Throughout his life, Longfellow was a deeply devout man who saw all of life directed by the hand of a wise and loving God who permitted even catastrophic events as part of a larger plan that would be consummated only in the other world. He remained true to the spiritual inclusiveness of his Unitarian heritage, and, to the end of his life, complained about the intolerance of Christian sects, none of whom—even Roman Catholicism—had a corner on the truth. For Longfellow, an upright life of love and compassion and trust in a merciful God was more important than subscription to doctrine and denomination. For him: "Life is the thing, and not the creed."[22]

～

Profile 23
Jefferson Davis

Born: Christian County, Kentucky, June 3, 1808
Died: New Orleans, Louisiana, December 6, 1889

The first and only president of the Confederate States of America followed the pattern, in his spiritual life, of many of his contemporaries, in that he was a religious man, married to an active church member, who made a public profession of his faith only in middle age. Davis, a Kentucky-born West Pointer who owned a large Mississippi plantation, had served as U.S. Senator and secretary of war (under Franklin Pierce) before he was called to take the reins of the Confederate government in 1861. At the time of his presidency, Davis was described as "a spare, thin-featured man with iron-grey hair and beard, and a clear gray eye full of life and vigor."[1] Only about five feet ten inches tall, his spare frame and erect posture made him appear taller than he was.

Davis's father, a veteran of the American Revolution, was a Baptist. His mother became an Episcopalian late in life. As a boy, Jeff was sent to St. Thomas Academy in Kentucky, which was run by Roman Catholic religious. He was, in fact, the only boy who was not a Catholic during the time he studied there. At one point he is said to have expressed his desire to become a Catholic to one of the priests, but was gently discouraged, probably because it seemed likely that the boy wanted to adopt the faith of all his friends chiefly out of a desire not to be different.

For the first five decades of his life, Davis was unchurched. He was married twice, both times to Episcopalians. His first wife, Sarah Knox Taylor, the daughter of future president Zachary Taylor, died after only a few months of marriage. The second, Varina Howell, nearly two decades his junior, would bear their six children. Even though he was given demerits at West Point for missing chapel on numerous occasions,[2] there is no evidence that he ever doubted or rebelled against the Christian faith. While serving as an officer in the Mexican War, Davis wrote his wife on August 16, 1846: "I have remembered your request on the subject of profanity and have improved. Have you remembered mine on the subject of prayer, and a steady reliance on the justice of one who sees through the veil of conduct to the motives of the heart? Be pious, be calm, be useful and charitable and temperate in all things."[3]

Though it may be difficult for some to understand how a man could own slaves and, at the same time, give even lip service to Christianity, Davis had no problem. He felt that the Southern gentry, in giving captive Africans the Christian faith, had performed a greater missionary service "than all the society missionaries of the world."[4] There is every evidence that he treated his slaves with kindness and that most of them liked him and entertained warm feelings toward him and his family even after they were free. Davis's attitude was much in keeping with the old feudal system. As master, he was charged with responsibility for the welfare of his "Negroes." In return for his kindness, he expected—and nearly always obtained—their loyalty. There was no thought of equality.

As civil war neared, Davis resigned from his seat in the U. S. Senate. While he was wrestling with this momentous decision, his wife Varina heard him murmuring, as he lay in bed, trying to sleep, "May God have us in his holy keeping and grant that before it is too late, peaceful councils may prevail."[5] Such proved not to be the case, and, upon becoming president of the Confederate States, he said, "I will do my best, and God will give me strength to bear whatever comes."[6] Like Lincoln, Lee, and other leaders, he acknowledged that the outcome of the war was in the hands of God, as he indicated in a letter to his wife in which he bade her, "Be of good cheer and continue to hope that God will in due time deliver us from the hands of our enemies and sanctify to us our deepest distress."[7]

During the first year of the war, Varina frequently observed her husband deep in prayer, and thought that the time was ripe to encourage him to join the church. She asked her pastor, Dr. Charles Frederick Ernest Minnegerode, rector of St. Paul's in Richmond, to talk to him. Davis told Minnegerode, "Before I became president, I felt that I was my own man. Now, perhaps, I should become God's man."[8] Although Davis expressed to Minnegerode his doubts about his worthiness to receive Communion, he decided to join the church. On May 9, 1862, after a private baptism at his home, he was confirmed at St. Paul's by the bishop. After the ceremony, Varina noted that "a peace which passed understanding seemed to settle in his heart."[9] Dr. Minnegerode wrote later, "From that day he never looked back. He never ceased trying to come up to his baptismal vow and lead a Christian life." Addressing the general perception that Davis was cold and hard and lacking in warmth, the pastor added, "His real nature was gentle, and conscience ruled him supreme."[10]

Davis continued the fight for Southern independence to the bitter end. As a Christian, he had not the slightest qualms about the amount of blood this cost. To an interviewer in July 1864, Davis said: "I desire peace as much as you do. I deplore bloodshed as much as you do; but I feel that not one drop of the blood shed in this war is on my hands— I can look up to my God and say this. I have tried all in my power to avert this war. I saw it coming, and for twelve years I worked night and day to prevent it, but I could not. And now it must go on till the last man of this generation falls in his tracks, and his children seize his musket and fight his battle, unless you acknowledge our right to self-government. We are not fighting for slavery. We are fighting for independence, and that or extermination we will have."[11]

Despite Davis's almost fanatically unyielding position, the cause was lost and the former president for a time was imprisoned under harsh conditions. Davis was allowed to keep only a Bible and prayer book as reading material, and these he kept constantly within reach. He told the prison doctor that he had come to realize that "without humility, the spirit of the Lord cannot dwell within one."[12] The physician, John Craven, observed, "There was then living no more devout exemplar of Christian faith and its value as consolation than Jefferson Davis." Craven said, "There was no affectation of devoutness or asceticism in my patient; but every opportunity I had of seeing him convinced me more deeply of his sincere religious convictions."[13]

After his release from prison, Davis lived nearly another quarter century. He continued active in the Episcopal church. While living in Memphis, Tennessee, he served as a vestryman of St. Lazarus Church. After moving to Biloxi, Mississippi, he served on the vestry of the Church of the Redeemer. His faith was evident as he faced devastating bereavements. He outlived all four of his sons. The oldest died in infancy before the war; another died at five, during the war, when he fell to his death from a balcony of the executive mansion in Richmond; still another died suddenly of diphtheria at ten, a few years after the war. When his last son, Jeff, Jr., died of yellow fever at twenty-one in 1878, Davis was crushed. He found himself almost tempted against faith, as he wrote his son-in-law, "The last of my four sons has left me. I am crushed under such heavy and repeated blows. I presume not God to scorn, but the many and humble prayers offered before my boy was taken from me are hushed in the despair of my bereavement."[14] Even though he could not understand why his Lord would deny his prayers and those of his friends, he did not scorn God. A month later, he wrote to one of his daughters how Jeff, Jr., died in the Christian faith, with "the comfort of our church," and affirmed that "his spirit passed from those who loved him here, but may we not hope, to a better world than ours." He recounted, "I have bowed to the blows, but in vain have sought for consolation. So many considerations, not selfish, plead for his longer stay on earth that I shut my eyes to what is not permitted me to see, and, stifling the outward flow, let my wounds bleed inwardly."[15]

In May 1881, he wrote his wife of their departed loved ones, declaring, "They are at peace, for whom we mourn, though today they are lost to us."[16]

Shortly after his eightieth birthday, Davis wrote his pastor that although he was impoverished, the circumstances of his life "are held subordinate to the cause of him who died for the redemption of fallen man."[17] It was this faith that enabled him to tell his wife, just before he died, "I am not afraid."

～

Profile 24
Andrew Johnson

Born: Raleigh, North Carolina, December 29, 1808
Died: Carter Station, Tennessee, July 31, 1875

When civil war broke out in 1861, Andrew Johnson of Tennessee was the only Southern senator who remained loyal to the Union. After federal troops recaptured part of his state, Johnson was appointed military governor of Tennessee. Chosen as Lincoln's running mate in 1864, he became president the next year when his predecessor was assassinated. President Johnson favored a policy of reconstruction of the South that favored the interests of the poor whites—at the expense of the blacks. He clashed with the Republican leadership of Congress, and, in the power struggle, was impeached by the House of Representatives. Although acquitted by the Senate, Johnson, for the rest of his term, was virtually powerless as Congress pursued its own plan for rebuilding the war-ravaged South.

Johnson was perhaps the only man to serve as president who (at least according to one report) publicly denied that he was a Christian.

While serving as military governor of Tennessee, he learned that Nashville was surrounded by rebels and on the verge of capture. He ordered a Methodist chaplain named Granville Moody to pray, and Johnson prayed along with him. When they were finished, Johnson declared: "Moody, I feel better. I'm not a Christian—no church—but I believe in God, in the Bible—all of it—but I'll be damned if Nashville shall be given up."[1] This is one of the few recorded statements Johnson made about his personal religious beliefs. There is no evidence that he ever joined a church or even was baptized.

As a legislator, he took some religious stands. He more than once opposed a resolution in the Tennessee legislature which called for daily prayer to open the sessions of the legislature.[2] He also spoke in defense of Roman Catholics. As a member of the United States Congress in 1844, he answered a representative from North Carolina who insisted that "foreign Catholics" were responsible for the election to the presidency of James K. Polk. Johnson defended his fellow-Democrat and went on to identify himself as "a member of a Protestant church." (If this was true, there is no record of it). He then declared: "The Catholics of this country had the right secured to them by the Constitution of worshiping the God of their fathers in the manner dictated by their own consciences....From whence or how obtained is the idea that Catholicism is hostile to liberty, political or religious? During the Reformation, did not the demon of persecution rage as fiercely among Protestants?...During our colonial state, when Protestants, Puritans, and Quakers were...waging a relentless war of persecution against each other, did not Catholic Maryland open her free bosom to all, and declare, in her domain, that no man should be persecuted for opinion's sake?...And is Catholicism a foe to liberty? Is Ireland's Catholic isle the nursery of slaves...? Was Catholic Poland the birthplace of slaves?...Were Lafayette, Pulaski, McNeill, DeKalb, and O'Brien [all well-known Roman Catholic leaders] foes to liberty? Was Charles Carroll of Carollton, the last survivor of the signers of the Declaration of Independence, a friend of despotism?"[3]

As governor of Tennessee in the 1850s, Johnson vigorously opposed the American Party (called the Know-Nothings because they took an oath to disclose no information about their organization), which opposed the immigration of "foreign Catholics." Johnson pointed out even Protestant reformers John Wesley and Martin Luther, if alive at the time, would fail to meet the approval of Know-Nothingism because they were foreigners.[4]

Like many of his contemporaries, Andrew Johnson was part of a marriage in which the wife was an active church member, but the husband maintained no formal church affiliation. Eliza, Johnson's wife, belonged to the Methodist church. When she was First Lady, however, she seldom, if ever, went to church or anywhere else, apparently because of poor health. The president attended church regularly, although not in the same place. Sometimes he attended St. Paul's Lutheran Church and sometimes Foundry Methodist, to whose building fund he contributed liberally.[5] His favorite place of worship was, however, St. Patrick's Roman Catholic Church. Johnson said he liked to worship there because the Roman Catholic church was a democratic church, which treated rich and poor alike and did not rent pews or reserve seats. Moreover, he liked the fact that the priests never preached on politics, but on "the fundamental virtues—lowly-mindedness and charity."[6]

Some have speculated that Johnson was a Catholic at heart. However, after his death, a local newspaper stated of the unchurched former president: "Those who knew him best are of the opinion that his religious belief conformed more nearly to the Swedenborgian faith than any other."[7] There was no elaboration. Emmanuel Swedenborg was an eighteenth-century Swedish scientist who claimed to enjoy "perfect inspiration" and insisted that "the inner sense of the Word of God has been dictated to me out of heaven."[8] He wrote more than thirty volumes of "heavenly doctrines," based on his private revelations. He claimed that his visions directed him to "explain to men the spiritual sense of the Scripture," insisting that Christ had actually come again, that the Second Coming was a new way of reading Scripture, and that he was supposed to teach humankind a method of understanding the Sacred Word in the light of its spiritual meaning.[9]

Despite their mystical teachings, the Swedenborgians believed that salvation does not depend upon private revelations or even by strict adherence to a formal creed, but by loving God, neighbor, and world.[10] In claiming that Johnson was a Swedenborgian, his friends may simply have meant that for the former president, deed was more imporant than creed.

The only time Johnson ever wrote with any detail about his own beliefs was two years before his death, when he was ill with cholera, and noted: "I have performed my duty to my God, my country, and my family. I have nothing to fear. Approaching death is to me the mere shadow of God's protecting wing. Beneath it I almost feel saved. Here, I know, no evil can come. Here will I rest in quiet and peace, beyond the reach of calumny's poisoned shaft, the influence of envy and jealous enemies, where treason and traitors in state, backsliders and hypocrites in church, can have no place; where the great fact will be realized that God is truth and gratitude the highest attribute of men."[11]

~

Profile 25
Edgar Allan Poe

Born: Boston, Massachusetts, January 19, 1809
Died: Baltimore, Maryland, October 7, 1849

The poet, short-story writer, and critic, who led an unhappy life cursed by poverty, alcoholism, and frequent bereavement, is generally not thought of as a religious man. He was apparently baptized at the age of three in Richmond's Monumental (Episcopal) Church, which he attended as a boy with his foster parents, and throughout his life seemed to consider himself an Episcopalian. Although he displayed familiarity with the *Book of Common Prayer* and the Bible and was said to be "a great lover of church music,"[1] he seldom went to church and once confided to a friend that the Bible was "all rigmarole."[2] He once said he liked Catholic priests because they "smoked, drank, and played cards like gentlemen, and never said a word about religion."[3] Nevertheless, Poe made occasional reference to God and religion in his correspondence. In one letter, he urged his mother-in-law to "trust God"; in another he told a friend that he was "grateful to God"; in others he spoke of "the religion we cherish," "the principles of our divine faith," and "the pure precepts of our holy religion."[4] He once called Christianity "that truest of all philosophies."[5] Although he seldom mentioned Christ, he did write a couple of short poems to the Virgin Mary.

After Poe became a widower, he dated for a while a woman in New York named Louise Shew, who was a devout Christian and who tried to convert him. She took him to a midnight service at the Episcopal Church of the Holy Communion in New York. She recounted that he observed the first part of the service "like a churchman," holding one side of her prayer book and singing the Psalms, but when the minister repeated the text from Isaiah, "He was...a man of sorrows and acquainted with grief," Poe suddenly "rushed out, too excited to stay."[6] Although Poe told Shew that she had "renewed [his] hopes and faith in God,"[7] she apparently gave up on him after be published *Eureka: A Prose Poem*, which contained his fullest statement of his religious beliefs.

In *Eureka*, Poe espoused what one critic described as "pantheistic transcendentalism." He declared that "Divine Volition" had willed a "primordial Particle" into being and diffused it into "the Universe of Stars." Atoms then began to form clusters of "nebulous matter," one of which became the solar system. Eventually, Poe contended, the universe will collapse into the "final globe of globes," which will, in turn, disappear, leaving God to remain "all and in all," to repeat this process forever and forever.[8] People, he believed, were "infinite individualizations" of the Godhead who would, after death, merge into a "general consciousness" which is identical with Divinity. Since people were individualizations of God, Poe believed that nothing exists greater than the individual soul. Each soul, he insisted, was "in part, its own God— its own Creator." The cosmically aware person "shall recognize his existence as that of Jehovah." Accordingly, Poe declared, "My whole nature utterly revolts at the idea that there is any Being in the Universe superior to myself!"[9]

At the end, when Poe, found in a stupor on a Baltimore street, was dying, apparently in *delirium tremens* in a hospital, the wife of his doctor came to see him and he asked her if there was any hope. She thought he was referring to his physical recovery and told him that her husband thought that he was "a very sick man." Poe responded, "I meant hope for a wretch like me beyond this life." She then read the fourteenth chapter of the Gospel of John to him, and he died not long afterward, praying, "Lord, help my poor soul!"[10]

~

Profile 26
Abraham Lincoln

Born: Hodgenville, Kentucky, February 12, 1809
Died: Washington, D.C., April 15, 1865

John Nicolay and John Hay, who served as secretaries to the Civil War president, in a magazine article they wrote some two decades after the death of their boss, conceded that Abraham Lincoln did not like to talk about his religious beliefs and probably never formulated or systematized his ideas into anything like a formal creed, but insisted that "he was a man of profound and intense religious feeling," whose every spoken expression demonstrated "that he held himself answerable in every act of his career to a more august tribunal than any on earth."[1]

Lincoln's religious beliefs were shaped, to a large extent, by his childhood experiences. In an 1889 interview, Dennis Hanks, a cousin who grew up with Lincoln, described Thomas Lincoln, the carpenter and farmer who was the father of the future president, as a man who did not drink, swear, play cards, or fight.[2] Hanks's daughter, who was interviewed at the same time, characterized the elder Lincoln as a man of high moral standards who was "kind and loving and kept his word." It was from him that "Uncle Abe got his honesty and his clean notions of living."[3]

Lincoln's mother, Nancy Hanks, was a devout Baptist, who was a member of the Little Mount Baptist Church of Knob Creek, Kentucky, where the Lincolns lived when Abraham was a small boy. He once told an acquaintance, "I had a good Christian mother, and her prayers have followed me thus far through life."[4] According to Dennis Hanks,

Lincoln's mother was an intelligent, aristocratic lady who was "as pretty as a picture and as smart as you'd find them anywhere." While Lincoln is recorded as saying that his mother could "read a little," Hanks insisted that she could both read and write and taught her son his letters using the Bible.[5]

A woman who worked as a maid in the Lincoln household during the decade before he went to the White House insisted, many years later, that Lincoln told her that among his earliest memories were the recollections of gospel meetings which he attended with his mother and sister. On the frontier, itinerant preachers called "Gospel Droners," would hold camp meetings during which people would fall unconscious during the energetic preaching, and awake, professing to be delivered of their sins "by a vision."

Lincoln recalled that his mother experienced visions and "often spoke of things that would happen," and even foretold, while still in apparently good health, her death at thirty-four.[6] After his mother's death, which occurred when Lincoln was nine, his father remarried to Sarah Bush Johnston, also a Baptist, and in 1823 the two of them joined the Pigeon Creek Baptist Church in Spencer County, Indiana. Shortly afterwards, Lincoln's sister, Sarah Lincoln Grigsby, joined the church, but Lincoln, although he seems to have served for a while as sexton of the congregation, never joined.[7]

In 1830, the Lincolns moved to Coles County, Illinois. One of the traveling clergymen they encountered there was a Roman Catholic, Father J. M. J. St. Cyr, who, the year after Lincoln's death, wrote an article insisting that the father and stepmother of Lincoln were both Roman Catholics, although "not well instructed in their profession." St. Cyr insisted that he "said Mass repeatedly in their house" and that "Abe," although not attracted to Roman Catholicism, occasionally helped him "in preparing the altar for Mass."[8] Allowing for the accuracy of St. Cyr's recollection that he did celebrate Mass in the Lincoln home, he certainly was mistaken in his assumption that Thomas and Sarah Lincoln were Roman Catholic. Sarah died a Baptist, and Thomas ended his days as a member of Shiloh Presbyterian Church in Coles County. There is no record of either belonging to any Roman Catholic Church.[9]

Though religious from boyhood, Lincoln never joined a church.

Growing up under circumstances in which his family had to rely upon the occasional ministrations of traveling clergymen of many denominations, Lincoln perhaps found it difficult to commit himself to the teachings of any one particular denomination. When he was an adult, he told a friend: "The fundamental truths reported in the four gospels…that I first heard from the lips of my mother are settled and fixed moral principles with me….I cannot without mental reservation assent to long and complicated creeds and catechisms."[10]

When Lincoln ran for the United States Congress against Methodist minister Peter Cartwright, his opponent accused him of being an "atheist." Lincoln rebutted this charge with a statement in the *Illinois Gazette* on August 15, 1846, in which he denied that he was an "an open scoffer at Christianity." He stated: "That I am not a member of any Christian Church is true; but I have never denied the truth of the Scriptures; and I have never spoken with intentional disrespect of religion in general, or of any denomination of Christians in particular."[11]

In this same statement, Lincoln also seems to refer to the fact that, as a young man, he toyed with the idea that events were predetermined, not by God so much as by some sort of natural law. He confided to a friend when he was in his forties: "Once I was led to believe by reading the wrong books, and not sticking to the most worthwhile book ever written, that science explained all." Later, he came to believe that "the power that operates the universe" was the will of a personal God.[12]

Cartwright tried to embarrass Lincoln when the latter attended one of his religious services by inviting everyone to stand up who wished to go to heaven, then asking everyone to stand up who did not wish to go to hell. Lincoln stood on neither occasion, and Cartwright asked, "May I inquire of you, Mr. Lincoln, where you are going?" Annoyed by the minister's politically motivated impertinence, Lincoln replied: "Brother Cartwright asks me directly where I am going. I desire to reply with equal directness: 'I am going to Congress.' "[13] When the ballots were counted that fall, it was Lincoln and not Cartwright who went to Congress.

Shortly after the conclusion of his single term in Congress, Lincoln and his wife, Mary Todd, suffered the loss of their son Edward (Eddie), who died at the age of four. Not long after Eddie's death, revival meetings were held at Springfield's First Presbyterian Church. The Lincolns attended both the services and the inquiry meetings and, afterward, Mary, who had been confirmed an Episcopalian, became a member. Although he rented a pew and accompanied his wife, Lincoln did not join. He was active in the life of the church, however. One evening, in the early 1850s, he gave a lecture on the Bible to a crowded congregation. Several ministers attended and called it "the ablest defense of the Bible ever uttered in the pulpit." Lincoln emphasized the superiority of the Ten Commandments to any other law code and insisted that a copy of the Bible should be placed in every home.[14]

Lincoln did not join the Presbyterian church partly because of his inability to subscribe to man-made creeds. He once declared: "If a church would ask simply for assent to the Savior's statement of the substance of the law, 'Thou shalt love the Lord thy God with all thy heart, and with all thy soul, and with all thy mind, and thy neighbor as thyself'—that church would I gladly unite with."[15] He allegedly remarked that if he joined any church, it would be the Baptist church— the church of his mother and stepmother.[16] Lincoln may have been uncomfortable with First Presbyterian for reasons other than doctrine. A maid claimed (many years later) that she heard him telling his wife, "I sometimes wonder if it is a church or a circus. They're all decked out in so much trappings and perform so."[17]

Lincoln's beliefs in providence and in heaven were evident in the letter he wrote late in 1850 to his stepbrother, who had informed him that his father was dying. "Tell him to remember to call upon and confide in our great and good merciful Maker, who will not turn away from him in any extremity. He notes the fall of the sparrow, and numbers the hairs of our heads, and he will not forget the dying man who puts his trust in him. Say to him...that if it be his lot to go now, he will soon have a joyous meeting with many loved ones gone before him, and where the rest of us, through the help of God, hope ere long to join him."[18]

Lincoln's belief that the affairs of humanity are in the hands of a just God was apparent in his reaction to his election as president in 1860. Just before election day, he remarked to a friend: "I know there is a God," he said, "and that he hates injustice and slavery. I see the storm coming, and I know that his hand is in it. If he has a place and work for me I believe I am ready. I am nothing, but truth is everything."[19]

Just before he left Springfield on February 11, 1861, he told his supporters, "I now leave, not knowing when or whether I may return, with a task before me greater than that which rested upon Washington. Without the assistance of that Divine Being, who ever attended him, I cannot succeed. With that assistance, I cannot fail. Trusting in him who can go with me, and remain with you, and be everywhere for good, let us confidently hope that all will yet be well."[20]

Lincoln was never baptized as a child. There is a tradition among the German Baptists, or "Dunkards," that Lincoln was baptized just before he left for Washington by Elder Daniel P. Saylor. Since the German Baptists of that time recorded the baptisms only of members of specific congregations, no record would exist of this event, allegedly done in secret for fear of offending Lincoln's wife, who wanted him to be a Presbyterian.[21] Lincoln had no doubt that the Civil War which soon broke out was being fought for "the preservation of [America's] precious birthright of civil and religious liberty."[22] Although he believed that slavery was evil, he admitted that the Bible did not provide a clear-cut answer.[23] The ungodliness of slavery, Lincoln felt, was evident through reason and common sense. In some of his speeches, Lincoln seemed to express the idea that blacks were inferior to whites. He certainly seemed to be opposed to what would later be called racial integration. However, the Negro's possible inferiority did not justify slavery. It was quite to the contrary. "Suppose it is true that the Negro is inferior to the white in gifts of nature," he suggested. "Is it not the exact reverse of justice that the white should for that reason take from the Negro any part of the little which he has given him? 'Give to him that is needy' is the Christian rule of charity; but 'Take from him that is needy' is the rule of slavery."[24]

How religious people could support the Confederacy was beyond Lincoln's comprehension. To a Tennessee woman who wanted him to free her husband, who was a prisoner of war, Lincoln said: "You say your husband is a religious man; tell him when you meet him that I say I am not much of a judge of religion, but that, in my opinion, the religion that sets men to rebel and fight against their government because, as they think, that government does not sufficiently help some men to eat their bread on the sweat of other men's faces is not the sort of religion upon which people can get to heaven."[25]

Lincoln's mind dwelt frequently on the fact that devout men and women on both sides of the conflict were calling upon God for victory. He commented that God "has before him a strange spectacle. We, on our side, are praying [to God] to give us victory, because we believe we are right; but those on the other side pray him, too, for victory, believing they are right. What must he think of us?"[26]

Although he believed that God was opposed to slavery and that the war was being waged for liberty, Lincoln hesitated to say that God was on his side. To a delegation of ministers, who urged him to abolish slavery outright (which he could not do constitutionally), he said: "These are not, however, the days of miracles, and I suppose...I am not to expect a direct revelation [from God]. I must study the plain, physical facts of the case...and learn what appears to be wise and right....Whatever shall appear to be God's will, I will do."[27]

On another occasion, a minister told Lincoln, "I hope the Lord is on our side." This prompted the president to respond: "I don't agree with you. I am not at all concerned about that, for we know that the Lord is always on the side of the right. But it is my constant anxiety and prayer that I and this nation should be on the Lord's side."[28]

He told Eliza Gurney, a Quaker friend, that he believed that he was himself "a humble instrument in the hands of our Heavenly Father," and that he desired "that all my works and acts may be according to his will." If, after seeking God's help in prayer and trying to do his best, he still found that his efforts failed, Lincoln concluded, "I must believe that for some purpose unknown to me, he wills it otherwise."[29]

In the early fall of 1862, George B. McClellan, the cautious commander of Lincoln's Army of the Potomac, fought Robert E. Lee's Army of Northern Virginia at Antietam Creek, near Sharpsburg, Maryland. Lee was forced back into Virginia, but McClellan failed to capture his army—as Lincoln and his advisors felt that he should and could have done. At this time, Lincoln made some notes for his own use, in which he mused: "The will of God prevails. In great contests, each party claims to act in accordance with the will of God. Both may be, and one must be wrong. God cannot be for and against the same thing at the same time. In the present civil war, it is quite possible that God's purpose is something different from the purpose of either party; and yet the human instrumentalities, working just as they do, are the best adaptation to effect his purpose. I am almost ready to say that this is probably true, that God wills this contest, and wills that it shall not end yet. By his mere great power on the minds of the now contestants he could have either saved or destroyed the Union without a human contest. Yet the contest began. And having begun, he could give the final victory to either side any day. Yet the contest proceeds."[30]

Lincoln found that he had to submit patiently to the will of God in the matter of the national bloodbath, but also in domestic tragedy. During the first year of the war, he and his wife were crushed when their eleven-year-old son Willie died. The distraught father told the child's nurse, "My poor boy, he was too good for this earth. God has called him home. I know that he is better off in Heaven, but then we loved him so. It is hard, hard to have him die. This is the hardest trial of my life." After Willie's funeral, he commented, "I now see as never before the preciousness of God's love in Jesus Christ, and how we are brought near to God as Father by him."[31]

A week later, both Lincolns were still prostrate with grief. Francis Vinton, rector of Trinity Episcopal Church in New York and a friend of Mary Lincoln's family, came down to try to comfort the grieving parents, and spoke sternly to the president, actually telling him that he was "unfitting himself for his high post by giving way to grief." After giving him some assurances from Scripture, Vinton left, and, from that time Lincoln—but not his wife—seemed to return to outward normality.[32]

Willie's death and Mary Lincoln's continued depression stimulated the interest of the president and First Lady in spiritualism. If the memoirs of Mariah Vance, their servant in Springfield, are to be trusted, both Lincolns dabbled in the occult after the death of Eddie Lincoln in 1850. When Lincoln confided to her that he and his wife went "to three good women who are in touch with the spirit world," she was horrified and asked how they could justify this activity, Lincoln told her: "The Bible says God is spirit. So if all things are created in his image and likeness...then his Son was spirit. Then we are spirit....Christ was crucified, returned, and ascended into heaven. Christ said we could do ever greater things than he did. If that is so, and I believe it is, for the world has only begun to touch the hem of his garment through faithful prayer, then why couldn't we, or our loved ones, return after the state called death?"[33]

Many historians do not trust the recollections of the aged Vance, who waited a half century to dictate them, but there is no doubt that the Lincolns consulted mediums and attended seances in the 1860s, for accounts were printed in the newspapers at the time. Interest in communication with the dead was so strong at the time that reports of seances in the White House drew little or no criticism.

Mary Lincoln had a dressmaker by the name of Elizabeth Keckley, who was a pillar of the Fifteenth Street Presbyterian Church, but was heavily involved in the occult. Allegedly she knew all the mediums in Washington, and encouraged the Lincolns to consult them.[34] *The Boston Gazette* of April 23, 1863, described in great detail a "spiritual soiree" held in the Red Room of the White House, conducted by medium Charles Shockle and attended not only by the Lincolns, but, among others, by Secretary of War Edwin Stanton and Secretary of the Navy Gideon Welles. For half an hour "tables were moved, and the picture of Henry Clay, which hangs on the wall, was swayed more then a foot, and two candelabras, presented by the Bey of Algiers to President Adams, were twice raised nearly to the ceiling."[35] However, although Lincoln appeared to be deeply interested in the occult, he seemed to reserve his judgment as to its authenticity.

On March 30, 1863, with the war going badly, Lincoln, at the suggestion of the Senate, proclaimed a National Fast Day. He declared: "It is the duty of nations as well as of men to own their dependence upon the overruling power of God; to confess their sins and transgressions in humble sorrow, yet with assured hope that genuine repentance will lead to mercy and pardon; and to recognize the sublime truth, announced in the Holy Scriptures and proven by all history, that those nations only are blessed whose God is the Lord." He continued: "And insomuch as we know that by his divine law, nations, like individuals, are subjected to punishments and chastisements in this world, may we not justly fear that the awful calamity of civil war which now desolates the land may be but a punishment inflicted upon us for our presumptuous sins, to the needful end of our national reformation, as a whole people? We have forgotten the gracious hand which preserved us in peace, and multiplied and enriched and strengthened us; and we have vainly imagined, in the deceitfulness of our hearts, that all these blessings were produced by some superior wisdom and virtue of our own. Intoxicated with unbroken success, we have become too self-sufficient to feel the necessity of redeeming and preserving grace, too proud to pray to the God that made us. It behooves us, then, to humble ourselves before the offended Power, to confess our national sins, and to pray for clemency and forgiveness."[36]

Three months later, after the Fourth of July saw the two great Union victories at Vicksburg and Gettysburg, Lincoln was convinced that the nation's prayers had been heard, that God had acted and permitted the U.S. Army and Navy to win such victories as to "furnish reasonable grounds" for increased confidence "that the union of these States will be maintained." Accordingly, he set aside August 6 as a day for the American people to assemble "in their customary places of worship, and, in the forms approved by their consciences" to "render homage due to the Divine Majesty for the wonderful things he has done in the nation's behalf" and to continue to beg God "to lead the whole nation through the paths of repentance and submission to the Divine Will back to the perfect enjoyment of union and fraternal peace."[37]

Lincoln's piety was private as well as public. He frequently begged people to pray for him and sometimes he was observed praying alone in his room on his knees. Along with his wife, he attended the New York Avenue Presbyterian Church, just a few blocks from the White House, which had recently been formed through a merger of the F Street Presbyterian Church and Second Presbyterian. The two younger boys, Willie and Tad, attended Sunday school, and when Willie died, Mary Lincoln donated the five dollars found in the boy's possession to the church.[38] Lincoln rented Pew Number 14, but still did not become a member.

It was clear that the presidency and the war led to a deepening of Lincoln's religious faith, and that sometime during his four years in the White House he moved from being simply a religious man to a committed Christian. His wife thought that this happened after Willie's death in February 1862. But Lincoln reportedly told a friend: "When I left Springfield, I asked the people to pray for me; I was not a Christian. When I buried my son—the severest trial of my life—I was not a Christian. But when I went to Gettysburg and saw the graves of thousands of our soldiers, I then and there consecrated myself to Christ."[39]

Lincoln's Second Inaugural Address, given on March 4, 1865, contains his best-remembered religious pronouncements. In it he made public his private concern about the purposes of God, who heard men and women and children from both sides pray for victory. "Both read the same Bible and pray to the same God," he said, "and each invokes his aid against the other. He continued: "The Almighty has his own purposes....If we shall suppose that American slavery is one of those offenses which, in the providence of God, must needs come, but which, having continued through his appointed time, he now wills to remove, and that he gives to both North and South this terrible war, as the woe due to those by whom the offense came."[40]

Lincoln seems now to have been almost certain that the war was in fact a punishment, and that its devastation was a judgment that penitent Americans were bound to accept in submission. The purpose of the Lord was becoming clear. His judgments were true and righteous.

Some time before his assassination, Lincoln was asked if he was ready to die. He answered: "No, I am not ready. Each day, as I look over its events and incidents, as I think of those I have made happy, of those I have made miserable, I see that I might have been truer to my neighbor, truer to my God."[41]

Lincoln was still not a church member at the time of his death. The Reverend Phinehas Gurley, pastor of the New York Avenue Presbyterian Church, insisted that Lincoln, who died on Holy Saturday, was planning to join his church and receive Communion on Easter—the next day.[42] Some of the German Baptists of Springfield insisted that he...had promised them that he would become a practicing Baptist after his years in Washington were over.[43]

Probably because he was never a member of any church, some writers have questioned Lincoln's religious commitment. One of the first was his former law partner, William (Billy) Herndon, who wrote a biography in which he claimed that Lincoln was a skeptic. This prompted

Lincoln's widow, then living in Germany, to write to a minister friend a letter describing her husband's religious faith as she saw it: "You who knew him so well [and] held so many conversations with him...know what [his religious views] were. A man who never took the name of his Maker in vain, who always read his Bible diligently, who never failed to rely on God's promises [and] looked to him for protection, surely a man such as this could not have been a disbeliever, or any other but what he was, a true Christian gentleman."[44] Such was her assessment of the man who has been characterized by at least two historians as "a man of more intense religiosity than any other president."[45]

~

Profile 27

Harriet Beecher Stowe

Born: Litchfield, Connecticut, June 14, 1811
Died: Hartford, Connecticut, July 1, 1896

Best known for her novel *Uncle Tom's Cabin*, which presented such vivid images of slavery that it served to further polarize a nation already dangerously divided along sectional lines, the author was characterized by Lincoln as "the little women who started the big war." Stowe, who claimed to receive inspiration for her most famous novel from a vision, was characterized by many who knew her as "a Christian of the highest order," and as a woman who lived "as nearly like Christ as anyone could."[1]

Harriet Beecher was one of eleven surviving children of Lyman Beecher, a Congregational minister who was one of the best-known clergymen of his time. All seven of her brothers became ministers, and two of her sisters were well-known writers and reformers. She grew up in an intensely intellectual household of spirited theological and philosophic discussions. Harriet, like most of her siblings, was a scholarly child.

Lyman Beecher believed strongly in the necessity of a personal conversion experience as a sign of the operation of God's grace in the
soul. Harriet, when she was fourteen, after hearing her father preach
on the topic, "Jesus as a soul friend offered to every human being,"
professed to be converted.[2] For many years thereafter, however, she
frequently questioned her experience, partly because relatives suggested
that conversion was not as simple as saying that she had given herself
to Jesus. In her thirties, now the wife of the Presbyterian theologian
Calvin Ellis Stowe, she underwent what she called the "baptism of the
Spirit," which she characterized as "a second conversion that is to the
Christian as real an advance as his first regeneration."[3]

Because of the importance that she attached to a tangible experience of God's grace, she was doubly anguished when her son, Henry,
drowned at nineteen in 1857. Although he was a religious young man,
he had never undergone a formal conversion experience. Stowe became convinced that the devil was "trying to separate me from the
love of Christ" and was sowing "the most...agonizing doubts of Henry's
state...into my mind—as if it had been said to me, 'You trusted in
God, did you? You had perfect confidence that he would never take
your child till the work of grace was mature—and now he has turned
him out without warning, without a moment's preparation—and where
is he?'" She concluded, however, that these thoughts were dishonor-
able to God, and it was her duty "to resist them and to assume and
sturdily maintain that Jesus had taken my dearest one in love to His
bosom."[4] After that, she was convinced that "He who has taken [him]
will care for him. He who has spared not his own son—how shall he
not...freely give us all things?"[5]

Eventually, she came to reject the Calvinistic belief that only those
who were given the gift of sanctity through a sudden, supernatural
infusion of divine grace could hope for heaven. She came to see the life
of the spirit as a ladder and sanctification as a gradual process by
which the soul ascended, "gradually outgrowing the human, rising
into the image of the divine."[6] She came to believe that if a mother
commended her child "with earnest devotion to her Savior and herself
to its Christian nurture," Christ "stands pledged and promised to ensure its eternal salvation."[7] Because its doctrines were more congenial,

from the age of about fifty, Stowe and most of her children attended the Episcopal Church, although she herself never requested confirmation.

At the center of the faith of Harriet Beecher Stowe was Jesus Christ. The essence of life was to adore "him as the image of the Invisible God."[8] "For who is this Jesus?" she wrote. "Not a man who died eighteen hundred years ago; but a living God who claims at this moment to be...the great reigning and working force, who must reign till he hath put all things under his feet."[9] She wrote her youngest son, "There is a hell, a fearful one—it is so certain a fruit of sinning that the only escape from it is escaping from sin and the only Savior who can save his people from their sins is Jesus."[10] She declared that "the atonement is not merely a contrivance by which we escape the punishment of sin—it is salvation from sin itself."[11] In her sixties, she wrote the British novelist George Eliot: "It is fifty years since Christ became a living presence to me and ever since he has been the inspirer, consoler, and strength of my life, and to read of those who struggle for goodness without knowing is painful to me as to read of those who die of hunger when there is bread enough and to spare. Christ is my life."[12] Stowe believed that the Bible was divinely inspired, and generally took it literally. Moreover she believed that Jesus Christ was to be seen in every supernatural incident that was recorded in the Old Testament.[13]

From 1864 until her death more than three decades later, Stowe owned a pew at St. John's Episcopal Church in Hartford, Connecticut, and she and her husband organized a community church in their winter home in Mandarin, Florida. Congregationalists, Baptists, Methodists, and Episcopalians were among those who comprised the congregation. She felt that one's denomination was unimportant as long as one had a saving relationship with Jesus Christ. She was, however, repelled by Unitarianism, which was popular in the New England of her day. She characterized it as "a denomination of skeptics and rationalisers of whom scarce any two believe alike," whose members are "wandering among the tombs of atheism."[14]

Although she was in some ways attracted to the Roman Catholic Church and believed that it preserved "all the essential beliefs necessary for our salvation,"[15] she was put off by what she felt was worship of the Virgin Mary. She was also cool to the practice of confession, which she felt could be effective only if the confessor were a "spiritual genius."[16] After a visit to Rome, she wrote: "Moody's Easter sermon which consisted of a simple homely earnest recital of the story of the Resurrection from the four gospels had more of Christ than I saw in Holy Week [in Rome] put together."[17] Ultimately, she believed that it was only devotion to Christ that mattered, a belief she had in common with Dwight Lyman Moody, the lay preacher of whose revivals she heartily approved.

Stowe believed that God intended women to minister equally with men, although she associated women with traditional roles. She wrote of "that pure ideal of a sacred woman springing from the bosom of the family, at once wife, mother, poetess, leader, inspirer, prophetess."[18]

Like many people of her generation, she was interested in spiritualism, and believed, at one time, that one of her friends was receiving messages from the late British novelist, Charlotte Brontë. She insisted that spiritualism was "the throbbing of the severed soul to the part of itself that has gone within the veil."[19]

Harriet Beecher Stowe's most famous novel *Uncle Tom's Cabin* came, she claimed, as a result of a spontaneous vision. She was taking Communion in the chapel of Bowdoin College, in Brunswick, Maine, where her husband was teaching in 1851, when she had a vision of a slave being subjected to a terrible beating, followed by a second vision in which the slave, dying, forgave his murderers.[20] She wrote the book "to show how Jesus Christ...has still a mother's love for the poor and lowly, and that no man can sink so low but that Jesus Christ will stop to take his hand."[21] She would insist that the novel was of supernatural origin: "God wrote it."[22]

Negroes, she believed, were special in that they are sort of a type of the suffering Christ. Speaking of the Passion of Jesus, she wrote: "While Europe [and Asia] clamored for his execution—Africa was represented in the person of Simon the Cyrenaean, who came patiently bearing after him the load of the cross; and ever since then poor Africa has been toiling on, bearing the weary cross of contempt and oppression after Jesus. But they who suffer with him shall also reign; and when the unwritten annals of slavery shall appear in judgment, many Simons who have gone meekly bearing their cross after Jesus to unknown graves shall rise to thrones and crowns."[23]

Stowe, four of whose children predeceased her, was very much concerned with the problem of human suffering. If Christians "profess to believe that they have an Almighty Friend perfect in wisdom and goodness and armed with almighty power," why then "are they not cheerful, exultant—why are they restless, uneasy, worried, worn with care?" She concluded that many sincere Christians suffer from "a divided heart—of something kept back from God" or lack "a full faith that things he says are so—and that the blessings he gives are real and are ours."[24] Achieving a full faith, she conceded, was difficult.

She felt that suffering, if yielded to God, yielded valuable fruits. Writing to a sister-in-law who had lost a child, she said that suffering without any earthly consolation leads a Christian to rely on God alone. "There is a tendency in the weariness of sorrow to despise and undervalue this affliction as of no use to us and only...a gratuitous torture." But, afterward, as the Bible tells us, it shall yield peaceable fruits and then may come a time, even in this life, when you shall bless your Heavenly Father even for this bitter sorrow."[25]

Even though God for her was love, this did not preclude the existence of hell. She wrote to her son Charles, who was a minister, "I advise you to preach a positive doctrine of retribution in the future, stated in the line of 'Whatsoever a man soweth, that also shall he reap.'...God is a loving father, but his laws are not to be trifled with."[26] If people rejected Christ, who is the only means of escape from sin, only judgment remained.

Stowe believed that in heaven, "our friends shall be restored to us in bodily form and shape, perfect in an immortal youth and bloom, never to die."[27] Writing to a friend late in life, she spoke of the "inconceivable loveliness of Christ" and of the "sphere" around him "where the enthusiasm of love is the calm habit of the soul, that without words, without the necessity of demonstrations of affection, heart beats to heart, soul answers soul, we respond to the Infinite Love, and we feel his answer in us, and there is no need of words."[28]

She believed in a sort of purgatory. "I do not...see any evidence in the Bible," she wrote, "that anyone at death goes directly to the states known as Hell or Heaven. It is remarkable that the doom of having gone to Hell so freely pronounced by theologians over this or that sinner is never pronounced of any one person in the Bible. Even Judas is simply said to have gone to his own place. It is only human imagination that changes that indefinite expression into Hell."[29]

The consciousness of Christ's love was evident during the years of physical and mental deterioration that preceded her death, during her lucid intervals. In her last days, she kept repeating, "Trust in the Lord and do good."[30] Not long before she lost the power of speech she told her nurses, "I have been waiting a long time to meet my Maker."[31]

~

Profile 28
Henry David Thoreau

Born: Concord, Massachusetts, July 12, 1817
Died: Concord, Massachusetts, May 6, 1862

The naturalist and philosopher, best remembered for his book *Walden* and his essay "Civil Disobedience," was coming from the woods one Sabbath day, carrying a pine sapling that he intended to transplant in his yard. He passed a church just as it was concluding its services. To neglect public worship and to labor on the Sabbath were still considered scandalous in Concord, Massachusetts, in the mid-nineteenth century—even among Unitarians—and Thoreau's aunt, who was among the offended worshipers, scolded him and prompted the response: "Aunt Louisa, I have been worshipping in my way and I don't trouble you in your way."[1] That sentiment expressed fairly accurately Thoreau's feelings about religion.

Although born and baptized a Unitarian, by his early twenties, he went to church only a few times, on a few special occasions, and was generally critical, if not outright hostile, to the idea of churches, clergy, and organized religion. Thoreau characterized ministers as men who could not butter their own bread,[2] and called the church a "baby-house made of blocks" which subsidizes "lifelong hypocrisy."[3] Worship, he felt, was a dynamic process by which one came to terms with the truth and with real goodness, which was as "original and free from cant and tradition as the air" and "heathen in its liberality and independence of tradition." Churches, after a fashion, tried to confine the truth, to bottle it, to package it, and once truth became "known and accepted," it began to have a "bad taste."

Those who held to ancient traditions and revelations, Thoreau said, only thought they loved God; actually they loved only his old clothes, "of which they make scarecrows for the children."[4]

One might imagine that Thoreau would have been sympathetic to the Quaker faith, but he was not. He felt that the Quaker meeting house was "an ugly shed," and that the "unworldliness of an aged Quaker has something ghostly and saddening about it, as it were a mere preparation for the grave."[5] The only Christian denomination for which Thoreau had the slightest respect was Roman Catholicism. He once commented that Catholic churches were "the only churches which I have seen worth remembering, which are not almost wholly profane."[6]

Although he once wrote that Lydia Emerson, wife of his friend Ralph Waldo Emerson, "almost persuades me to be a Christian," he confessed that he always fell back "into heathenism."[7] He felt that it was "constitution and temperament" that led some people to embrace Christianity, but that some people had "no genius for it." Jesus he revered as "the prince of reformers and radicals" and "a brother of mankind" who "taught mankind but imperfectly how to live." However, "his thoughts were directed to another world. There is another kind of success than his."[8]

Thoreau said that what was religion in others was love of nature in him.[9] In fact, an acquaintance characterized Thoreau as a man who "experienced nature as other men are said to have experienced religion."[10] He told another friend: "I would fain improve every opportunity to wonder and worship, as a sunflower welcomes the light."[11] Another time he declared: "God exhibits himself to the walker in a frosted bush today as much as in a burning one to Moses of old." He wrote: "There are, from time to time, mornings, both in summer and winter, when especially the world seems to begin anew....Mornings when men are new-born, men who have the seeds of life in them. It should be part of my religion to [be] abroad then."[12] It was statements like this that led one biographer to conclude, "If a pantheist is one who worships nature, because nature is life, and life is all there is that matters, then Thoreau was a pantheist."[13]

Other biographers insist that Thoreau believed that God was distinct from nature. "If nature is our Mother," the philosopher wrote, "is not God much more?"[14] He once referred to God as "the Artist who made the world and me"; other times he referred to "the Maker of this earth"; "the great Benefactor and Intelligence that stands over me, the human insect."[15] For Thoreau, God was "the everlasting Something to which we are allied, at once our maker, our abode, our destiny, our very Selves."[16] He had a "constant" desire to communicate with this "everlasting Something," and suggested that the best way to do this was through the contemplation of nature.

Thoreau believed in life after death. Commenting on a shipwreck, which took the lives of many immigrants bound for America, he declared that the victims had "emigrated to a newer world than ever Columbus dreamed of, yet one of whose existence we believe there is more universal and convincing evidence—though it has not yet been discovered by science—than Columbus had of this."[17]

Thoreau, who had suffered from tuberculosis most of his life, was ill continuously the last year of his life, and during his declining days, he remained unshaken in his beliefs. Earlier, he had expressed the opinion that "sin...is not in overt act, or indeed in acts of any kind, but in proportion to the time which has come behind us and displaced eternity, to the degree in which our elements are mixed with the elements of the world."[18] When, now that he was sick, someone suggested that he seek out someone to hear his confession, Thoreau replied, "I have nothing to confess."[19] When his aunt asked him if he had made his peace with God, he answered, "I did not know we had ever quarreled."[20]

When a friend asked him about his relationship with Jesus Christ, Thoreau said, "A snowstorm is more to me than Christ."[21] Nevertheless, Thoreau's happiness in his last months impressed all his visitors. Emerson commented that he "never saw a man dying with so much pleasure and peace."[22] He told one friend, "It is just as good to be sick as to be well,"[23] and wrote another, that although he did not expect to live much longer, "I am enjoying existence as much as ever, and regret nothing."[24] He refused to take painkillers, declaring he preferred to endure the "worst penalties of suffering" rather than be "plunged into a turbid dream of narcotics."[25]

Two friends skated down a frozen river to visit the ailing philosopher, who told them, "You have been skating on this river; perhaps I am going to skate on some other....Perhaps I am going up-country."[26]

A few days before he died, when another friend asked him how the "opposite shore" might appear to him, Thoreau replied, "One world at a time."[27] At the sight of a robin, he remarked, "This is a beautiful world, but I shall see a fairer."[28] When he died quietly, his sister said, "I feel as if something very...beautiful happened—not death."[29]

At the eulogy given at the First Parish (Unitarian) Church of Concord, Massachusetts, Thoreau's friend, Ralph Waldo Emerson, characterized him as a man who "was bred to no profession; he never married; he lived alone; he never went to church; he never voted; he refused to pay a tax to the State; he ate no flesh, he drank no wine, he never knew the use of tobacco; and though a naturalist, he used neither trap nor gun....He concluded that his "soul was made for the noblest society; he had in a short life exhausted the capabilities of this world; wherever there is knowledge, wherever there is virtue, wherever there is beauty, he will find a home."[30] At the grave site, Emerson declared of Thoreau, "He had a beautiful soul."[31]

~

Profile 29
Frederick Douglass

Born: Tuckahoe, Maryland, February 17, 1818
Died: Washington, D.C., February 20, 1895

The experience of the abolitionist and reformer as a slave during his first twenty years of life helped to prejudice him against orthodox Christianity. Born in Talbot County, Maryland, the son of a white father whom he was unable or unwilling to identify and a slavewoman, Frederick Bailey (who changed his surname to protect his identity when he ran away from his master) was reared by his grandmother Bailey until he was six, after which he was separated from any sustained relationship with family members. As a child he was taught by his master to "cling to everything good and forsake all evil." He was taught not to steal and that "servants should obey their masters."[1] Even as a child he was repelled by the gross inequality he saw about him. When he was hungry and his master had more than enough, why was it a sin to take some of his excess food? A slave friend convinced him that since both he and his master's pig were his master's property, it was no sin to steal and eat the pig.[2]

At twelve, Frederick began to experience "religious feelings."[3] During the next few years, when he was in service to a family in Baltimore, his attraction to Christianity increased. He was befriended by a white itinerant Methodist evangelist named Hanson. Despite threats by his master to punish him for wasting time, the boy spent hours praying and reading Scripture in an alley with a black coachman and lay preacher known as Father Lawson. Another black lay preacher named Charles Johnson led Frederick Bailey to a formal acceptance of Christ as Savior.[4]

For a time, young Bailey seemed to be enthusiastic about his professed faith. He began to attend a Sunday-school class for black children at the Dallas Street Methodist Church in Baltimore, and, at fourteen after he was sent to live across the bay in the town of St. Michael's, Maryland, he prayed passionately for the conversion of his master, Thomas Auld. He reasoned, "If he has got religion, he will emancipate his slaves, and if he should not do as much as this, he will, at any rate, behave towards us more kindly."[5] To Frederick's delight, Master Auld was converted at a camp meeting and began to go to church and even organize family devotions. But his treatment of his slaves remained unchanged. In fact, when he learned that Frederick had organized a Sunday school for slave boys, Auld stormed into the meeting and broke it up.

By the time he ran away, Frederick Bailey was already put off by the Christianity he observed. When he was fifteen, he was mercilessly beaten by a man named Edward Covey, to whom he had been hired out, and who was active in the Methodist church. He observed, "Of all the slaveholders whom I have ever met, religious slaveholders...are the meanest and basest, the most cruel and cowardly."[6] After he was living as a free man in New Bedford, Massachusetts, he still retained some ties to organized religion. He and his wife attended the Elm Street Methodist Church. However, along with other people of color, they were forced to sit in the balcony and wait until the whites had taken Communion before they were admitted to the Lord's table. And so they left to attend Zion Chapel, an all-black Methodist church. There Douglass was active for a time and was even given "authority to act as an exhorter,"[7] and allowed to address the congregation. Soon, however, he became completely alienated from the church. Not only was he infuriated that many Christians owned slaves and many other Christians, who did not, took no action to abolish slavery, he was incensed when he learned that the American Bible Society, for fear of aggravating the sectional conflicts of the time, refused to distribute Bibles to slaves. In a speech in Syracuse, New York, early in his career as an orator for abolition, Douglass declared, "I despise that religion that can carry Bibles to the heathen on the other side of the globe and withhold them from the heathen on this side—which can talk about human rights yonder and traffic in human flesh here."[8]

When it was pointed out that slavery was not explicitly condemned in the New Testament, Douglass objected that if he could be convinced that the Bible "sanctioned" slavery, "then I will give the Bible to the flames and no more worship God in the name of Christ!"[9] He insisted that because slavery in America, "with all its hell-black horrors...found no more secure shelter anywhere than amid the popular religious cant of the day."[10] At thirty-four, he railed in one of his speeches, "These ministers make religion a cold and flinty-hearted thing, having neither principles of right action nor bowels of compassion. They strip the love of God of its beauty and leave the throne of religion a huge, horrible repulsive form. It is a religion for oppressors, manstealers, and thugs."[11]

Douglass, early on, was aware that many people considered him an atheist, and, in an appendix to the autobiography he wrote at twenty-seven, he admitted that he had written in such a way as to lead many to suspect that he was "an opponent of all religion." This he denied. He drew a distinction between the "slaveholding religion of this land" and "Christianity proper," and went on at some length to demonstrate the hypocrisy of the many ministers and lay Christians who owned slaves or condoned slavery."[12]

Douglass held, for most of his life, that human beings are responsible for their destinies, rather than God. When slavery was abolished and black men given the right to vote, he shocked many of his friends by refusing to thank God for such signal graces. In one of his speeches he said, "I dwell here in no hackneyed cant about thanking God for this deliverance. I object to it largely because I find that class of men who have done nothing for the abolition of slavery...want us to join in thanking God for the deliverance."[13]

Douglass associated God with the laws of the universe. He felt that one came to know God through a scientific study of the laws of the universe, which, he said, "seem to teach that the mission of man's improvement and perfection has been wholly committed to man himself." Man was on his own. Each individual was "his own savior or his own destroyer," and "has neither angels to help him nor devils to hinder him."[14] He scoffed at the idea of ascribing good or ill fortune directly to supernatural intervention, which made man "a very insignificant agent in his own affairs." To attribute events to God was for him nothing but superstition. The idea of going to church to meet God and that God was present in any special way in church was a belief on the same order as Haitian voodoo.[15]

For Douglass, the "laws of God" were "perfect and unchangeable." The intelligent person had "little use for altars or oracles" and knew that "health is maintained by right living; that disease is cured by the right use of remedies; that bread is produced by tilling the soil; that knowledge is obtained by study; that wealth is secured by saving; and that battles are won by fighting." For him "the lazy man is the unlucky man and the man of luck is the man of work."[16] People create their own destiny.

Like many nineteenth-century liberals, Douglass felt that the world was getting better. He seemed to believe that, after ending slavery, humankind would ultimately go on to eliminate poverty, prejudice, war, disease, and all the other evils of existence. Humanity, he proclaimed, was "ever moving onward," increasing in the "perfection of character and grandeur of achievement."[17] He conceded: "I do not know that I am an evolutionist, but…I certainly have more patience with those who trace mankind upward from a low condition, even from the lower animals than with those who start him at a high point of perfection and conduct him to a level with the brutes. I have no sympathy with a theory that starts man in heaven and stops him in hell."[18]

In Douglass' day, many conservative Christians insisted that the Book of Genesis provided a literal and physical description of the creation. Not surprisingly, Douglass, in a speech in 1883, insisted, "Men are compelled to admit that Genesis by Moses is less trustworthy as to the time of creating the heavens and the earth than are the rocks and the stars."[19] Flatly denying the infallibility and inerrancy of the Scriptures, he railed against people reactionary enough to hold to old-fashioned, outmoded beliefs and reject "the revision of the Scriptures."[20] Douglass seems to have believed that traditional Christianity exerted a "baleful influence" on the world, in that it held back progress and made people think less of themselves than he thought they should.

Douglass held that the universe was governed by a natural law that "in all directions is imperative and inexorable, but beneficial withal," a law which "accepts no excuses, grants no prayers, heeds no tears, but visits all transgressors with cold and iron-hearted partiality."[21] There was no place for prayer in Douglass' universe. There was no place for miracle. There was no place for sin. There was no place for rendering thanks to God. Douglass scoffed that "all the prayers in Christendom cannot stop the force of a single bullet, divest arsenic of its poison, or suspend any law of nature."[22] Any good thing that any human being enjoyed came from his own effort and not from God.

The very concept of faith, according to Douglass, struck at "fundamental progress," and should be discarded, "removed from the minds of men."[23] The idea of penitence was "absurd." If people believed that the consequences of violating a moral law "may all be removed by a prayer, a sigh, or a tear, the result is about the same as if there were no law. Faith, in that case, takes the place of law, and belief, the place of life. On this theory, a man has only to believe himself pure and right, a subject of special divine favor, and he is so," claimed Douglass, and this he felt was ridiculous.[24] The fact that Douglass' God was totally impersonal, and revelation the phantasm of unenlightened minds did not mean moral anarchy for Douglass. It seems as if he felt that logic or reason or common sense revealed what was right and what was wrong.

Douglass was not completely hostile to all organized religion. He approved of churches that taught people to reform society and make the world better. But he had a concept of the separation of church and state quite similar to that embraced by many late twentieth-century jurists and legislators. "My command to the church, and all denominations of the church, whether Catholic or Protestant is, hands off this Government. And my command to the Government is, hands off the Church." Accordingly, he opposed the use of the Bible in the public schools.[25]

Douglass' attitude repelled many of his supporters. Appalled that he had refused to offer thanks to God for the end of slavery and for the Fifteenth Amendment to the Constitution (which permitted men of color to vote), and horrified that he wanted the Bible removed from public schools, a convention of freedmen, meeting at Bethel African Methodist Episcopal Zion Church in Philadelphia in 1870 adopted the resolution "that we will not acknowledge any man as leader of our people who will not thank God for the deliverance and enfranchisement of our race, and will not vote to retain the Bible, the book of God, in our public schools." As the minister who presided over the meeting explained, "While we love Frederick Douglass, we love truth more. We admire Frederick Douglass, but we love God more."[26]

There is little indication that advancing age affected Douglass' beliefs. Late in life, he spoke positively about the Roman Catholic Church, because it "welcomes to its altar and communion men of all races and colors and would contradict its assumption of being the universal church if it did otherwise."[27] He seemed genuinely attracted to a denomination known as the Old Catholic Church. While in Paris in his fifties, he actually found himself regularly attending a church of this persuasion, which maintained the traditional liturgy, but allowed priests to marry and liberalized somewhat its theology. Douglass become a friend of Father Hyacinthe, who was the pastor of the Paris congregation. Late in life, on at least one occasion, Douglass suggested that the Old Catholic Church would do well in America.[28]

During his last years, one of Douglass' close friends was the Rev. Francis J. Grimké, pastor of the fashionable Fifteenth Street Presbyterian Church in Washington. Dr. Grimké, a blond, blue-eyed former slave of European appearance and Princeton education, some three decades Douglass' junior, was a frequent visitor at Douglass' estate, Cedar Hill, which overlooked the Anacostia River, across from Washington. Grimké idolized Douglass, and in years to come, wrote and spoke extensively about him. For example, in an address to Washington school children in February 1908, Grimké spoke of his friend's "beautiful character and life." He commended Douglass as a man who "believed in work," as "a self-respecting man...an honest man..." a man "pure, chaste in character and life." But, significantly, in the three addresses on Frederick Douglass that have been preserved, Grimké never said a word about Douglass' religious faith.

However, according to Grimké, in his last years, Douglass became fond of the Gospel hymns popularized by the revivals of Moody and Sankey. Grimké was the guest of Frederick and Helen Douglass at Cedar Hill in January 1895, when, after dinner, "we had music on the piano and music on the violin, and singing." The attention of all the guests were riveted to Douglass, when he positioned himself in the doorway between the parlor and the hall, and, accompanying himself with his violin, sang, with great emotion, the explicitly Christian hymn by Fanny Crosby, "In Thy Cleft, O Rock of Ages." He sang all three verses "with a pathos that moved us all."[29]

On the basis of this incident, Grimké seems to have believed that Douglass, somehow, had a conversion experience. Certainly, Douglass, who was an accomplished musician, was unlikely to have been carried away by the simple melody by Robert Lowry. Nor could he have sung the hymn out of nostalgia for his boyhood days in the Methodist church, for the hymn was of recent composition. Whether Douglass' moving rendition of "In Thy Cleft, O Rock of Ages" was an indication of a change of heart, no one will ever know, for just weeks later, after coming home from a meeting, Frederick Douglass, at the age of seventy-seven, without warning, dropped dead in his home.

~

Profile 30
Mary Ann Todd Lincoln

Born: Lexington, Kentucky, December 13, 1818
Died: Springfield, Illinois, July 16, 1882

The wife of Abraham Lincoln was one of the most controversial First Ladies in American history. Many people who venerate her husband as a near-saint think of her only as an ill-tempered, unbalanced woman who, along with the Civil War, was one of the sorrows with which that patient man had to contend.

An intelligent, aggressive, strong-willed, and outspoken woman in a day when the general public had little tolerance for women of that character, she was an even stronger champion of Negro freedom than was her husband. Many considered her an outright abolitionist. During the war, she felt that her husband was moving too slowly toward ending slavery. When abolitionist Frederick Douglass complained that the President was not acting fast enough to abolish slavery, the First Lady conceded, "Oh, yes, Father is slow."[1]

Early in the war, she diverted funds set aside for soldier care to an organization to provide for housing, education, and employment for freed slaves, thereby, in the words of one author, risking "a scandal of national and political proportions."[2] Moreover, the First Lady spent nearly every day nursing the sick and wounded in the numerous military hospitals in Washington. One newspaper recorded, "It may not be known that Mrs. Lincoln has contributed more than any other lady...from her private purse, to alleviate the sufferings of our wounded soldiers."[3]

Mary Lincoln had, however, a very sad life. Her mother died in childbirth when she was six. Of her own four children, three would predecease her, and, from the fourth she would eventually be estranged. To her horror, eight of her fourteen siblings supported the Confederacy, and three of her half brothers would die in action. Although she considered these family members traitors, she herself was labeled a traitor and a Confederate spy by many in the North. In addition, she suffered from frequent migraine headaches and other painful physical problems, and from severe depression that left her moody, abrasive, and sometimes hysterical.

Mary Lincoln, like her husband, was deeply religious, and most of her spiritual energy was devoted to coping with suffering. She was raised an Episcopalian, but joined the First Presbyterian Church of Springfield in the early 1850s, because of its pastor, the Rev. James Smith, who consoled her on the death of Eddie, the first of her children to die.

Even as a very young woman, before her marriage, Mary Todd was concerned with the hollowness of earthly pleasures that did not satisfy. In July 1840, she wrote a friend that although she was happy at the moment "in this dull world of reality," it was best "to dispel our delusive daydreams as soon as possible." She sought to "turn my thoughts from earthly vanities, to one higher than us all," since "every day proves the fallacy of our enjoyments, and that we are living for pleasures that do not recompense us for the pursuit."[4]

Throughout her life she believed that God permits suffering to wean mortals away from the world. In this vein, she wrote a friend in November 1867, "It is the lot of humanity to suffer; otherwise we would cling too fondly to earth and its transitory pleasures."[5] Three years earlier, to another friend who had just lost a son, she wrote, "Our Heavenly Father sees fit, oftentimes to visit us, at such times, for our worldliness. How small and insignificant all worldly honors are when we are thus so severely tried."[6]

Mary Lincoln had not the slightest doubt that afflictions were ordered directly by God. Even so, submission to God's will was difficult, and much of Mrs. Lincoln's life was spent in an effort to resign herself to it. At times, she was tempted to rebel. When her son Willie died in the White House at the age of eleven, she wrote a Washington society lady, "How often I feel rebellious, and almost believe that our Heavenly Father has forsaken us, in removing so lovely a child from us!"[7] In this crisis, she felt it was the calmness and equanimity of her youngest son, Tad, that taught her "a lesson in enduring the strokes to which we must submit."[8]

When her husband was assassinated, she wrote: "The deep waters of affliction have almost overwhelmed us and we find it very difficult to bow in submission to our Heavenly Father's will....[Yet] our Heavenly Father has so disposed events...."[9] She conceded that it was God who "removed my idolized husband from me."[10] Even so, as she confided to her former pastor, James Smith, now in Scotland, "I fear 'calmness and resignation' can never visit this troubled spirit...."[11] She wrote Rhoda White, a judge's widow from Suffern, New York, "I am endeavoring to look upward and be submissive to the will of the Heavenly Father, whom, we are taught to believe, does not willingly afflict us. Pray for me....Broken-hearted as we both are, our only refuge in our distress is in the Savior, who suffered and died for us. Our sorrows must certainly draw us very near to the loved ones who have only 'gone before.' "[12]

In an attempt to look heavenward and draw near to the loved ones gone before, Mary Lincoln turned to mediums and fortunetellers. According to a maid who worked for the Lincolns in Springfield and dictated her recollections many years later, after the death of Eddie in 1850, both Abraham and Mary were seeing three mediums, who were "in touch with the spirit world," and in Abraham's words, "straighten us out."[13] After Willie's death in 1862, she looked to the occult more than ever. It is believed that she was involved in at least eight seances in the White House, some of which were attended by her husband.

Mary Lincoln claimed in 1863, in a letter to her sister Emelie, that she had frequent visions of her dead children. Speaking of Willie, she wrote, "He comes to me every night, and stands at the foot of my bed, with the same sweet, adorable smile he has always had; he does not always come alone; little Eddie is sometimes with him."[14] She told a friend in November 1869, however: "I am not...a spiritualist—but I sincerely believe—our loved ones, who have only 'gone before' are permitted to watch over those who were dearer to them than life."[15] Later in life she had a photograph taken of her by a "spirit photographer," which showed a ghostly image of her husband hovering over his black-clad widow.

When her youngest son, Tad, died in 1871 at the age of eighteen, she was completely devastated. Her world, she said, was now "complete darkness."[16] Four years later, she suffered an apparent breakdown and was placed in a mental hospital by her remaining son, Robert. After she took legal action to free herself, she was permanently estranged from "that wretched young man...old in sin."[17]

During her last years, Mary Lincoln spent much of her time in Europe. In a letter to a grandnephew, Edward Lewis Baker, she stated that, in observance of the Sabbath, she never traveled on "this sacred day."[18] She also revealed, in another letter to him, her attraction to the ceremonial aspects of Roman Catholicism: "This is a fête day among the Catholics, and the grandest procession, quite a mile in length, passed this street....Two or three bands of music were interspersed in the line. Can I say to you how I wished your Grandma [Mary's sister] and yourself had witnessed it?"[19]

It is not recorded where or whether she worshiped publicly during her long sojourn abroad, but it is clear that her soul was absorbed with an intense longing for heaven. "My 'Gethsemane' is ever with me," she wrote her sister Elizabeth Todd Edwards from France, "and God can *alone* lighten the burden until I am reunited to my dearly beloved husband and children."[20]

She dwelt constantly on her husband, in his "glorious home," a home "prepared for all those who truly love and serve him here on earth," where he was "rejoicing before the throne of God and the Lamb for evermore."[21] Even before Tad died, she wrote from Frankfurt, Germany, "*In God's own time* the veil will be removed, and the chastenings that we are *now* so grievous to be borne, will be made clear to us. 'Over the river' our loved ones are watching and waiting for us. But yet that time of that reunion appears so far distant."[22] From her home in France in April 1877, she wrote her grandnephew, "The time will come when the severance will be over, together husband, wife, and children—never more to be separated."[23]

In 1880, Mary Lincoln, now physically ill, returned to America. On the same ship was the famed French actress, Sarah Bernhardt. One day, the sea was so rough that both women were knocked off their feet, and Mary Lincoln was kept from falling down a steep staircase when the actress grabbed her by the skirt. When Bernhardt told her, "You might have been killed, Madame," Lincoln replied sadly, "Yes, but it was not God's will,"[24] giving the Frenchwoman the impression that she was sorry that she had been spared from death. After two more years of failing health, the longed-for moment came on July 16, 1882, when she died in her sister's home in Springfield—the same house in which she had been married.

∼

Profile 31
Susan Brownell Anthony

Born: Adams, Massachusetts, February 15, 1820
Died: Rochester, New York, March 13, 1906

The feminist, reformer, and women's rights' leader was a lifelong Quaker, and her ideas and outlook were shaped by her faith. Among the tenets of the Society of Friends is that all people—including women—are equal before God. Quakers also teach that the individual conscience of a man or woman is more important than formal creeds or confessions. They also hold that religious beliefs need to be translated into concrete physical action to right the wrongs of the world. Anthony, whose father, during most of her formative years, ran a cotton mill in a small town in upstate New York, grew up in a household in which both parents supported the right of women to vote and approved of the struggle to abolish slavery. As a young girl, she came in contact with many of the prominent reformers of the day who visited in her home.

Anthony once said, "Theories, theosophies, and theologies, they are all Greek to me."[1] Another time she said, "I was born and reared a Quaker, am one still...but today all sectarian creeds and all political policies sink into utter insignificance compared with the essence of religion and the fundamental principle of government—equal rights.[2] A "deeder, not a creeder," she believed in what she called "Prayer in Action." Like Frederick Douglass, she felt that it was useless to sit in church or at home and address petitions to God. If conditions in the world were to be changed, it was up to the individual to work to change them. She sometimes recounted a story that Frederick Douglass told her, how, when he was under the influence of the Methodists, he used to pray to God to bring him liberty, but how "God never answered his prayers until he prayed with his heels."[3] Anthony insisted: "I pray every single second of my life; not on my knees, but with my work. My prayer is to lift women to equality with men. Work and worship are one with me. I cannot imagine a God of the universe made happy by my getting down on my knees and calling him 'great.' "[4] For her, "doing the work of righteousness—feeding the hungry—clothing the naked—visiting the sick and in prison—undoing the bonds of the Slave and letting the oppressed go free" was more important than "the Law, Judgment, Mercy, and Faith," or belief in the traditional creeds and doctrines.[5]

Anthony, in the words of a biographer, "opposed the traditional religiousness which took people away from the world and reform."[6] She felt that women needed to go "outside the four walls of home and the other four of the church into the great world," instead of "living in the air with Jesus and the angels."[7]

The Bible she saw as a "human production,"[8] and not the divinely inspired Word of God. "The Friends consider the book as historical, made up of traditions, but not as a plenary inspiration," she explained.[9] The belief that the Bible was directly and totally inspired by God and without error was, for her, a superstition, whose "lingering skeleton" she hoped to see crumble away.[10] She was particularly concerned with the passages of Scripture which she felt degraded women. She considered these passages no different from civil laws that were discriminatory.[11] Accordingly, she supported *The Woman's Bible*, which eliminated those texts which supposedly reflected gender bias.

The essence of Susan Anthony's religion was benevolence—working to make the world better. She had an inner conviction, which she put on the level of revelation, "that it is through woman that the [human] race is to be redeemed."[12] Once women were empowered politically, she believed, they would bring about "social purity" and reform many of the ills of society that were being neglected by men.

Although she always considered herself a Quaker, when she lived in Rochester, New York, during the last part of her life, she usually worshiped in a Unitarian church, apparently because it was more socially active than the local Quaker meeting. Publicly and privately, she rarely spoke about heaven or God,[13] and she could not understand a religion that was concerned primarily with otherworldly things. One of her friends was the theosophist Annie Besant, who claimed that her "aura" frequently traveled in the world beyond. Exasperated, Anthony asked her one day, "Annie, why don't you make that aura of yours do its gallivanting in this world, looking up to the needs of the oppressed, and investigating the causes of present wrongs."[14] Besant replied that it was useless "to deal with individuals here" in this world. Anthony answered, "But Annie! We are here. Our business is here!"[15]

As to the world to come, Anthony once observed that she had "an intuitive feeling that we [are] not to cease to exist when the body dies."[16] Another time she said, "If it be true that we die like the flower, leaving behind only the fragrance...while the elements that compose us go on to form new bodies, what a dream is the life of man!"[17] She wrote Isabella Beecher Hooker, who was heavily involved in spiritualism: "Of the before and after I know absolutely nothing, and have very little desire and less time to question or study. I know this seems very material to you, and yet to me it is wholly spiritual, for it is in giving time and study rather to making things better in the between which is really all that we can influence...."[18]

In her final hours, Anthony said to her friend, Anna Howard Shaw: "Anna, if there is a continuance of life beyond and if I have any conscious knowledge of this world and of what you are doing, I shall not be far away from you, and in times of need I will help you all I can."[19] She saw before her the faces of women who had been a part of the women's suffrage movement. Just before she lost consciousness, she told Shaw, "I wonder if we shall know each other in the hereafter. Perhaps I can do more over yonder than I have done here."[20] This was in keeping with her lifelong belief, for she had said many years before, "I've always felt sure that if I entered the other life before women were enfranchised, nothing in the glories of heaven would interest me so much as the work for women's freedom on earth."[21]

⌒

Profile 32
Frances Jane (Fanny) Crosby

Born: Gayeville, New York, March 24, 1820
Died: Bridgeport, Connecticut, February 12, 1915

Called by one contemporary writer "the most wonderful person living," and known as the Methodist Saint, the Queen of Gospel Singers, and the Mother of the Gospel Hymn, Fanny Crosby wrote the words to as many as nine thousand hymns, some of which became the mainstay of the evangelical campaigns of Dwight Lyman Moody, the lay preacher, and his minister of music, Ira D. Sankey.

In the early nineteenth century, the singing of hymns by congregations during church services was uncommon in America. Especially in New England it was considered bad taste to sing "human hymns"—that is, hymns composed by persons outside the biblical canon. Gradually, many churches began to accept hymns which were paraphrases of the Psalms, such as those of the eighteenth-century English minister Isaac Watts. Later, formal and majestic hymns of praise, such as those of Charles Wesley, were accepted in many quarters. Around the time of the Civil War, however, in camp meetings and other revivals, a different type of hymn became popular—one informal, related to the singer's personal feelings, and set to a tune in the popular style. After the war, when Moody and Sankey began their revivals, they began to use these songs, which were set to simple tunes and easily sung, and they became all the rage in Protestant Christendom.

Moody, who was without musical background or talent, felt that congregational singing was so essential to Christian worship that he gave his chorister Sankey equal billing for years, insisting that he, Moody, would preach the Gospel, and Sankey would sing it. Sankey made use of the popular hymns of the time and began to publish collections of the hymns used in the meetings. He issued several series of *Gospel Hymns*. Soon the musical idiom that publisher Hubert Platt Main called "music for the masses"—hymns that could be sung and enjoyed by people who were not musicians—came to be called "gospel hymns"—after the popular songbooks. They were also called "Sunday school hymns," because many ministers still felt that they were unfit for use in the main services but acceptable in the Sunday school. By the end of the century, however, the Gospel hymn came to be widely accepted in most Protestant churches in America and the British Empire.

George Coles Stebbins, who composed the music to many Gospel hymns, wrote that without them Moody would not have been as successful as he was. A disproportionate number of the lyrics in the *Gospel Hymns* collections and other sacred songbooks of the time were written by one person, who was acknowledged to be a major factor in the success of the Moody-Sankey campaigns. This one person, who wrote under more than two-hundred pen names as well as her own name, was a dwarflike teacher of the blind— herself sightless—named Frances Jane Crosby, and universally known as "Fanny" or "Aunt Fanny."

Crosby, who was distantly related to the much younger "Bing," was born in a village called Gayeville, not far from the modern town of Brewster, New York. She never knew her father. Her mother, whose maiden name was Mercy Crosby, always told Fanny that her father's name was John Crosby and that he died when Fanny was a baby.

Shortly after her birth, it was obvious that there was something wrong with the child's eyes. Because they seemed to be inflamed, a local folk practitioner applied hot poultices, which burned the infant's eyes. And so, Fanny Crosby came to be known to the villages of eastern New York and western Connecticut where she lived with her mother as the "Blind Girl."[1] Despite her handicap and her nurture in a single-parent household, Fanny Crosby grew up a happy, well-adjusted child.

First as a student and then as a teacher at the New York Institute for the Blind in Manhattan, Fanny Crosby earned a reputation as America's Blind Poetess, traveling as far as Washington, D.C., to give recitals of her poetry and writing two volumes of verse. She also wrote the lyrics to several popular songs of the day, including "There's Music in the Air," which was popular well into the twentieth century. Eventually, she came into conflict with the superintendent of the Institute, and she was fired. At the same time, at age thirty-eight, she married twenty-seven-year-old Alexander Van Alstyne, a former student, but never adopted his surname except for strictly legal purposes. They lived apart in later years.

Although successful as a poet as well as an educator, Fanny Crosby at thirty, was still dissatisfied and depressed. A fellow teacher from the Institute invited her, during the fall of 1850, to attend a series of revivals at the Broadway Methodist Temple at 30th Street. Crosby had been introduced to Methodist services eleven years earlier, when she consented to provide music (she was an accomplished pianist, organist, and harpist) for the class meetings of the Eighteenth Street Methodist Church. Twice, at the invitation at the Tabernacle, she went forward to the altar to be prayed over, and nothing happened. Desperately, she presented herself at the altar for a third time and remained there for hours. Still nothing happened, until the congregation began to sing the Isaac Watts's hymn, "Alas, and did my Savior bleed/ And did my sovereign die?/ Would He devote that Sacred Head/ For such a worm as I?" At the last stanza, Crosby felt "my very soul flooded with celestial light." From that day on, she said, "The Lord planted a star in my life and no cloud has ever obscured its light."[2]

Fanny began to write hymns at forty-four, first supplying music publisher William Bradbury, then, after his death, the firm of Bigelow and Main and other publishers of church music. Since she had the ability to think and talk in verse, she was frequently able to turn out several hymns a night, after she spent her day working in the missions of Manhattan with the homeless, whom she called "my boys." What little money she made from her hymns she gave away to the poor and chose to "live on faith," praying for her immediate needs. Eventually, she came to travel extensively around the Northeast, speaking in churches, missions, prisons, and YMCAs. Despite her blindness, until her very last years, she usually traveled alone, on trains and streetcars, with the help of only a cane.

At least two thousand of her hymn poems were set to music and published, and many are still popular in evangelical circles. Methodist, Baptist, and Bible-church hymnals still contain such works as "Blessed Assurance," "Pass Me Not, O Gentle Savior," "To God Be the Glory," "I am Thine, O Lord," "He Hideth My Soul in the Cleft of the Rock," "All the Way My Savior Leads Me," "Jesus, Keep Me

Near the Cross," and "Some Day the Silver Cord Will Break." Her favorite, popular in the nineteenth century, but not so much today, was "Safe in the Arms of Jesus." Like many of her most effective hymns, Crosby claimed that this was dictated by the Holy Spirit. The songwriter William Howard Doane came to her flat on Varick Street, on the West Side of Manhattan, one day, and played a tune. Within fifteen or twenty minutes (by most accounts) Crosby had the words. Many of her lyrics were born this way. She insisted that her songs came from God to save the souls of human beings. She often said that she prayed to God that her hymns would "save a million men," and she liked to hear accounts about people, previously hardened and godless, who gave their lives to God when they heard her hymns and found their hearts melted.

Crosby's mother and grandparents were, like most members of their community, Presbyterians. During her childhood, Fanny attended a Quaker meeting when she and her mother lived in Connecticut. After she went to live in New York, it is not clear where she worshiped, although one suspects that the Institute, like nearly all schools of the time, had regular chapel services and that she attended.

For the sixty-five years that remained to her life, Fanny Crosby enjoyed what has been called "divine intimacy." She actually felt the sustained presence of God. She lived her life almost constantly in prayer, conversing with God as "friend with friend." Fanny Crosby gave people the impression that she was continually in the presence of God. She seemed constantly happy and joyful and seemed to live the chorus of one of her songs: "This is my story, this is my song / Praising my Savior all the day long!" In fact, some of those who knew her testified that at times, especially late in life, Crosby literally and physically glowed with a visible radiant aura.[3]

Although she was without the gift of physical sight, Crosby at times had visions. She would go into a dreamlike state in which she would communicate with her "Angel Guardian." For example, she once said: "I was walking beside a clear river with a spirit or an angel guide. On the other side of the river were beautiful trees, perfect ones, with no sign of age or decay; and under the trees people were walking; they were perfect, too, and it looked so peaceful and so lovely that I said to my guide, 'Let me cross over the river into that beautiful land.' But the guide replied, 'Not yet. Go back to your work. Fulfill your mission; then you may cross.' "[4]

Another vision, when she was about forty, foretold her life's work as a hymnwriter: "I was in an immense observatory, and before me was the largest telescope I had ever imagined. I could see everything plainly....At last we came to a river and paused there. 'May I not go on?' I asked of my guide. 'Not now, Fanny,' was the reply. 'You must return to the earth and do your work there, before you enter those sacred bounds; but ere you go, I will have the gates opened a little way, so you can hear one burst of celestial music.' Soon there came chords of melody such as I never had supposed could exist anywhere; the very recollection of it thrills me."[5] Although she wrote very little music—a few hymn tunes—she said that this particular vision inspired her to write sacred lyrics.

Crosby was never the least unhappy about her blindness, at least after her conversion. "A great many people sympathize with me," she frequently said, "but, although I am grateful to them, I really don't need their sympathy. What would I do with it?"[6] At eighty-three she told an interviewer: "Although it may have been a blunder on the physician's part, it was no mistake of God's. I believe it was his intention that I should live my days in physical darkness so as to be better prepared to sing his praises and to incite others to do so."[7] Just before she died she declared: "I believe the greatest blessing the Creator bestowed upon me was when he permitted my external vision to be closed. He consecrated me for the work for which he created me."[8]

Many people asked Crosby about her theology, prompting her to say that she seldom thought about theology. She said she never worried about *what* she believed, but about in *whom* she believed. Her faith was based on Scripture and her own personal experience. She felt that "character and kindness" and "purity of life and deed" were more important than the subscription to a particular creed.[9]

The ultimate authority in Crosby's life was the Bible, which she had memorized—in its entirety—as a girl. "This Book is to me God's treasure home. It is my bread of life, the anchor of my hope, my pillar of fire by night, my pillar of cloud by day. It is the lantern that lights my pathway to my paradise home."[10]

Crosby had trouble with the denominationalization of Christianity. To her, everyone who loved Christ was her "Brother" or "Sister," and she never made much distinction between churches. She always identified herself as a Methodist, but attended many different congregations of many different persuasions. She did not formally become a church member until she was approximately sixty, when she was received into the Cornell Memorial Methodist Church in upper Manhattan. When she moved to Bridgeport, Connecticut, around 1900, she transferred her membership to the First Methodist Church. However, she seldom attended. A grandniece who lived with her the last eight years of her life later recalled that she almost never attended church during those years, even though she was physically active and traveling all over the Northeast during most of that time. She preferred to worship at home. Many felt that she became disillusioned with the "liberalism" that was beginning to affect Methodism and other Protestant denominations. She seemed to admire the Roman Catholic faith as "a good strong religion," and in her last years, it was a Roman Catholic priest who regularly called on her.[11]

Prayer was very important for Fanny Crosby. She urged people to pray both morning and evening. "The good will come out of it, and he will answer the prayer much better than you think.[12] Of suffering she said, "Our Lord afflicts his children only to bring them closer to him. I walk by faith, not by sight. I am ready to suffer, if only for his glory."[13] Suffering was no sign of God's displeasure. "If I had no troubles, I'd think the Lord didn't love me," she once remarked.[14] Although her life was full of external and temporal suffering, she remarked, late in life, "I am happy as a lark, for he who takes care of the sparrow will never forget Aunt Fanny. Many a storm has beaten on this old bark of mine, but I always entered the harbor. Many sorrows which have been heart-rending have crossed my path, but out of Gethsemane I have reached Olivet, where angel voices have beckoned me to the lands of eternal sunshine."[15]

Fanny Crosby's was an active faith. She believed that communion with God resulted in a life lived for others. For many years, she spent her days in the home missions in New York's seedy Bowery district, simply "being there" for the homeless persons who sought shelter in those institutions. Frequently, she gave talks in the mission chapels in which she invited the drunkards, the vagrants, and the prostitutes to give their lives to God. She also spoke in YMCAs, in prisons, and in churches. When she moved to Bridgeport, Connecticut, she was a regular speaker at the Christian Union on South Main Street, near Fairfield Avenue.

Clarice Bray Griffins, who was living in Long Hills, Connecticut, in 1971, recalled the days when, as a teenaged girl, she played the piano at the services, which were held every night. The audience was composed mainly of street people. After being led to the podium, Crosby would greet them invariably with the words, "Dear Friends, I am so happy to see you!" Then she would recite a passage from sacred Scripture, and then preach in a voice that was strong and steady, even into her nineties. Griffins recalled that Crosby "was a good talker. She took away all self-consciousness. She spoke about salvation, about what the Lord would do for them. She was very short and very slim, and always dressed in black and wore a bonnet tied under her chin. She used to tell me, 'If you play at my mission, you're my girl.' She told the men, 'This is my mission and you're my men!' She was very sweet, very cheerful, very happy. She would tell the men why they should be Christians. After she finished preaching, she gave an invitation, and usually one or two men were converted. She was very calm, never emotional. She was usually the only speaker."[16]

A man who wished to remain anonymous provided an account around 1950 of his boyhood encounter with Fanny Crosby. He remembered her as a tiny figure, dressed in black, "her eyes...sealed with dark glasses." She seemed quite unprepossessing until "she lifted a frail little hand and in a voice as sweet as the song of a bird, as calm with spiritual assurance as if angels had inspired her." The effect of her brief talk was electrifying. "I can never get away from the spell that was cast over my soul by Fanny Crosby's quoting this [hymn]. My life was literally remade!"[17]

Crosby traveled and spoke almost up to the time of her death. She still journeyed along on the New York subway until she was ninety-one. At the end, she was so frail that she had literally to be carried from her car or carriage to the hall where she was to speak. Weakened by a failing heart, during the last few months of her life she was confined to the house in Bridgeport where she lived with the family of her step-niece. Needless to say, death held no terrors for her, immersed as she was in "the ocean of God's love."[18]

On February 7, 1915, a journalist called on Aunt Fanny for an interview. Now nearly ninety-five, she breathed with difficulty and was wasted away almost to a skeleton. Yet she was cheerful and ebullient and protested that she was in danger of a swelled head when the interviewer read her a flattering note from evangelist Billy Sunday. "Pray for me," she asked, "that I may be kept at the feet of Jesus."[19] Three days later a Congregational minister visited and found the dying woman "full of radiant light" as she expressed her concern for four categories of persons whom she hoped to remember especially in heaven: railroad men, policemen, prisoners, and the poor. When the minister said, "I hope sometime to reach heaven," and asked her if she would remember him, she replied, "Why, of course I shall remember you...and all whom I have known and loved here."[20]

On the eleventh of February she did not leave her bed and would not eat. The pastor of St. Patrick's Roman Catholic Church came for a last time and spent some time with her. Her family never knew the subject of their conversation.

That evening her niece's husband looked in on her and she said to him, "All right, Governor."[21] After a few hours, she got up, staggered into the hallway, and collapsed into the arms of her niece, who carried her back to bed and summoned a doctor, who diagnosed a massive stroke. Two hours later, very peacefully, and with a smile on her face, she breathed her last.

Her funeral was said to have been the largest ever seen in Bridgeport up to that time—even larger than that of P. T. Barnum two decades earlier. Since her favorite flower was the violet, those who came to pay their respects as her body lay in state in the First Methodist Church were encouraged to bring a violet to drop into her open casket, so that by the time it was closed, Aunt Fanny appeared to be sleeping in a bed of violets. After a service in the packed church, which concluded with the singing of her favorite hymn, Father Frederic William Faber's "Faith of Our Fathers," her casket, no bigger than a child's, was conveyed to Mountain Grove Cemetery, where, on her instructions, no tombstone was erected only two tiny markers, one of which designated her grave as that of "Aunt Fanny," and the other which bore the words by which she hoped that her life would be remembered: "She did what she could."

∼

Profile 33
Ulysses Simpson Grant

Born: Point Pleasant, Ohio, April 27, 1822
Died: Mount McGregor, New York, July 23, 1885

T he victorious commander of Union troops in the Civil War who went on to serve two undistinguished terms as president was never a religious man. Although his mother, sister, and wife were devout Methodists, he was never even baptized. During his administration, Grant became a friend of the Rev. Dr. John Philip Newman, pastor of the Metropolitan Methodist Church, where his wife, Julia, worshiped. The president himself attended Metropolitan, which was then located in Judiciary Square between the Capitol and the White House, but "no more often than he had to," for the sake of appearances.[1] Unlike many people of his time, he did not refrain from work on Sunday. This horrified some people, including millionaire financier Jay Cooke, who protested to the Republican National Committee, "God will not reward us unless our rulers are righteous."[2] Grant had, in fact, twice accepted invitations by the evangelical preacher Dwight Lyman Moody to appear on the platform with him. Moody was in the habit of inviting noted celebrities to sit on the raised platform, facing the public, behind the pulpit where he preached, as a sort of endorsement of his message. But, while sympathetic to Moody's work, Grant never made a public or private confession of faith in Christ.

After Grant left office, his friend Dr. Newman, whom he had appointed Inspector of U.S. Consulates, was appointed pastor of the Central Methodist Episcopal Church in New York, and appointed the former president, who also made his home in the city, a trustee of the church, even though he was not a member. Early in 1885, Newman became concerned when he learned that Grant was dying and was determined to make one final effort to lead him to a profession of Christian faith. The clergyman resolved that he would do his best to persuade General Grant to accept Christ as savior. During his visits with Grant, Newman noted that the general, who was suffering from throat cancer, "manifested more dependence upon God in prayer than I have ever known him to do."[3] Grant knew that he was dying, for he told Newman, "I shall soon be through with the things of this world, but it seems strange that I must agonize for some days longer."

In early April, Grant's condition deteriorated to the point that death was believed imminent. Julia Grant begged Newman to baptize her husband, which the minister promised to do, but only if the sick man showed some signs of consciousness. He told her that he could not baptize an unconscious man. However, as the pastor was praying by his bed, the general opened his eyes and looked at him. Newman then said, "General, I am going to baptize you." Grant responded, "I am much obliged to you, Doctor."[4]

After his baptism, Grant rallied, and regained enough strength to complete his memoirs, the royalties from which would provide for his family in the coming years. Grant, in fact, improved so much that Newman, for one, dared to hope that God was going to bring about a miracle of healing. He suggested this possibility to Grant, who said he did not believe he had cancer, but asked if God could heal it if he did.

"Why not?" answered Newman. "You must hold on to him by prayer and faith."

Grant lived less than four months after his baptism. Newman, and other friends of Grant, continued to agonize over whether the general was really saved. One of Grant's friends, Senator Jerome Chaffee was unconvinced and believed that the general allowed himself to be baptized and was receptive to prayer simply to please his wife and because he did not want to hurt the feelings of an old friend.[5]

But Grant, during the last months of his life, did make statements that seemed to indicate a sense of sincerity. When Newman urged him to receive holy Communion, Grant refused. The general, for whom speech was now extremely painful, wrote him a note, "I would be only too happy to do so if I felt myself truly worthy. I have a feeling in regard to taking the sacrament that no worse sin can be committed than to take it unworthily. I would prefer not to take it, but have the funeral service performed when I am gone."[6]

Another time, Grant told Newman, "Doctor, I am going. I hope the prospect of the future is clear and bright."[7] He also, on at least one occasion in his illness, spoke of the Bible, and said, "I believe the Scriptures, and whoever lives by them will be benefited. I do not argue with men's interpretation of them, for the interpretation is human: but the Scriptures are man's best guide. I have endeavored so to live as not to injure anyone and when I found that I have, I suffer more than they do."[8]

After Grant died peacefully on July 23, his wife found a note that he had scribbled to her during his last days: "Look after our dear children and direct them in the paths of rectitude. It would distress me far more to hear that one of them could depart from an honorable, upright, and virtuous life than it would to know that they were prostrated on a bed of sickness from which they were never to arise alive. They have never given us any cause for alarm on this account, and I trust they never will. With these few injunctions and the knowledge that I have of your love and the dutiful affection of all our children, I bid you a final farewell until we meet in another, and, I trust, better world...."[9]

Grant was certainly neither atheist nor agnostic. Nor was he even indifferent to religion. He believed in the Scriptures. He believed in a life after death. He was pious enough to believe himself unworthy of taking Communion. Yet his convictions seemed so vague, perfunctory, and unenthusiastic that his great friend Dr. Newman confided to his diary that his ministry to General Grant in his last days represented a "singular failure to bring a soul to Christ."[10]

~

Profile 34

Thomas Jonathan
(Stonewall) Jackson

Born: Clarksburg, Virginia, January 21, 1824
Died: Guiney's Station, Virginia, May 10, 1863

The man many consider the most brilliant general to fight for the cause of Southern independence was called "Stonewall" because he refused to order a retreat during the First Battle of Bull Run and caused his lines to hold fast against a Federal advance, standing, in the words of another general, "like a stone wall." Although notorious as an aggressive and ferocious fighter, Jackson was equally famed for his deep religious commitment. Jackson's brother-in-law, General Daniel H. Hill, said, "I never knew anyone whose reverence for the Deity was so all pervading, and who felt so completely his entire dependence upon God."[1] Moses D. Hoge, a Presbyterian minister, wrote, "To attempt to portray the life of Jackson while leaving out the religious element would be like undertaking to describe Switzerland without making mention of the Alps."[2] A few months before he was killed, Jackson wrote his wife, "If I know my unworthy self, my desire is to live entirely and unreservedly to God's glory."[3]

A native of Clarksburg, in what is now West Virginia, Jackson lost both parents before his eighth birthday and was reared by an uncle. Young Jackson was inspired, he later said, by the memory of his mother, who evidently came from a Methodist background and joined a Presbyterian church shortly before she died. Even as a boy, he liked to read the Bible, and while at West Point, he was said to have been "observant of the decencies of religion."[4] However, it was not until he was stationed in Mexico, during America's successful war with that country, that Jackson, in his mid twenties, became truly serious about religion. He was first drawn to Roman Catholicism and sought to investigate the teachings of that denomination through several sessions with the archbishop of Mexico City. He found the archbishop sincere, honest, affable, able, and learned,[5] but concluded that Roman Catholicism was "irreconcilable" with the Bible and constituted an "apostasy from the system of Holy Writ."[6]

After his study of Roman Catholicism, he began to study the Bible every night, a practice he continued for the rest of his life. One year after he left Mexico, while stationed in New York City, he requested the sacrament of holy baptism, which was administered at St. John's Episcopal Church on April 29, 1849. After he became a professor at Virginia Military Institute, he was received into the Presbyterian church in Lexington. From that time on, Jackson considered his pastor his spiritual commander, to whose "orders" he was bound in obedience.[7]

A member of the church he attended later commented, "It would be difficult to find in the entire ranks of Presbyterians, any other member who disciplined himself so strictly, obeyed what he believed to be the will of God so absolutely, prayed so fervently, or found so much happiness in his religion."[8] For the rest of his life, Jackson contributed at least ten percent of his income to church and charity, and attended not only the Sunday services but the Wednesday prayer meetings as well, and he was elected a deacon in December 1857. Although he fervently embraced the doctrines of the Presbyterian church, Jackson was not a sectarian. He believed that the Bible and those beliefs that all Christians held in common formed the basis for unity, and, during the war, he opposed the appointment of military chaplains who held a narrow, sectarian point of view.[9]

Shortly after he joined the Presbyterian church, Jackson organized a young men's Bible class. In 1855, he organized a Sunday school for slaves, despite a Virginia law that forbade the public gathering of persons of color. Jackson once told a friend that he felt sorry for black people and that he believed "they should be free and have a chance." He also believed that slaves should be taught how to read, so that they could study the Scripture.[10] Nevertheless, unlike many men of his time, Jackson did not have a guilty conscience about the institution of slavery. He himself owned a handful of slaves. Although slavery was "not a thing desirable in itself," it was not condemned by Scripture and thus, according to one biographer, Jackson believed it was "allowed by Providence for ends which it was not his business to determine.[11]

Jackson believed that everything that happened in life was God's will. This was not always easy to accept. When his first wife died shortly after giving birth to their first child—a stillborn girl—he wrote a friend, "I do not see the purpose of God in this, the most bitter, trying affliction of my life, but I will try to be submissive, though it break my heart."[12] At the same time, he wrote down in a notebook: "Objects to be effected by Ellie's death: to eradicate ambitions; to eradicate resentment; to produce humility."[13] Within a few years he married again. He thought of his wife as "a gift from our Heavenly Father," and, in a letter to her, added, "How delightful it is, thus to associate every pleasure and enjoyment with God the Giver! Thus will he bless us and make us grow in grace, and in the knowledge of him, whom to know aright is life eternal."[14] The firstborn child of his second marriage did not live, and Jackson got to see his third child only a few times before he was killed when she was less than six months old.

Jackson believed in praying at all times. Everything he did he accompanied with a silent prayer. He told a friend, "When I take a draught of water, I always pause, as my palate receives the refreshment, to lift up my heart to God in thanks and prayer for the water of life. Whenever I drop a letter into the box at the post office, I send a petition along with it, for God's blessing upon its mission and upon the person to whom it is sent. When I break the seal of a letter just received, I stop to pray to God that he may prepare me for its contents, and make me a messenger of good. When I go to the classroom and await the arrangement of the cadets in their places, that is my time to intercede with God for them. And so of every other familiar act of the day."[15]

During the war, Jackson could often be heard in his tent praying aloud. Frequently, he would chose a prayer partner, because of the promise of Christ that "if two of you shall agree on earth touching anything that they shall ask, it shall be done for them of my father which is in heaven."[16] A comrade said of him, "when Jackson knelt, the heavens came down indeed into communion with earth."[17]

Jackson believed that the Bible furnished human beings with rules and examples to govern every aspect of life. He told one of his officers that the Bible even provided a model for official reports of battles. "Look, for instance, at the narrative of Joshua's battle with the

Amalekites," he said. "There you have one. It has clearness, brevity, fairness, modesty; and it traces the victory to its right source, the blessing of God."[18]

One grievance Jackson had against the United States (and later Confederate) government was the Sunday mail. In those days post offices were open and mail was delivered on Sundays. For Jackson this comprised a violation of the commandment enjoining humankind to keep the Sabbath holy. He would not send letters late in the week, for fear they might be in transit on Sunday. Once he was on his way to church with a friend, who announced his intention to stop at the post office to see if he had any mail. Jackson dissuaded him from doing this, so the friend picked up his mail Monday and received two letters. The first, which he would have retrieved on Sunday, reported the serious illness of a family member. The second, which had arrived on Monday, brought news that the health crisis reported in the first letter had been favorably resolved. Jackson used this as an example of how God blessed those who honored the Sabbath; "Now had my friend causelessly dishonored the Sabbath, he would have suffered a day of harrowing anxiety, which the next day's news would have shown utterly groundless, but God relieved him from this gratuitous suffering."[19]

Jackson's favorite saying was, "Duty is ours. The consequences are God's."[20] Because of his attitude, he had a personality that was compared to "calm sunshine."[21] Jackson declared, "I am confident that I am reconciled and adopted through the work of Christ. Therefore, inasmuch as every event is disposed by omniscience guided by redeeming love for me, seeming evils must be real blessings; it is not in the power of any earthly calamity to overthrow my happiness."[22] Accordingly, he never worried about other people or himself. During the war, he wrote his wife, "It is a great comfort to me to know that though I am not with you, yet you are in the hands of one who will not permit any evil to come nigh to you. What a consoling thought it is, to know that we may, with perfect confidence, commit all our friends in Jesus to the care of our Heavenly Father, with an assurance that all shall be well with them."[23]

It was not that he denied that bad things happened to faithful Christians. After all, by his late thirties, he had lost, in early childhood, both parents and an infant sister; as a teenager, his older brother; in early adulthood, a wife, two children, and the uncle who raised him (who died in the California Gold Rush). He felt that God would give him the grace to endure anything it was his will to send.

A friend once challenged him on this. Knowing that Jackson suffered from eye problems, he asked what would he do if he lost his sight. Jackson replied that God would give him the strength to endure total blindness. The friend went on to ask what Jackson would do if he was stricken with catastrophic illness, if he lost all his money, if he became "dependent on others for his every need" for the rest of his life. "If it were the will of God to place me there," said Jackson, "He would enable me to lie there peacefully a hundred years."[24]

He most devoutly believed that God would recompense the faithful Christian in the world to come for what was suffered on earth. In May 1859, he wrote his wife: "See if you cannot spend a short time each evening after dark in looking out of your window into space, and meditating upon heaven with all its joys unspeakable and full of glory, and to think what the Savior relinquished in glory when he came to earth, and of his suffering for us; and seek to realize with the Apostle, that the afflictions of the present life are not worthy to be compared with the glory which shall be revealed in us."[25]

Jackson taught at VMI for ten years, where he was famous not only for his religious zeal but also for his boring lectures and for his mild eccentricities. In the spring of 1861, civil war broke out. Like Lee, Jackson believed that secession was a mistake, but he also believed in states' rights, and was convinced that the use of force by the federal government to thwart the secession of the Southern states was illegal. But, for him, it all boiled down to the will of God. "Why should Christians be disturbed about the dissolution of the Union?" he asked. "It can come only by God's permission, and will only be permitted if for his people's good."[26]

Like Lee and Lincoln—but even more strongly—Jackson believed that the war was a punishment for America's sins. He wrote his wife, "Peace should not be the chief object of prayer in our country. It should aim more specially at imploring God's forgiveness of our sins, and praying that he will make our people a holy people. If we are but his, all things shall work together for the good of our country, and no good thing will he withhold from it."[27] He was even more specific in a letter to a friend: "I greatly desire to see peace—blessed peace. And I am persuaded, that if God's people throughout our Confederacy will earnestly and perseveringly unite in imploring his interposition for peace, we may expect it. Let our Government acknowledge the God of the Bible as its God, and we may expect soon to be a happy and independent people."[28] One reason, he felt, that God willed the breakup of the Union was the policy of separation of Church and state under "the old United States." Jackson believed in "the union of Church and State," and wanted the Confederacy to declare itself a Christian nation.[29]

Because the breakup of the Union was God's will, Jackson was, therefore, engaged in a holy war, like those fought by the Israelite armies of Old Testament times. He urged that the Confederate army slaughter all prisoners, just as David, Joshua, Gideon and other Old Testament warriors had done. "Let us make thorough work of [the] enemy," he urged, "invade his country, and do him all possible damage in the shortest possible time."[30]

Those who knew Stonewall Jackson felt that there was no conflict between his role as a Christian and his role as a soldier. John B. Gordon, a general who served under him, commented, "There is in all his mental and moral characteristics the most perfect harmony.[31] In other words, his ferocity as a soldier was consistent with his religious beliefs. Jackson was inspired by Old Testament accounts of kings and warriors, apparently inspired by God, who smote their foes "hip and thigh," wreaking bloody havoc upon them and their land. This was the way Joshua and David waged war, through the command of God, and it was the way Stonewall Jackson believed in waging war.

He was not totally confident of victory. According to historian and biographer James I. Robertson, Jackson believed that "victory would come, and the curse of God [which caused the war] would be lifted, when one side demonstrated its worthiness to be called the blessed people of Providence."[32] God would not grant victory to the South unless her people totally consecrated themselves to him. Part of the total consecration he sought for the Confederacy was the banning of Sunday mails. He wrote a congressman, "I do not see how a nation that thus arrays itself, by such a law [mandating the delivery of mail on Sunday] against God's holy day, can expect to escape his wrath."[33]

Stonewall was very careful to ascribe all glory to God after his victories. After the First Battle of Bull Run, he wrote his wife, "Yesterday we fought a great battle, for which all the glory is due to God alone."[34]

Curiously, he was not averse to waging battles on Sunday. After a successful Sabbath attack, he wrote, "I felt it my duty to do it, in consideration of the ruinous effect that might result from postponing the battle until the next morning. So far as I can see, my course was a wise one, though very distasteful to my feelings, and I hope and pray to our Heavenly Father, that I may never again be circumstanced as on that day. I believed that so far as our troops were concerned, necessity and mercy both called for the battle." There were other Sunday battles to come. So that the Sabbath could be kept holy, Jackson, after Sunday battles, would designate another day in the week as a Sabbath for himself and his men.

Jackson wanted a "converted army." He insisted on the hiring of regimental chaplains to direct frequent religious services. He encouraged his units to erect log chapels, and contributed at least $500 of his own money toward expenses and supplies for promoting the Christian faith within his ranks.[35] Daily religious services were held at his headquarters, which all of his men were encouraged, but not required, to attend. Jackson liked to sit, not among his officers, but among common soldiers during the services. During the winter of 1862–1863, a religious revival broke out among his troops, and by spring Jackson was confident that he was now commanding "an army of the living God."[36]

Jackson never worried about falling in battle. After he was slightly wounded at First Bull Run, he commented, "My religious belief teaches me to feel as safe in battle as in bed. God has fixed the time for my death. I do not concern myself about that, but always to be ready, no matter when it may overtake me....That is the way all men should live, and then all would be equally brave."[37]

In May 1863, toward the end of a victorious battle at Chancellorsville, Virginia, Jackson was struck by friendly fire. After his mangled left arm was amputated near the shoulder, he seemed to hold his own for a few days. He told his chaplain, "You see me severely wounded, but not depressed; not unhappy. I believe that it has been done according to God's holy will, and I acquiesce entirely in it."[38] He went on to say that "the child of God can, in the midst of severest sufferings, fix the thoughts upon God and heavenly things, and derive great comfort and peace, but that one who had never made his peace with God would be unable to control his mind under such sufferings so as to understand properly the way of salvation, and repent and believe in Christ."[39]

At first Jackson thought he was going to live. He thought God had further work for him to perform. But his condition worsened. He developed pneumonia. Then he asked his wife, who had come to his side, to sing a favorite hymn. As he grew worse, his wife asked, "Do you know the doctors say you must very soon be in heaven? Do you feel willing to acquiesce in God's allotment, if He wills you to go?" Jackson, who was by then nearly speechless, looked her in the face and said, "I prefer it. I prefer it. It will be an infinite gain to be translated."[40]

When his wife bent over him and asked for "one final assurance" that his Savior was present with him, the dying soldier gasped, "Yes." In response to her question as to whether she and their baby daughter should live with her father, Jackson answered, "Yes, you have a kind and good father; but no one is so kind and good as your Heavenly Father." When she asked if he wanted to be buried in Lexington, he answered, "Yes, in Lexington." Then, when his daughter was brought to him, he tried to embrace her and smiled and said, "Little darling." Then he passed into a semi-coma.[41] Sometime after that, Thomas Jonathan Jackson, the warrior of God, emerged from the coma and said, "Let us pass over the river and rest under the shade of the trees." Then he looked at his wife and died.

∼

Profile 35
Andrew Carnegie

Born: Dunfermline, Scotland, November 25, 1835
Died: Lenox, Massachusetts, August 11, 1919

A native of Scotland who emigrated to America with his parents when he was thirteen and went to work in a factory for $1.20 a week, Carnegie "pulled himself up by his bootstraps" to become America's leading steel manufacturer. Of the $500 million that he made when he sold his business when he was sixty-five, he gave away approximately $350 million to charitable causes during the last eighteen years of his life. The self-made man had self-made religious beliefs.

The Carnegies were nominal Presbyterians in Scotland, and, upon arrival in Allegheny, Pennsylvania, Andrew's father and other relatives joined the "New Church" of the Swedenborgian Society. Andrew's mother attended no church and strove to live by the precept of Confucius: To perform the duties of this life well, troubling not about another."[1] Even so, she encouraged her sons to go to church and Sunday school. Carnegie recalled later that for a time he was "deeply interested in the mysterious doctrines of Swedenborg," but quickly rejected the teachings of the Society as "man-made theology."[2] Along with the teachings of Swedenborg, he, like his mother, rejected the Bible.

As a young man he found himself "all at sea" as to what he believed, until he studied the works of Charles Darwin, the biologist who described the theory of evolution, and Herbert Spencer, the British writer who tried to apply the theory of evolution to human behavior. Carnegie came to believe in "an Inscrutable Existence everywhere manifested," to which humankind "can neither find nor conceive either beginning nor end." This Inscrutable Existence was the "Infinite and Eternal Energy from which all things proceed."[3]

Accordingly, Carnegie rejected all theology, which he dismissed as "man's dim, distorted, and, in some instances, debasing misconceptions." True religion, he believed, would become clearer with the progression of scientific discovery. Like many men of his time, he believed that the world was getting better and better with the passing years and the increase of scientific knowledge. He seemed to feel that the problems of humanity would be solved by the advance of human knowledge and wisdom. Carnegie claimed that all religion was beneficial, and that "almost any system of religion would make one good enough if it were properly obeyed."[4]

Religion for Carnegie was a philosophical system to promote ethical behavior. The industrialist was frankly hostile to Christianity, probably because the teachings of Christ are impossible to reduce, with any degree of intellectual honesty, to a system of ethics. "The whole scheme of Christian Salvation is diabolical, as revealed by the creeds," he complained. "An angry God—imagine such a creator of the universe! Angry at what he knew as coming and was himself responsible for. Then he sets himself about to beget a son, in order that the child should beg him to forgive the Sinner. This, however, he cannot or will not do. He must punish somebody—so the son offers himself up [and] our creator punishes the innocent youth, never heard of before—for the guilty and became reconciled to us. 'Very good, my demon, you may be reconciled to me. But I am not reconciled to you.' I decline to accept salvation from such a friend. This is the natural reply that rises in my heart."[5] And so Carnegie dismissed all traditional Christian creeds and doctrines, along with the Bible, as "libelous" to the "Unknown."[6]

Carnegie believed that the Great Unknown had revealed his design for humanity through Herbert Spencer, whom he regarded as a kind of prophet. According to one biographer, for Carnegie "the only sin was ignorance, and man's mind was his endowment of divinity; his salvation lay in education and his evolutionary progress towards perfection." Since mankind now generally understood the laws of nature and evolution, progress toward perfection would now move at a faster rate.[7]

Because he believed that the human race would perfect itself, he tended to think of earth as heaven. He cautioned that people tended to dwell too much on the life beyond to the neglect of the present life. "Here in this life all our duties lie, none has yet been given us pertaining to another [life] for which we hope,"[8] he wrote. He did not reject outright the idea of life after death. "We have here an everlasting indestructible universe, not an atom ever destroyed," he insisted. "We have been placed in this world, we know not why or how. There would be no violation of the known law should we be ushered into another world as we have been into this, nor in our being endowed with everlasting existence like the universe of which we are a part."[9] He believed, however, that there was no proof of life after death, and therefore men and women should concentrate on an attempt to assist the improvement of the human race on earth. A few years before his death he wrote a friend that he was sad that he was not going to be "allowed to live here in this heaven on earth forever, which it is to me. None other is satisfactory."[10] To another friend he wrote, "More and more I realize we should think less [and] less of 'Heaven our Home' and more [and] more of 'Home our Heaven.' Wish I could get an option to leave this heaven only when I wisht."[11]

The outbreak of World War I, which was an obvious setback in the human progress to perfection, reportedly troubled Carnegie deeply. There is no evidence, however, that even in his final years he modified his beliefs.

∽

Profile 36
Samuel Langhorne Clemens
(Mark Twain)

Born: Florida, Missouri, November 30, 1835
Died: Redding, Connecticut, April 21, 1910

Samuel Clemens, who wrote under the pen name of Mark Twain, once wrote, "The cat's tail is only an incumbrance to her, yet she thinks it is the most precious thing she has got. Just so with man and religion."[1] Although the author, both in his work and in private, frequently railed bitterly at religion, there were times when he seemed to feel genuine regret that he was not a believer. He seems to have made a brief attempt—out of love for his wife—to cultivate religious faith early in his marriage, but soon returned to the skepticism in which he was raised, and in which he would die.

Clemens's father was an unbeliever. So, apparently, were his older brother and sister. So was the uncle with whom Sam lived for a time during his youth. Out of all his family, only his mother had even a semblance of religious faith. When Sam was five, she joined the Presbyterian Church in Hannibal, Missouri, and forced him to attend with her. Even so, there were some aspects of the Christian faith with which she admitted to having a problem. "Religion is a jugfull; I hold a dipper-full," she said. "I know a person that can turn his cheek is higher and holier than I am…but I…wouldn't have him for a doormat."[2]

Clemens's early impressions of religion were negative. According to one biographer, in his youth he knew "a succession of clergymen, not particularly intelligent, each contradicting half of what the others [stood] for."[3] The only thing they seemed to agree upon was the image of an angry God who delighted in casting people into hell and causing wars, accidents, fires, earthquakes, and epidemics. His mother forced young Sam to read through the Bible from cover to cover, and he resented that.[4] Then, too, he came into contact with the religious superstitions of the Negroes of Hannibal, Missouri, who believed in ghosts, hauntings, spells, and curses.[5] Thus, long before he was an adult, Sam Clemens had a decidedly negative view of Christianity and all organized religion in general.

When he was in his thirties, he married Olivia Langdon, who had grown up in a liberal Congregational church in Elmira, New York. Because he loved her dearly, Clemens at first tried to be religious. During his engagement, he wrote, "Don't be sad, Livy. We'll…make the Spirit of Love lord over all the realm…be of good heart. Turn towards the Cross and be comforted—I turn with you—what would you more? The peace of God shall rest upon us, and all will be well."[6]

For a time after his marriage, Sam Clemens read the Bible with Livy and prayed with her. He told her that he would become a church member, but, although he rented a pew at the Asylum Hill Congregational Church near their home in Hartford, Connecticut, he never joined. In fact, shortly after his marriage, when a friend remarked on the fact that he was saying table grace, Clemens confided to him that he did it to please Livy and that it meant nothing to him.[7] After eight years of marriage, he gave up the pretense, and told the minister of the Asylum Hill Church, "Joe, I'm going to make a confession, I don't believe in your religion at all....I've been living a lie right straight along whenever I pretended to. For a moment, sometimes, I have been almost a believer, but it immediately drifts away from me. I don't believe one word of your Bible was inspired by God any more than any other book."[8]

During the first year of their marriage, Livy Clemens prayed daily for her husband's conversion. Then she seemed to lose her faith. She stopped attending church, and never sent their daughters to Sunday school. In fact, she once told her husband, "Well, if you are to be lost, I want to be lost with you."[9] When their daughter Susy died suddenly in 1896, she still believed in life after death, and Clemens was prompted to write her, "I will believe in it with you. It has been the belief of the wise and thoughtful of many countries for three thousand years; let us accept their verdict; we cannot frame one that is more reasonable or probable. I will try never to doubt it again."[10] However, the time came when Clemens said to Livy, "If it comforts you to lean on the Christian faith, do so, and she replied that she hadn't."[11]

Throughout life, Clemens, though a professed unbeliever, railed against God for the calamities of life. It is hard to tell whether he really did not believe in God or whether he was simply angry at him. When his daughter Susy died, he denounced God as a "malign thug."[12] When someone objected that God does not willingly punish mortals, Clemens retorted, "Well, why does he do it, then? We don't invite it."[13] He could not understand why God would permit the San Francisco earthquake in 1906, and was reminded "that in Biblical times, if a man committed a sin, the extermination of the whole surrounding nation—cattle and all—was likely to happen." This thought prompted him to write a friend, "I never count any prospective chickens when I know that Providence knows where the nest is."[14]

When he was in his forties, Clemens wrote his brother that he did not "believe in the divinity of the Savior."[15] Clemens seemed to believe that the Nazarene was nonetheless—in some sense—a Savior. Indeed, he once wrote that although he did not believe that Christ was divine, "no matter, the Savior is none the less a sacred personage, and a man should have no desire or disposition to refer to him lightly, profanely, or otherwise than with the profoundest reverence."[16]

But Samuel Clemens did believe that there was a God, though not in the "God of the Bible," whom he saw as "jealous, trivial, ignorant, revengeful."[17] Late in life, he wrote a sort of creed, in which he declared:

> I believe in God Almighty. I do not believe he has ever sent a message to man by anybody, or delivered one to him by word of mouth, or made himself visible to mortal eyes at any time in any place. I believe that the Old and New Testaments were imagined and written by man, and that no line in them was authorized by God, much less inspired by him.
>
> I think the goodness, the Justice, and the mercy of God are manifested in his works: I perceive that they are manifested toward me in this life; the logical conclusion is that they will be manifested toward me in the life to come, if there should be one.
>
> I do not believe in special providences. I believe that the universe is governed by strict and immutable laws. If one man's family is swept away by a pestilence and another man's spared it is only the law working; God is not interfering in that small matter, either against the one man or in favor of the other.[18]

At the age of sixty-three, he wrote in a notebook: "The Being who to me is the real God is the One who created this majestic universe and rules it....He is the only Originator—He made the materials of all things; He made the laws by which, and by which only, man may combine them into machines and other things which outside influence may suggest to him. He made character—men can portray it but not 'create' it, for He is the only Creator. He is the perfect artisan, the perfect artist. Everything which He has made is fine, everything which he has made is beautiful."[19]

For Clemens, God's Bible was nature. "We read it every day," he wrote, "and we could understand it and trust in it if we would burn the spurious [Bible] and dig the remains of our insignificant reasoning faculties out of the grave where that and other man-made Bibles have buried them for 2000 years and more."[20]

As for man, he once wrote that "man is himself a microbe, and his globe a blood corpuscle drifting with its shining brethren of the Milky Way down a vein of the Master and Maker of all things, whose body, mayhap—glimpsed partwise from the earth by night, and receding and lost to view in the measureless remoteness of space—is what men name the Universe."[21]

At other times, Clemens could be much more gloomy. In his story, "The Mysterious Stranger," which he wrote late in life, he has Satan, who is portrayed sympathetically, declare, "There is no God, no universe, no earthly life, no heaven, no hell. It is all a dream—a grotesque and foolish dream. Nothing exists but you and you are but a thought— a vagrant thought, a useless thought, a homeless thought, wandering forlorn among the empty eternities!"[22] It is not clear how much this reflects Clemens's thinking. He seems to have believed that the cosmos was real. But he believed that everything that happened was predetermined. "Each event has its own place in the eternal chain of circumstances, and whether it be big or little, it will infallibly cause the next event, whether the next event be the breaking of a child's toy or the destruction of a throne."[23]

To the end of his life, however, Samuel Clemens, despite the bitter comments he made about organized religion, seemed to be in search of God. He was interested in extrasensory perception, faith healings, dreams, and he attended seances. He was favorably impressed by Christian Science. Although he sometimes criticized that religion, he once wrote a friend that Christian Science was a boon to humanity. "Mary Baker Eddy organized and made available a healing principle that for two thousand years has never been employed, except as the merest kind of guesswork. She is the benefactor of the age."[24] Yet, of all denominations, he seemed to respect Roman Catholicism most of all. When his daughter Jean was being educated in a convent school, he wrote his wife that he was glad, and "way down deep in my heart I feel that if they make a good strong unshakable Catholic of her, I shan't be the least sorry. It is doubtless the most peace-giving and restful of all the religions. If I had it I would not trade it for anything in the world."[25]

Clemens's views of the afterlife were as variable and tentative as his ideas on other aspects of religion. His daughter Clara—the only one of his four children who survived him—wrote, "Sometimes he believed that death ended everything, but most of the time he felt sure of a life beyond."[26] Late in life, he told a friend: "As to a hereafter, we have not the slightest evidence that there is any—no evidence that appeals to logic and reason. I have never seen what to me seemed an atom of proof that there is future life....And yet—I am strongly inclined to expect one."[27] When, just before Christmas, 1909, his daughter Jean, who suffered from epileptic seizures, was found dead, he blurted out to the housekeeper, "Oh, Katy, she's in heaven with her mother."[28] Some time after that he wrote a friend, "For one who does not believe in spirits, I have had a most peculiar experience. I went into the bathroom [apparently the one where Jean had been found dead] and closed the door. You know how warm it always is in there, and there are no draughts. All at once I felt a cold current of air about me. I thought the door must have been open; but it was closed. I said, 'Jean, is this you trying to let me know that you have found the others?' Then the cold air was gone."[29] Yet, shortly after that, just a month before he died, he wrote another friend, "Isn't this life enough for you? Do you wish to continue the foolishness somewhere else? Damnation, you depress me."[30] Even so, his very last words, to his daughter, hours before his death, were, "Goodbye, dear. If we meet...."

Samuel Clemens seems to have been a man desperately in search of a spiritual peace that he never found. Perhaps his psyche was too deeply scarred by his negative experience of what passed for Christianity when he was a boy to bring himself to any commitment of faith. His writings and his comments convey the strong impression that he was angry with God, but they also show that he never really denied God's existence. Some of the harsh things he said and wrote about God—and man, as well—appear to be the result of his bitterness more than any real convictions of unbelief. On one level, he apparently wanted to believe. He compared the "calm concidence" of Christian believers to aces, and described such faith as "wonderful to observe."[31] Nonetheless, for some reason, he could never bring himself to make an act of faith.

～

Profile 37
Dwight Lyman Moody

Born: East Northfield, Massachusetts, February 5, 1837
Died: Northfield, Massachusetts, December 22, 1899

The best-known and most influential religious leader in America during the last third of the nineteenth century, often called the Protestant Pope, was neither a clergyman nor theologian, but a former shoe-salesman-turned-lay preacher. D. L. Moody, who sought to unite all men and women in the love of Christ, led thousands of people in the United States and in Great Britain to commit their lives to Christ as their personal savior. He drew on the support of people of all denominations, both liberal and conservative, from the worldly Episcopalian financier J. P. Morgan to the Quaker poet, John Greenleaf Whittier (who commended the preacher for turning drunkards and gamblers into decent fathers and husbands),[1] to the editors of Britain's Roman Catholic *The Tablet*, who called his religious campaigns "a thing of God, a testimony to Jesus,"[2] to the prominent Negro Presbyterian minister Francis Grimké, who wrote in his diary, "D. L. Moody was a soul-winner. He was ever looking out for opportunities to point men to Jesus.…That was his business; he lived for no other purpose."[3]

Moody, one of a number of children of a farming family in what was then the backwoods of Massachusetts, was baptized by a Unitarian minister in a Unitarian church, but (he was given to understand) "in the name of the Father and of the Son and of the Holy Ghost."[4] Even as a child, D. L. was precociously religious, recruiting children from the neighborhood for the Sunday school at the Unitarian church which his family attended. His trust in God impressed his family even at the age of eight, when he and an older brother were returning late at night after cutting corn on a farm some miles from their own home, and boarded a ferry to convey them across the Connecticut River, only to discover that the ferryman was drunk and unable to control the boat. D. L. assured his terrified brother that God would take care of them and was perfectly calm throughout the frightening and hazardous crossing.[5]

Although Moody's mother (his father had died young) was very religious, the concept of the "regenerating work of God's Spirit by a definite acceptance of Christ" was alien to the experience of the Moodys.[6] Young Moody had hated to go to church, but his mother forced him. "I thought it was hard to have to work in the field all week and then be obliged to go to church and hear a sermon I didn't understand." He fully expected to put the practice of churchgoing behind him once he was on his own, but found that, by force of habit, he was unable to stay away from religious services.[7]

When he was nineteen and working in a shoe store in Boston, a Sunday-school teacher from the Mount Vernon Congregational Church, where he was attending, called on him when he was wrapping shoes in the stock room and successfully persuaded him to make a definite commitment of his life to Christ. "Before my conversion," he later declared, "I worked to be saved, now I worked because I am saved." He recalled, "I remember the morning on which I came out from my room after I had first trusted Christ. I thought the old sun shone a good deal brighter than it ever had before. As I walked out upon Boston Common and heard the birds singing in the trees, I thought they were all singing a song to me…. I had not a bitter feeling against any man, and I was ready to take all men to my heart. If a man has not the love of God shed abroad in his heart, he has never been regenerated."[8]

Later, when he heard a minister declare, "The world has yet to know what God can do with and for and through a man who is fully and wholly consecrated to him," Moody declared himself to be that man.[9] When he was in his mid thirties, Moody underwent another religious experience, sometimes referred to as his "second conversion," sometimes as his "baptism in the Holy Spirit." According to his great friend, Daniel Webster Whittle, "God blessed him with a conscious incoming to his soul of a presence and power of his Spirit such as he had never known before. His heart was broken by it. He spent much time in just weeping before God, so overpowering was the sense of [God's] goodness and love."[10] Many people who knew Moody believed that he lived in "continuous communion" with God.

When Moody went to live in Chicago as a young man, working as a sales representative for a shoe company, he joined the Plymouth Congregational Church and hired a pew (in those days many churches generated income by renting pews) and filled it with street urchins. Soon he had rented four pews, all of which were filled with the children of the street. Then he started a Sunday-school class, just for the boys known as "hoodlums." Within a short time he had five hundred, then fifteen hundred. Moody refused to recognize denominations in the Sunday school and used only the Bible for instruction. Because many of the boys came from a Roman Catholic background, Moody encountered some opposition from people of that denomination, but, after meeting with Bishop James Duggan, he obtained the support of the Diocese of Chicago for that work. By early 1861, Moody's Sunday school was so renowned that it was visited by president-elect Lincoln. Soon Moody gave up his lucrative job, which was paying him $5,000 a year, to devote all of his time to religious work. Not only did he conduct his Sunday school, he visited his boys in their homes and also visited the prisons, talking with the inmates, reading and praying.

When the Civil War broke out, Moody decided that he would not take up arms. "There has never been a time in my life when I felt that I could take a gun and shoot down a fellow being."[11] Moody decided to worked for the "Christian Commission" as a lay chaplain. He ministered to the wounded, distributed hymnals, and preached at the various prayer meetings that became popular in many of the camps. The men were drawn to his preaching. General Oliver Otis Howard, a fellow New Englander and fellow Christian, who later served as the head of the Freedmen's Bureau, later wrote that Moody showed his solders how to give their hearts to God. "His preaching was direct and effective, and multitudes responded with a promise to follow Christ."[12]

When, in the early 1870s, he responded to an invitation to preach at religious rallies in Britain, he attracted huge crowds and gained international renown as a revival preacher. His "campaigns," as he called his meetings, were made particularly effective by his practice of having Ira David Sankey, a former government worker with a beautiful voice, "sing the Gospel." The songs that Sankey sang were supplied by the poet Fanny Crosby and musicians William Howard Doane, Robert Lowry, and George Stebbins. Moody and Sankey began publishing these hymns, and, although the sales of these songbooks produced substantial revenue, Moody donated everything to charity.

Moody's appeal was apparently not enhanced either by his physical presence, erudition, or oratorical skills. Most people who knew him found him physically unprepossessing. A man who met him late in life described him as "one of the shortest, fattest men I ever saw."[13] He had a thick New England brogue which hearers from other regions of the country found difficult at first to understand. Criticized for grammatical mistakes, he allegedly once told someone, "I wish you would try to save as many men with your grammar as I am without it." His sermons were described as disjointed, repetitious, and made up largely of illustrations. Yet people came.

Moody eschewed the practice of altar calls and hated high pressure tactics to force conversions. He set up inquiry rooms which a Roman Catholic observer called "Protestant confessionals," in which the anxious were to meet in small groups or even individually with Moody and his associates to pray and discuss spiritual problems. Unlike many other evangelists, Moody refused to count converts. That, he believed, was between the individual and God. Statistics show that church membership increased significantly in cities where Moody had held campaigns, although this increase often did not prove permanent.[14] It is believed that Moody had his greatest success with middle-class people who were lapsed or nominal Christians. He seemed to be less effective with people with no religious background and those hostile to religion.

Moody compared the faith of the Christian with the trust of the little boy who "when his coat and pants are worn out believes his mother will provide him with others."[15] The faith of a Christian, Moody insisted, takes God without any "ifs."

Perhaps the thing that Moody emphasized the most was the love of God. Early in his career, Moody stressed the wrath of God, threatening his hearers with hellfire and damnation, but soon came to emphasize the love of God. "I used to preach that God was behind the sinner with a double-edged sword, ready to hew him down. I have got done with that. I preach now that God is behind him with love, and he is running away from the God of love."[16] When Moody did speak of hell, it was always with tears in his eyes.[17] He emphasized that the believer must identify with the sufferings of Christ on the cross. In one of his sermons, Moody said, "I must die for my sins or find some substitute to die in my stead. I cannot get this man or that man to die for me, because they have sinned themselves, and would have to die for their own sins. But Christ was without sin, and therefore he could be my substitute."[18] He frequently repeated in sermons, "Because he died for me, I love him. Because he died for me, I will serve him. I will work for him. I will give him my very life."[19]

Moody emphasized the love of God, the Father. "I remember for the first few years after I was converted," he recalled, "I had a good deal more love for Christ than for God, the Father, whom I looked upon as the stern Judge, while I regarded Christ as the mediator who had come between me and the stern Judge, and appeased his wrath; but when I got a little better acquainted with my Bible, these views all fled. After I became a father and woke up to the realization of what it cost God to have his son die, I began to see that God was to be loved just as much as his Son was."[20]

The Holy Spirit was very important in Moody's preaching. "We would in reality not know Christ but for the Holy Ghost," he said. The principal work of the Spirit was to "impart love." The Spirit also prepared the individual for conversion by making him sensitive to his misdeeds. The Spirit, in fact, enabled the individual to believe. "There is no life or power for a man to serve God until he is first born of the Spirit, until he has been quickened by the Holy Ghost," Moody insisted. Moreover, the Holy Spirit imparted, joy, peace, patience, goodness, and the power to do whatever God has called a person to do, and cast out fear.[21]

Even though Moody preached that no one could come to Christ unless drawn by the Holy Spirit, he rejected the idea of the Calvinists, common in his youth, that God predestines some people to Hell. He believed salvation was an act of will. He taught that "man is born with his back towards God. When he repents and turns right around and faces God."[22] This reorientation of the will to God, although effected by the Holy Spirit, was still a matter of personal choice. "When we search for God with all our hearts, we are sure to find him," he said.[23] He compared conversion to walking through a doorway. "One minute he is on this side, the next he is on that side," he said of the believer. If a man or woman was truly saved, this would be evident through good works. "After a man's saved, he can't help working for God," he insisted.[24]

Moody was not much for what came to be called social activism or the social gospel. He tried to stay out of the movement for civil rights for people of color. Moody was an abolitionist before the war and personally believed in racial equality. He did not discriminate in the educational institutions he founded. For instance, in what later became known as the Moody Bible Institute in Chicago, the student body in the 1890s included Japanese, Chinese, Asians, Indians, Africans, and American blacks. Mary McLeod Bethune, who attended the Institute in the 1890s, recalled, "There were no feelings of race at Moody. There we learned to look upon a man as a man, not as a Caucasian or a Negro. My heart had been somewhat hardened...here under this benign influence of...Dwight L. Moody, a love for the whole human family, regardless of creed, class, or color, entered my soul."[25]

Moody at times invited prominent Negro leaders to share his pulpit in some of his northern campaigns. Yet in the South, he sometimes gave in to the practice of segregation. Early in his career, when preaching in Augusta, Georgia, he was horrified when local authorities put up barriers, separating black and white members of his audience. He ordered the barriers taken away and warned the whites that they "might possibly be astonished some day to see these blacks marching into the kingdom of heaven while they themselves were shut out."[26] However, his friend and associate, D. W. Whittle, insisted that unless he acquiesced to local custom, no whites would come to hear him. After that, when in the South, Moody often allowed his audiences to be segregated, or preached in separate buildings to each group.[27]

Moody's priority was conversion. Reform of society could come only through a regeneration of the heart. If large numbers of people sincerely turned to Christ, he believed, the world would change. This, he was convinced, was the solution to the world's problems: war, racism, crime, alcoholism. "If it were not for unbelief," he insisted, "there would be no drunkards, prostitutes, and other unfortunate and undesirable persons."[28] It was useless to attempt to change society until the hearts and minds of men and women were turned to God. He declared, "And there is no reform until God has been found."[29] He even felt that conversion to Christ was the solution to poverty: "Whenever you find a man who follows Christ, that man you will find a successful one."[30]

Moody was a "premillenialist." In other words, he interpreted the twentieth chapter of Revelation in such a way that he expected Christ to return bodily to earth to bring about a thousand years of peace for God's people.[31] Before the Civil War, many Christian leaders were "post-millenialists" who believed that "the age of gold" would come about as the result of human effort, and, only then, after a thousand years, would the Lord return to earth. Moody and others among his contemporaries popularized the premillenial conception of Christ's return.

Moody believed that all Christians should be familiar with the Bible, and understand God's will from reading it without any preconceived notions.[32] Faith and belief must be the result of private study and prayer rather than the dogma or creed of any particular sect. He told an assembly of college students in Springfield, Massachusetts, in the summer of 1886: "Become an independent reader and feed yourselves and grow in strength. Too many Christians everywhere get their religious food by ecclesiastical spoon-feeding. They take only that which is fed them from the pulpits one day in the week. Take, read, feed on the whole word of God. Don't throw this and that passage in the Book aside. If you can't explain, can't understand it, don't try; don't worry because of it. There are depths in the Bible no one, however acute his theology, can sound."[33]

He believed that the Bible was divinely inspired and without error. He told one of his sons that if the Bible had said that Jonah had swallowed the whale, he would believe it.[34] Yet, when the same son asked about the apparent conflict in Matthew and Acts concerning the death of Judas, Moody snorted, "What difference does it make what happened to a rascal like Judas?"[35]

Although he disagreed with them, he often invited liberals, advocates of the social gospel, higher criticism, and evolution to speak at his conferences. Almost everyone who dealt with him agreed that Moody was "fair and brotherly" even when he disagreed or offered criticism.[36] He once said, in fact, that "higher criticism"—which he criticized because it seemed to depend on the prejudices, opinions, and reasoning of the scholar and because it was often incomprehensible to the ordinary man or woman—was "less dangerous than unchristian attacks upon it."[37]

Sectarian divisions among Christians were anathema to Moody. "If I thought I had one drop of sectarian blood in my veins, I would let it out before I went to bed," he said.[38] "Although he identified himself, usually, as a Congregationalist (although, because of his pacifism, he sometimes called himself a Quaker), he felt that it was important that Christians of all denominations cooperate in the work of leading souls to Christ. "I hope to see the day when all bickering, division, and party feeling will cease, and Roman Catholics will see eye to eye with Protestants in this work," he declared. "Let us advance in a solid column—Roman Catholics, Protestants, Episcopalians, Presbyterians, Methodists—against the ranks of Satan's emissaries."[39]

Accordingly, he objected vigorously to the tendency among many conservative Christians—who later called themselves "fundamentalists"—to separate from other Christians who did not believe as they did. He is said to have begged, in his later years, Christians of different persuasions to put aside their feuding for ten years to unite in leading people to salvation.

At a time when relations between the two branches of western Christianity were hostile and suspicious, Moody sought, and in some cases obtained, friendly relations with Roman Catholics. When he began his ministry in Chicago in the early 1860s he was frustrated when he visited many sick persons who were Roman Catholic and who refused to allow him to pray with him because of the difference in faith. He arranged a meeting with James Duggan, the Irish-born bishop of Chicago. When Duggan urged Moody to unite with the true church—the Roman Catholic Church, Moody told him, "Well, Bishop, this is a very important matter, and ought to be attended to at once. No man wants to belong to the true church more than I do. I wish you would pray for me right here, that God would show me his true church, and help me to be a worthy member of it." The bishop and the lay preacher knelt down and prayed together for each other. Although Moody never became a Roman Catholic, Duggan did encourage members of his diocese to pray with him and his workers and cooperate with his ministry.[40]

For Moody, Christ's true church consisted of all those who committed their lives to Jesus Christ and were bound in love by the Holy Spirit. God's blessings could be obtained only when Christians laid aside "all differences, all criticism, all coldness and party feeling" and came "to the Lord as one"[41] The true church was defined by love, and this is where Moody felt "the churches have all gone astray."[42]

Moody preached three times a day, five times a week, and four or five times on Sunday. He rose early each day to study the Bible and pray. He made notes of all the good things he had read and heard during the day. He would not play checkers, cards, or billiards; he did not smoke, drink, or dance; he disliked Sunday papers because he insisted that they "demoralize the Church of God" by reporting "murders, divorces, and football games."[43] He never insisted that this somewhat ascetical lifestyle was necessary to salvation, however.

For years he seemed a dynamo of creative energy. He founded a Bible institute and a nondenominational church in Chicago, as well as the Mount Hermon and Northfield Schools in his hometown of Northfield, Massachusetts. In his early sixties, he began to slow down, but still refused to give in to failing health. "People say to me, have you the grace to die?" he declared. "I say, No, I have only grace now to hold this meeting. The Lord promises to give grace when we need it and not before, and when death comes and not before, will He give us dying grace."[44]

In 1899, when he learned of the death of Robert Ingersoll, a prominent lawyer who lectured around the country, espousing agnosticism, he mused: "My feeling toward him has always been that of deepest pity, for a life like his seems so barren of everything that has made my life joyous and blessed. He chided those who wanted to consign the Great Agnostic to Hell, affirming, "We are not his judges. It is for God alone to judge him."[45]

Moody preached for the last time in Kansas City, Missouri, in November 1899. In one of his last sermons, he declared: "We say this is the land of the living! It is not. It is the land of the dying. What is our life here but a vapor? A hearse is the most common sight. Families broken into. Over there is one who has lost a father, there a mother, there is a place vacant, there a sister's name is no more heard, there a brother's love is missed. Death stalks triumphant through our midst, in this world. Only yesterday I met a mother who had lost her babe. Death in front of us, death behind us, death to the right of us, death to the left of us. See the hospitals in our land and the asylums for the insane and blind and the aged. See the great number of jails in our land....But look at the other world. No death, no pain, no sorrow, no old age, no sickness, no bending forms, no dimmed eyes, no tears. But joy, peace, love, happiness. No gray hair. People all young. River of life for the healing of the nations, and everlasting life. Think of it! Life! Life without end!"[46]

Moody soon became too ill to continue and returned to his Massachusetts home, where he lingered a month, troubled by a failing heart. Then, three days before Christmas, he awoke from sleep and said slowly and distinctly: "Earth recedes; Heaven opens before me." When his son tried to rouse him, thinking that he was dreaming, the dying man said, "No, this is no dream, Will. It is beautiful. It is like a trance. If this is death, it is sweet. There is no valley here. God is calling me, and I must go." After giving instructions to various family members, he exclaimed: "This is my triumph; this is my coronation day! I have been looking forward to it for years." Speaking of two baby grandchildren who had recently died, he said joyfully: "Dwight! Irene!—I see the children's faces." After telling his wife, "Mamma, you have been a good wife to me!" he lost consciousness, only to be resuscitated by the doctors. Bewildered and not a little annoyed, he demanded, "What does all this mean? What are you all doing here?" He refused further medical assistance and threatened to dismiss his doctor unless he cooperated with his wishes. Further prolongation of his life, he said, would only keep the family in anxiety.[47] Soon afterward he began to sink again, and this time the physicians allowed him to go. He died "quietly and peacefully," as if only falling asleep.[48]

Some time before he died he had said, "Some day you will read in the papers that D. L. Moody…is dead. Don't you believe a word of it! At that moment I shall be more alive than I am now. I shall have gone up higher, that is all—out of this old clay tenement into a house that is immortal; a body that death cannot touch, that sin cannot taint, a body fashioned like unto His glorious body. I was born of the flesh in 1837. I was born of the Spirit in 1856. That which is born of the flesh may die. That which is born of the Spirit will live forever."[49]

～

Profile 38
Stephen Grover Cleveland

Born: Caldwell, New Jersey, March 18, 1837
Died: Princeton, New Jersey, June 24, 1908

The only man to serve two nonconsecutive terms as president of the United States, Grover Cleveland was a blunt, gruff man with cold, piercing eyes whose face and form reminded some observers of a bulldog. One author described him as a man with little of the charm associated with most politicians; he was "not the grinner, nor a hand-waver, not an active hat tipper."[1] The Democrat was known for his honesty and hard work, and his willingness to do what he believed was right, even at the expense of popularity and political future. Although he seldom talked about spiritual matters, he was deeply religious.

His father, who died when "Grove" was a teenager, was a Presbyterian minister, and Cleveland, although never a member of any church,[2] frequently attended services of worship throughout his life. His mother was also very devout, and when he went away from home, she gave him a small Bible, which he would carry with him everywhere he went for the rest of his life. When he took his oath of office as president, he did so with his left hand on that Bible, which he had opened to Psalm 112, which begins: "Praise the LORD! Happy are those who fear the LORD, who greatly delight in his commandments."[3]

As a young man, Cleveland worked at the New York Institute for the Blind as an aide to his brother, who taught there, as well as to the preceptrix Fanny Crosby. The future president and the future hymnwriter became lifelong friends.

While president, Cleveland regularly attended the First Presbyterian Church. A long-time friend observed that although he "seldom talked about his religious convictions," he had an "absolute, undoubting...faith,"[4] a faith that "never questioned the truth or soundness of those fundamental teachings that had come down to him through generations of orthodox clergymen." He had, in fact, an abhorrence of those scholars who tried to demythologize the supernatural or miraculous accounts in the Scriptures. Cleveland once commented, "The Bible is good enough for me: just the old book under which I was brought up. I do not want notes, or criticisms, or explanations about authorship or origin, or even cross-references. I do not need or understand them, and they confuse me."[5]

Cleveland also believed that the United States was a Christian nation. "It would not be in existence and it could not hope to live if it were not Christian in every fiber," he said privately. "That is what has made it and what will save it in all its perils. Whenever we have departed from this conception of life and thought, nationality has suffered, character has declined, and difficulties have increased. While slavery remained, we could not hope fully to work out Christian ideals, and whenever we overlook the fact that 'righteousness exalteth a nation,' we pay the penalty."[6]

Cleveland's administrations coincided with a huge influx of Jewish immigrants, and this prompted him to tell his associates, "I welcome people from every land and of every form of faith, but I firmly believe that, as we have done in our political ideas, we shall assimilate them to our religion, by demonstrating—as Christianity at its best estate has always done—its superiority and its power."[7] Needless to say, Cleveland was a great supporter of foreign missions, and was occasionally criticized for declaring publicly the "duty" of trying to convert the world to the Christian faith.[8]

After leaving the White House, Cleveland and his family retired to Princeton, New Jersey, where they attended the First Presbyterian

Church. Cleveland had married late, and his first child, Ruth, was born when he was past fifty. Fanny Crosby wrote a poem about "Baby Ruth," and a candy bar was named in her honor. Ruth Cleveland lived only to the age of twelve. When she died, unexpectedly, of diphtheria, her father was crushed. He wrote in his diary on the day of her burial, "I had a season of great trouble in keeping out of my mind the idea that Ruth was in the cold cheerless grave instead of in the arms of her Savior." But a few days later, he was able to record, "God has come to my help and I am able to adjust my thoughts to dear Ruth's death with as much comfort as selfish humanity will permit. One thing I can say: Not for a moment since she left us has a rebellious thought entered my mind."[9]

The former president was ill for some time before he died. A few weeks before the end, he asked for one of the hymnals used for family devotions when he was a boy. A friend recalled, "As weakness more encroached, he faced toward the inevitable with trust in the Almighty and with good will to mankind. The intent look on his face was not due to apprehension."[10] The last words he spoke to his wife were: "I have tried so hard to do right."[11]

Fanny Crosby had visited Cleveland a few weeks before his death. When she learned of his passing, she told reporters that she knew him as a "lovely, noble character" and a "noble, faithful Christian gentleman." They had a "deep, warm friendship that death cannot break, for the cords will be united and we shall see and know each other in the land of the blest."[12]

Profile 39
John Pierpont Morgan, Sr.

Born: Hartford, Connecticut, April 17, 1837
Died: Rome, Italy, March 31, 1913

The banker and financier who helped to organize U.S. Steel, the first billion-dollar corporation in the United States, was also a celebrated art collector and yachtsman. Few people who knew him personally found J. P. Morgan an appealing character. Many thought of him as the very caricature of the arrogant capitalist—a cold, brusque, overbearing man who allegedly remarked, when urged to use his wealth to alleviate the plight of the public: "I owe the public nothing!" One biographer depicted him as wallowing in every one of the seven deadly sins except sloth, of which not even his most bitter enemies could accuse him.

Despite his ruthlessness and his lack of apparent sympathy for the unfortunate, Morgan considered himself a good Christian. He was the chief financial support of his own congregation, and also contributed several million dollars to the building fund of the Cathedral of St. John the Divine in New York City. He contributed millions to the Lying-In Hospital and endowed a sanitarium for the treatment of tuberculosis.[1] He also contributed prodigiously to New York's Metropolitan Museum of Art and Metropolitan Opera. Every Christmas Eve, he loaded a carriage with toys and food for the poor.[2] For all his philanthropies, Morgan insisted on absolute privacy.

Born a Congregationalist, at twenty-four Morgan became an Episcopalian, joining St. George's Church at Stuyvesant Square in Manhattan, where he was active the rest of his life. When he was in New York, he went there nearly every day to pray or meditate while the organ played.[3] He attended services every Sunday morning, and Sabbath evenings he led family devotions with his wife and children, fervently rendering his favorite hymns in his deep, tuneless voice. He attended most of the conventions of the Episcopal Church and often sought the company of bishops. Despite his chronic marital infidelities, he helped to organize the New York Society for the Suppression of Vice, which fought pornography and prostitution.[4] Morgan was also a major financial backer of Dwight Moody and Ira Sankey's religious campaigns, and frequently attended their revival meetings, sitting in the front row on the platform, along with prominent ministers, and fervently joining in the singing of the Gospel hymns.[5]

When he visited the Holy Land in 1882, Morgan wrote to his wife about the Holy Sepulchre: "There is the slab on which [Jesus] was laid. Impelled by an impulse impossible to resist, you fall on your knees before that shrine."[6] Morgan insisted that he believed every word in the Bible. When his secretary asked if he believed the story of Jonah and the whale, he replied: "If the time comes when I cannot believe every word in the Bible, then I could believe none of it."[7] Yet, at the same time, he was fascinated by the occult, believed in horoscopes, and regularly hired an astrologer named Evangeline Adams.[8] At times, he expressed an interest in reincarnation.[9]

In the early 1880s, William S. Rainsford was hired as rector of St. George's. For years, Morgan, as the chief financial support of the congregation, acted as if he owned it. In the pastor's absence, he stood outside to greet the congregation "like a feudal lord of the manor with his tenantry."[10] Despite the fact that the rector's salary and the financial health of his congregation were at the mercy of Morgan's good graces, Rainsford insisted that St. George's end the practice of renting pews, and demanded that its well-heeled members welcome the poor and homeless.[11] Morgan acquiesced to the rector's demands, but balked when Rainsford wanted to give all members, rich and poor, the opportunity to serve on the vestry (church council). Morgan objected, "I do not want the vestry democratized. I want it to remain a body of gentlemen whom I can ask to meet me in my study—gentlemen who...could make up deficits out of their pockets."[12] That was too much for the capitalist. In a snit, Morgan resigned as senior warden, and he refused to speak to Rainsford in anything but grunts and monosyllables. However, just before he set sail for a European vacation, Morgan invited his pastor to see him off. In his state room, the financier threw his arms around the minister and cried, "Pray for me! Pray for me!"[13]

Rainsford later wrote of Morgan that he believed that Morgan was sincerely religious, but "had no vision of reforms and generally little sympathy for reformers." Moreover, "on the religious side of his nature," the financier was "intensely conservative" and "had the peace and power of religious assurance, while the very nature of his assurance precluded in him the possibility of spiritual development." Rainsford did not think Morgan a hypocrite, but saw him as a man who compartmentalized his life: "His religion was a talent to be wrapped in its own napkin and venerated in the secret place of his soul; laid aside in safe disuse, rather than passed from man to man."[14] The Episcopal Church Morgan saw, not as "an active, reforming spirit, but a repository of ancient beauty, powerful because it was archaic and unchanging."[15] He was, in fact, attracted to the "very archaic element" of Episcopal worship, "its atmosphere of withdrawal from the common everyday affairs of man."[16]

There is no evidence that Morgan ever found his life inconsistent or that his conscience ever troubled him. He never doubted that he would go to heaven. A physically unattractive man with beady eyes, a face disfigured with acne, and a huge nose that looked like a raspberry, some believed he looked forward to being reborn into a beautiful and unblemished body.[17] Just before he died, he wrote his will, in which he declared: "I commit my soul into the hands of my Savior, in full confidence that having redeemed it and washed it in his most precious blood, he will present it faultless before the throne of my Heavenly Father; and I entreat my children to maintain and defend, at all hazard and at any cost of personal sacrifice, the blessed doctrine of the complete atonement for sin through the blood of Jesus Christ, once offered, and through that alone."[18]

～

Profile 40
John Davison Rockefeller, Sr.

Born: Richford, New York, July 8, 1839
Died: Ormond Beach, Florida, May 23, 1937

The billionaire oilman from earliest childhood seemed obsessed with making money. At the age of seven, he was earning a few pennies by digging potatoes and managing a flock of turkeys, and with his earnings he bought candy by the pound and sold it to his brothers and sisters by the piece.[1] At the age of thirteen, he was lending $50 at compound interest.[2] At fourteen, he moved, with his mother and siblings to Cleveland, Ohio, where he attended high school. His classmates found him "money-mad."[3] Asked what he wanted to be, he told fellow students, "I want to be worth a hundred thousand dollars, and I'm going to be, too!"[4]

After graduation, he obtained a job as a clerk accountant, making $3.50 a week. Soon he became a commission merchant, selling produce. When the Civil War broke out, he made a handsome profit by selling salt and pork to the Union Army, so that at twenty-four, he was able to buy a small oil refinery. Oil was then in demand, not yet for gasoline, but for lighting, paint bases, and as an industrial lubricant, and Rockefeller began quickly to acquire more and more oil refineries. Soon after his acquisition of his first refinery, someone saw him alone in his office, thinking himself unobserved. He was jumping up and down, shouting, "I'm bound to be rich! Bound to be rich!"[5]

After he organized Standard Oil, he began to drive his competitors out of business, until he established a monopoly in the business of oil refining. He made many enemies because of the ruthless way he and his aides did business, but, since everything he did was legal at the time, he never felt any compunctions about his sharp practices. Once, fairly late in life, Rockefeller, testifying in court, noticed in the audience a small Ohio refiner whom he had driven out of business years before. After he got off the stand, he went up to the man and held out his hand, with the words, "How are you, Mr. Rice? You and I are getting to be old men, are we not?" Rice refused to shake the billionaire's hand and bitterly complained, "You said you would ruin my business and you have done so." Rockefeller shook his head and protested, "Not a word of truth in it!"[6]

Rockefeller, who owned an estate near Cleveland, a townhouse in Manhattan, homes in Seal Harbor, Maine, Ormond Beach, Florida, and Lakewood, New Jersey, and a 4,180 acre compound at Pocantico Hills, Westchester County, New York, was known for his parsimony toward his hired help. Typical of his dealings with his staff was the five-dollar Christmas bonus he once gave his groundskeeper, which was wiped out by five dollars in docked pay because the man chose to spend the holidays with his wife and children. Instead of giving his employees time off on holidays, he typically said, "Instead of spending money on amusements, my employees will be given an opportunity of adding to their savings. Had they been given a holiday, no doubt their money would have been spent foolishly."[7]

Yet Rockefeller lived a lifestyle much less lavish than that of many of the super rich. He was sparing in food and drink, and, other than keeping accounts and buying and selling stock, his only hobby was golf. Faithful to his wife, he was a devoted father to his children. He was also a deeply devout man, whose love of money was rivaled only by his love of God. Frequently, his critics quoted the passage from Luke 18:25, in which Jesus declares, "It is easier for camel to go through the eye of a needle than for someone who is rich to enter into the kingdom of God." When asked to respond, Rockefeller invariably quoted his favorite verse, "Do you see those who are skillful in their work? They will serve kings" (Proverbs 22:29).[8]

From the time he moved to Cleveland, Rockefeller attended the working-class Erie Street Baptist Church with his family, and there he was baptized at the age of fifteen. Shortly afterward, he was named the clerk of the church and began teaching Sunday-school class. For thirty years, he served as superintendent of the Sunday school. Even when he was making $3.50 a week, he tithed, and this practice continued for the rest of his life. He was also a faithful money raiser. When the minister announced that the church would have to close its doors unless the congregation could raise $2,000, Rockefeller, then about nineteen, planted himself at the door and buttonholed every member, begging for a contribution, recording the pledges in a little ledger book. During the next few months, he pursued the members to collect the pledges, and was able to raise the entirety of the sum that was needed to keep the church going."[9]

Throughout his life, Rockefeller never missed a service unless he was ill. When he began spending large portions of his year in New York City, he became a member of the Fifth Avenue Baptist Church. He did not teach Sunday school there, but opened his home for the meetings of all sorts of church societies and committees—for prayer meetings, temperance meetings, missionary society meetings.[10] He and his wife always invited visiting ministers home for dinner. "You have fed us, now let us feed you," they said.[11] When at his Florida home, he attended Union Baptist Church, where all the regular worshipers, except for him, were black.[12] He seldom read books, but he loved sermons. He declared that he needed "good preaching to wind me up, like an old clock, once or twice a week."[13] Many of his friends and associates criticized him for continuing his Baptist affiliation. Baptist churches were seen as poor people's churches. The Episcopal Church was considered the place of worship of choice for the rich. When a friend told him, "John, you are too big for the Baptist Church," Rockefeller responded, "I hope I'm big enough for the Baptist Church."[14]

Of the church Rockefeller once said, "I cannot understand a church where people get up and march out. There ought to be something that makes a church homelike. Friends should be glad to see each other and to greet strangers. There should be something every time to make people want to come back."[15]

Rockefeller never had a single qualm about his massive accumulation of wealth. He insisted that he made his fortune so that he could give to charitable causes,[16] and referred to his fortune as "God's Gold."[17] He insisted that a man should "get all the money he honestly can" and then use it to extend charity to the poor.[18] In 1905, he told a reporter, "God gave me my money. I believe the power to make money is a gift from God, to be developed and used to the best of our ability for the good of mankind. Having been endowed with the gift I possess, I believe it is my duty to make money and still more money and use the money I make for the good of my fellow man according to the dictates of my conscience."[19] He could not understand why people criticized him and he likened attacks on his ruthless operation of Standard Oil to a "crucifixion."[20]

Rockefeller's religion colored his private life. He held family Bible readings every morning and fined any child or grandchild a penny for being late. Every Friday evening he held a prayer meeting. He was a strict observer of the Sabbath. Not only did he insist on cold meals on Sunday (because cooking would constitute a violation of the Sabbath), he refused to allow maintenance people to work then, although he was known to insist that they begin their work at 12:01 midnight Monday morning![21]

Rockefeller continued to tithe throughout his life. From thirty-five cents a week at the time of his first job, his tithe grew steadily with his income. By the time he was in his early forties, he was giving $65,000 a year to church and charity. By his fifties, his tithe amounted to $1.5 million a year,[22] and by 1905, when he was sixty-six, his contributions amounted to more than $100 million a year.[23] Until he was well past seventy, nearly all his donations were made without publicity. Then, at a time when he was held in the deepest contempt by the public as a rapacious and predatory financial pirate, his public relations agent convinced him to allow the public to know the extent of his philanthropies, and, gradually, in the last twenty years of his life, he came to be seen as a philanthropist and humanitarian.

The earliest objects of his generosity, when he was in his early twenties, besides his own church, were a Methodist church, a Negro congregation, and a Roman Catholic orphanage.[24] A firm believer in racial equality, in 1881 he established Spelman College in Atlanta (named in honor of his wife, Cettie Spelman) for black women. A grandson later remarked, "It's marvelous now to think of Grandfather giving money to a college for black women when higher education for either blacks or women was unheard of."[25] In 1887, he donated $600 million to the University of Chicago,[26] an institution that continued to be the recipient of his prodigious benefactions. In 1901, through the Rev. Frederick T. Gates, whom he hired to administer his charities in 1891, he set up the Rockefeller Institute for Medical Research, which, within four years, developed a serum to treat meningitis. Through Gates, the General Education Board was set up to donate millions each year toward Negro education. The Rockefeller Sanitary Commission was established, which proved instrumental in eliminating hookworm in the American South.[27]

John D. Rockefeller, Sr., lived to be nearly ninety-eight years old. His shrunken and wizened form was frequently seen on newsreels, giving away dimes with the admonition, "A dime for the bank, a penny to spend."[28] While his son built the large, impressive Riverside Church in New York, the old man preferred to attend Union Baptist Church at his Florida home, joining his hoarse, rasping voice to those of his friends in a hearty rendition of spirituals and gospel songs.[29] "I was right," he said toward the end of life. "I knew it as a matter of conscience. It was right between me and my God."[30]

～

Profile 41

William McKinley

Born: Niles, Ohio, January 29, 1843
Died: Buffalo, New York, September 14, 1901

All but forgotten except by students of history, the Republican president from Ohio was reluctantly responsible for the war with Spain in 1898 by which the United States annexed Puerto Rico, Guam, and the Philippines, and made Cuba an American protectorate. It was also under his administration that Hawaii was annexed.

Even those who opposed his policy of "imperialism" had to admit that he was one of the nicest men ever elevated to the presidential dignity. An assistant secretary of state, David J. Hill, said of him, "If the Lord ever breathed the breath of life into a more gracious and amiable man than Mr. McKinley, I have yet to find it out."[1] A committee clerk who had frequent dealings with the president pointed out that "in powerful contrast to the rudeness so prevalent in Washington," McKinley was "the incarnation of courtesy to clerks and other obscure men."[2] When he had to deny a favor to a senator or representative, McKinley looked so unhappy that the person who had been disappointed actually felt sorry for him.[3]

Once, during a presidential campaign, he was riding in a closed carriage from one speaking engagement to another on a cold day, and noticed a reporter shivering outside. Even though he knew this reporter was responsible for covering his campaign in a spirit of vicious hostility, he invited the man into his coach. The reporter protested, "I guess you don't know who I am. I have been with you on the whole campaign, giving it to you every time you spoke, and I am going over tonight to rip you to pieces." "I know," said McKinley, "but you put on this coat and get inside and get warm so that you can do a good job."[4] Of course, these incidents reveal a shrewd political instinct, but even his enemies admitted that William McKinley was truly a good-hearted and compassionate individual.

He was also one of the most religiously observant men to occupy the White House. During the four and a half years that he served as president, when he was in Washington, he missed only two Sundays at the Metropolitan Methodist Church, where he was a regular communicant. A prominent Democrat who was a bitter political enemy attended Metropolitan Methodist one Communion Sunday and recounted: "I watched the President....I gave close attention to his countenance and attitude during all the opening service and his interest in the earnest words which were spoken before the sacrament of the Lord's Supper was administered. And, after a while, when I saw William McKinley get up from his place and go and kneel down at the altar, humbly, with the rest, and reverently take the Communion, and then, when he arose, quietly wipe away the traces of emotion from his eyes, his whole countenance and attitude showing the deepest religious emotion, I confess...I said to myself, 'A country which has a man like that at the head of its affairs is not so badly off, after all.'"[5]

On May 26, 1899, midway through his first term, McKinley wrote and signed a slip of paper which he enclosed in his letterbook. It read: "My belief embraces the divinity of Christ and a recognition of Christianity as the mightiest factor in the world's civilization."[6] His belief was nurtured from his earliest childhood by his pious mother, a devout Methodist who hoped that he would become a bishop some day. He remained deeply attached to her until her death shortly after he became president. During a revival at their church in Poland, Ohio, thirteen-year-old William made a decision to commit himself to Jesus Christ, and arose in church and testified: "I have not done my duty. I have sinned. I want to be a Christian, for I believe that religion is the best thing in the world. I give myself to my Savior, who has done so much for me."[7]

William McKinley never wavered in his faith, which found expression in the Methodist church, for the rest of his life. After settling in Canton, Ohio, where he practiced law, he became an active member of the First Methodist Church there, where he served as Sunday-school superintendent and on the board of trustees and board of stewards. Even after he entered politics, he remained an active member.

Many of his friends felt that McKinley's faith was sorely tried in his relationship with his wife, the former Ida Saxton. The McKinleys were devoted to each other, but Ida, who lost two babies early in their marriage, suffered for many years from seizures and circulatory ailments and lived the life of an invalid. Many found her a silly, childish, whining woman who was excessively demanding of her husband's attentions. She herself told an interviewer, "If anyone could know what it is to have a wife sick, complaining always, an invalid for twenty-five years, seldom a day well…and yet never a word of unkindness has ever passed his lips."[8] McKinley devoted himself to the demands of his frail wife with what his friends considered saintly devotion.

When McKinley, who had served as a congressman and as Ohio's governor, was running for president, partly because of his wife's condition, he did not travel around the country campaigning, but gave speeches to delegations from various localities in front of his home. He refused to receive delegations on Sunday. Once, when a group from Detroit appeared one Sunday morning, he told them, "This is the Sabbath day, and I cannot receive delegations, much less would I have you come to me with a band of music on the Sabbath. I cannot, in any event, see you this morning, for I must go to church. I attend the First M.E. Church and would advise you to be present."[9] One of his handlers, who had known the candidate since the two were army buddies during the Civil War, commented, "Major McKinley is a quiet man upon religious subjects, but he is a religious man. I have been with him many times and during all his campaigns. We have frequently attended political meetings and banquets, and have often retired at a late hour, but I have never known him to go to bed until he had read from his Bible and knelt in prayer."[10]

When McKinley was inaugurated in 1897, he opened the Bible to the passage in the first chapter of Second Chronicles, in which Solomon prays, "Give me now wisdom and knowledge, that I may go out and come before this people: for who can judge this people that is so great."[11] He told friends, "I pray to God every day to give me strength to do this work, and I believe he will do it."[12] He believed that his responsibility to God came before all else—even his responsibility to his office (although he made no distinction, for in carrying out his duties as president, he was doing his duty to his God). "I place the cross higher than the flag," he said.[13]

Like most nineteenth-century people, he tended to be optimistic, especially about the progress of the world. Even before his elevation to the presidency, he had spoken sanguinely about the growing influence of Christianity in an address to the YMCA of Youngstown, Ohio, in which he declared, "It is another recognition of the Master who rules over self, a worthy tribute to him who came on earth to save fallen man and feed him to a higher plane….The religious believer commands and receives the highest consideration at the hands of his neighbors and countrymen, however much they may disagree with him; and when his life is made to conform to his religious profession, his influence is almost without limitation, widespread and far reaching."[14]

As we have seen, although he retained his membership in the First Methodist Episcopal Church of Canton, he regularly attended Metropolitan Methodist in Washington. Every Sunday evening he gathered his friends and those members of Congress who cared to attend to hymn-sings in the White House.[15] His favorite hymns were "Nearer, My God, to Thee," "Lead, Kindly Light," "Jesus, Lover of My Soul," and "There's a Wideness in God's Mercy."[16]

McKinley's faith was evident during the closing days of his life. Six months into his second term as president, he was shot by a terrorist while shaking hands in a reception at the Pan American Exposition in Buffalo, New York. On the eighth day after the attack, McKinley, realizing that the end was near, asked to see the entire team of doctors and surgeons who were treating him. "It is useless, gentlemen; I think we ought to have prayer." He smiled and crossed his hands on his chest, as he led them in the Our Father. Afterward Ida was sent for. She leaned over the bed and the two kissed for the last time. "Goodbye, all," he said. "It is God's way. His will, not ours, be done." Then, after singing a few lines of "Nearer, My God, to Thee," he whispered, "That has been my inextinguishable prayer.... It is God's way." He never spoke again.[17]

∼

Profile 42

Thomas Alva Edison

Born: Milan, Ohio, February 11, 1847
Died: West Orange, New Jersey, October 18, 1931

From what is known of his early life, most of Edison's early influences served to prejudice him against Christianity and religion in general. His father was an unbeliever, but his mother was a devout Presbyterian, who made young Alva, the youngest of several children, read the Bible and attend a church whose pastor constantly presented the picture of a furious God who mercilessly punished sinners in an eternity of hellfire.[1] Edison was sent to the Family School for Boys and Girls, which was run by George Engle, a minister who whipped the boy so frequently and so severely that, after a few months, he ran away.[2] As a child, he was in terror of the ghosts of the dead, and, after he obtained his first job as a vendor on a train, when he was returning home at night and passed a cemetery, he closed his eyes and allowed the horse to proceed on its own, for fear of seeing ghostly apparitions.[3] An inveterate reader, at thirteen he read Thomas Paine's *The Age of Reason* and became a believer in materialism. Paine's philosophy dissipated young Edison's fear of hell, damnation, ghosts—and churchly religion. After that, the only religious organization to which he was ever attracted was Madame Helena Blavatsky's Aryan Theosophic Society, which taught a blend of spiritualism, Hinduism, and Buddhism, and tried to blend science and theology.[4] Active in the society in his early thirties, Edison quickly lost interest.

Edison, in his mature years, believed that the mind consisted of "subparticles of matter, somewhat like electrons." These particles traveled "through space," bringing to earth the wisdom of other worlds. Coalescing into swarms, they lodged in people's brains, and created "intelligence." Traits were inherited when these "little people" passed from one human being to another, and genius was the result of a particularly fortunate grouping of these "little intelligences."[5] Sometimes some of the intelligences within a certain person could not agree. As a result, "They fight out their differences, and then the stronger group takes charge. If the minority is willing to conform, there is harmony. But minorities sometimes...refuse to do their appointed work in the body, and the host sickens and dies." After that, all the intelligences were free to seek new experiences elsewhere, traveling like "swarms of bees" through space until they found another host.[6]

In an interview with Edward Marshall of the *New York Times*, Edison, at sixty-three, insisted, "There is no 'supernatural'....[A]ll there is, all there has been, all that ever will be, can or will, sooner or later, be explained along material lines."[7] The inventor denied the individuality of the human being, and, as proof, referred to the billions of intelligences that comprise each person.[8] Thus, for him, there was no immortality of the soul. "I am not an individual. I am an aggregate of individuals. Will New York City go to heaven?...[A]ll this talk of an existence for us, as individuals, beyond the grave is wrong. It is born of our tenacity of life—our desire to go on living—our dread of coming to an end as individuals. I do not dread it, though. Personally, I cannot see any use of a future life."[9]

For Edison, the brain was a "mere machine." As for the will, he felt it "may be a form of electricity, or it may be a form of some other power of which we as yet know nothing. But whatever it is, it is material."[10] Although in another interview, five years later, he said he believed in "a personal God" and that "nature and science both affirm his existence."[11] For Edison, God was the laws that govern the universe. God was nature. "Nature made us...not the gods of the religions. And nature did it mercilessly; she had no thought for mercy or against it."[12] Nature was neither kind, nor merciful, nor loving.

Even so, Edison had great respect for Jesus. He conceded that "we have the teaching of a few men with great minds whom we call prophets and whose leadership of thoughts has been of incalculable value to the world."[13] The greatest of these prophets were Christ, Buddha, Confucius, and Mohammed. "That the teachings of these leaders have maintained their powerful influence through the generations and the centuries is proof enough that they contain some truth,"[14] Edison wrote when he was nearly eighty. Christ was the greatest of these teachers. He claimed, "The teachings of Christ have shown a greater vitality than any other, for they are accepted annually today by more new minds than any others."[15] He insisted that Christianity produced the "world's best leadership" and Christian nations "are the wisest nations."[16]

Edison revered Christ for his moral code. But he, like Jefferson, felt that Christ's teachings had been deformed by his followers. He had harsh words for theologians, whom he defined as people "who have attempted to interpret [the teachings of Christ] for other people." These people "have disagreed more widely and bitterly with regard to what is truth than the leading interpreters of any of the other teachers."[17]

When, late in life, he was asked to comment on the fact that a recent poll revealed that church membership was no longer growing, he said, "People are drifting away from superstition and bunk; increase in scientific knowledge is responsible."[18] Nonetheless, Edison saw a future for organized Christianity. Edison's "church of the future" would teach morals and science, like Thomas Paine's Theophilanthropists. Of the new church, the inventor said: "I believe that a great change must and will occur....[C]reeds and ceremonies will become less and less important...and...the religion of the future...will be more and more an education in established truth....Somehow I cannot be impressed by the idea that merely spoken prayers are likely to be answered, but I am absolutely sure that lived prayers are certain to be answered....

Convince boys and girls and men and women that if they are not straight and square and honest, if they are not reasonably unselfish and inclined to follow the great precept of the Golden Rule, they cannot possibly be happy, and you will accomplish about all that is necessary about religious teaching."[19] Ministers should focus on the Sermon on the Mount...and concern themselves with "morals rather than creeds."[20] Sermons should be about "the beauties and wonders of the natural world around us."[21] Nature "can teach us more about God Almighty in a day than all the textbooks of the theological seminaries can teach us in ten years....[A]n oak leaf, or the busy efforts of a squirrel to lay up food for the winter, might form a better text for an inspiring sermon for a summer's day, or the infinite beauty of a snowflake on a Sunday morning in the winter, than any sentence from...Jeremiah's pessimistic Lamentations."[22]

For Edison, religion was living according to Jesus' moral code, expressed in the Sermon on the Mount (which was apparently, along with the Ten Commandments, the only part of the Bible to which he attached any importance), and learning, through scientific investigation, about a God who was synonymous with nature. Nevertheless, Edison, at least in later years, was somewhat open to the possibility of the immortality of the soul, at least in some form. But he felt that if the soul was, in fact, immortal, there must be some way of demonstrating this scientifically. "Nothing should be based upon belief which is not, in its turn, based on truth," he said.[23] And so, in his seventies, he began to talk about inventing a device for psychic researchers, like "a very sensitive Ouija board," sensitive to "psychic energies," that would enable the dead to communicate with the living.[24] Needless to say, he never succeeded. Just before he died, emerging from a coma, he looked up, and said to his wife, "It is very beautiful over there."[25] Some felt that he was referring to the grounds of his mansion in West Orange, New Jersey. Others felt that, on the point of death, he had experienced a vision.

Profile 43

Booker Taliaferro Washington

Born: Hale's Ford, Virginia, April 5, 1856
Died: Tuskegee, Alabama, November 14, 1915

Dwight Lyman Moody had just opened a week's revival on March 13, 1898, at the Grand Central Palace in New York, on Lexington Avenue, and had just begun to speak when he recognized a latecomer who was just entering the hall. The evangelist announced that Booker T. Washington was present, and insisted that he take a seat on the platform along with other dignitaries and then would give a short talk.

Washington, then forty-two, had been principal of the Tuskegee Normal and Industrial Institute of Alabama for nearly two decades, and, now at the height of his fame, was the best-known African American leader. Instead of demanding equal rights for the Negro, Washington urged the people of his own race to accept the inequities of segregation and concentrate on developing marketable skills and, through thrift and hard work, attain economic power. Because of his timid attitude toward the evils of segregation, he was quite popular with whites, who did not always heed his exhortation to them to show preference in hiring black skilled labor over that of foreign birth.

The impromptu talk that Washington gave at Grand Central Palace that winter's day illustrated his attitude to the social problems of his day, as well as to religion. "I well remember the first prayer I heard from my mother's lips," he began. "I was a slave. As I look back now, I can see my mother bending over me as I lay on my pallet in the poor little cabin in which we lived. She is about to leave me for a day of hard labor and she bends over me and her lips move in prayer. I hear her as she prays that Mr. Lincoln will succeed, and set us free. She prayed that at least her child might be free."

He continued: "I remember also the second prayer I heard from her lips. Mr. Lincoln had triumphed and we were free American citizens. She prayed then that her child might be educated. Both prayers were answered. If there is one thing the Negro race can teach the white race, it is simple faith. We believe in the Bible and in God." Washington demonstrated this point through a story. "A white man once went into a Negro church where the people were enthusiastic and began shouting. [He asked,] 'Why do you people do that way?' 'Well, Boss,' a Negro said, 'we ain't got no better sense.' We believe simply and devoutly. The Russian sometimes appeals to dynamite and the Irish to agitation, but the simple Negro appeals to God in his midnight prayers."[1]

Washington's religious faith was based on a simple belief in a merciful God and in prayer. Washington was attracted to religion at an early age. At eight or nine, he was baptized at the African Zion Baptist Church of Tinkereville, West Virginia. While a student at Hampton Normal and Agricultural Institute in Virginia, he was deeply influenced by one of his teachers, a woman by the name of Nathalie Lord, who encouraged him to devote forty-five minutes a day to reading the Bible and to join her and other students in prayer meetings in her room for the conversion of those students who were not Christians. After he was graduated from Hampton, Washington attended Wayland Seminary in Washington, D.C., which trained black men for the Baptist ministry. He left after a year, however. Whereas Douglass was alienated from organized religion because of the acquiescence to the institution of slavery by most white churches, Washington was alienated because of the unspiritual nature of most black churches.

Even as a boy, Washington was disenchanted by the emotionalism of the services of his home church. He never forgot the day when his mother barely escaped serious injury at the hands of a preacher, who worked the congregation into a frenzy. Then the preacher took the big pulpit Bible and "threw it into space," roaring, "Here, God, take this Bible!" The Bible struck Washington's mother on the arm with such force that she had to seek medical assistance. The arm, at first thought broken, was found to be only badly bruised. However, the young Washington was appalled when nobody in the congregation faulted the preacher, because he was "in the spirit."[2]

Throughout his career, Washington criticized the black clergy and overly emotional black church services. In an article that he wrote for the *Christian Union* on August 14, 1890, Washington contended that many black Baptist ministers and Methodist clergy were "unfit, either mentally or morally, or both" to preach the Gospel to anyone."[3] He insisted that their "greatest object was to collect their salaries. "They care no more for the moral and intellectual training of the people than they care for the snap of their finger."[4] He went on to say that "with few exceptions, the minister considers himself successful in proportion as he is able to set the people in all parts of the congregation to groaning, uttering wild screams, and finally going into a trance."[5]

Because of such clergy and such services of worship, Washington offered that most people of color in the South—even church members—were "just as ignorant of true Christianity, as taught by Christ, as any people in Africa or Japan, and just as much in need of missionary efforts as those in foreign lands."[6] As a consequence, throughout his life, Washington urged the creation of nondenominational Bible training schools to teach black ministers about the Bible, how to prepare sermons, how to read hymns, how to study, and how to reach and help people "in an unselfish Christian way."[7]

This attitude was reflected at Tuskegee, of which he wrote in his autobiography, "The school is strictly undenominational, but it is thoroughly Christian, and the spiritual side of the students is not neglected. Our preaching services, prayer meetings, Sunday school, Christian Endeavor Society, YMCA, and various missionary organizations testify to this."[8] Washington required his students to attend twenty-five–minute services at the college chapel on Tuesdays and Thursdays, at which he frequently spoke. He also held short prayer services every evening except Saturday.

Typical of Washington's chapel talks was one that he gave two years before his death, in which he said: "I suspect that each of your parents would like to know that you are learning your Bible; not only to read it because you have to, but to read it every day of the year because you have learned to love the Bible; because you have learned day by day to make its teachings part of you....[N]o matter how busy the day may be, no matter how many mistakes, no matter how many failures you make in other directions, do not fail to find a few minutes to study or read your Bible. The greatest people in the world...are persons who are not ashamed to let the world know not only that they believe in the Bible, but that they read it."[9]

Prayer and Bible reading were the core of Washington's religious experience—far more important than identification with any organized church or denomination. He led family prayers each morning and each evening. His daughter recalled that he read the Bible each day at breakfast. "Really, he prayed all the time,"[10] she asserted. In every room of his mansion, the Oaks, there was a Bible, so that family, friends, and visitors could occupy any spare moments in the study of God's word. Tuskegee's campus barber reminisced about Washington, "If he was sitting down when you walked in, you at almost any time would see him reading [the Bible]."[11]

There is no evidence as to how Washington interpreted the Bible. Obviously, he was enough of a traditionalist to believe that God was accessible and answered prayer. We have seen how he attributed the end of slavery and his own success in life to prayer. He believed that the Bible provided the key to an ethical and successful life. He seemed to believe that Christian faith would not only result in material success for the Negro, but that it would diminish the hostility of whites. Noting the increased number of lynchings in the United States, and growing hostility between blacks and whites, he spoke of the possibility of a "reformation," insisting, "Nothing but the spirit of religion and education vitalized in every community, North and South, will do it."[12]

As he made clear at the Moody revival meeting, Booker T. Washington had a simple faith, centered around prayer and Scripture reading. The man or woman or child who put trust in God and read the Scriptures would be reformed not only spiritually but socially. While he nowhere taught that material blessings are the right of everyone properly disposed toward God, he strongly felt that any earthly success achieved by a man or woman is due to prayer and the ensuing grace of God. And he likewise felt that racial harmony could never be attained except through spiritual reformation on the part of both blacks and whites.

～

Profile 44

Louis Dembitz Brandeis

Born: Louisville, Kentucky, November 13, 1856
Died: Washington, D. C., October 5, 1941

Associate Justice of the Supreme Court for more than two decades, Louis Brandeis was the first Jew to serve on that body. A native of Kentucky, he came from a family of assimilated German Jews who never attended religious services and who celebrated Christmas as a secular holiday for the exchange of gifts.

Brandeis's mother wrote, "I do not believe that sins can be expiated by going to divine service and observing this or that formula." She insisted that the only thing that mattered was "goodness and truth and conduct that is humane and self-sacrificing," and that "our errors can only be atoned for by acting in a more kindly spirit."[1] For Brandeis, who never studied Hebrew or had a bar mitzvah, religion was a matter of ethical conduct.

Until he was in his fifties, Brandeis seemed to regard his Jewishness as unimportant. He expressed no objection when his brother married a Gentile, and later approved of his daughter's marriage to a Christian. His wife was Jewish, but they were married in a civil service by the founder of the New York Society for Ethical Culture.[2]

Just before his appointment to the Supreme Court, Brandeis became involved in Zionism, the movement to establish a national homeland for Jews. He expressed a desire to create a small, self-governing nation that would exemplify the values of Judaism, as well as provide a home for persecuted Jews from various nations.[3] He hoped this homeland would prove to be a New Athens, which would exemplify democracy and preserve the Jewish heritage.

For Brandeis, this heritage was mainly cultural, rather than religious. He declared that the Jews "gave to the world its three greatest religions, reverence for law, and the highest concepts of morality.... Our teaching of brotherhood and righteousness has, under the name of democracy and social justice, become the twentieth-century striving of America and of western Europe. Our conception of law is embodied in the American constitution which proclaims this to be 'a government of laws and not of men.' "[4]

To the end of his life, Brandeis was nonobservant. He never attended synagogue and continued to set up Christmas trees in his home, a practice which, according to one of his daughters, had "no religious significance whatsoever."[5] Those who knew him well said that he was "puzzled by people who relied on God and religious institutions."[6] Late in life, he told an acquaintance, "I do not understand what you mean by experiencing God's presence. I have faced many trials, had to make grave decisions, tasted of the sweet and bitter, was depressed and elated, worked and studied, and thought and meditated. I have lived through many a moment in which, according to the faithful, God should have spoken and helped." He found no evidence of divine intervention in his life. "I sensed no power outside myself working along me with," he continued. "Nor would I describe what was going on in me as supernatural, irrational, or mysterious. I believe that I was reasoning through by concentrating and recalling what good men had said and done before me."[7]

Similarly, Brandeis was critical of the idea of resurrection. "I know how we love our precious little body," he said, "how much attention some bestow on it, and how loath we are to part from it, if part we do. I am not unacquainted with the weakness of man and his conceitedness and I can understand that in the infancy of the race he was impelled to mistake death for a long sleep. But that human beings should be under the illusion to this day attests [to] both the deep darkness in the human mind and the failure of education and science."[8]

Brandeis' secular approach to Judaism was reflected in his funeral, which took place in his Washington apartment. No rabbi officiated. An assistant secretary of state spoke the eulogy. A violin quartet played selections from Beethoven.

～

Profile 45
Thomas Woodrow Wilson

Born: Staunton, Virginia, December 28, 1856
Died: Washington, D. C., February 3, 1924

The former president of Princeton University and governor of New Jersey who occupied the White House during the years of World War I was one of the most outspokenly Christian men to hold the office of the American presidency. The son of a Presbyterian minister, Woodrow Wilson was active throughout his life in the denomination in which he had been reared. He served at one time as an elder in the Second Presbyterian Church of Princeton, New Jersey, and, upon moving to Washington, continued his lifelong habit of Sunday worship. He first attended the New York Avenue Presbyterian Church, near the White House, but, nine months after his inauguration, he laid the cornerstone for the new Central Presbyterian Church, of which he became an active member when it opened. Whether in Washington, at his summer home in Cornish, New Hampshire, or on the road, he faithfully attended services of worship, despite the annoyance of gawkers and secret service agents.

A rare exception to his habit of worship occurred in January 1914, when he failed to attend services in a Mississippi town. He apologized in writing to the Presbyterian pastor there, who had been expecting him and his family. He explained: "We have such a feeling for the Sabbath and for the sacredness of worship that it is peculiarly distasteful to us to have our attendance on church made a spectacle of. We have known that inasmuch as we were expected at your church it was surrounded by photographers and moving picture men and persons curious merely to observe us, and it is that circumstance and that alone...which has kept us away."[1] In Washington and in Cornish, however, the press proved cooperative and allowed the Wilsons to worship in peace.

Not only did Wilson attend Sunday services, he led his family (he had three daughters by his first wife) in morning and evening prayers, and made it a habit of reading a portion from the Scriptures just be-

fore going to bed. A strict observer of the Sabbath, he not only re-
frained from official business on Sunday but also refused to attend
sports or theatrical events as well.[2]

During his presidency, Wilson remarked to friends, "My life would
not be worth living, if it were not for the driving power of religion, for
faith, pure and simple. I have seen all my life the arguments against it
without ever having been moved by them." He once told a friend,
"Never for a moment have I had one doubt about my religious beliefs.
There are people who believe only so far as they understand—that
seems to me presumptuous and sets their understanding as the standard of the universe. Why shouldn't Helen's dog Hamisch here set up
his understanding as a standard? I am sorry for such people."[3] Wilson
always referred to Jesus Christ as his "Lord and Savior." In a speech in
Denver in May 1911, he spoke of the Savior as "a man marked in the
history of mankind as the chosen instrument of God to do justice and
exalt righteousness in the people."[4] In another speech in the same year,
he declared: "Jesus came, as the Scriptures themselves say, in the fullness of time, after mankind had gone through the long struggle...
typified in the characters and the history of the Old Testament. He
had not come unbidden. He did not come unheralded. The world had
been struggling toward him. Then he stepped out as one who should
say, 'I am He'; one who would illustrate what mankind was striving
for in all the dim history of the past."[5]

Woodrow Wilson believed that Christianity was "the most vitaliz-
ing thing in the world," the only force that could transform life and
bring about a prosperous nation and a peaceful and happy world. He
told a gathering of the Federal Council of Churches in Columbus,
Ohio, in December 1915, that "Christianity is a vital body of conceptions, which can be translated into life for us—life in this world and a
life still greater in the next. Except as Christianity changes and in-
spires life, it has failed of its mission. That is what Christ came into the
world for, to save our spirits."[6] "Christianity," he declared, was the
"only force in the world that does actually transform the life," as a
result of which "men begin suddenly to erect great spiritual standards
over the little personal standards which they heretofore professed and
will walk smiling to the stake in order that their souls may be true to

themselves."[7] That "one man's soul is of equal value with another man's soul," Wilson insisted, was "the discovery of Christianity," a religion "based upon the proposition that every man stands directly responsible to his Maker, and that therefore his standard of right is external to himself and eternal in the heavens."[8] The Bible reveals "a standard set for us in the heavens...which is the fixed and eternal standard by which we judge ours lives."[9]

By transforming the lives of individuals, Christianity transforms the world—and saves humankind. He told an audience in Buffalo, New York, in November 1916, that "Christianity was just as much intended to save society as to save the individual."[10] Wilson felt that the only thing that separated races and nations was "difference of thoughts, difference of point of view, prompted by difference of traditions, difference of experiences, difference in instruction." If, however, "all the world had a common literature [and]...had drunk at the same sources of inspiration and suggestion, many lines of division would... disappear." He therefore felt that the world must be Christianized, believing that "in proportion as men yield themselves to the kindly light of the Gospel, they are bound together in the bonds of mutual understanding and assured peace." He wished to spread the Gospel "to make all the nations of the world of one mind, of one enlightenment, of one motive, driven through every effort of their lives by one devotion and one allegiance—to Jesus Christ."[11]

Wilson believed that scholarship was most fruitful when it was conducted under Christian auspices, a point which he made at the opening of the American University in Washington in May 1914. He insisted that "scholarship has never, as far as I can...recollect, been associated with any religion except the religion of Jesus Christ."[12] Moreover he told a conference of Methodist leaders in Baltimore in March 1915 that wars will never have any ending until human beings cease to hate one another, and that this would come about through "the single supreme plan of peace, our relation to our Lord and Savior, Jesus Christ."[13]

Wilson was outspoken in his insistence that "America was born a Christian nation," he declared in a speech in Denver in the spring of 1911. "America was born to exemplify that devotion to the elements of righteousness which are derived from the revelations of Holy Scriptures." Accordingly, progress could never be divorced from the Christian faith.[14]

Citizens of the United States had an obligation to study the Bible. "Part of the destiny of America lies in daily perusal of this great book of revelations—that if they would see America free and pure they will make their own spirits free and pure by this baptism of the Holy Scripture."[15] When, in 1917, Wilson led the country into the Great War, he saw to it that service people were issued Bibles, accompanied by his personal message: "The Bible is the word of life. I beg that you will read it and find this out for yourself—read, not little snatches here and there, but long passages that will really be the road to the heart of it.... When you have read the Bible you will know that it is the Word of God, because you will have found it the key to your own heart, your own happiness, and your own duty."[16] He felt that people who rejected the Bible were "simply groping and staggering in their ignorance to a fearful day of judgment."[17]

As might be imagined, Wilson's religious views had political ramifications. He seemed at times to feel that he was a messenger of God, especially after he involved the nation in the World War. At first, he sincerely tried to keep America out of war. Shortly after hostilities broke out in Europe, Wilson set aside October 4, 1914, as a day of prayer, in which he requested "all God-fearing persons to repair on that day to their places of worship there to unite their petitions to Almighty God that he vouchsafe his children healing peace again and restore once more that concord among men and nations."[18]

When, however, two and a half years later, he entered the war, he did not, like Lincoln, agonize over God's will. On the contrary, Wilson had no doubt that the United States and her allies were on the side of God. Even before the war, before he was elected president, Wilson, in a campaign speech, spoke of his "confident hope" that the United States was "prominently chosen to show the way to the nations of the world how they shall walk in the paths of liberty."[19] Now he called on America to fight to "make the world safe for democracy." He equated American-style democracy with Christian civilization, and in this spirit, in a speech to Confederate veterans in June 1917, he declared that "we are to be an instrument in the hands of God to see that liberty is made secure for mankind."[20]

When the war was over, Wilson, who personally attended the peace conference in Paris, seemed to feel that his own peace proposals embodied God's own plan for world peace. French Premier Georges Clemenceau privately complained of Wilson, "He thinks he is another Jesus Christ come upon the earth to reform men."[21] Unhappy and disappointed at being forced to compromise with his allies, Wilson returned to the United States convinced that the hope of humanity lay in his country's consent to be a part of the League of Nations that he had proposed. His struggle to make the Senate approve the peace treaty without altering his plans in any way took on the aspect of a holy crusade, and ended by alienating the Republican opposition to the point of destroying any chance of ratification—and bringing on a major stroke that incapacitated him physically and mentally. When the Senate rejected his version of the League of Nations, the ailing president was convinced that this action was tantamount to a rejection of God's will. He remarked to his doctor, "The devil is a busy man."[22]

Although Wilson was a sincere and devout Christian, his personality led many of his opponents to accuse him of hypocrisy. He impressed many people as being a cold, inflexible man. He once told a friend who reminded him that there were two sides to every question, "Yes— the right and the wrong."[23] When his ambassador to Great Britain tried to get him to listen to opinions different from his own, Wilson, "sprung up, stuck his fingers in his ears, and, still holding them there, ran out of the room."[24]

Because Wilson seemed so self-righteous, failings which in others might be attributed to the weaknesses of human nature seem magnified in him. For instance, despite his lofty talk of universal brotherhood, Wilson was generally regarded by black Americans as a cruel bigot, who supported racial segregation and endorsed the grotesquely negrophobic movie, *Birth of a Nation*.[25] When delegates from the National Independence Equal Rights League, led by black activist William Monroe Trotter, appeared at the White House in November 1914 to protest segregation in offices, cafeterias, and toilets in various government buildings, Wilson was completely unsympathetic. He told the delegation that the policy of segregation, endorsed by his administration, was "not to put the Negro employees at a disadvantage," but to "make arrangements which would prevent any kind of friction between the white employees and the Negro employees."[26] He went on to say, "I want to help the colored people in every way I can, but there are some ways, some things that I could do myself that would hurt them more than it would help them"[27] When the delegation warned that he would lose the support of Afro-American voters, Wilson was offended, and urged black people to vote for someone else if they did not like his policies. When Trotter accused Wilson of taking a position inconsistent with his professed Christianity, the president exploded in anger and ordered the delegation out of his office.

Wilson did not think of himself as narrow or bigoted, however. Reportedly, he told another group of Negro leaders, "Segregation is not humiliating, but a benefit, and ought to be so regarded by you gentlemen."[28] In November 1915, a year after his meeting with Trotter, in an address on preparedness, he declared, "We should rebuke not only manifestations of racial feeling here in America where there should be none, but also every manifestation of religious and sectarian antagonism." In denouncing religious bigotry, he said, "We agree to differ about methods of worship, but we are united in believing in Divine Providence and in worshiping the God of Nations."[29] He believed that if each individual read the Bible, directly drinking "at the sources of divine inspiration without overmuch intervention and interpretation,"[30] there would be greater harmony among the different sects of Christians.

Wilson was a private man. Although he tended to be cold—even arrogant and supercilious—to strangers, he could be warm and loving to family and friends. Most of his published statements about religion were given in public addresses, but there is abundant evidence that his faith permeated his entire existence. He was aware of his temper and frequently regretted his outbursts. He was aware that he was a sinner sustained only by the saving mercy of his Savior, to whom he looked for forgiveness and help.

He felt that God had a hand in everything, good or evil, that happened. When his first wife died, he wrote a friend, "God has stricken me almost beyond what I can bear."[31] He later wrote her that "faith in

God's providence" sustained him more than anything else. Without such a faith, he confided, "I think I should go mad."[32] Two years later he told the Confederate veterans, "The wise heart never questions the dealings of Providence, because the great long plan, as it unfolds, has a majesty about it and a definiteness of purpose, an elevation of an ideal, which we were incapable of conceiving as we tried to work things out with our own short sight and weak strength."[33]

Two years after he left office, still incapacitated, he wrote his pastor, "I sometimes get discouraged at the exceedingly slow progress of my recovery, but I am ashamed of myself when I do because God has been so manifestly merciful to me, and I ought to feel much profound gratitude. I believe that it will turn out well, and that whether well or ill, it will turn out right."[34] His health never improved, and, less than a year later, he died. When his doctor told him that he was dying, he said, "I am ready. I am a broken piece of machinery. When the machinery is broken....I am ready. You have been good to me. You have done everything you could."[35] A little later, seeing that his house on S Street, NW, in Washington was crowded with specialists, he remarked, "Sometimes too many cooks spoil the broth."[36] He spoke for the last time to his dearly loved second wife, Edith. He had written to her, shortly before their marriage in 1915, "God comes to a man, I think, through the trust and love of a sweet, pure woman. Certainly God seems very near when I am with you."[37] It was to her that Woodrow Wilson spoke his last word: "Edith."

～

Profile 46
William Howard Taft

Born: Cincinnati, Ohio, September 15, 1857
Died: Washington, D.C., March 8, 1930

The only individual to date to hold (at different times) the offices of president of the United States and chief justice of the Supreme

Court has been characterized as a man of "childlike frankness" who displayed "unstudied naturalness," who—almost unheard of in a politician—"said what he thought without the slightest regard for how it would sound or read."[1] He was born into a wealthy and prominent Cincinnati family that has been described by a biographer as "not...religious."[2] His father, Alphonso Taft, who served as attorney general and then secretary of war under Ulysses Grant and minister to Austria-Hungary and later Russia under Chester A. Arthur, was a Unitarian. "Big Bill" and his siblings attended the Western Unitarian Conference Church along with their parents. Biographer Henry Pringle, writing shortly after the statesman's death, concluded that throughout his life, for Taft and most of his family, "religion...was a matter of relatively slight importance."[3]

When he was in his early forties, Taft summarized his beliefs in a letter to one of his brothers: "I am a Unitarian. I believe in God. I do not believe in the Divinity of Christ, and there are many other of the postulates of the orthodox creed to which I cannot subscribe. I am not, however, a scoffer at religion, but, on the contrary, recognize, in the fullest manner, the elevating influence that it has had and always will have in the history of mankind."[4] Because of his rejection of Christ's divinity, there were many who opposed his candidacy for president in 1908 solely on the grounds that he was an unbeliever. Taft refused to discuss his religion during the campaign. He wrote one of his supporters, "Of course, I am interested in the spread of Christian civilization, but to go into a dogmatic discussion of creed I will not do, whether I am defeated or not....If the American electorate is so narrow as not to elect a Unitarian, well and good. I can stand it."[5] With the solid backing of his predecessor, Theodore Roosevelt, whom he had served as secretary of war, Taft captured the White House.

Taft, during his many years in Washington, both as president and chief justice, attended All Souls Unitarian. His wife and daughter were active in the Episcopal church.

William Howard Taft was not so casual as that about his religion. He was a strong believer in the ethical teachings of the Bible and in "Christian civilization." He also believed that God had a hand in the affairs of human beings. In 1925, the chief justice, whose health was beginning to fail, wrote his son, "...when I wake up in the morning and get dressed and come to breakfast, I thank the Lord for another day."[6]

A short address that he gave to the youth group at All Souls, just a few months before his death, reveals the sentiments of Taft, at least as an old man, that religion is a life of integrity and service. He told them: "You are already dreaming of what you are going to accomplish in life. I hope your dreams will come true; but, remember, you do not make a failure because those dreams do not come true—if you really make yourself useful to all about you, and have character, strength, honesty, religious feeling, and obligation to God so that you are serving somebody else besides yourself. After all, when you come to the end of your life, the only comfort, the only real satisfaction you have, is in the good you have done for others."[7]

～

Profile 47
Theodore Roosevelt

Born: New York, New York, October 27, 1858
Died: Oyster Bay, New York, January 6, 1919

To do justice and to love kindness, and to walk humbly with your God"—these words from Micah 6:8 were the favorite Bible verse of the scientist-soldier-writer-explorer-public servant who served as America's twenty-sixth president. Of that verse he commented, "That is my religion, my faith. To me it sums up all religion, it is all the creed I need. It seems simply and easy, but there is more in that verse than in the involved rituals and confessions of faith of many creeds we know."[1]

Although he was faithful in his outward performance of his religious duties, T.R. was notoriously reluctant to talk about his personal beliefs or spiritual life, even with his own family. One of his sons was able to recall to a biographer only that his father stressed that a person's actions "talked" more than words.[2] It seems clear that Theodore Roosevelt's religion was one of deed rather than creed.

When he was forty-two and a candidate for vice president, he wrote in an article in *Century* magazine, "The prime worth of creed is to be gauged by the standard of conduct it exacts among its followers toward their fellows."[3] Seven years later, when he was president, in a talk at his alma mater Harvard, T.R. said, "The religious man who is most useful is not he whose sole care is to save his own soul, but the man whose religion bids him strive to advance decency and clean living and to make the world a better place for his fellows to live."[4]

For him, a true Christian was one who lived in such a way "that when death comes he may feel that mankind is in some degree better because he has lived."[5] This is what T.R. strove to accomplish in his public career. He was one of the first presidents to believe that the role of government is to help people in need. He fought to protect "the little man" by regulating business and industry and by promoting legislation to conserve natural resources and to ensure the public's access to wholesome food and drugs. He literally fought to advance his ideals when he resigned his position as assistant secretary of the Navy in 1898 to raise a regiment to fight in Cuba so that the people of that island might enjoy the benefits of democracy. He was willing to take up arms again during the First World War, which he regarded as a battle between the righteousness of democracy and the evil of militaristic tyranny. His commitment to justice, mercy, and humility was evident also in his private life. There was never so much as a whisper of a scandal in sexual or financial affairs. Everyone who knew him testified to the moral purity of his life. He never told bawdy stories and would not permit others to tell them in his presence.[6] No one ever heard him use interjections stronger than "By George!" or "Bully!"

Roosevelt believed that it was important for people to go to church. Churchgoing built those moral qualities essential for the just and democratic society that he strove to promote. Late in life he wrote that "a community where men have abandoned...their religious needs is a community on the rapid down grade."[7] He urged all Americans to go to church or synagogue: "I know all the excuses, I know that one can worship the Creator and dedicate oneself to good living in a grove of trees or by a running brook, or in one's own house, just as well as in church. But I also know that as a matter of cold fact the average man does not thus worship or thus dedicate himself."[8]

Roosevelt was a lifelong member of the Dutch Reformed Church, and, while president, each Sunday he was in town, he walked, accompanied by a few secret service agents, several blocks from the White House to Grace Reformed Church. According to those who observed him, "he always went through all of the ritual" and regularly partook of holy Communion.[9] He frequently read the Bible on his own, but nobody ever saw him pray, except in church. One friend told an interviewer, "I never saw him in formal prayer, but as prayer is the desire of the heart, [I] think he prayed without ceasing, for the desire of his heart was always to do right."[10] For T. R., true prayer was putting the moral teachings of the Bible into practice.

Roosevelt believed strongly in religious toleration: "I have the profoundest respect for all denominations: Protestant, Catholic, and Hebrew. In my individual contact with men I have found the most splendid people imaginable holding these various beliefs."[11] He insisted that "the greatest enemy of true democracy is religious prejudice."[12] He took pride that his cabinet included representatives of all three faiths. "In no case does the man's religious belief in any way influence his discharge of his duties save as it makes him more eager to act justly and uprightly in all his relations to all men," he insisted.[13] Outraged that any American would vote for or against any candidate on religious grounds, in a speech to the Knights of Columbus (a Roman Catholic organization) in 1915, he declared: "The Constitution explicitly forbids the requiring of any religious test as a qualification for holding office. To impose such a test by popular vote is as bad as to impose by law."[14] On another occasion he wrote: "To discriminate against a thoroughly upright citizen because he belongs to some particular church is an outrage against that liberty of conscience which is one of the foundations of American life. You are entitled to know whether a man seeking your suffrages is a man of clean and upright life, honorable in all of his dealings with his fellows, and fit by qualification and purpose to do well in the great office for which he is a candidate; but you are not entitled to know matters which lie purely between himself and his Maker."[15]

Accordingly, Roosevelt believed strongly in the separation of church and state. He alienated many religious people when, during his presidency, he tried to end the practice of imprinting the words, "In God We Trust" on United States coins, believing that the practice served no useful purpose, trivialized religion, and was contrary to the "spirit of reverence."[16] Although he had no objection, in places "where local sentiment favors it" to the practice of teachers reading "a few verses of the ethical or moral parts of the Bible, so long as this causes no offense to any one," he felt that it was "entirely wrong" to legislate compulsory Bible reading or prayer. "I believe in absolutely nonsectarian public schools," he wrote in 1915. "It is not our business to have the Protestant Bible or the Catholic Vulgate or the Talmud read in those schools."[17]

For Roosevelt, the essence of religion was upright conduct. His was a totally this-worldly faith. He had little interest in spiritual or supernatural matters. According to his friend, William Allen White, T.R. defined God as "the personality" of "the moral government of the universe."[18] Another friend related that for Roosevelt, God was "the Great Power behind the universe" that "makes for righteousness."[19] He never discussed the divinity of Christ. Those who knew him best felt that the subject did not interest him. One friend explained, "He did not endeavor to explain the godward side of Jesus, but was attracted to and imitated his manward side of service."[20]

Roosevelt was impatient with the sort of faith that "subordinated the development of the race on this earth to the well-being of the individual in the next."[21] T.R. apparently did not believe in life beyond the grave. When he was in his twenties and feeling guilty about his marriage to Edith Carow so soon after the death, in childbirth, of his first wife Alice Lee, he wrote his sister, "Were I sure there were a heaven, my one prayer would be that I might never go there, lest I meet those I loved on earth who are dead."[22] On another occasion, he spoke of death as "the everlasting darkness."[23]

"Death is always and under all circumstances, a tragedy," he wrote an English friend when he was a young man, "for if it is not, then it means life itself has become one. But it is well to live bravely and joyously, and to face the inevitable end without flinching when we go to join the men and tribes of [time] immemorial."[24] Such was

Roosevelt's attitude twenty years later when, shattered by the death of one of his sons in war as well as by numerous ailments and injuries, he felt the approach of death, which, like life, he professed to be "a part of the same Great Adventure."[25] Just before the end, he wrote a friend, "It is idle to complain or rail at the inevitable; serene and high of heart we must face our fate and go down into the darkness."[26]

For Theodore Roosevelt, religion was moral conduct; it was righteous living; it was social justice. Not long before his death he declared that "the essence of religion" was "to be just with all men, to be merciful to those to whom mercy should be shown, to realize that there are some things that must always remain a mystery to us, and when the time comes for us to enter the great blackness, to go smiling and unafraid."[27] From all evidence, as Theodore Roosevelt faced the expected prospect of eternity, he did so with the satisfaction that in his sixty years on the earth he had done justly, loved mercy, and walked humbly with his God.

～

Profile 48
William Jennings Bryan

Born: Salem, Illinois, March 19, 1860
Died: Dayton, Tennessee, July 26, 1925

Despite his three unsuccessful attempts to capture the presidency, the Great Commoner was one of the most influential statesmen of the first quarter of the twentieth century. Beginning his career as a congressman from Nebraska, he first gained national prominence through his advocacy of the interests of America's rural heartland. Through most of his career, he fiercely supported the rights of the majority against the tyranny of big government, big business, and, also, as we shall see, big religion. The pinnacle of his public career was his appointment as secretary of state under Woodrow Wilson in 1913. During the last decade of his life, Bryan devoted most of his energies to the propagation of the Christian faith, and incurred much ridicule from intellectuals for his forceful opposition to the theory of evolation.

Bryan played a leading role in bringing about such reforms as the regulation of railroads, prohibition, voting rights for women, the income tax, and the election of U.S. Senators by the voters of each state (instead of the legislatures)—all of which were intended to benefit the common citizen. Bryan also believed that each citizen had the right to worship as he or she pleased, without government interference.

Bryan, the son of a judge in rural Illinois and one of several children, was the product of a religious home. The family prayed at the beginning of each day, at noon, and at night, when the parents read to the children from the Bible just before bedtime.[1] Bryan's father was a Baptist and his mother was a Methodist, and the children had to attend the Sunday school of each parent. Participating in two Sunday-school classes each Sunday, far from generating resentment in young Will, gave him, as he claimed in later years, "a double interest in Sunday-school work."[2] It also gave him an ecumenical outlook. For him, the most important thing was that a man or woman make a commitment to Christ as Savior. Denomination was relatively unimportant. Although he later came to describe Roman Catholicism as "the greatest branch of the Christian Church,"[3] he was never a member of that denomination, perhaps because its leaders did not share his ecumenicity.

At fourteen, Will Bryan joined a Presbyterian church near his home in Salem, Illinois. Church membership did not change his habits of life or thought, Bryan later affirmed, for he did not "know of a virtue that came into my life as a result of joining the church, because all the virtues had been taught me by my parents."[4] Bryan therefore never had a real conversion experience because he never rejected or ignored the teachings of his devout parents.

Bryan later claimed, "I passed through a period of skepticism when I was in college."[5] This occurred when he studied Darwin and found it difficult to reconcile the theories of the British scientist with the teachings of his parents. After a short period of soul-searching, however, Bryan committed himself to his boyhood teachings, rejected totally the teachings of Darwin, began to attend Sunday school at the local

Presbyterian Church, and told his friends that he believed that God was calling him, not to be a minister, but a Christian politician.[6]

Bryan, who with his wife, Mary Baird, was a member of the Westminister Presbyterian Church in Lincoln, but frequently attended a small Methodist church near their home, Fairview, continued, with their three children, the devotional practices that he had learned from his parents. The family opened the day with devotions. Bryan read from the Bible, then Mary gathered the family around the piano to sing hymns before the short service was concluded with prayer.[7] Later in life, when he and his wife were living in Miami, Florida, he taught a Tourist Bible Class. Throughout his life, he spoke at churches and Chautauqua assemblies, and for many years published syndicated Sunday-school lessons.

Bryan's daughter Grace characterized him as "a Christian statesman before he was a Democrat, and, patriot though he was, his God came before his country."[8] He often stated that he was ready to sacrifice his political career, and even his respect, to advance his religion. Many felt that he was, certainly in his later years, more of an evangelist than a politician. He was an approachable man, witty and playful, who did not smoke, drink, curse, or tell or listen to dirty jokes. He had a warm and faithful relationship with his wife, who was an attorney and his chief political advisor. He was uncommonly devoted to her, especially during the last years of their married life, when she was confined to a wheelchair because of arthritis. Norman Vincent Peale, the celebrated preacher and author, said that Bryan had "the peace of God inwardly."[9]

Bryan felt strongly that a Christian's beliefs should be reflected in actions and in interpersonal relationships. Christians were obliged to work to change society and help the unfortunate. Late in life he wrote a friend, "The Christian must live his religion in business as well as at home."[10] Christ's commandment to love one's neighbor as oneself meant that Christians were to attempt to "solve every problem economic, social, political, and religious."[11]

A major focus for Christian social action, Bryan believed, was the prevention of war. "The Gospel of the Prince of Peace gives us the only hope that the world has…of the substitution of reason for the arbitrament of force in the settlement of international disputes," he declared.[12] Bryan opposed the Spanish-American War and the American occupation of the Philippines. As secretary of state, he vigorously opposed American involvement in World War I, and eventually resigned in protest over Wilson's aggressive policy. He was appalled at the grisly carnage taking place. Speaking in Madison Square Garden, he declared, "They have exhausted human ingenuity to find new ways in which man may kill his fellow man. And these are not barbarous nations, they are among the Christian nations of the globe...."[13] Although he opposed war and fought policies and decisions that made war likely, if not inevitable, once the United States was formally at war, Bryan supported his government, even to the point of actually joining the armed services in the Spanish-American War and offering to do so when American entered the World War I. "Gladly would I have given my life to save my country from war," he said at the time, "but now that my country has gone to war, gladly will I give my life to aid it."[14]

All the reforms which Bryan backed were an extension of his religious involvement. Some of Bryan's positions would not be popular in the late twentieth century. For instance, he was a strong supporter of Prohibition. Although he was more responsive to the concerns of Black citizens than his contemporaries in the White House—Roosevelt, Taft, and Wilson—he did not endorse the idea of equal political rights for the Negro in the South, insisting that blacks, as a group, were unprepared to exercise political power. He also wanted immigration from Asia curtailed. He felt, however, that these policies reflected what was best for the majority of Americans, and he tended to believe that "the voice of the people is the voice of God."

In his understanding of Christianity, Bryan adhered firmly to what came in his day to be known as "fundamentalism." In the early twentieth century, Christians in America and western Europe came to be divided into "modernist" and "fundamentalist" camps. Modernists tended to believe that religious practice should reflect the ideas of the time. Many modernists supported the ideas of Scripture scholars who dismissed as mythic or inauthentic many passages in the Bible. Whereas Thomas Jefferson tended to reject any part of Scripture that did not accord with reason, the modernists of Bryan's day also tended to reject what they found at variance with their interpretation of scientific inquiry. Fundamentalists, on the other hand, took the position that everything in the Scriptures was written under divine inspiration and was therefore without error. Conservative theologians subscribing to this position published a series of 135 essays, early in the century, which came to be known as *The Fundamentals*. They insisted that, to be a Christian, one had to subscribe to the following propositions: (1) the inerrancy of the Bible; (2) the Virgin Birth; (3) the substitutionary atonement (that Christ died as a substitute for the guilty human race, which he thereby restored to union with God); (4) the physical Resurrection; and (5) the Second Coming of Christ. William Jennings Bryan subscribed to these fundamentals.

Bryan believed in the divinity of Christ. He also believed that Christ worked miracles in the present day and could heal in response to prayer.[15] If a person denied one miracle recorded in Scripture, he thereby denied the possibility of all miracles.[16] He believed in heaven and hell, and, shortly before his death, revealed his attitude toward the future life in a letter to an old friend, when he wrote, "Old age would be unbearable if it brought an end to so intimate a relationship, but we have the satisfaction of believing that death is only a narrow starlit strip between the companionships of yesterday and the reunions of tomorrow."[17] He believed that the Bible furnished "an infallible guide throughout life"[18] and "a code of morality superior to anything the world has ever known."[19]

Later in life, Bryan's religious agenda tended to focus on one issue: the opposition to the idea of evolution, as taught by Charles Darwin. He claimed that "Darwinism is the greatest menace to the Christian church and to civilization."[20]

Bryan felt that Darwin's teachings about evolution were of dubious validity and credibility. "To believe in the idea of natural selection," he insisted, "requires more faith in chance than a Christian is required to have in God."[21] His greatest objection was because of its effects on those who subscribed to it. "The objection to evolution," he wrote "is not primarily that it is not true....The principal objection to evolution is that it is highly harmful to those who accept it."[22] Bryan felt that Darwin's theories put "the creative act so far away that reverence for the creator is likely to be lost."[23] Darwin's insistence that human beings evolved from lower forms of life made man just another animal, and, according to Bryan, robbed him of "dignity, uniqueness, and superiority."[24] He was especially disturbed by the attempts of those people who called themselves "Social Darwinists" to apply Darwin's ideas to human relationships. He felt that Social Darwinism condoned the oppression of the poor and weak by the rich and strong, strengthened "class pride and the power of wealth," and undermined democracy.[25] He noted with horror that Social Darwinism had taken strong root in Germany, which had become infected with "that damnable doctrine that might makes right."[26] He felt that the World War I was largely to be attributed to the effects of Social Darwinism. In the 1920s, the horrors of Communism in Russia, labor violence in many countries, and the violent, racist, nationalistic, totalitarian ideology increasingly popular in Germany, he laid squarely at the door of Charles Darwin and his theory of evolution. "The Darwinian theory," he cried, "represents man as reaching his present perfection by the operation of the law of hate—the merciless law by which the strong crowd out and kill off the weak."[27] Despite the depth of his feelings, Bryan was not a fanatic. To a liberal minister who wrote him a letter, criticizing his views, Bryan responded, "I hope that we are in agreement on this, that God overrules in the affairs of men and will bring victory to which ever side is right...I am more anxious that the right shall triumph than that my view shall, if I am mistaken."[28]

As a delegate to the annual General Assembly of the Presbyterian Church in the USA in 1922, 1923, and 1924, Bryan demanded unsuccessfully that the assembly pass a resolution condemning Darwinian evolution. He was especially concerned about the teaching of evolution in public schools. Believing that Christian taxpayers should insist on complete neutrality on religious issues on the part of teachers,[29] he felt that the teaching of evolution was the result of school boards, influenced by a religious elite of modernist theologians, imposing upon the public an idea that was rejected by a majority of Americans. Just as he wanted to take government out of the hands of political bosses, he wanted "to take the church out of the hands of the [religious] bosses and put it in the hands of worshippers."[30] This assumption was, to a large extent, behind his effort to persuade state legislatures to curtail the teaching of evolution.

In June 1923, Oklahoma banned textbooks favorable to evolution. Then Tennessee passed a law banning the teaching of evolution outright. Thereupon the American Civil Liberties Union, condemning the ban, offered to provide counsel to any Tennessee teacher willing to defy the new law so that its constitutionality could be tested. John Scopes, a science teacher in Dayton, Tennessee, was persuaded to stand as defendant. The defense team included the flamboyant and irreligious trial lawyer, Clarence Darrow. Bryan, although now seriously ill with diabetes and heart trouble, eagerly accepted the invitation to join the prosecution team. And, so, in July 1925, the Monkey Trial became a media circus whose proceedings were broadcast over the radio waves and occupied the attention of the American public for days.

Bryan declared that the real issue was "the right of the people, speaking through the legislature, to control the schools which they create and support";[31] whether "a minority in the state can come in and compel a teacher to teach that the Bible is not true and make the parents of these children pay the expenses."[32]

Before the trial ended in the upholding of Scopes's conviction and the ban on the teaching of evolution in Tennessee (which would persist for another forty years), it degenerated into a sort of carnival when Clarence Darrow was allowed to cross-examine Bryan on his own beliefs. Responding to a question by Darrow, Bryan answered, "I believe everything in the Bible should be accepted as given there; some of the Bible is given illustratively. For instance, 'Ye are the salt of the earth.' I would not insist that man was actually salt or that he had flesh of salt, but it is used in the sense of salt saving God's people."[33] He admitted that he believed that "a big fish" swallowed Jonah and added that if the Bible stated that Jonah himself swallowed the fish or whale, he would not hesitate to believe it. When Darrow asked him if he believed that God actually made the sun stand still—literally and physically—Bryan explained that the Bible was using language that people of the time could understand.[34] Trying to make Bryan appear ignorant, Darrow questioned him on the age of various world civilizations, and asked other questions to which his antagonist could not provide an intelligent answer. At the end of the two-hour ordeal, Bryan seemed to many ignorant and unprepared, and Darrow (who, at one point, shouted, "I am examining you on your fool ideas that no intelligent Christian on earth believes"[35]) seemed spiteful, petty, and vindictive. Most people felt that Bryan's performance at the Scopes Trial was not one of his most effective. Many arch-conservatives were disappointed that he insisted that certain passages of Scripture were symbolic. Others felt that some of his responses reflected a lack of study and preparation. Bryan was, in fact, quite ill by then. He seemed untroubled by criticism. After all, the ban on the teaching of evolution in the schools of Tennessee was upheld. In the next few months, three other Southern states would pass similar laws. Besides, Bryan insisted, the most important thing in life was not winning, but, rather, keeping the faith.[36]

Bryan survived the Scopes Trial by but five days. Just before retiring for a nap from which he never awoke, he told his son: "Seems there's hardly time enough for resting, none at all for dying."[37] And so concluded a life spend in behalf of his God and of his people, whom he tried to defend from political, business, religious, and scholarly minorities, to further a democracy of Bible-believing, God-fearing people, which he believed America to be. His bones lie in Arlington National Cemetery, beneath a simple marker reading: "Bryan—He kept the faith."

～

Profile 49
Jane Addams

Born: Cedarville, Illinois, September 6, 1860
Died: Chicago, Illinois, May 21, 1935

The social reformer is best remembered for the Hull-House settlement house which she opened in Chicago in 1889. Hull-House provided such services as social clubs, daycare, medical services, cooking and sewing courses, boarding-house facilities, a playground, and a gymnasium for the working-class people who lived in the neighborhood. Addams also fought for child-labor laws, the recognition of labor unions, industrial safety laws, improved welfare legislation, and successfully lobbied for the creation of the nation's first juvenile court.

Addams, whose mother died when she was very young, was raised by her father, who, on alternating Sundays, attended all four churches (Methodist, Lutheran, Evangelical, Presbyterian) in town and contributed to each, but considered himself Quaker. When she was a little girl, she was troubled when other children spoke of predestination and hellfire. When she asked her father about predestination, he told her that he "didn't have the mind that would ever understand it," and he advised her not to waste too much time thinking about it. It did not matter, he said, "whether one understood foreordination or not," but he insisted that it was "very important not to pretend to understand what you didn't understand, and that you must always be honest with yourself inside."[1] When she told a lie, she lay awake, thinking of what the other children had told her about hell, until she got up and woke her father to confess her misdeed. Her father, who never talked of hell, simply told her that if he "had a little girl who told lies," he was very glad that she "felt too bad to go to sleep afterwards."[2]

Addams attended Rockford Female Seminary, which was founded by Presbyterian and Congregational ministers and had a very strong, traditional religious emphasis, with daily chapel, weekly prayer meetings, a regular monthly fast day, an annual prayer week, in addition to the compulsory Sunday services. While she was there, Addams was under pressure from faculty and other students to "convert" to traditional Christianity, to commit herself to a personal relationship with Jesus Christ. "I was singularly unresponsive to all these forms of emotional appeal," she wrote years later, and was "unspeakably embarrassed" when, on one occasion, a teacher came to her during the "silent hour" which students were required to observe every evening, and tried to press her to make a decision.[3]

She wrote: "The only moments in which I seem to have approximated in my own experience to a faint realization of the 'beauty of holiness,' as I conceived it, was each Sunday morning between the hours of nine and ten, when I went into the exquisitely neat room of the teacher of Greek and read with her from a Greek [New] Testament."[4] None of her teachers or classmates could dissuade her from

her conviction that religion was a matter of actions rather than experiences. She wrote her friend, Ellen Starr, "You long for a beautiful
faith, an experience....I only feel that I need religion in a practical
sense."[5] Another time she wrote: "I have been trying an experiment. I
didn't pray, at least formally, for almost three months, and was shocked
to find that I feel no worse for it."[6] And so, in college she resolved to
shape her own religion, to "go ahead building my religion wherever I
can find it, from the Bible and observation, from books and people,
and in no small degree from [Scottish author Thomas] Carlyle."[7] She
was later strongly influenced, especially in her ideas on pacifism, by
Russian writer Leo Tolstoy.

In her twenties, she decided to join a church, and was baptized and
accepted into membership at the Cedarville Presbyterian Church in
her hometown. Shortly before, she wrote a friend, "I am always floun-
dering when I deal with religious nomenclature or sensations simply
because my religious life has been so small."[8] Later she wrote that
joining church involved "little assent to dogma or miracle." She sought
membership, rather, as "an outward symbol of fellowship, some bond
of peace, some blessed spot where unity of spirit might claim right of
way over all differences."[9] In Chicago, at least during the early years
of Hull-House, she frequently attended All Souls Unitarian Church
and Fourth Presbyterian. For several years she led an evening Bible
class and prayer meeting at Hull-House, and, although she did not
have any formal religious services or instruction, she did make space
available for use by any religious group.

Addams' conception of God was quite vague. Early in life she described God as "a primal cause—not nature exactly, but a fostering
Mother, a necessity, brooding and watching over all things, above every human passion."[10] Not long before she died, she replied to a niece:
"Not a personal one." Pressed to answer whether she believed in any
God at all, she answered, "Part of the time I do and part of the time I
don't."[11] The funeral eulogies that she gave, from time to time, for
friends and supporters, which she published three years before she
died, indicate that she believed that dying was going into the "unknown."

Yet Addams considered herself a Christian. To be sure, she did not believe that Christ was divine. As a young woman she wrote a friend: "Christ don't help me in the least. Sometimes I can work myself into great admiration for his life, and occasionally I can catch something of his philosophy, but he doesn't bring me any nearer to the Deity."[12] She thought of Jesus "simply as a Jew living hundreds of years ago, surrounding whom there is mystery and a beauty incomprehensible to me." Her feelings for and toward Christ were similar to her feeling about "very fine music—that I am incapable of understanding."[13] She believed "in keeping the events, the facts of Christ's life before us and letting the philosophy go."[14]

Addams believed that to be a Christian was to promote the kingdom of God by (in the words of one biographer) "improving working conditions, building better housing and sewerage systems and eventually eliminating poverty."[15] She founded Hull-House as a religious act, as part of what she saw as a "renaissance" of Christianity, as it was originally taught. She wrote in her autobiography about "the impulse to share the lives of the poor, the desire to make social service, irrespective of propaganda," which expressed the true "spirit of Christ." She wrote: "Jesus had no set truths labeled 'religious.' On the contrary, his doctrine was that all truth is one, that the appropriation of it is freedom. He himself called it a revelation—life." Revelation, Addams believed, had to be expressed in concrete action, for "action is the only medium man has for receiving an appropriating truth." She characterized the early Christian believers as "preeminently nonresistant." Moreover, they "believed in love as a cosmic force....[I]t never occurred to them...to regard other men for an instant as their foes or as aliens."[16]

The Christianity of Jane Addams was therefore a totally secular faith. She rejected the assumption "that Christianity is a set of ideas which belong to the religious consciousness, whatever that may be." Christianity could not be practiced "apart from the social life of the community."[17] It involved a commitment to social action, to improving physical conditions in society, and showing love and compassion to all, embodying "the hope of the world and the protection of all who suffer."[18]

∼

Henry Ford

Born: Dearborn, Michigan, July 30, 1863
Died: Dearborn, Michigan, April, 1947

The automobile manufacturer who, through the use of the assembly line and mass production, made the car affordable for the average American, was born on a farm in Michigan. His father, who came to America from Ireland during the potato famine in the 1840s, was a Protestant. In Michigan, William Ford became a warden in the local Episcopal church, but was said to have been a freethinker and an active Mason.[1]

Although Henry, as a young man, used to walk four miles to church each Sunday with his best friend, he admitted that it was for social reasons and that he was "not very religious."[2] Although he was later married and buried according to the rites of the Episcopal church, his religious beliefs were always unconventional, if not bizarre.

In an interview when he was sixty-three, Ford said, "I think the real power of human lives is hidden away with the soul....There are actual entities all about us, entities of force, intelligence....When a man is doing good, they swarm to help him....We rush too much with nervous hands and worried minds. We are impatient for results. What we need...is reinforcement of the soul by the invisible power waiting to be used."[3]

Ford was a fervent believer in reincarnation. "Everything is indestructible," he insisted. "Nothing is ever lost. Souls come and go, and they come again."[4] Ford told a relative, "You know when a person dies, I think their spirit goes into a newborn baby. I think that's why some people are so much further advanced in knowledge than others and are gifted. A man when he dies, if he is a genius, his spirit will go into a newborn baby and that person will be an expert like Einstein or Edison."[5] One of his proofs for reincarnation: "When the automobile was new and one of them came down the road, a chicken would run straight for home—and usually get killed. But today when a car comes along, a chicken will run for the nearest side of the road. That chicken has been hit in the ass in a previous life."[6] He insisted that he was the reincarnation of a soldier killed in the Civil War, which is why he was a pacifist,[7] but attributed his genius to the fact that in a still earlier lifetime, he had been none other than Leonardo da Vinci.[8]

Ford described Jesus as "an old soul."[9] In other words—Jesus was a man who had been incarnated many times before and thus had unusual wisdom because he embodied the learning of so many other lifetimes. He believed that one came into communion with the "Supreme Being" through meditation. He insisted that "if I quietly withdrew from the nervous anxiety over things, inventions, and the business that drives from every side, there was a renewal of strength in the thought of being part of the great unseen power."[10] He cautioned against meditating too much, however. "If one meditates too much," Ford declared, "there is not likely to be much work done."[11]

Many of Ford's convictions seemed superstitious and bigoted. He became alarmed if a black cat crossed his path. He was afraid of walking under ladders. If he found he had put on a sock inside out, he would not change it for the rest of the day. He did not like to leave his house on Friday the thirteenth. When he saw a red-haired person, he looked for a white horse, and when he saw a white horse, he looked for a red-haired person.[12] He harbored a hatred of fat people, and frequently insulted workers whom he considered too heavy. Once he refused to hire an electrician until he lost a substantial amount of weight. When the man complied and Ford noticed that his clothes no longer fit him, he snidely remarked, "You're leaving those clothes on because you want to eat your way back into them."[13] The subject of Ford's persecution later died, at least partly as a result of his weight loss.

After he had some difficulties with a bank loan, the industrialist began to attribute many of his problems to a "Jewish plot," and disseminated anti-Jewish publications. When a Jewish journalist claimed that these articles were helping to provoke violence against Jews in Europe, Ford promised to take back everything he had circulated if the journalist could bring him proof that anything he had ever caused to be printed had hurt anyone. When confronted with the evidence, Ford promised to stop the anti-Semitic publications.[14] Harry Bennett, for many years Ford's chief aide, recalled, "He became bigoted about Jews, and just as much so about Roman Catholics, though the latter aspect of his intolerance was never so well known to the public."[15]

Ford was not particularly consistent in his prejudices, however. Bennett recounted, "Mr. Ford did, of course, like many Jews and Catholics. But he always had an out. When he liked a Jew—as he did Harry Newman and Hank Greenberg and Judge Harry Keyden and others— he'd say to me, 'Oh, he's mixed, he's not all Jewish.' When he liked a Catholic—as he liked Frank Nolan, a company lawyer, and many others—he'd say, 'Oh, he isn't good Catholic.' "[16]

Ford was furious when the renowned Roman Catholic priest and writer, Fulton Sheen, expressed the hope that the elder Ford would become Roman Catholic. The automaker had given the clergyman that impression when, upon meeting him, he said, "Well, now, you've got the best religion in the world." But he happened to say that to any clergymen he met, of whatever faith or persuasion.[17] So, to squelch the rumor that he was sympathetic to the Roman faith, Ford, who had been an inactive Mason, decided to "go all the way" and become a Thirty-Third Degree Mason, since membership in the Lodge is forbidden to members of the Catholic Church.[18]

Ford seems to have been less bigoted toward Negroes, since he took action to stamp out the Ku Klux Klan in his plants and was a close friend of the black scientist, George Washington Carver. Ford grew even more eccentric with age, however. He became violently opposed to drinking milk and using sugar, and lived on a diet of cracked wheat, insisting, "You can live as long as you want, as long as you eat only cracked wheat."[19] He never softened in his opposition to traditional Christianity, and remarked, not long before he died, that "cows, horses, pigs, and creeds will someday disappear from the earth."[20]

~

Profile 51
George Washington Carver

Born: Diamond Grove, Missouri, (probably) July 12, 1864
Died: Tuskegee, Alabama, January 5, 1943

The agricultural chemist who served for nearly a half century on the faculty of Alabama's Tuskegee Institute has been credited with devising hundreds of products from the peanut and sweet potato. The child of a slave, he was orphaned in infancy, and raised by a white couple who owned a farm. The elder Carvers were, by most accounts, not churchgoers, but, even before he made a religious commitment, young George displayed a strain of mysticism that would characterize the entirety of his life. He believed that the truth was often revealed to him in dreams. For instance, when he was a small boy he was distressed when he could not find his pocketknife. Then he dreamed that he saw it protruding from a half-eaten melon. When he awoke, the boy rushed to the place shown in the dream, and there was the melon and in it was the knife.[1]

Carver was "converted" when he was ten years old. Writing about the experience as an adult, he explained: "God just came into my heart one afternoon while I was alone in the 'loft' of our big barn, while I was shelling corn....One of our neighbors, about my age, came by one Saturday morning and in talking and playing he told me he was going to Sunday school tomorrow morning. I was eager to know what a Sunday school was. He said that they sang hymns and prayed. I asked him what prayer was and what they said. I do not remember what he said; I only recall that as soon as he left, I climbed up into the 'loft,' knelt down by the barrel of corn and prayed as best I could. I do not remember what I said. I only recall that I felt so good that I prayed several times before I quit."[2]

Throughout his career as a scientist, Carver relied on divine inspiration for scientific insights. He said that he was not of the class of scientist who "believed that the world is merely the result of chemical forces...."[3] As we come in closer touch with nature and its teachings, he insisted, "we are able to see the Divine and are therefore fitted to interpret correctly the various languages spoken by all forms of nature about us."[4]

For the Tuskegee professor, the God revealed by nature was the God of the Bible. The study of science only confirmed the truths of sacred Scripture, and therefore scientific research was a means of learning God's will. He insisted that the mysteries of God could be better understood through the study of nature. In fact, he called his laboratory God's Little Workshop. "I am not interested in science, or anything else, that leaves God out of it," he said.[5] He wanted his students to "study the great Creator through the things he has created."[6]

For example, in December 1927, in a letter to a friend, he described how contemplating a sunset constituted a religious experience: As he watched the glory of the setting sun and its awe-inspiring brilliance and color, he remained for a time "unconscious of everything except the scene." Then, when he came to himself, he said aloud, "O God, I thank thee for such direct manifestation of thy goodness, majesty, and power."[7]

Before he entered his workshop, Carver prayed. In a lecture to the Women's Board of Domestic Missions at the Marble Collegiate Church in New York City in November 1924, he said that all his discoveries were a direct revelation from God, that he had no great mind and never used a book in his laboratory. It was God who revealed his discoveries to him and showed him the method.[8] When the editors of the *New York Times* criticized Carver for being unscientific, he wrote back, giving an example of how God inspired his discoveries: "While in your beautiful city, I was struck with the large number of Taros and Yautias displayed in many of your markets; they are edible roots imported to this country largely from Trinidad, Puerto Rico, China, Dutch Guina [sic], and Peru. Just as soon as I saw these luscious roots, I marveled at the wonderful possibilities for their expansion. Dozens of things came to me while standing there looking at them....I know of no one who has ever worked with these roots in this way. I know of no book from which I can get this information, yet I will have no trouble in doing it. If this is not inspiration and information from a source greater than myself...kindly tell me what it is."[9] Another time he said: "I discover nothing in my laboratory. If I come here of myself I am lost. But I can do all things through Christ. I am God's servant, his agent, for here God and I are alone. I am just the instrument through which he speaks, and I would be able to do more if I were to stay in closer touch with him. With my prayers I mix my labors, and sometimes God is pleased to bless the results."[10]

Carver claimed to have conversations with God in his laboratory. He recounted more than once in lectures how God told him about the peanut. Carver told God that he wanted to know all about the peanut, and God said that he would give Carver a handful of peanuts. He continued: "I carried the peanuts into my laboratory and the Creator told me to take them apart and resolve them into their elements. With such knowledge as I had of chemistry and physics I set to work to take them apart. I separated the water, the fats, the oils, the gums, the resins, sugars, starches, pectoses, pentosans, amino acids. There! I had the parts of the peanut all spread out before me. I looked at him and he looked at me. 'Now, you know what the peanut is.' "

"'Why did you make the peanut?"

"The Creator said, 'I have given you three laws; namely, compatibility, temperature, and pressure. All you have to do is to take these constituents and put them together, observing these laws, and I will show you why I made the peanut.' "[11]

Carver even went so far as to say that God directly told him how to make specific products. When Carver asked him, "Can I make milk out of the peanut?" God answered, "Do you have the constituents of milk?" When Carver answered that he did, God told him to go ahead and Carver created peanut milk.[12]

The scientist constantly read the Bible and said that his slogan passages were: Proverbs 3:6 ("In all your ways acknowledge him, and he will make straight your paths."); Philippians 4:13 ("I can do all things through him who strengthens me."); and Psalm 119:18 ("Open my eyes, that I may behold wondrous things out of your law.").[13]

Carver insisted: "I always sleep over a problem....[T]he next morning I see the method and the new perspective which usually clears it up. I didn't do it. God has only used me to reveal some of his wonderful providences."[14] "I love to think of nature as an unlimited broadcasting station," he said, "through which God speaks to us every hour, if we will only tune in. Pursue truth with a new zest and give all the credit for the answers to the greatest of all teachers."[15]

Carver wrote that the secret of true happiness was "the joy of coming into the closest relationship with the maker and preserver of all things." He told his students, "Begin now to study the little things in your own door yard, going from the known to the nearest related unknown, for indeed each new truth brings one nearer to God."[16] He wanted his students "to get the fullest measure and success out of life" and that came through a relationship with Christ. "I want them to find Jesus and make him a daily, hourly, and momently part of themselves."[17]

In 1907, he organized a Bible class at Tuskegee. Students used to come to him on Sunday afternoons to ask about the relationship between science and nature. He started with six or seven people, and within a few months he had over three hundred, and these numbers continued for years. His class met for twenty to twenty-five minutes on Sunday evenings between supper and chapel services. Sometimes he acted out the roles of various biblical characters. Describing the story of the Israelites in the wilderness, he showed the young men a sample of what he believed manna (the mysterious food provided by God) to be. He was known to end his recounting the story of the destruction of Sodom and Gomorrah by touching off some chemicals in a huge cloud and sulphur and flame.[18]

He was frequently asked, "How can we know God?" and he frequently replied: "God is always there—just waiting for you to make contact. He is all around you, in all the little things you look at but don't really see. God is here. The seed that made this flower was created millions of years ago. It survived drought and blizzards and the assaults of man himself. And in this flower is the beginning of a seed that will grow millions of years after all of us are gone. Can any of you believe that the miracle of this flower is no more than an accident?"[19]

Carver, who believed that there was no conflict between science and revealed religion, said he believed "in the Biblical account of creation as found in Genesis."[20] However, he believed in evolution and insisted that this was supported by Scripture. Of course, he believed that nothing happened by chance and that it was the hand of God that caused life to evolve from single-cell organisms to humans. He used to explain the story of creation using maps, charts, plants, and geological specimens to show that the findings of science were in harmony with revealed truth.[21]

Carver never identified with any particular sect, although he once told a Presbyterian minister that he was a Presbyterian.[22] He worshiped regularly at the Tuskegee Chapel. One author describes his religion as "mystical and nondenominational." Because he believed that there was more than one true way to relate to God, on occasion he expressed support and admiration for the Baha'i faith and for the Rosicrucian Fellowship. He also expressed interest in George Baker, who called himself "Father Divine" and who attracted a large following in the 1920s and 1930s, claiming to be "God Incarnate."[23]

Each morning at four, he arose and went into the woods to pray. "Alone there with the things I love most," he said, "I gather my specimens and study the lessons nature is so eager to teach us all. Nothing is more beautiful than the loveliness of the woods before sunrise. At no other time have I so sharp an understanding of what God means to do with me as in the hours of dawn. When other folk are still asleep, I hear God best and learn his plan."[24]

When a minister wrote from Kansas City, Missouri, to ask about his method of prayer, Carver, just about a year before he died, wrote back: "My prayers seem to be more of an attitude than anything else. I indulge in very little lip service, but ask the Great Creator silently, daily, and often many times per day to permit me to speak to him through the three great Kingdoms of the world which he has created...the animal, mineral, and vegetable kingdoms; their relations to each other, to us, our relations to them and to the great God who made all of us. I ask him daily and momently to give me wisdom, understanding, and bodily strength to do his will."[25]

Carver believed that "the Love of Christ" would transform people into what he would wish them to be, and that people would be drawn to those so transformed, for they would see and seek Christ in them.[26] He wrote a friend, "Don't get alarmed...when doubts creep in. That is Old Satan. Pray, pray, pray. Neither be cast down or afraid if perchance you seem to wander from the path. This is sure to come if you trust too much in self."[27]

Indeed, Carver tried not to trust in himself. We have seen how he denied that he had a great mind and how he attributed all his success to the direct inspiration of God. When people sent him money, he often gave it away to the poor, who were numerous in the area where he taught. "O God, this is your money," he said. "What shall I do with it that will bring the greatest returns for him?"[28] But he was far from destitute. During his lifetime he was involved in at least four commercial ventures and obtained at least three patents and had enough worldly substance to contribute $60,000 toward a foundation grant in his name.[29]

Carver was an eccentric man, a loner, who liked to work by himself in his laboratory, and, to the horror of some serious scientists, kept no records of his experiments or of the formulae for the products that he produced.[30] Throughout his life, he was subjected to many slights and insults because of his color, but he generally tried to ignore them. "If I used my energy struggling to right every wrong done to me, I would have no energy left for my work."[31] He frequently declared, "No man can drag me down so low as to make me hate him."[32] However, he once replied to a group of white southern clergymen who asked him how they could promote favorable race relations: "Your actions speak so loud I cannot hear what you are saying. You have too much religion and not enough Christianity—too many creeds and not enough performance. This world is perishing for kindness."[33] Yet he was confident that: "Divine love will one day conquer the world."[34]

Death, for George Carver, was a passage "into the fullness of joy."[35] A few hours before the end, the scientist summoned his valet, James Lomax, and asked him what he was doing. The valet answered that he was preparing Carver's meal. "Yes," replied the dying man, "they are also preparing for me in the other world." He never spoke again.[36] So passed from the earthly scene a man who was characterized by educator and civil rights activist Mary McLeod Bethune as "a giant in the field of creative achievement," who "believed that all science pointed to God" and who was "a demonstration of the simplicity of eternal faith."[37]

∼

$\mathscr{Profile}$ 52
Warren Gamaliel Harding

Born: Blooming Grove, Ohio, November 2, 1865
Died: San Francisco, California, August 2, 1923

Although he seems to have been reasonably well-liked in his time, Harding today is regarded generally with less respect than any other president. His administration was disfigured by numerous scandals, and he himself has been criticized not only for his ineptitude as an administrator, but for his fondness for alcohol and his frequent all-night poker parties. The former senator from Ohio seems to have been a likeable man, but somewhat superficial.

In his way, Harding was a religious man. Both of his parents were physicians, and each belonged to a different church. His father was a Baptist, his mother a Methodist who later became a Seventh Day Adventist. His mother's influence was the strongest on young Warren, as she told him stories from the Bible and encouraged him to memorize passages from Scripture. She wanted him to become a minister, and she had cause to hope when, at fourteen, Warren was converted at a local revival.[1] But the thought of the ministry never appealed to him, and he entered the field of journalism (he became the editor of the Marion, Ohio, *Star*) and then politics.

While attending Iberia College, young Harding studied evolution, and, as a result, considered himself an atheist for a while.[2] Then he started attending a Methodist church. After he settled in Marion, he joined the First Baptist Church (now Trinity Baptist). A biographer wrote, "Religion was for Harding like the Constitution, something to be honored and left alone....There must be some reason for everything, he believed—in the odd moments when he thought about it—a God somewhere, an afterlife somehow in which one would not be judged too harshly."[3] That he believed in eternal life is evident in a letter he wrote his sister after their mother died in 1910, in which he reveals his realization of his own spiritual inadequacy. After recounting his mother's last words (spoken in reply to a question as to

266

whether she were praying), which were, "No, I am only trusting," Harding declared: "She could and she had the right to trust...and surely...there are for her all the rewards in eternity that God bestows on his very own. I could not speak for myself, but dear, dear Mother will wear a crown if ever a Christian woman does—and I can believe in eternal compensations for such as her."[4]

For many years, Harding worshiped regularly at the First Baptist Church of Marion, where he served as trustee. He established the following code for his newspaper reporters and writers: "Above all, be clean. Never let a dirty word or suggestive story get into type. I want this paper so conducted that it can go into any home without destroying the innocence of any child."[5] Throughout his life, he was generally a man of clean speech. His attorney general insisted that he never heard him use "an oath."[6]

When he was told of his election to the presidency, Harding commented, "It is not time for exultation but for prayer to God to make me capable of playing my part."[7] However, the first Sunday after his inauguration, reporters were disappointed when he failed to show up at Calvary Baptist Church, which he had designated as his place of worship in Washington. His explanation was that he was just too busy with the duties of the presidency to attend.[8]

During his brief administration, Harding made several public statements on religion. In April 1921, he told a convention of Presbyterian laymen in Marion: "I want you to believe that there is an individual here who believes in the reconsecration of a religious Republic. I have for my inheritance a Christian belief....Sometimes I think the world is adrift from its moorings of religion, and I know it will help, if there comes a great revival of faith....I do not see how a government can exist in the world without coming in contact with God....I rejoice in the inheritance of a religious belief and I do not mind saying that I gladly go to God Almighty for guidance and strength in the responsibilities that are coming to me."[9]

In 1922, he spoke at Calvary Baptist and declared: "If I were to utter a prayer for this Republic tonight, it would be to reconsecrate us in religious devotion and make us abidingly a God-fearing, God-loving people." Despite "our complete divorcement of Church and State, quite in harmony with our religious freedom there is an important relationship between church and nation, because no nation can survive if it ever forgets Almighty God."[10]

Again, on June 24, 1923, in an extemporaneous speech at Colorado Springs, Colorado, the president declared: "I should like to have America a little more earnest and thoroughly committed to its religious devotion. We were more religious one hundred years ago than we are today. We have been getting too far away from the spiritual and too much absorbed in our material experience. It tends to make us a sordid people....I tell you, my countrymen, the world needs more of Christ; the world needs the spirit of the Man of Nazareth, and if we could bring into the relationship of humanity among ourselves and among the nations of the world the brotherhood that was taught by Christ, we would have a restored world, we would have little or none of war, and we would have new hope for humanity throughout the world."[11]

A few weeks later Harding, who had a badly diseased heart, suddenly died, but he had just completed a message which he was never able to deliver, in which he insisted that America needed less of "religion" and more of Christianity: "We need less of sectarianism, less of denominationalism, less of fanatical zeal and its exactions, and more of the Christ spirit—more of the Christ practice and a new and abiding consecration of reverence to God."[12]

Perhaps the deficiencies in his own life helped Harding to see a need for spirit revival and reconsecration in the world. He seems to have become sincerely convinced that what Americans needed was a wholehearted return to the faith in Jesus Christ.

∼

Profile 53
William Edward Burghardt Du Bois

Born: Great Barrington, Massachusetts, February 23, 1868
Died: Accra, Ghana, August 27, 1963

The educator, writer, and civil rights leader who helped to found the NAACP, and vigorously opposed Booker T. Washington's policy of accommodation to racial segregation by demanding for the Negro every political, civil, and social right that belonged to any other American, was baptized in an Episcopal church in his hometown of Great Barrington, Massachusetts. When he was about ten, his mother began to attend the First Congregational Church of that town, where she became a member and he attended Sunday school. The pastor of the church was Evarts Scudder, who preached traditional Christian doctrines, such as the divine authority of the Scriptures and salvation through Christ alone.[1]

Young Du Bois, at the age of seventeen, went to Fisk University, where he taught Sunday school for a time and wrote to Pastor Scudder, asking for his prayers and mentioning the anticipated arrival of D. L. Moody on campus.[2] However, he became indignant when he was criticized for planning a dance, and was angered when he learned that an Episcopal priest from New York, whose book on religion and politics was used at Fisk, was charged with heresy,[3] and by the end of his college years he had rejected orthodox Christianity. Although he always maintained high ethical and moral standards, he believed that he was captain of his own soul.[4] Late in life, he wrote a friend that in his youth, he assumed that human beings "could alter and direct the course of events so as to better human conditions." Believing that "this power was limited by environment, inheritance, and natural law," he concluded that from "the point of view of science, these occurrences must be a matter of chance and not law." He went on to say, "I did not rule out the possibility of some God also influencing and directing human action and natural law. However, I saw no evidence of such divine guidance."[5]

269

Horace Bumstead, who was president of Atlanta University when Du Bois went there to teach, described him as apparently "one of those persons who, when asked about their religion, reply that they have none to speak of."[6] A biographer has written, "At best [Du Bois] recognized a vague presence manifesting itself in laws slowly revealed through science."[7] Although at Atlanta he refused to lead morning prayers, as members of the faculty were expected to do occasionally, once he offered a short prayer at commencement: "Give us grace, O God, to dare to do the deed which we know well cries out to be done."[8]

The Credo he published in 1904 had mainly to do with racial and humanistic themes. For instance, he declared: "I believe in liberty for all men; the space to stretch their arms and souls; the right to breathe and the right to vote, the freedom to choose their friends, enjoy the sunshine, and ride on railroads uncursed by color," but he did preface the testament by declaring that he believed in "God, who made out of one blood all races that dwell on earth."[9]

After Atlanta was devastated by riots in 1906, when white mobs stormed black neighborhoods, destroying property and attacking and even killing people of color, Du Bois composed a litany in which he both berated God for allowing the catastrophe and accused him of being dead. "Is this thy justice, O Father," he cried, "that guile be easier than innocence and the innocent be crucified for the guilt of the untouched guilty?" He then declared, "a mobbed and murdered people, straining at the armposts of thy throne, we raise our shackled hands and charge thee, God, by the bones of our stolen fathers, by the tears of our dead mothers, by the very blood of thy crucified Christ: what meaneth this? Tell us the plan; give us the sign! Keep not thou silent, O God!" He concluded: "Hear us, Good Lord! In night, O God of a godless land! Amen! In silence, O silent God!"[10]

In January 1945, Du Bois, then in his late seventies, replied to John R. Timpany, a Roman Catholic priest, who urged him to unite with his faith: "I cannot assent to any creed which demands that I accept on faith the elaborate doctrine and dogma of the Catholic Church. As a scientist I am perfectly aware there are some things in this world we must accept on faith so long as we rigorously test them by the data of experience. Beyond that I cannot go."[11]

In 1948, Du Bois received a letter from E. Pina Moreno, a Baptist minister from Cuba, who asked him about his belief in God and his opinion about the Lord Jesus. Du Bois responded, "If by being 'a believer in God' you mean a belief in a person of vast power who consciously rules the universe for the good of mankind, I answer No; I cannot disprove this assumption, but I certainly see no proof to sustain such a belief, neither in history nor in my personal experience. If, on the other hand, you mean by 'God' a vague force which, in some uncomprehensible way, dominates all life and change, then I answer, Yes; I recognize such force, and if you wish to call it God, I do not object."[12] He said nothing about Christ, but from this and other statements, it is seems obvious that he rejected the notion of Jesus' divinity.

Late in life, Du Bois was attracted to Communism. On September 26, 1957, when he was nearly ninety, he wrote in the *Literary Gazette of the Soviet Union*: "I stand with bared head before the miracle of the Union of Soviet Socialist Republics; before a great nation which in forty years...has raised itself from superstition, disease, and poverty to health and industry; from almost ninety percent illiteracy to an intelligent people with probably the best system of education in the world; from a degraded peasant agriculture to an economy of farm and factory which is becoming the most efficient in the world."[13] Du Bois, in fact, joined the Communist Party at the age of ninety-three, and drew up a list of ten demands he would make as a member of the American Communist Party. One of them was "No dogmatic religion."[14]

Eventually Du Bois left the United States to live in the African nation of Ghana, where he intended to edit an *Encyclopedia Africana*, a project he was unable to finish by the time death intervened, when he was ninety-five. Even in his closing days, Du Bois displayed no interest in religion. Just before he died, he told his wife, "You must not grieve because that time is coming. I've lived longer than most men and we've shared so much together. You and others will complete what I have left unfinished, perhaps better than I should have done."[15] To Ghanian leader Kwame Nkrumah he said, "I want to thank you for all you've done to make the ending of my life bountiful and beautiful. I rejoice that I have seen the pilot light you're raising here in Ghana. I have only one regret: I failed you—my strength gave out before I could carry out our plans for the encyclopedia. Forgive an old man."[16] Thus, without fear, regret, apparent belief in an afterlife, or the consolations of religion, W.E.B. Du Bois approached the end of a long and eventful life.

~

Profile 54

John Calvin Coolidge

Born: Plymouth, Vermont, July 4, 1872
Died: Northampton, Massachusetts, January 5, 1933

The former governor of Massachusetts who succeeded to the presidency on the unexpected death of Warren Harding was a taciturn, sour-looking native of Vermont who was said to look as if he had been "weaned on a pickle." So spare with words was Silent Cal that the story was circulated about a woman who sat next to him at dinner and told him that she had bet a friend that she could coax more than two words from him, only to have the president quack, in his Yankee twang, "You lose!" The Republican president is also famous for saying, "The business of America is business."[1] During the 1920s, he presided over a prosperous economy which he and his advisors hoped would spread its benefits to all classes of society as the government worked to ensure the growth of big business.

Calvin Coolidge was often described as a Puritan in the sense that he displayed unimpeachable moral standards and embodied the ethics of frugality and hard work (although he is alleged to have spent less time in his official duties than almost any other chief executive). However, despite his given names, there is no evidence that he was a doctrinaire Calvinist. In fact, he never belonged to a church until he was president. The little town where he grew up was so small that it could not support an organized church, but depended on traveling ministers—mostly Congregationalists, Baptists, and Methodists—to conduct worship services. There was a Sunday school, and young Calvin attended, and he also learned to read the Bible.

According to biographer William Allen White, who characterized him as a "religious" but not "pious" man, "Religion was part of the spiritual air men breathed" in the New England of Coolidge's youth,[2] and, although he never sought formal doctrinal or denominational connections, Coolidge, throughout his life, embraced a general, non-sectarian Christianity, which biographer Gamaliel Bradford described as the "orthodoxy of the middle nineteenth century," which consisted of "the unshaken belief in an anthropomorphic God who guides the destinies of nations and also the petty affairs of individuals, and to whom it is of real importance what you or I or Calvin Coolidge may do and not do."[3] Although there is no record of any conversion experience, Coolidge believed in God, prayed to him in time of crisis,[4] and, after his marriage attended the Jonathan Edwards Congregational Church near his home in Northampton, Massachusetts. Grace Goodhue Coolidge joined the church, but Calvin never did.

After he became vice president in 1921, the Coolidges attended the First Congregational Church of Washington, and became friends of the pastor, Jason Pierce. Although he had never been confirmed in any church, Coolidge regularly took Communion at first. When he became president, Pierce persuaded his congregation to vote Coolidge into the congregation without a public profession of faith and accepted the new First Lady as an associate member. This pleased Coolidge, who later wrote, "Had I been approached in the usual way to join the church...I should have been feared that such action might appear to be a pose, and should have hesitated to accept."[5] In other words, although he was pleased to be a church member, he did not want to make a formal request for membership at that stage of life, fearing that press and public would believe that the president was joining a church for the first time at age fifty-one merely for appearance's sake.

As president, Coolidge began the tradition of lighting the national Christmas tree and of giving a Christmas message to the American people.[6] He spoke of his faith in an interview in September 1926, in which he said, "It would be difficult for me to conceive of anyone being able to administer the duties of a great office like the presidency without a belief in the guidance of a divine providence."[7] He believed strongly that American society was founded on biblical teaching and could not function without this support, as he said in a letter in the spring of 1927 in which he declined an invitation to attend the Bible class at the Episcopal Church of the Epiphany: "The foundations of our society and our Government rest so much on the teachings of the Bible that it would be difficult to support them if faith in these teachings should cease to be practically universal in this country."[8] He elaborated on this position in an address he gave in Washington before the National Council of Congregational Churches in 1925. He argued that the law could punish criminals, and should, but that it could not reform them; only religion could. Without the support of religion, "political effort would be practically fruitless." When he spoke of "religion," he went on to say, he was not referring to it "in any denominational or any narrow and technical sense," but meant "to include all that can be brought within that broad definition." He concluded: "I can conceive of no adequate remedy for the evils which beset society except through the influences of religion. There is no form of education which will not fail, there is no form of government that will not fail, there is no form of reward which will not fail."[9]

Coolidge's religious faith was broad, general, and non-creedal. He seldom if ever spoke of Jesus Christ. After he left the White House to return to Northampton, he attended the Edwards Congregational Church nearly every Sunday, but those close to him were of the opinion that he "spent as much time when in church figuring out who was absent as in listening to the sermon."[10]

The life of this laconic president had its share of heartbreak. His mother died when he was twelve and he lost his sister, his only sibling, a girl of fourteen, when he was seventeen. The greatest sorrow of his life came during the first year of his presidency when his sixteen-year-old son Calvin died of a blood infection. A few years later his wife, Grace, was able to express her feelings about their son in a poem:

> You, my son, have shown me God.
> Your kiss upon my cheek
> Has made me feel the gentle touch
> Of Him who leads us on.[11]

Whether her husband shared in these sentiments is not known. His friends and associates knew that he was devastated by the boy's loss, but that he suffered the loss in silence. Once he was heard to say, "The ways of providence are often beyond our understanding."[12]

Although Calvin Coolidge's ideas about God and religion were, in the words of one biographer "mystically vague,"[13] he did believe in a providence that governed the affairs of humanity; he believed that individuals had a duty before God to act in the best interests of others; and he believed that the moral and spiritual principles of the Bible were the foundation of American civilization and could not be discarded without disastrous consequences. And so, while not a "pious" man in the sense that he had little interest in creeds, doctrines, or religious exercises or observances (or at least formal ones), he had, according to biographer Gamaliel Bradford, a religious outlook on life. Bradford wrote, "It is impossible to question the absolute sincerity and profound conviction of his religious attitude. It is not only believed, but lived, and no man ever carried his convictions into his life with more fervor or reverent piety than Calvin Coolidge."[14]

⁓

Profile 55

Herbert Clark Hoover

Born: West Branch, Iowa, August 11, 1874
Died: New York, New York, October 20, 1964

Asked about his religious affiliation late in life, the engineer, humanitarian, and former president chuckled and admitted, "I was raised a Quaker, but I never worked very hard at it."[1] Herbert Hoover spent his early childhood in West Branch, Iowa, one of three children of a devout Quaker couple. The father, Jesse, died when the boy was only six, leaving mother, Huldah, to raise her family in poverty. She was a deeply religious woman, who dedicated her life to the service of the Lord at eighteen, who taught Sunday school, and who held prayer meetings in her home.[2] Writing to relatives, she confessed that although she was so poor that she sometimes could not afford postage stamps, "we know not what is before us, but as children of the Lord we can trust it all to him who knows what is best."[3]

Young "Bert," who under the guidance of his mother, read the Bible in its entirety, wrote in his autobiography that the Quakers around whom he spent his boyhood held to a "literal belief in the Bible, great tolerance, and a conviction that spiritual inspiration sprang from the 'inward light' in each individual."[4] He did not particularly enjoy the meetings: "Those who are acquainted with the Quaker faith and who know the primitive furnishing of the Quaker meeting-house, the solemnity of the long hours of meeting awaiting the spirit to move someone, will know the intense repression upon a ten-year-old boy who might not even count his toes."[5]

When Bert was ten, Huldah died, and he shortly afterward went to live with his mother's brother, Henry John Minthorn in Oregon. A physician, he too was a devout Quaker. On the wall of young Hoover's room hung two mottoes: "Do not cast me off, do not forsake me, O God of my salvation" from Psalm 27 and "I will never leave you or forsake you" from Hebrews 13. As in Iowa, the entirety of Sunday was spent in religious observance: Sabbath school, attendance at meeting, Bible study, and participation in a children's temperance organization.[6] Young Bert was enrolled at the Friends Pacific Academy, a Quaker school, and on New Year's Day, 1887, at twelve, was accepted as a member of the Newberg Monthly Meeting of Friends.[7]

Hoover's outlook changed after he went away to college to study engineering. At Stanford University, "I attended many lectures on biology, evolution, and the reconciliation of science and religion. The impact of the university upon fundamentalist religion of the times brought spiritual conflicts to many young people. The Quaker 'inner light' as the basis of faith, however, suffered much less than some others. I much more easily adapted fundamental natural law into my spiritual complex than those whose early training was in the more formalistic sects and of wider doctrinal base."[8]

After Hoover was graduated from college, there is no evidence that he attended religious services of any kind for at least twenty years.

Contrary to the practice of his mother and uncle, he smoked, drank alcoholic beverages, attended the theater, and used Sunday as a day of recreation.[9] A niece later recalled that her family was "reverent but not religious." One of his sons, many years later, recalled that in his family religion was never discussed "at any time."[10]

Hoover did admit that he believed in "the divine within each individual,"[11] and maintained that he cultivated "peace at the center," which allowed him to avoid hatred and resentment toward his enemies and "drop hostilities in this deep pool of inner quietness."[12] When he was bitterly attacked for his handling of the Depression, his wife, the former Lou Henry, who had become a Quaker when she married him, explained, "Bert can take it better than most people because he has ingrained in him the Quaker feeling that nothing matters if you are 'right with God.'"[13]

When Hoover accepted the presidential nomination from the Republican Party in 1928, he declared: "In this land, dedicated to tolerance, we still find outbursts of intolerance. I come of Quaker stock. My ancestors were persecuted for their beliefs. Here they sought and found religious freedom. By blood and conviction I stand for religious tolerance, both in act and in spirit. The glory of our American ideals is the right of every man to worship God according to the dictates of his own conscience."[14] He tried scrupulously to keep the issue of religion out of the campaign, in which his opponent was New York governor Al Smith, a Roman Catholic, whom some voters opposed solely of the basis of his religious affiliation. Hoover blamed Smith, however, for raising the religion issue in his campaign.[15] Most historians feel that Smith lost mainly for reasons other than his religious affiliation.

When Hoover became president, he and his wife "frequently" attended the new Friends Meeting, opened on Florida Avenue, in Northwest Washington. Most people who knew him, however, believe that Hoover's Quaker faith was most clearly discernible in his policy as president.

A rather cool, detached, reticent man known for his quiet, plain, blunt speech, Hoover came into the White House with the reputation of being a humanitarian. During and immediately after World War I, he coordinated the operation of several relief agencies to save millions of Europeans from starvation. When, however, in the first year of his administration a worldwide depression broke out, Hoover was criticized. Although his administration became the first in American history to take steps intended to involve the government in helping the economy, many hoped that Hoover would support efforts at the direct relief of the unemployed. This he was unwilling to do, preferring to support government efforts to aid businesses in the hopes that this would stimulate the economy and provide more jobs. Hoover's belief in helping the needy indirectly was, many believe, an outgrowth of his early training, which stressed self-reliance, individual responsibility, and hard work.

His Quaker upbringing, it was felt, was also evident in his approach to the Bonus March. When thousands of veterans converged on Washington during the summer of 1932, in support of a bill before Congress that would have paid each veteran the pension owed him many years in the future, Hoover opposed the measure, on the grounds that the government simply did not have the money. The idea that the government should go into debt was abhorrent to him. He was, moreover, bitterly criticized and lost all hope of reelection when he refused to reprimand Army Chief of Staff Douglas MacArthur for acting against his expressed orders and using force against a number of veterans who would not disburse. MacArthur and Secretary of War Patrick Hurley convinced Hoover that the veterans were Communist-inspired and planned a violent confrontation with the government.[16]

Hoover was called by some a "sham Quaker" because he was willing, at times, to resort to force, but, he pointed out that not all Quakers believe in "extreme pacifism." The uncle with whom he lived in Oregon when he was a boy used to tell him, "Turn the other cheek once, but, if he smites it, then punch him!"[17] According to one historian, Hoover's foreign policy was to "reduce and eliminate the causes of conflict by supporting arbitration, arms limitation, and...a deterrent defense force."[18] He wanted American forces strong enough to prevent an enemy attack anywhere in the Western Hemisphere, but was criticized for his unwillingness to use the military to preserve international peace, especially when Japan invaded Manchuria (in China) in 1931.[19] Throughout his administration, Hoover tried in vain to obtain international agreements to ban air warfare, chemical warfare, and the use of tanks and large mobile guns.[20]

Out of office, he worked to keep the United States out of World War II and criticized his successor, Franklin Roosevelt, for being much too belligerent. When war finally broke out, he supported the effort, but felt that the United States could have done more to try to negotiate a peace with Japan before using the atomic bomb, a course of action which he claimed "revolts my soul" and besmirched America's reputation.[21]

In later years he was, like many men of his generation, concerned with the spread of Communism. After the halfhearted and unsuccessful attempt to overthrow the Castro regime in Cuba through the Bay of Pigs invasion, Hoover was critical of the Kennedy administration, and remarked, "You know, I'm a Quaker and I loathe war, but, by heavens, if I were President of the United States, I would order the necessary forces into the Bay of Pigs, and I would decimate that Cuban army while they're there."[22] He expressed to Pope Pius XII his fear of "the tide of Red agnosticism sweeping over Europe." When the pontiff remarked that he found this statement unusual coming from a Quaker, the former president answered that although Quakers were only a small minority of the world's faithful, they too depended for their existence on "the moral foundations of the world."[23]

Hoover's faith was concerned more with morality and conduct than with doctrine and creed, with relieving the suffering of this world. His concept of spirituality was of an inner light—with him, apparently of conscience and considered intelligent judgment—that enabled him to take public positions that may not have been popular at the time, which served the good of humanity.

Hoover spoke most explicitly and in the greatest detail about his personal religious beliefs in an interview in his late seventies. He declared: "My professional training was in science and engineering. That is a training in the search for truth and its application to the use of mankind. With the growth of science we have had a continuous contention from a tribe of atheistic and agnostic philosophers that there is an implacable conflict between science and religion in which religion will be vanquished. I do not believe it."

The former president went on to argue that he believed "not only that religious faith will be victorious, but that it is vital to mankind that it shall be." Although individuals, he said, may differ "in form and particulars, there is one foundation common to all religious faith."

Hoover believed that the principles of democracy were a direct result of such a faith, and that America had grown strong because of it. "Always growing societies record their faith in God," Hoover observed. "Decaying societies lack faith and deny God." American, he believed, remained strong because "its faith is in compassion and in God's intelligent mercy."[24]

~

Profile 56
Albert Einstein

Born: Ulm, Germany, March 14, 1879
Died: Princeton, New Jersey, April 18, 1955

The German-born physicist, celebrated for his theory of relativity, who taught at Princeton University during the last two decades of his life and became a United States citizen in 1940, believed in what he called Cosmic Religion. The son of secularized, nonpracticing Jews, he received some exposure to Christianity when he attended the public schools of Munich, where Bavarian law mandated instruction in the Roman Catholic faith. He received private instruction at home on the essentials of Judaism, but never had a bar mitzvah or learned Hebrew. Nevertheless, when he was eleven, he became intensely interested in his ancestral faith, even foregoing the eating of pork and composing hymns which he sang on his way to school. But, within a year, he lost interest.[1] Later, he wrote, "Through the reading of popular scientific books, I soon reached the conviction that much in the stories of the Bible could not be true."[2]

Despite his rejection of traditional Judaism, Einstein believed in

God—in his own way. At the age of eighteen, he wrote, "Strenuous labor and the contemplation of God's nature are the angels which, reconciling, fortifying, and yet mercilessly severe, will guide me through the tumult of life."[3] Later in life, he characterized himself as a "deeply religious nonbeliever."[4] When he was in his late forties, he wrote, "My religious feeling consists in a humble admiration for the infinitely superior spirit manifesting itself in the little of reality that we are able to recognize with our weak and frail reason."[5] A few years later he wrote, "A knowledge of the existence of something we cannot penetrate, our perceptions of the profoundest reason and the most radiant beauty, which only in their most primitive forms are accessible to our minds— it is this knowledge and this emotion that constitute true religiosity; in this sense, and in this alone, I am a deeply religious man."[6] His conviction that "the laws of nature manifest a spirit which is vastly superior to man, and before which we, with our modest strength, must humbly bow."[7] This acknowledgment of Something infinitely greater than human experience, this awe at the beauty and immensity of the universe, Einstein called "Cosmic Religion."

For Einstein, a religious person was one "who has, to the best of his ability, liberated himself from the fetters of his selfish desires and is preoccupied with thoughts, feelings, and aspirations to which he clings because of their close superpersonal value." The thoughts, feelings and aspirations of such a person have an "overpowering meaningfulness," even if they are not united with belief in a "divine being." The religious person, for Einstein, was "devout in the sense that he has no doubt of the significance and loftiness of those superpersonal objects and goals which neither require nor are capable of rational foundation."[8] He claimed that religious geniuses of all ages were "distinguished by this kind of religious feeling, which knows no dogma and no God conceived in man's image, so there can be no church whose central teachings are based on it."[9] Interestingly, he considered Saint Francis of Assisi such a religious genius.[10]

Since Cosmic Religion had "no anthropomorphic conception of God corresponding to it," it was a faith that was difficult to communicate from one person to another. Einstein felt that art and science were uniquely capable of awakening this feeling and keeping it alive in those who are receptive to it.[11] In fact, he believed that scientists often had "a religious feeling of a specific kind," which differed "essentially from the religiosity of more naive people."[12] In fact, he felt that "the cosmic religious feeling is the strongest and noblest motive for scientific research,"[13] and that the "only creative religious activity" of his time was in scientific investigation.[14]

Einstein's conception of God was quite similar to those of Thomas Paine, Frederick Douglass, Andrew Carnegie, Thomas Alva Edison, and, to a large extent, Thomas Jefferson. God was the mover of an orderly and harmonious universe who could best be known through scientific investigation. Einstein could not conceive of a God who rewarded or punished, or who had a will similar to that of human beings.[15] He rejected the notion of a God who "interferes in the course of events."[16] He did not believe in prayer, and answered a girl who wrote him a letter in which she asked whether scientists prayed, insisting, "A scientist will hardly be inclined to believe that the course of events can be influenced by prayer—that is, by a wish addressed to a supernatural being."[17] Nor did he have any interest in life beyond the grave. He wrote that he did not "want to conceive of an individual that survives his physical death." For him, belief in an afterlife was for "feeble souls," who believe out of "fear or absurd egoism."[18] The idea of a personal God he dismissed as "childish" and superstitious.[19]

Einstein held that the Bible, "in part beautiful, in part wicked," was "an interesting monument to past times," but felt that belief in it as "eternal truth" would have vanished "a long time ago [had] its conservation not been in the interest of the privileged classes."[20] Free will he rejected. "Human beings in their thinking, feeling, and acting are not free, but are just as...bound as the stars in their motions,"[21] he insisted. Because people were not responsible for their actions, he could not hate his enemies. "I cannot hate [my enemy] because he must act as he does."[22] He did not believe in sin. However, he did concede that nations had the right to pass laws to protect society from those who practiced unsocial behavior. He felt that his belief that free will was illusory was a great consolation. Not only did it mitigate feelings of hatred and resentment, it also brought comfort in the face of tragedy and disaster, because everything that happened was fated to occur as it did. It also led to humility, for with such a belief, it was impossible for human beings to take themselves too seriously.[23]

The physicist always identified himself as a Jew. For him, Judaism was a "way of sublimating everyday existence, and it entails no narrow discipline in doctrinal matters affecting one's personal view of life," and "demands no act of faith."[24] He believed that the essence of the Jewish religion was a belief that "the life of the individual only has meaning in so far as it aids in making the life of every living thing nobler and more beautiful. Life is sacred, that is to say, it is the supreme value, to which all other values are subordinate."[25]

On the other hand, Einstein seemed to have a negative opinion of priests, whom he accused of teaching a religion of fear and perpetuating ancient, outmoded superstition solely for their own material advantage and power.[26] He urged religious leaders to give up their notions of a personal God and teach morality. Einstein's Cosmic Religion was an offense to many orthodox Christians and prompted Boston's Cardinal William O'Connell to insist that Einstein's teachings produced "doubt about God and Creation."[27]

Although he rejected revealed religion and the idea of a personal God, he rejected atheism as well and insisted that "the man who regards his own life and that of his fellow creatures as meaningless is not merely unhappy, but hardly fit for life."[28] He believed that the universe was orderly and harmonious and this fact was proof that it was guided by a superior force. He believed, moreover, that the cosmos was a source of marvel and wonder, and that in awe of the immensity and beauty of creation, intelligent men and women should be inspired to rise above self-interest to live in the service of humanity. This, then, was Einstein's Cosmic Religion which emphasized ethical values, the sacredness of all life, and underpinned by his conviction that "only a life lived for others is a life worthwhile."[29]

～

Profile 57
Douglas MacArthur

Born: Little Rock, Arkansas, January 26, 1880
Died: Washington, D.C., April 5, 1964

The general who commanded American forces in the Pacific during World War II and again in the Korean War was baptized an Episcopalian, but, although he was familiar with the Bible and held regular family devotions with his wife and son, using the Scriptures and the *Book of Common Prayer*, he never went to church.[1] He nevertheless considered himself a religious man.

When, in 1942, he found his troops in a demoralized condition, he wrote an artist friend in New York, asking him to paint some pictures that would inspire the spirits of his men. When the artist wrote back, asking him what kind of thoughts and sentiments he wanted him to convey, MacArthur replied: "Two thousand years ago a man dared stand for truth, for freedom of the human spirit, was crucified and died, yet this death was not the end, but only the beginning....For twenty centuries, the story of the man of Galilee has served for all Christians as lesson and symbol so that today when we stress the spiritual significance of our united efforts to reestablish the supremacy of our Christian principles we can humbly and without presumption declare our faith and confidence in God's help in our final victory."[2]

MacArthur's conception of Christianity centered upon its ethical teachings and was for him inseparable from his concept of democracy. This was very apparent during the time that he was serving as commander of the Allied Occupation Forces in Japan and announced that it was his intention to Christianize the Japanese. Having told the Joint Chiefs of Staff that it was his policy to "increase greatly the Christian influence,"[3] he facilitated the entry of missionaries into the conquered land until, within four years, there were more than twenty-five hundred. He promoted Christian missions through press releases, messages to American church organizations, and personal communications with the Pentagon, Congress, and prominent religious leaders. Supporting such organizations as the American Bible Society, the Gideons, and the Pocket Testament League, he announced a goal to have ten million Bibles distributed among the Japanese.[4] He even helped plan the International Christian University, which opened in 1953 near Tokyo. He ordered, in fact, that statements derogatory to Christianity be expunged from Japanese schoolbooks and replaced with references favorable to the teachings of Christ.[5]

In keeping with his identification of Christianity with western democracy, he told Father Edward Flanagan, founder of Boys Town, that "democracy can never succeed in Japan until the country is Christianized."[6] He was very much concerned with preventing a Communist takeover in Japan, and only the growth of Christianity, he believed, could prevent that.

In his autobiography, MacArthur explained that before and during the war, Japan was controlled "by a feudalistic overlordship of a mere fraction of the population, while the remaining millions, with a few exceptions, were abject slaves to tradition, legend, mythology, and regimentation."[7] This system, shattered by the war, MacArthur associated with the traditional Japanese religions of Shinto and Buddhism, which were not only undemocratic, but promoted lax morals.[8] Defeat had left a spiritual vacuum which, he felt, if not filled with Christianity, would be filled with Communism.[9]

MacArthur wrote: "From the beginning I guaranteed that every Japanese could worship as he wished. I knew however that true religious freedom could never be achieved in Japan until drastic revision was made in the ancient, backward, state-controlled subsidized faith known as Shintoism....The Japanese people were told that the Emperor was divine himself and that the highest purpose of every subject's life was death in his service. The militarists who had led Japan into war had used this religion to further their efforts, and the state still subsidized it."[10]

Accordingly, "while making no theological stand," MacArthur "ordered state subsidization to cease." And, shortly afterward, Emperor Hirohito publicly renounced his own divinity.

Despite the General's boast, "I could make the Emperor and seventy million people Christian overnight, if I wanted to use the power I have,"[11] Japan did not become Christian—or Communist either, for that matter. By November 1949, MacArthur conceded that "Japan would not be Christianized in any conceivable period of time."[12] He felt it was sufficient, however, if the Buddhists and Shintoists came to practice the moral conduct and right living attributed to Christianity. Moreover, he believed that he had made a positive contribution by awakening the Japanese "to a more positive and progressive rule."[13] In the end, he believed that he had successfully reformed Japanese society by breaking the idols of their "legendary ritualism" and teaching them the "maturity of enlightened knowledge and truth."[14]

Douglas MacArthur claimed to "adhere entirely" to the teachings of Christianity.[15] Nearly everyone who knew him agreed that, although he never attended church while he was trying to make Christians out of the Japanese, he sincerely believed in the existence of a God who controlled human affairs and in the moral and ethical teachings of Jesus. Many, however, felt that his religious outlook was tinged with egotism. Journalist John Gunther wrote that the General thought that there were two "leading representatives of Christianity in the world today"— himself and the pope.[16] And biographer William Manchester, while conceding that MacArthur's belief in "an Episcopal, merciful God" was genuine, "he seemed to worship only at the altar of himself."[17]

～

Profile 58
Franklin Delano Roosevelt

Born: Hyde Park, New York, January 30, 1882
Died: Warm Springs, Georgia, April 12, 1945

Elected president four times, the man who guided America through the Great Depression and World War II said and wrote surprisingly little about religion. Although he was lifelong member of St. James Episcopal Church near his estate at Hyde Park, New York, where he was elected senior warden the year before he became president, the four volumes of his personal letters, edited by one of his sons and published a few years after his death, reveal next to nothing about his religious convictions.

Even in the major crises and crossroads of his life, in reaction to deaths of family and friends or the illness that left him permanently crippled in his late thirties, he made no reference to God or to any religious beliefs. His public speeches contain only the conventional references to God made by all politicians. Few of his biographers have anything substantial to say about his spiritual convictions. Such a dearth of information about his faith might easily incline one to the conviction that he had none, that Franklin Delano Roosevelt was a man who cared or thought little about spiritual things, but such is not necessarily the case.

Frances Perkins, Roosevelt's secretary of labor, once commented to his wife, Eleanor, that "Franklin is a very simple Christian," prompting the First Lady to respond, "Yes, a *very simple* Christian."[1] Although Perkins "never developed the point further with her,"[2] a conversation reported later by Eleanor Roosevelt sheds some light on what she meant. Early in their marriage, she asked him about the sort of religious instruction they should arrange for their children. Franklin told her, in effect, "They should go to church and learn what I learned." When she asked, "But are you sure that you believe in everything you learned?" he answer, "I really never thought about it. I think it is just as well not to think about things like that."[3]

In her memoir, *This I Believe*, Eleanor Roosevelt wrote that her husband "believed in God and in his guidance. He felt that human beings were given tasks to perform and with those tasks the ability and strength to put them through. He could pray for help and guidance and have faith in his own judgment as a result."[4]

Frances Perkins, who devoted a chapter to Roosevelt's faith in her memoirs of him, recalled, "He read the Bible a good deal. He knew a good many phrases and passages by heart. He loved the *Book of Common Prayer*, read it frequently, and often quoted from it. His Thanksgiving Day proclamations on at least two occasions when he was governor of New York were drawn largely from prayer-book sources, one of them being a paraphrase of the General Thanksgiving. The hymns, psalms, and canticles of common use in the [Episcopal] Church were all a satisfaction and comfort to him. He loved the system of the Church and its order."[5] She also recounted that F.D.R. "was able to associate himself without any conflict with all expressions of religious worship. Catholic, Protestant, and Jew alike were comprehensible to him, and their religious aspirations seemed natural and much the same as his own. He had little, if any, intellectual or theological understanding of the doctrinal basis of the major religions. But he had a deep conception of the effect of religious experience upon person's life, attitudes, moral sense, and aspirations."[6]

When he was at home at Hyde Park, he almost always attended Sunday services at St. James. While he was assistant secretary of the navy during World War I, F.D.R. attended St. Thomas Episcopal Church in northwest Washington where he was a junior vestryman, but, after he became president, after worshiping a few times early in his first administration at St. Thomas, aside from Christmas services at one of the big Baptist or Methodist churches, where he enjoyed the hymns and carols, he seldom went to church in Washington because he felt that the stares of celebrity-seekers made him too nervous to worship. He confided to Frances Perkins: "I can do almost everything in the 'Goldfish Bowl' of the president's life, but I'll be hanged if I can say my prayers in it. It bothers me to feel like something in the zoo being looked at by all the tourists in Washington when I go to church."[7] His sensitivity about his difficulty in walking added to his reluctance to attended church services.

However, on the morning of his inauguration—March 4, 1933—F.D.R. himself organized a special service of "worship and intercession" for his family and the members of his cabinet and their families at St. John's Episcopal Church, across Lafayette Square from the White House. He invited Endicott Peabody, headmaster of Groton, the prep school he had attended as a teenager, to lead the service. Frances Perkins described the occasion as simple, but memorable. The service consisted of hymns, psalms, and prayers from the *Book of Common Prayer*, selected by Roosevelt and Peabody. The worshipers included Protestants, Roman Catholics, and Jews, but Perkins recalled "I doubt that anyone remembered the difference." Everyone prayed together that God supply the grace to enable Roosevelt to be a good president.

Roosevelt found that service so meaningful that he organized similar gatherings on each of his three subsequent inaugurations.

Roosevelt's religion was simple in that he had absolutely no interest in theology or church politics. He was indifferent to the distinctions between denominations and even religions. He believed in God, but never troubled to contemplate his nature nor ponder the precise role of Jesus nor his relationship to the Godhead. He never troubled over the inerrancy of Scripture. He simply felt that people should read the Bible to learn how to live and pray to God to guide them and direct them in life. He did believe very strongly in freedom of religion, that everyone everywhere in the world had a fundamental right to worship God in the way he or she desired, as he emphasized in his speech on the "Four Freedoms."

Roosevelt was deeply concerned about countries where religious freedom was lacking. When diplomat Maksim Maksimovich Litvinov of the Soviet Union explained that no one was actually punished for going to church in the USSR, but that the government strongly discouraged the practice, Roosevelt told him: "Well, now, Max, you know what I mean by religion. You know what religion gives a man. You know the difference between the religious and the irreligious person. Why, you must know, Max. You were brought up by pious parents. Look here, some time you are going to die, and when you come to die, Max, you are going to remember your old father and mother—good, pious Jewish people who believed in God and taught you to pray to God. You had a religious bringing up, and when you come to die, Max, that's what is going to come before you, that is what you are going to think about, that's what you are going to grasp for. You know it's important."[8]

There is a record of F.D.R. reading only one religious writer and that was the Danish philosopher Søren Kierkegaard, who was recommended by a priest at St. John's as one who could explain the evils of the Nazis. "Kierkegaard explains the Nazis to me as nothing else ever has," he confided to Perkins about the mid-nineteenth century author. "I have never been able to make out why people who are obviously human beings could behave like that. They are human, yet they behave like demons. Kierkegaard gives you an understanding of what it is in man that makes it possible for these Germans to be so evil."[9]

There is no evidence of any outward sign of deepening piety as Roosevelt's health declined precipitously during the last year of his life. Nevertheless, his widow wrote: "I am quite sure that Franklin accepted the thought of death as he accepted life."[10] She went on, in her memoir, to describe him as a genuinely religious man: "He had a strong religious feeling and his religion was a very personal one. I think he actually felt he could ask God for guidance and receive it. That was why he loved the Twenty-Third Psalm, the Beatitudes, and the thirteenth chapter of First Corinthians. He never talked about his religion or his beliefs and never seemed to have any intellectual difficulties about what he believed."[11]

Eleanor went on to describe a conversation he had with her about spiritualism as characteristic of his attitude toward religion. People were always sending the president and the First Lady accounts of conversations with the dead in seances and through mediums, and Eleanor, in ridiculing one such communication that had reached her desk, was cut short by Franklin, who told her, "I think it is unwise to say you do not believe in anything when you can't prove that it is either true or untrue. There is so much in the world which is always new in the way of discoveries that it is wiser to say that there may be spiritual things which we are simply unable now to fathom. Therefore I am interested and have respect for whatever people believe, even if I cannot understand their beliefs or share in their experiences."[12]

~

Profile 59
Felix Frankfurter

Born: Vienna, Austria, November 15, 1882
Died: Washington, D.C., February 22, 1965

The jurist, a native of Vienna, Austria, was brought to America by his parents when he was a boy, and served for many years as professor of law at Harvard, where he became famous as a supporter of liberal causes; a founder of the American Civil Liberties Union; a backer of the Zionist movement, which worked for the establishment of a Jewish homeland in Palestine; and an advocate of Franklin Roosevelt's New Deal. For the last twenty-three years of his active life, he served as associate justice of the U. S. Supreme Court and was one of the most influential members of that body.

Frankfurter, who was Jewish, told an interviewer late in life that he came from "an observant, not an orthodox...Jewish family." When he was a boy, "I wouldn't eat breakfast until I had done the religious devotions in the morning." For him and for his family, religion was "a kind of family institution, a kind of emotional habit. It had for me the warmth of the familiar, the warmth of the past, and of the association to family festivals."[1]

Especially meaningful to him was the family celebration of Passover, led "with great gayety...and lively playfulness" with his father, who had "a very sonorous singing voice." Frankfurter, in later years, described the feast as "a joyous and pleasantly sad recital, in prayer and anecdote and song, of the story of the days of the children of Israel in Egyptian slavery and their triumphant escape." When he was in his first year at Harvard and unable to be present at the family celebration, "there was an aching loneliness, as of a dog away from its home."[2]

However, young Frankfurter, in his readings, was influenced by the "Victorian agnostics." Even by that time, he went to synagogue only on holy days. Then, when he was a junior in college, he was attending the all-day Yom Kippur observance and "looked around as pious Jews were beating their breasts with intensity of feeling and anguishing sincerity." He then decided "that it was unfair of me, a kind of desecration...to be in the room with these people to whom these things had the meaning they had for them, when for me they had no other meaning than adhering to a creed that meant something to my parents but had ceased to have meaning for me." He felt that he "no longer had roots in that kind of relation to the mysteries of the universe," and thought to himself, "It's a wrong thing for me to be present in a room in holy service, to share these ceremonies, these prayers, these chants, with people for whom they have inner meaning as against me for whom they have ceased to have inner meaning."[3] And so, Frankfurter left in the middle of the service, and never again, for the rest of his long life, returned to the synagogue. But he remained "interested in theological matters."

He professed to have "a great interest in the history of religion and theological controversies." He declared, "I don't believe in spiritual Messiahs, I don't believe in economic Messiahs, I don't believe in political Messiahs. I don't believe that poor fallible man, however great, wise and deep his insight, is endowed with ultimate wisdom."[4]

One of Frankfurter's closest friends was Reinhold Niebuhr, a liberal Protestant minister who taught theology for many years at Union Theological Seminary in New York, and the two men frequently had long talks. Once he went to hear Niebuhr preach, and after the service, told him, "Reinie, may a believing unbeliever thank you for your sermon?"[5] Indeed, the justice explained, "If one has to put a label on complicated processes or complicated beliefs, or feelings about complicated aspects of life," he preferred the label of "reverent agnostic."[6]

Even so, despite his agnosticism, his failure to attend synagogue, and his marriage to a Gentile, Frankfurter considered himself a Jew. He insisted, "I came into the world a Jew and I want to leave it as a Jew," and left instructions that at his funeral, which was held in his apartment, that the traditional Jewish Mourner's Prayer be read, which affirms life and glorifies the name of God, declaring, "May His great name be blessed forever and to all eternity."[7]

~

Profile 60

Harry S. Truman

Born: Lamar, Missouri, May 8, 1884
Died: Kansas City, Missouri, December 26, 1972

I am not a religious man."[1] This is the way that the outspoken senator from Missouri, who succeeded to the presidency upon the death of Franklin Roosevelt, described himself to a friend.

Truman's parents were Baptists, but for a time, when he was a boy, the family lived in an area where the most convenient church was Presbyterian, and he attended it. During his boyhood, he read through the Bible twice. Later he recalled he "knew a lot of stories in it which were not particularly stressed in Sunday school—for example, the final ending of old man Lot's march out of Sodom and David's terrible treatment of Uriah." However, he was impressed by "the system of morals" taught by Moses in the chapter twenty of Exodus and the Sermon on the Mount, as reported Matthew.[2]

Living in Grandview, Missouri, Truman joined the Baptist church there when he was eighteen, and kept his membership apparently for the rest of his life, during which he attended church sporadically and prayed when he needed guidance. In his twenties, he wrote Bess Wallace, his future wife and the only woman in whom he ever had a romantic interest: "I like to play cards and dance as far as I know how and go to shows and do all the things [the Baptists] said I shouldn't but I don't feel badly about it. I go when I feel like it....You see, I'm a member but not strenuous one."[3]

Much later, in an autobiographical sketch, he explained: "I'm a Baptist because I think that sect gives the common man the shortest and most direct approach to God. I've never thought the Almighty is greatly interested in pomp and circumstance, because if he is, he wouldn't be interested in 'the sparrow' alluded to in Matthew's Gospel."[4] In his diary, on April 13, 1952, after attending St. John's Episcopal Church across from the White House, Truman further elaborated: "I've never been of the opinion that Almighty God cares for the building or the form that a believer approaches the Maker of Heaven and Earth. 'When two or three are gathered together' or when one asks for help from God he'll get it just as will panoplied occupants of any pulpit. Forms and ceremonies impress a lot of people, but I've never thought that the Almighty could be impressed by anything but the heart and soul of the individual. That's why I'm Baptist, whose church authority starts from the bottom—not the top."[5]

His wife, Bess, was an Episcopalian, who likewise was sporadic in her attendance. When their daughter, Margaret, was a teenager, Harry was insistent, however, that she join a church. He wrote Bess, "I don't care whether she's an Episcopalian or Baptist but she ought to be one or the other and the sooner she starts the better."[6] (Margaret apparently never developed an interest in either.) One of the things Truman disliked most about formal religion was emotionalism, of which there was a great deal in the Baptist congregations of his boyhood, where people shouted, jumped, and clapped. Such noisy services he characterized as "mostly excitement and when the excitement wears off people are as they always were....I think religion is something one should have on Wednesday as well as Sunday."[7] In an autobiographical sketch Truman commented, "I'm not very much impressed with men who publicly parade their religious beliefs. My old grandfather used to say that when he heard his neighbor pray too loudly in public he always went home and locked his smokehouse."[8]

While Truman attended church when he was in the mood, throughout most of his life he was active in a number of social and fraternal organizations: the Elks, the American Legion, the Veterans of Foreign Wars, and, above all, the Masons. According to biographer David McCullough, Truman "took the ritual and spiritual teachings of Freemasonry with extreme seriousness," and rose to the Thirty-Third degree."[9]

Most important to Harry Truman was moral conduct. "Since my childhood, at my mother's knee," he commented, "I have believed in honor, ethics, and right living as its own reward."[10] Late in life he observed, "Three things ruin a man. Power, money, and women. I never wanted power. I never had any money, and the only woman in my life is up at the house right now."[11] He maintained a reputation for moral and continent behavior even when he was in the Army in Europe. A fellow officer in World War I observed, "Personally, I think Harry is one of the cleanest fellows...morally that I ever knew or saw. I never saw him do anything out of the way that would be questionable in the way of a moral situation. He was clean all the way through. I always admired him for that quality and you know when a man's in the Army...his morals get a pretty good test."[12] Throughout his life Truman insisted, "A man not honorable in his marital relations is not usually honorable in any other."[13]

Less than three months after he became vice president, the death of

Franklin Roosevelt elevated Truman to the presidency, an office he always said he never sought. The day after his accession, he told a crowd of reporters, "Boys, if you ever pray, pray for me. I don't know whether you fellows ever had a load of hay fall on you, but when they told me yesterday what had happened, I felt like the moon, the stars, and all the planets had fallen on me."[14] When he made his first address to Congress he declared: "At this moment I have in my heart a prayer. As I have assumed my duties, I humbly pray Almighty God, in the words of King Solomon, 'Give therefore thy servant an understanding heart to judge thy people that I may discern between good and bad: for who is able to judge this thy so great a people?' I ask only to be a good and faithful servant of my Lord and my people."[15]

Truman's wholehearted support for the creation of the nation of Israel was apparently influenced, at least in part, by his religious views. Clark Clifford, who served as Truman's legal counsel affirmed: "His own reading of ancient history and the Bible made him a supporter of the idea of a Jewish homeland in Palestine, even when others who were sympathetic to the plight of the Jews were talking of sending them to places like Brazil. He did not need to be convinced by Zionists. In fact, he had to work hard to avoid the appearance of yielding to Zionist pressure."[16]

The attitude of the president toward the Vatican had a drastic effect on his church attendance. He had been attending First Baptist Church on Sixteenth Street. He claimed that he enjoyed going there because the pastor, Edward Hughes Pruden, treated him not as a celebrity but as an ordinary parishioner. He had begun to attend regularly and even occasionally give talks to the Sunday-school children when he decided to establish diplomatic ties to the Vatican, a move which was criticized by many Baptists. Dr. Pruden went to the White House one day to see the president, and when, departing, the reporters asked him about the purpose of his visit, the minister told them, "I came to dissuade the President from sending an ambassador to the Vatican." When Truman read of the interview in the paper, he fell into a rage and spouted, "Damn it, this is a violation of confidence!" Never again did he set foot in First Baptist.[17]

A similar breach of confidence led to permanent alienation from the most prominent member of his denomination, Billy Graham. Invited to the White House in 1950, Graham, then in his early thirties, came with two aides. "The President stood and greeted us and told us he was a Baptist himself," the evangelist later recalled. "Well, I immediately began trying to preach to him." After a minute or two, Truman interrupted him brusquely. "He said he lived by the Sermon on the Mount and the Golden Rule, and then repeated he was a Baptist," Graham recounted. "Would it be all right if we just had a word of prayer before we leave, Mr. President?" ventured the preacher. Without waiting for a response, he made bold to put his arm around the President, and prayed that God would bless him and his administration and "give him of his wisdom in dealing with all the difficulties in the country and the world." While he prayed, his aide, Cliff Barrows, kept up the typical Baptist ejaculatory prayers that Truman hated: "Yes, Lord! Amen!"[18]

When he left the White House, Graham was greeted by reporters and recounted everything that went on. Already annoyed by Graham's manner, Truman was furious when he learned of the interview and gave orders that the evangelist was never again to be admitted near his presence.[19] Graham and Truman did meet again in 1967 when the evangelist visited the former president and apologized for his indiscretion. Truman always disliked Graham, however, and late in life characterized him as a "counterfeit."[20]

On the day that he left office in 1953, Truman, his wife, his cabinet, and a few friends attended a private and unpublicized prayer service at St. John's Episcopal Church, across from the White House. Truman joined in the singing of "O God, Our Help in Ages Past," and while his wife and daughter knelt beside him, sat with his head bowed while the prayers were offered.[21]

There is little written about Truman's churchgoing or religious activity in the nearly two decades he lived after leaving the presidency. When, in June 1963, in the *Murray v. Curlett* Decision, the Supreme Court forbade the use of the Lord's Prayer and Bible readings as public school requirements, Truman found himself on the same side as the outraged Billy Graham. The former president was quoted as saying that prayer "never hurt anyone" and made "good citizens out of them."[22]

To the end, Truman maintained his belief that "The Sermon on the Mount is the greatest of all things in the Bible, a way of life, and

maybe some day men will get to understand it as the real way of life."[23]
His religion was centered on conduct in this world rather than on the
spiritual or supernatural, and what he held to be of utmost importance is underscored in a prayer which Truman said through much of
his life: "Oh! Almighty and Everlasting God, Creator of Heaven, Earth,
and the Universe: Help me to be, to think, to act what is right, because
it is right; make me truthful, honest, and honorable in all things; make
me intellectually honest for the sake of right and honor without thought
of reward to me. Give me the ability to be charitable, forgiving, and
patient with my fellowmen—help me to understand their motives and
their shortcoming—even as Thou understandest mine!"[24]

∼

Profile 61

Anna Eleanor Roosevelt

Born: New York, New York, October 11, 1884
Died: New York, New York, November 7, 1962

The wife of Franklin Delano Roosevelt and the most active and
influential First Lady in American history, she served, after his
death, as delegate to the United Nations and played an important role
in drafting the Universal Declaration of Human Rights, earning her
the sobriquet "First Lady of the World." In an interview in 1952, she
said, "I grew up in a family where there was a very deep religious
feeling. I don't think it was spoken of a great deal. It was more or less
taken for granted that everybody held certain beliefs and needed certain reinforcements of their own strength and that came through your
belief in God and your knowledge of prayer."[1]

Eleanor's parents, alcoholic playboy Elliott Roosevelt, brother of
Theodore Roosevelt, and socialite Anna Hall were not the sort of people
in whom one would expect to find a meaningful spiritual commitment, but both were actually somewhat observant. Elliott, after his
separation from his wife, regularly attended an Episcopal church near

his home in Abingdon, in southwestern Virginia, where he sang in the choir and was popular with the local clergy.[2] Both Elliott and Anna Roosevelt urged Eleanor to memorize the Twenty-Third Psalm. Anna Roosevelt felt that the Bible was "useful" in "anchoring" children "to the right."[3] When "Nell" was eight years old, shortly after her mother died, one of her brothers also was taken, and she wrote her father, "We must remember Ellie is going to be safe in heaven and to be with Mother who is waiting there, and our Lord wants Ellie Boy with him now. We must be happy and do God's will."[4]

By the time she was ten, her father, too, was dead and she was living with her maternal grandmother, Mary Ludlow Hall, whom she characterized in later years as "a good women with a great and simple faith."[5] Grandmother Hall conducted prayer services at the beginning and end of each day, devotions that everyone in her household—including the servants—was required to attend.[6]

"But as I grew older I questioned a great many things that...my grandmother...had taken for granted,"[7] Eleanor Roosevelt said later in life. After she married her distant cousin, Franklin Roosevelt and began a family, she agonized over whether to give her children religious instruction. Her husband told her, "It didn't do you any harm to learn those things, so why not let your children learn them? When they grow up, they'll think things out for themselves."[8] This advice gave her the feeling "that perhaps that's what we all must do—think out for ourselves—what we could believe and how we could live by it. And so I came to the conclusion that you had to use this life to develop the very best that you could develop."[9]

Throughout her life, Eleanor Roosevelt continued to attend Episcopal services. "Mother seldom missed Sunday services,"[10] her oldest son recalled. One of her granddaughters, in an attempt to explain the religion of Eleanor and Franklin, later wrote, "The Victorian-age people...believed in the concept of loyalty, not only to the family but to institutions such as the church....I think it was a question of loyalty, of feeling part of the group. My grandparents were religious in the old sense. It was something you did, it was something you kind of accepted—and you could interpret intellectually any way you wanted, but you still did it. It was part of your life and your responsibility."[11]

Holy Communion was very important to Eleanor Roosevelt, although she considered it a "symbol," rather than the physical reality of the presence of Christ. "Taking Communion with other people around the rail was one way she felt a part of the whole fabric of human relationships,"[12] her granddaughter observed.

Although she was an Episcopalian, Mrs. Roosevelt felt comfortable in just about any church. She seemed to dislike Roman Catholicism, however, because she felt that its leaders tended to meddle in politics.[13] In 1949 she and Francis Cardinal Spellman, archbishop of New York, angered each other when he urged government aid for parochial schools and she publicly disagreed, insisting that this would violate the separation of church and state prescribed in the Constitution. "Spiritual leadership," she wrote, "should remain spiritual leadership and the temporal power should not become too important in any church."[14] Eleven years later, she was still sufficiently distrustful of Roman Catholics in public office to express reservations about John F. Kennedy's bid for the White House, even though he was a fellow Democrat.[15]

Mrs. Roosevelt observed once that there was little in common between the organized church and the teaching of Christ. Although she found it "meaningful" to worship in church, especially in beautiful structures in which she could derive a sense of the "sublime,"[16] she confided to friends that she got more out of reading the Bible and praying alone than she did from going to church.[17]

Each evening she knelt by her bed to pray. Before giving a speech, she would pray for God's help in "saying something that would be meaningful" to the audience.[18] "A prayer for me," she wrote, "is not something to be recited only in church. It should be a continuous influence, something carried in the heart and mind all the time, shaping one's active life."[19] On her bedside table and in her purse she kept a copy of the Prayer of Saint Francis (which begins, "Lord, make me an instrument of Thy peace..."). She also kept on her person an observation by the eighteenth-century Quaker John Woolman that prayer and submission to God's will were the surest remedies for all problems, and that God was able to deliver not only people, but also nations who came to him in prayer.[20] She wrote out a prayer that reads in part: "Our Father, who hast set a restlessness in our hearts and made us all

seekers after that which we can never fully find, forbid us to be satisfied with what we make of life. Draw us from base content, and set
our eyes on far-off goals. Keep us at tasks too hard for us, that we may
be driven to thee for strength. Deliver us from fretfulness and self-pity;
make us sure of the good we cannot see....Save us from ourselves and
show us a vision of the world made new. May thy spirit of peace and
illumination so enlighten our minds that all life shall glow with new
meaning and new purpose, through Jesus Christ Our Lord."[21]

In 1952 she told an interviewer, "I don't know whether I believe in
a future life. I believe that all that you go through here must have some
value, therefore there must be some reason." She explained that she
tried not to worry about the future. "I think I am pretty much of a
fatalist," she added. "You have to accept whatever comes and the only
important thing is that you meet it with courage and with the best that
you have to give."[22] However, shortly before her death in 1962 she
took her father's old Bible to her priest to ask about getting the cover
repaired. After describing her father's failings, she asked the priest if
he thought that they would keep him out of heaven. When the priest
told her that he thought that her father's weaknesses, in light of what
she told him of his faith, would not bar him from heaven, she seemed
"visibly pleased at the thought that she would see her father again
someday."[23] On another occasion, however, she told a senator that she
"had no expectation of being united" with her husband in the next
world.[24]

Eleanor Roosevelt said that as long as a person does "the best that
you were able to do" that "was what you were put here to do and that
was what you were accomplishing by being here."[25] When she was
racked by the agonies of her final illness, and told her nurse that she
wished to die and heard the reply, "The Lord who put you in this
world will take you from it when you have finished the job for which
you are here," she looked at her intravenous tubes and oxygen tank
and retorted, "Utter nonsense!"[26] Those were her last recorded words.

～

Profile 62
Hugo La Fayette Black

Born: Harlan, Alabama, February 27, 1886
Died: Bethesda, Maryland, September 25, 1971

Associate Justice of the Supreme Court for thirty-four years, Black was bitterly criticized by Christian conservatives when in 1962 he wrote the majority opinion for *Engel v. Vitale,* the first of several court decisions that effectively banned the practice of prayer from public schools in the United States. Although condemned by some as an atheist, Black was conversant with the Bible and considered himself a religious man.

The son of a father who did not go to church and a mother who was a devout Baptist, young Black grew up in Alabama and attended a Baptist church in the morning and Methodist services in the afternoon. When he was a young man, he joined the Baptist church in Ashland, Alabama, chiefly out of respect to the memory of his mother, who had recently died. Before applying for membership, he conferred with the pastor, expressing his concern that he would be required "to confess a religious faith greater than I had" or be forced to pretend "that I had been a heavy sinner simply because I had sometimes played cards or danced."[1] The minister agreed to accept him on his terms, and, in the next few years, the young lawyer became church clerk, Sunday-school teacher, and Sunday-school organist. For sixteen years, he taught Sunday school at the First Baptist Church of Birmingham, where he was then living.

In a talk to his students during the 1920s, he held forth on his religious convictions: "Religion is a vital part of the warp and woof of our national existence. Its glowing, burning truths inspired the hearts of the American pioneers. Its sacred precepts established our home life; shaped our infant institutions and nourished a spirit of equality and democracy. The voice of Roger Williams and his followers played no small part in impressing the principles and policies that molded our institutions and crystallized our sentiments into a written Constitution and laws. The Bible penetrated the trackless forests with the pioneers and strengthened the sturdy character of our early settlers. In the name of religion and freedom of religion, laws were resisted to cross a tempestuous ocean to an unknown land. Our country has grown great, wealthy, and prosperous...under a government instituted by readers and lovers of the Bible."[2]

Around the same time that he was active in the Baptist church, Black joined the Ku Klux Klan. When, later in life, he was criticized for this affiliation, he explained that he was an active Mason, and that in the Alabama of the 1920s, the Klan was organized and run by the lodge.[3] Moreover, he was told, "If good men like you don't join the Klan, it will be left to some of the roughnecks."[4] It should be pointed out, in Black's defense, that the Klan was popular in the 1920s as a superpatriotic organization, and many people joined it who were not violent bigots.

When Black moved to Washington, D.C., he attended All Souls Unitarian Church, where he became a friend of the pastor, Dr. Duncan Howlett. Black's second wife observed, "Hugo says he's going to hold on to Dr. Howlett because he's his closest connection to God."[5] Throughout his life, Black read the Bible frequently. He frequently remarked, "When in trouble, read your Bible."[6] His favorite passage was 1 Corinthians 13:13: "And now faith, hope, love abide, these three; and the greatest of these is love."[7] The justice seems, however, to have looked to the Bible only for the inspiration of its ethical teaching. One biographer commented that "a more formally irreligious man [than he] would be hard to find."[8] Black, who "never quite felt there was a hereafter," once said: "I can't exactly believe and I can't exactly not believe."[9]

Black was involved in the church-state controversy as early as 1947, when he wrote an opinion in *Everson v. Board of Education* supporting the Court's decision to uphold a New Jersey law that authorized local school boards to reimburse parents for the cost of public transportation of students to both public and private schools—including church schools. Black wrote: "Neither a state nor the federal government can set up a state church. Neither can pass laws which aid one religion, or prefer one religion over another....Neither a state nor the

Federal Government can, openly or secretly, participate in the affairs of any religious organizations or groups or vice versa. In the words of Jefferson, the clause against establishment of religion by law was intended to erect 'a wall of separation between Church and State.' "[10] Black, however, agreed with his colleagues that this "wall of separation" had not been breached by the state of New Jersey, and that state aid to a public safety measure which was designed to protect students could not be construed as aid to church schools.[11]

Black, however, insisted that the "wall" had been violated by a prayer recommended, but not required, for public-school students, by the New York State Board of Regents in the early 1960s. He wrote the majority opinion for *Engel v. Vitale* in April 1962, insisting that the suggested prayer was, in fact, an "establishment of religion," banned by the Constitution. Since the "daily invocation of God's blessings" was a religious activity, "it is no part of the business of government to compose official prayers for any group of the American people to recite as a part of a religious program carried on by the government."[12] He cited the First Amendment to express his conviction that the framers of the Constitution believed that religion was "too personal, too sacred, too holy to permit its 'unhallowed perversion' by a civil magistrate."[13]

The justice wrote a niece: "The basic premise of the First Amendment is that people must be left to say their prayers in their own way, and to their own God, without express or explicit coercion from any political office holder. There are not many people with religion and intelligence who will think this constitutional principle wrong on mature second thought."[14]

Speaking to a group of Baptist ministers, Black said that he hoped the Court decision would not cause people to "lose their religious convictions," because "religious people conceived the Constitution."[15] But he seemed to feel that religious practices and convictions were appropriately expressed in private, and that in the interest of freedom of religion, all formal public religious observances were out of order, and that religious persecution would result if this were not the case. He explained, "People [have] been tortured, their ears lopped off, and sometimes their tongues cut or their eyes gouged out, all in the name of religion....When one religion gets predominance, they immediately try to suppress others."[16]

Shortly after *Engel v. Vitale*, Justice Black received an angry letter from a woman who warned him that he would go to hell. He answered her, in keeping with his apparent sentiment that religion was to be practiced in private. Mrs. Black described her husband's reply in her diary: "If she would go to the library, as he was sure she didn't have it in her house, and ask for a book called the Bible, she could read where it said, 'Pray in your own closet.'"[17]

∼

Profile 63
Marcus Moziah Garvey

Born: St. Ann's Bay, Jamaica, August 17, 1887
Died: London, England, June 10, 1940

The Jamaican editor who lived several years in New York and who founded the Universal Negro Improvement Association "to improve the spirit of pride" among people of color was never an American citizen, but his ideas were extremely popular among some African Americans. It was the goal of Marcus Garvey to establish worldwide unity among Negroes and to create an independent black state in Africa (which was then almost entirely colonized by European powers) whither the oppressed people of the black diaspora could find fulfillment.

Garvey, whose parents were Methodist, attended schools run by the Methodist Church.[1] As an adult, he complained that traditional Christianity taught "all that is good is white and all that is bad is black,"[2] and argued that the teachings of Jesus needed to be rescued from the corruptions imposed by whites. In his "School of African Philosophy" he taught what he called "Black Fundamentalism."

Garvey affirmed that "there is a God and we believe in him. He is not a person nor a physical being. He is a spirit and he is a universal intelligence." Human beings were created in the likeness of God in

terms of their intelligence, which is "a unitary particle of God's universal intelligence." Because they are "only units of God and God is the
whole," God cannot be questioned. Garvey thought it "presumptuous" therefore when human beings question God.[3]

He contended, "Man never dies. Nothing dies. Man is made of body
and spirit. The spirit is God. It is intelligence. The body of man is
matter. It changes from living matter in the man to the other matter in
the soil. It is always the same matter. It doesn't die in the sense of how
we understand death. It changes."[4] One should not fear death, "because what you call death is only change and you are still in the universe." He urged, "Do not be more cowardly than the rose, the apple,
the coconut, the sheep, the fish or the cow to do that which all [things]
must, and which we call death....If you are going to weep to die, then
the rose should weep to die. If you weep, you are a coward."[5]

Garvey was not entirely without hope of eternal life, at least in a
purely spiritual form. He conceded that "good souls" may in fact "pass
into some higher realm of usefulness, probably to become an angel or
to be used by God in some higher sphere." The wicked soul, however,
never lives as a soul again, but is "judged before it completely disap-
pears, and will recognize its punishment in the judgment before God,
then is obliterated completely."[6]

Christ, Garvey believed to be a "superior creature," who had "in
his veins the blood of all mankind and belonged to no particular race,"
who lived an "exemplary" life, "faultless to a word." Christ, according to Garvey, was divine in that his "free-will soul," which he shared
with other mortals, never disobeyed "the Holy Spirit guide of God."[7]

Christ taught the greatest philosophy in history: to love one's neighbor as oneself, to treat others as one would wish, in turn, to be treated.
His mission was "to redeem man from sin and place him back on the
pinnacle of goodness as God intended when he made the first two
creatures." This was accomplished chiefly through example, as Jesus
showed that man "could lift himself by obedience to the highest soul
expression in keeping with the Holy Spirit of God of which he is a part."[8]

The symbol of Christ was the cross. "The black man has a greater
claim to the cross than all other men," insisted Garvey "If it is a symbol of Christ's triumph, then the Negro should share in that triumph."[9]

Garvey believed in the Trinity, which he taught was "not commonly understandable to the ordinary mind. Each person, Garvey contended, possesses "the Holy Spirit of God," which can neither sin nor die. What sins is the mind, which rebels against the Holy Spirit within. For Garvey, it seems as if the goal of human beings was to harmonize the mind and will with the Holy Spirit, and, thereby, through this effort, achieve salvation. "You can worship God by yourself," he said. "You are responsible to God by yourself. You have to live your own soul before God. Nobody but yourself can save your soul."[10]

Garvey taught that "the shortest prayer we may give to God, even if we never pray otherwise, is by making the sign of the cross and by saying, at the same time, in the name of the Father, the Son, and the Holy Ghost." This, in itself, "is a powerful prayer" which "supersedes all others." He insisted, "if the words are repeated sincerely and earnestly from the heart, God answers that prayer."[11]

Perhaps the most controversial tenet of Garvey's Black Fundamentalism was his belief that Christ ought to be portrayed, artistically, as a black man. He urged the depiction of black Madonna and of black angels. "Whilst our God has no color," he explained, "yet it is human to see everything through our own spectacles, and since the white people have seen their God through white spectacles, we have only now started out to see our God through our own spectacles....We Negroes believe in the God of Ethiopia. The everlasting God—God the Father, God the Son, and God the Holy Ghost—that is the God in whom we believe, but we shall worship him through the spectacle of Ethiopia."[12]

The core of the "Black Fundamentalism" of Marcus Garvey seems to have been salvation through right living. If one wished to commune with God, Garvey taught he should make an altar of his heart, soul, and mind, and "express it in the following way:

> I've built a sacred place all mine,
> To worship God, who is Divine,
> I go there every day, in thought,
> Right to my own, dear sacred heart—
> MY ALTAR.[13]

~

Walter Perry Johnson

Born: Humboldt, Kansas, November 6, 1887
Died: Washington, D.C., December 10, 1946

Considered by many to have been the greatest of all pitchers, the mainstay of the Washington senators won more than four-hundred games in a twenty-year career. A mild and dignified man, in contrast to his contemporaries Ty Cobb and Babe Ruth, Johnson was a man of unimpeachable reputation. In all of the literature of professional sports, there seems never to have been written a word detrimental to his character. All who knew him agreed that the Big Train was amiable, even-tempered, and a well-adjusted family man. His daughter, Carolyn Johnson Thomas, wrote, "He...lived the Golden Rule every day of his life. He was kind and considerate to everyone and, although he himself adhered to the highest moral standards, I never knew him to be judgmental toward others. His close friends ranged from a fox-hunting country bar owner to a prominent minister."[1]

Johnson was not, however, a conventionally religious man. Although his children were baptized at St. John's Episcopal Church in Bethesda, Maryland, and attended Sunday school there, he was not a church-goer. His religion seems to have been the golden rule—treating others the way he would have liked to be treated. This idea was evidently instilled in him by his parents. When he was growing up on farms in Kansas and California, formal religion played only a little role in the life of his family, but Walter and his siblings were taught to live according to ethical standards.[2]

Johnson told one of his daughters, "It is more important to demonstrate goodness in your daily life than to proclaim your purity primarily on Sundays."[3] Another daughter, when a young girl, asked him whether it was really necessary to go to church, and received "his thoughtful and candid reply" that "you could be really a good person and still not go to church."[4]

Johnson was not hostile to the church. After he moved his family to Germantown, Maryland, he expressed his pleasure that one of his daughters chose to attend services at a nearby Methodist church.[5] It was simply that he felt that deeds were more important than creeds. He seemed to believe that it was desirable that men and women live virtuous and benevolent lives, whether this was inspired by a formal religious commitment or some other means.

"Whatever faith Dad harbored was sorely tested," Carolyn Johnson Thomas wrote, by the death of a baby daughter in 1921 and by the sudden passing of his wife, Hazel, in 1930. "His letters to Mother after their little daughter Elinor's death are heartbreaking," she wrote, and "it is understandable that Mother's cruelly early death bewildered him and led him to wonder 'how God could do this to me.' He was so kind and gentle, and would never knowingly have inflicted pain on anyone. It would have been difficult to acknowledge a just God under the circumstances."[6]

Daisy Bardwell Jones, who served as Johnson's private duty nurse during the pitcher's last illness, devoted a chapter in her autobiography to her experiences at his bedside. During much of the time her patient was speechless, but when he spoke, he did not mention God or religion. However, the Reverend Edward Duff, a hospital chaplain, reported that Johnson, aware that he was approaching the end of life, told him, "Father, I guess I'm gonna be seeing Hazel....[I]t's been a long time."[7] Of this remark, Carolyn Thomas wrote, "He may have found solace in at least the hope, if not the belief, that he would one day rejoin those he had so deeply loved."[8]

～

Profile 65
Knute Kenneth Rockne

Born: Voss, Norway, March 4, 1888
Died: Bazaar, Kansas, March 31, 1931

The celebrated head coach of the Notre Dame football team worked for a university that was run by a Roman Catholic religious order and had a student body that was overwhelmingly Roman Catholic. For most of his life, however, Rockne, a native of Norway who had been brought to America by his parents at the age of five, was a nominal Lutheran, but was never pressured by his employers to adopt their religious affiliation. He was married to a Roman Catholic, but, far from pushing him to convert, when he suggested, shortly after their wedding, that "it might be a good idea" for him to embrace her faith, his wife suggested that he wait. Finally, in the spring of 1925, he informed her, "I'm going to do it. Right away, before I get sidetracked. It's right now."[1]

The coach was inspired in his decision by the example of his players, many of whom took holy Communion every day. "I'd begun to realize how incongruous it must have appeared," he explained, "when we arrived in another city for a game and the public saw my boys rushing off to church the moment they got off the train while the coach rode to the hotel and took his ease."

One night, before an important game, Rockne was nervous and unable to sleep, and got dressed and went to the lobby of the hotel where the team was staying. As he explained in a talk shortly after his commitment to Catholicism: "About five-thirty in the morning, while pacing the lobby, I unexpectedly ran into two of my players hurrying out. I asked where they were going at that hour—although I had a good idea. Within the next few minutes, a dozen more hurried out and I suddenly decided to go with them. They didn't realize it, but these youngsters were making a powerful impression on me with their devotion, and when I saw all of them walking up to the Communion rail, and realized the hours of sleep they'd sacrificed, I understood for the first time what a powerful ally their religion was to them in their work on the football field."[2]

Rockne asked his friend, Father Vincent Mooney, who was a former football player, to instruct him, and three nights a week, for several months, the two men met. The coach's daughter recalled: "I remember my mother telling me what an intellectual approach my father took to his conversion. It would have been simple for him to do some of the reading and merely make [the] most of the sessions with Father Mooney. But he never missed a night. He could have accepted everything at face value quite dutifully and with a minimum of extra time spent. After all, he was a terribly busy man. But Daddy was too curious and too sensitive for that. Every time Father Mooney got off onto some new bit of religious philosophy, Daddy insisted on doing as much reading as possible on that phase of it. He'd come home with all sorts of big books, even during football season, and wade into them because he wanted to know all the underlying thoughts and subtleties connected with whatever discussion was lying ahead. Then he'd go to Father Mooney feeling that he was better able to understand the precepts and dogma he was being asked to accept."[3]

In those days, people embracing Roman Catholicism from other Christian denominations were almost always asked to undergo a second, conditional baptism, and this sacrament was administered to Rockne at the Old Log Chapel on the afternoon of November 20, 1925. The next day he took his first Communion at St. Edward's Hall on the campus. It so happened that the coach's young son was to take his first Communion that day, also. But Rockne kept the news of his intended reception of the Eucharist a secret not only from his friends but from his children as well, and when he started to walk beside Knute, Jr., to the Communion rail, the horrified boy whispered nervously, "Daddy, you know you can't come up there with me. Only Catholics can receive Communion." Knute, Sr., confidently whispered, "Don't worry—Father Mooney will tell you all about it." As the two Rocknes knelt together at the rail, Knute, Jr., watched uneasily as Father Mooney approached with the ciborium, the container from which he distributed the consecrated wafers. "It's all right, son," the priest explained. "Your father was baptized yesterday."[4]

That day Notre Dame played Northwestern University, which was run by Methodists. At halftime the Fighting Irish were losing, and their coach inspired them, declaring: "As you all know by now, I received my first Communion this morning...and obviously this is a helluva religion I've gotten myself into! Losing to a bunch of Methodists out there." Notre Dame rallied and won, 13–10. After the game, Rockne told fullback Rex Enright, who had played an important role in the victory, "It was nice for a good Presbyterian like you, Rex, to save the new Catholic's ballgame from those Methodists."[5]

Rockne remained an active Roman Catholic during the few years that remained to his life, and it was said that when his body was identified amid the rubble of a Kansas plane crash, the beads found in his fingers indicated that during the last seconds of his life, as his plane foundered and plunged to earth, he was praying the rosary.[6]

~

Profile 66

Irving Berlin

Born: Mohilev, Siberia, Russia, May 11, 1888
Died: New York, New York, September 22, 1989

The composer of "White Christmas" and "Easter Parade" was probably the greatest songwriter of his time. The son, grandson, and great-grandson of cantors, he was born in the town of Mohilev, Russia, with the name of Israel Baline, but emigrated as a small child, along with his parents and elder siblings, after their home was burned by a Russian mob during the reign of the anti-Jewish Emperor Alexander III. Although he was raised in a Jewish neighborhood in Manhattan by Orthodox parents, like many Jews of his generation, he did not practice his faith as an adult, even though he continued throughout his extremely long life to identify himself as a Jew.

He was married twice, both times to Gentiles. His first wife died shortly after their marriage; the second, who preceded him in death after more than sixty years of marriage, bore him three daughters as well as a son who died shortly after birth. Ellin Mackay Berlin was from a Roman Catholic family, but, like her husband, did not practice her religion for much of her life. When their oldest daughter was born, however, she did suggest raising her as a Roman Catholic, provoking a violent reaction from her husband. According to their daughter, they had "such a terrible fight...that she did not ask again."[1] The Berlins decided that they would rear their children in "the moral and ethical values common to all great religions." They determined to give their children a sense of what was right and what was wrong and to raise them not to be good Jews or good Catholics, but to be good human beings.[2]

Although Berlin seldom if ever attended religious services, Ellin took the children to New York's fashionable Temple Emanu-El. They did not celebrate Easter, but observed Yom Kippur, Succoth, Hanukkah, and Christmas. During Hanukkah, the menorah was set up in a windowsill in the living room and Ellin read the children the story of Judas Maccabaeus, explaining "how, out of such a bloodthirsty history, could come peace and hope." At Christmastime she read the account of the birth of Jesus in the Gospel according to Luke.[3] The children were taught that the Christ Child was a "symbol of hope" and that he grew up to be "the greatest of the Jewish prophets who... rose from the dead and went to heaven."[4] The children were taught to recite the Lord's Prayer and "Now I Lay Me Down to Sleep," and when the second child, a boy, died shortly after birth, the oldest daughter, Mary Ellin, was told that he had been "taken by the angels and was in heaven."[5]

Nearly all the religious instruction came from the mother. Berlin himself, although he identified himself as Jew, professed to being an agnostic. When his wife, late in life, became a practicing Roman Catholic, he was unhappy. Some years later, however, he told one of his daughters, "Remember how upset I was, what a fuss I made, when your mother went back into the church? I'm glad now she has that."[6]

In 1944, Berlin traveled to Italy to entertain American troops in Italy. While in Rome, he thanked Pope Pius XII for all that he had done in behalf of Jews in Italy. (To the end of his life, he rejected the accusations that the pontiff had closed his eyes to the Holocaust.)[7] Later, he wrote his wife about "a visit to one of your cousins, John something....He lives close to a famous monastery....I spent some time with the priest there. It was very interesting."[8]

Ellin's cousin was Count Giovanni Telfner. The town was San Giovanni Rotondo (in south central Italy), and the priest was the renowned Padre Pio. Pio was a Capuchin friar, one year older than Berlin, who for more than twenty years had borne on his hands, feet, and side spontaneous wounds known as the stigmata, wounds suggestive of the Passion of Christ. Padre Pio was renowned for miracles of healing, for prophecies, for a mysterious "aroma of paradise" that, at times, could be perceived by people throughout the world whenever Pio was praying for them, as well as for his ability to "read souls." As a consequence, even during wartime, crowds of people surrounded the friary where Pio lived and worked, often waiting for days to line up to make their confession to him and to attend the Mass that the beloved priest celebrated at five in the morning.

Berlin apparently asked to meet Padre Pio, and the two men talked for a time through an interpreter. Nobody knows what was said. At the end of the interview, Padre Pio kissed Berlin on both cheeks and blessed his journey home.[9] Padre Pio was famed for being the agent— on occasion—of instant conversions, but there is no evidence that Berlin was converted. He evidently had an amicable talk with Padre Pio, but, in the forty-five years that remained to his life, he continued to describe himself as an agnostic, who observed some Jewish and Christian holidays as secular and cultural affairs.

～

Profile 67

Rose Fitzgerald Kennedy

Born: Boston, Massachusetts, July 22, 1890
Died: Hyannis Port, Massachusetts, January 22, 1995

The matriarch of the Kennedy family—daughter of the mayor of Boston, wife of a banker and businessman who served as U. S. ambassador to Great Britain, and mother of three United States senators, one of whom became president—was a devout Christian and practicing Roman Catholic throughout her extremely long life. She treated her religious background and her faith in eloquent detail in her memoirs, which she wrote in her eighties.

Her father, John Francis Fitzgerald, she described as a "devout and dutiful Catholic who took Holy Communion regularly and observed the holy days and obligations of the Church calendar," but who was "so deeply involved in the affairs of the world that he took religion for granted without thinking about it." For him, going to church was an opportunity "of communicating not only with God but with many of his friends and political constituents."[1]

It was Rose's mother, Mary Hannon Fitzgerald, who imparted to her the "precious gift" of "a deep faith in the Church and its teachings and practices." For her, "the Church was a pervading and abiding presence." Rose's mother taught her children their catechism and religious lessons and explained to them the fasts and feasts of the Church. "May was the month of the Blessed Virgin. There was a little shrine to her in our house, with her statue, and all month we kept it decorated with fresh flowers and offered a prayer there each night. Every night during Lent my mother would gather us in one of the rooms of the house, turn out the lights—the better to concentrate— and lead us in reciting the Rosary." Although Rose's knees ached and she sometimes wondered "why I should be doing all the kneeling and studying and memorizing and contemplating and praying," she appropriated the faith that her mother taught her, and, in time, became "understanding and grateful," and tried, in her turn (with varying success) to pass on to her own nine children "this precious gift of faith."[2]

Rose Kennedy did not consider herself particularly religious—just "an ordinary, staunch, believing Irish Roman Catholic." Her faith had great importance to her and she tried to make it important to her offspring. "Religion was never oppressive or even conspicuous in our household," she wrote, "but it was always there, part of our lives, and the Church's teachings and customs were observed. We went to Mass on Sundays, holy days, First Fridays. We said grace before meals....I would choose a different child each time to say grace. At Sunday dinner after Mass, we generally had a little discussion of what the sermon had been about, what the Gospel message meant, so the children would pay attention during Mass. If it was a holy day or a favorite saint's day, we discussed its meaning and asked what the saint's life could teach us. At Easter, of course, we asked the meaning of the Resurrection and life everlasting....Faith, I would tell them, is a great gift from God and is a living gift, to sustain us in our lives on earth, to guide us in our activities, to be a source of solace and comfort, so we should help it grow and flourish, and try never to lose it."[3]

She wanted the children to have at least a few years in good Catholic schools "where, along with excellent secular education, they would receive thorough instruction in the doctrines of their religion and intelligent answers to any doubts or perplexities," but her husband, while allowing the girls to spend some time at convent schools, insisted that the four sons be educated almost entirely in secular schools.[4]

"I'm sure God wants us to be happy and take pleasure in life," Rose Kennedy wrote. "He doesn't want us to be sad....I see no reason to doubt it. God made the world and made us to live in it for a while. We owe him infinite thanks and obligations and duties. Surely among these is the appreciation of the delights of life."[5]

Rose Kennedy, who outlived her husband and four of her children, had, of course, her share of heartbreak. One of her greatest griefs was the mental disability of her oldest daughter, Rosemary. Nonetheless, "Rosemary's misfortune did not incline me in the least toward doubt," she wrote. "If anything [it] strengthened my belief and sheltered my spirit from despair. I asked myself endlessly why this had to happen to her. I felt it was so unfair for her to have so many handicaps and the others to be so blessed. The more I thought, the clearer it became to me that God in his infinite wisdom did have a reason, though it was hidden from me, and that in time, in some way, it would be unfolded to me. 'God wants something different from each of us.' "[6]

For Mrs. Kennedy, the most important thing in human life was faith. "If God were to take away all his blessings, health, physical fitness, wealth, intelligence, and leave me but one gift, I would ask for faith— for with faith in him, in his goodness, mercy, love for me, and belief in everlasting life, I believe I could suffer the loss of my other gifts and still be happy—trustful, leaving all to his inscrutable providence. When I start my day with a prayer of consecration to him, with complete trust and confidence, I am perfectly relaxed and happy regardless of what accident of fate befalls me because I know it is part of his divine plan and he will care for me and my dear ones."[7]

For Rose Kennedy, faith was the continuing awareness of the existence of God, not in some far-off and unrelated manner but as the object of a spiritual experience in which she was personally involved. She was as confident of God's existence as she was of her own, "and I see him as Lord and Savior relating lovingly to all who are created by his hand." Christ revealed himself through the Bible "and for Catholics especially he reveals himself also in his Church." Both Scripture and Church, she believed, had to be "experienced in faith to comprehend the riches they enfold."[8]

"We must guard against the thought that faith is mere credulity or that we can simply talk or reason ourselves into possessing it," she wrote. "The truth is that just as it centers upon God, so too it comes from him to those who seek it." A person could not be born into faith. Even children thoroughly instructed in the truths of the Christian faith "at some time in his or her development" had to "pray for the gift of faith" and "personally accept the gift of faith and cherish it as his or her own." In trouble, a person "must turn to God in faith, knowing that his loving-kindness is never far from us and that his providence never allows us to be tested beyond our strength. If we can truly believe in his presence and goodness to us, we are never alone or forsaken."[9]

The three religious practices that were most meaningful to Rose

Kennedy were the rosary, a book of meditations by John Henry Cardinal Newman, the nineteenth-century English religious leader, and the Stations of the Cross. "The rosary has helped me to lead a happy life devoted to the love of God and for the benefit of my family and my friends, and the welfare of my neighbor," she insisted. She conceded that some people might find the praying of the rosary silly, "but for me, if I cannot sleep—if I am worried on a plane, if I am pacing the floor overwrought in thinking of my husband's illness—I hold the rosary in my hand, it gives me comfort, trust, serenity, a sense of understanding by the Blessed Mother because as I have talked and prayed to her all my life, in happy successful times. I know now she will understand and comfort me and bring me solace."[10] She found Newman's meditations helpful when she was discouraged and "in an inexplicable dilemma." She loved to go to church to kneel before the fourteen pictures representing the events in the last hours of the life of her Lord, and found that meditating and praying before each brought her comfort and consolation. At the final station where she saw the Virgin Mary view her Son in the tomb, she thought of the resurrection of the dead.

"In the Resurrection of Christ," she wrote, "we find our sure hope in the immortality of the individual soul, as well as the promise of a resurrection of our own bodies, to enjoy forever the presence of God in heaven, above the grave." Such a faith gave her life "a sublime meaning and a source of wonderful strength."[11] When she came to the fourteenth station, Mrs. Kennedy affirmed, "I take a renewed strength and courage in the thought that as Jesus Christ rose from the dead, my husband and I and our sons and daughters will one day rise again and we all shall be happy together, never more to be separated. My spirits are lightened and my heart rejoices, and I thank God for my belief in the Resurrection."[12] The promises of Christ were her steady source of guidance and inspiration throughout her extended lifetime. In such a faith Rose Fitzgerald Kennedy lived and died.

～

Profile 68
Earl Warren

Born: Los Angeles, California, March 19, 1891
Died: Washington, D.C., July 9, 1974

The former governor of California, who presided over the Supreme Court for sixteen years and is perhaps best known for writing the majority opinion in the *Brown v. Board of Education* Decision which made racially segregated schools illegal, was attacked as an atheist for several decisions in the 1960s, which effectively banned formal prayers and religious observances in public schools.

None of Warren's biographers have much to say about his religious beliefs, nor does Warren himself in his memoirs. It is clear, however, that he was neither atheist nor agnostic. The son of devout Methodists, he was married in a Baptist church to a wife who was a practicing member of that denomination all her life. It is not clear whether Warren himself attended, but he was said to have read the Bible a few minutes every day.[1] Though one biographer characterized him as a man who "never made a display of piety," he was said to have lived "by a strict moral code."[2] His son characterized him as "the most religious man I ever knew. He was raised on the Bible."[3] Although Warren said little about his religious beliefs or affiliations in his memoirs, he did record that he joined the Masonic Order after World War I and was elected Grand Master of Masons for California in 1935.[4]

Warren, who wrote none of the opinions in the court decisions regarding school prayer, supported the decisions, declaring in his autobiography, "The majority of us on the Court were religious people, yet we found it unconstitutional that any state agency should impose a religious exercise on persons who were by law free to practice religion or not without state interference."[5] He actually told a friend that he felt that "it was good that people said their prayers in school or any time," and that he "disliked" the decisions, but concurred in them because he "had no alternative." He insisted, "I had to live up to the Constitution."[6]

Profile 69
George Herman (Babe) Ruth, Jr.

Born: Baltimore, Maryland, February 6, 1895
Died: New York, New York, August 16, 1948

The pitcher-turned-outfielder who was the cornerstone of the New York Yankees baseball dynasty, who amassed a lifetime total of more than 700 home runs, along with a .342 career batting average, was certainly the best-known athlete of his time. The product of a violent and impoverished home, Ruth grew up a wild boy in the slums of Baltimore until he was placed, as an incorrigible, in St. Mary's Industrial Home, where he spent most of his formative years.

Ruth's father is believed to have been of Lutheran background and his mother of Roman Catholic heritage. There is no evidence, however, that the elder Ruths, whose contact with their son was so minimal that most people considered Babe an orphan, attended church regularly or influenced him spiritually. It was at St. Mary's, which was run by the Congregation of St. Francis Xavier, that young Ruth received religious instruction. Biographers mention that he made his first Communion there and was confirmed a Roman Catholic.

Babe Ruth did not impress most people as a religious man. For most of his adult life, he was notorious for heavy drinking and an unrestrained, riotous lifestyle. Yet, in his own way, he was religious. He always held the Brothers of St. Mary's in highest respect, and maintained a lifelong friendship with Brother Matthias, who taught him how to play baseball and whom he considered the greatest man he ever knew. Thomas Hilary Kaufman, a priest of the Dominican order who ministered to Ruth during the last summer of his life, insisted that throughout much of his career Babe went to Mass and received Communion every Sunday, wherever his team happened to be. When the Yankees were playing in Washington, the Bambino invariably communed at the Church of St. Thomas the Apostle at 27th Street and Woodley Road, NW, a few blocks from the Wardman Park Hotel, where visiting teams stayed.[1] According to Ruth's own memoirs,

Kaufman was overly generous in his description of his churchgoing habits. "I had drifted away from the Church during my harum-scarum early years in the majors. I'd go to Mass now and then, and, believe me, I never missed a night without saying my prayers."[2]

Ruth's religious convictions affected his marital relations. He separated from his wife, Helen Woodford, in 1923. There was apparently no thought of divorce and remarriage. This was (and still is) forbidden by the Church. Ruth cared enough about his relationship with his Church to abide by its rulings—on some things. He married his second wife Claire only after Helen died.

Ruth told a friend that he valued his religion because, like a batting average, it set a standard by which he could measure himself.[3] Whether he was troubled by the discrepancy between his behavior and the standards of conduct taught by his faith is unclear. Most of those who knew Ruth did not consider him a man given to introspection.

As Ruth's health failed when he was in his early fifties, he decided to put his house in order. Before a serious operation, he made a conscious decision to rededicate himself to God.[4] Father Kaufman, a teacher, was on summer assignment to the Church of Saint Catherine of Siena on East 68th Street in New York, when, on August 1, 1948, he called on Ruth, who was a patient at the Memorial Hospital for Cancer and Allied Diseases. Ruth was then deathly ill, but enjoyed visits from the "Long Boy from Baltimore," which is what he called the tall young priest.[5] Years later Kaufman recalled that Ruth's sickroom "looked like a religious articles store," full of holy pictures, medals, and statues.[6] Babe's favorite image, which he kept next to his bed, was that of Martin de Porres, a black Peruvian lay brother who was later made a saint.[7]

Kaufman characterized Ruth as "a little rough," but "very devout, very good, and very pious." He said that Ruth trusted Christ as his Savior.[8] In an interview he gave on the day of Ruth's death, Kaufman recalled that Babe was "sincerely and unostentatiously religious." He continued to say, "It was inspiring the way he prayed....He knew toward the end that he was dying and he was ready without complaint. Saturday night, I blessed him with a relic of Mother Cabrini [who had recently been made a saint], and that made him happy."[9]

On Monday night, August 16, Ruth was in his death agony. From 6:20 to 7:20, Kaufman recalled, the dying man prayed "fervently," over and over, "My Jesus, mercy!" Finally, "his voice faded away. At 7:30 he went into a peaceful sleep. [Shortly after that] he died a beautiful and a happy death."[10]

~

Profile 70

Oscar Hammerstein II

Born: New York, New York, July 12, 1895
Died: Doylestown, Pennsylvania, August 23, 1960

Trained as a lawyer, Hammerstein wrote the lyrics to some of Broadway's most successful musicals, including *Show Boat* (with Jerome Kern) and *Oklahoma, Carousel, South Pacific,* and *The Sound of Music* (with Richard Rodgers). Most of his songs have a bright, optimistic, positive tone, and this attitude is reflected in the statement of his personal philosophy which he furnished for the collection, *This I Believe,* in the early 1950s. Entitled "Happy Talk," after a song in *South Pacific,* he declared: "I have an unusual statement to make—I am a man who believes he is happy.

"What makes it unusual is that a man who is happy seldom tells anyone. The unhappy man is more communicative. He is eager to recite what is wrong with the world, and he seems to have a talent for gathering a large audience. It is a modern tragedy that despair has so many spokesmen and hope so few. I believe, therefore, that it is important for a man to announce that he is happy, even though such an announcement is less dramatic and less entertaining than the cries of his pessimistic opposite.

"The conflict of good and bad merges in thick entanglement. You cannot isolate virtue and beauty and success and laughter and keep them from all contact with wickedness and ugliness and failure and weeping. The man who strives for such isolated joy is riding for a fall.

He will wind up in isolated gloom. I don't believe anyone can enjoy living in this world unless he can accept its imperfection. He must know and admit that he is imperfect, that all other mortals are imperfect, that it is childish to allow these imperfections to destroy all his hope and all his desire to live."[1]

This philosophy of making the best of an imperfect world seems to have a secular rather than religious basis. However, Maria Trapp, on whose life Hammerstein based his last musical, *The Sound of Music*, found the lyricist to be a very spiritual man. A devout Roman Catholic, Trapp said of Hammerstein shortly after he died: "I can only tell you what is in my heart and not in my head. I am a Catholic and I would say that he was a living saint. That means that a person is as close to perfection as one can get and still be alive. It emanated from him and I'm sure he didn't know it himself."[2]

Although many of those who knew him considered Hammerstein to be "religious," his religion was never associated with any church or creed. His father was from a Jewish background, but never practiced his religion. His mother was an Episcopalian, and Oscar was baptized in that church. The family seldom attended services, and Oscar and his brother were apparently never confirmed. Their mother apparently saw that they fasted on Good Friday and abstained from fish every Friday. Beyond that, there is no evidence of any religious training.[3] As an adult, Hammerstein, considered a decent, moral, and amiable man, never joined a church or attended services on any regular basis.[4] His spirituality seems to have been unspoken, implicit, and secular, but sufficiently distinct to be perceptible to Trapp and others who knew him.

His attitude to death was similar to his attitude to life. Ill with cancer, he told his daughter shortly before he died: "I've had a happy childhood. I've had a good time as a young man. And I've had a terrific middle age. The only thing I'm disappointed in is that I was looking forward to having a really good old age, too." Continuing, he told her, "I know I'm going to die. I don't want to die, but I know I'm going to. But I've been a very lucky man. I've had the work that I wanted to do. I've been married to the woman I love and I've had a good life. I've had everything. I'd like it to last longer, but it isn't, I'm not dissatisfied."[5]

～

Ethel Waters

Born: Chester, Pennsylvania, October 31, 1896
Died: Chatsworth, California, September 1, 1977

The singer, actress, and entertainer was described by musician Gloria Gaither in the following way: "More than a great performer, sensational singer, skillful communicator—she was a great soul. And the compassion of her heart came through her voice, and her words, and her performances to touch people, soul to soul, intimately, because we who heard her somehow knew she had hurt where we hurt; she had known pain and struggle and joy and victory as we knew them. She knew Jesus and it was his ability to touch people at the core of their being that we felt when we heard her."[1]

This brilliant and gifted artist has been described as a woman of many contradictions. One of her friends characterized her as "mean, tough, strong, sweet, and very lovable. When she spoke there was always a purpose....[H]er words were always given with an inner love which she possessed very strongly."[2] Most of those acquainted with her agreed with Jarrell McCracken, a Texas book and music publisher, who was struck by her "captivating presence" and her "zest for life," as well as her "obvious happiness, and her spiritual peace."[3]

Waters, who disliked the term "black" and described herself as a "Negress," spent a bleak childhood in the slums of Chester, Pennsylvania, the daughter of a young girl who had been raped by a friend of one her sisters. Young Ethel lived most of the time with her grandmother, who was a devout Christian. Her grandmother and most of the family were Roman Catholics, but Ethel's mother was a Protestant (variously described as a Baptist or a Methodist). As a result, there were sometimes sectarian disputes in the family that helped to create in young Ethel a permanent aversion to denominations and churchgoing. She was baptized a Roman Catholic and educated by nuns, and was, in fact, a nominal Catholic all her life, but never truly identified with her church or any other denomination. From a very early age, she recognized the value of the religious traditions of both her mother and grandmother. While the religious experience of the grandmother seemed to emphasize good works, the presence of God seemed more real in the experience of her mother.

On those occasions when she went with her mother to worship in storefront churches, she was fascinated: "The beauty that came into the tired faces of the very old men and women excited me....The emotion that invaded them was so much bigger than they. Some would rock. Some would cry. Some would talk with eloquence and fire, their confusions and doubts dispelled."[4] Although her logic and reasoning led her to question much of the doctrine, she was impressed by the fact that these worshippers seemed particularly "close to God."[5]

When she was twelve, she attended, with her friends, a children's revival in a Methodist Church in Chester, led by the Reverend R. J. Williams, a dynamic preacher. Services were held for several consecutive nights, and at the conclusion of each, Williams would invite all the children who were not "out and out" Christians to come to the "mourner's bench" for prayer. Waters went forward each night, but nothing happened. As she declared in one of her autobiographies, "All the rest of the people were jumping up like Russian dancers," but for her nothing happened and she did not want to pretend.[6]

On the last night of the revival, she experienced a wonderful reaction. "Love flooded my heart and I knew I had found God and that now and for always I would have an ally, a friend close by to strengthen me and cheer me on....I don't know exactly what happened or when I got up. I don't even know whether I talked. But the people who were there that night were astounded. Afterward they told me that I was radiant and like one transfixed. They said that the light in my face electrified the whole church. And I did feel full of light and warmth."[7]

As a result of this experience, Waters started to attend the Methodist church every Sunday, but, shortly afterward, another girl provoked a fight with her, and, because she felt that she could never forgive the hostile child, she stopped going to church—forever.[8]

Having gone on to become a star of stage and screen, Waters remained generally religious. Whenever she performed in public, she prayed, "Oh, dear Lord, please let me earn my salary. Let me please the people. Help me do my best." When she left the stage, she prayed, "Oh, thank you Lord for helping me please the people."[9] She supported financially her mother, other relatives, and needy friends and colleagues. She had the sense that God was watching over her and protecting her, but it was in a vague, general sense.

In May 1957, Ethel Waters was unhappy, dissatisfied, and lonely. She was depressed by the loss of her beauty. Her health was poor, and she had lost the lithe figure for which she had been known as "Mama Stringbean." It was then that she decided to attend the Billy Graham Crusade, which was being held at Madison Square Garden in New York. "Even though I had never stopped for one minute—either praying or believing—something was missing....I had tried...all through the years of my professional career to be a good Christian. You talk about works? I worked at it. I gave to charities even when I had to borrow the money." Nevertheless, she did not feel at peace.[10]

The Crusade lasted several months, and Waters sang in the choir for sixteen weeks. "I didn't hear any voices from heaven," she later wrote, "but the first thing I knew I was kind of arguing with the Lord."[11] She was concerned about whether, as a Christian, she could, in conscience, sing secular music. It was then that Waters decided to give up her career in show business. She later declared, "Jesus said you can't follow God and mammon. And singing songs like 'St. Louis Blues' and 'Heat Wave' and shaking my hips and making a whole lot of money is mammon to me. That's what all that means to Ethel Waters. Singing secular songs was not only my livelihood, it was all I had. I gave it up and I was sincere."[12]

For the rest of her life, except for some performances in a production called *Member of the Wedding*, in which she found no material injurious to faith or morals, and some television appearances, Ethel Waters sang only at nondenominational religious gatherings. She became a member of the Billy Graham team and was celebrated for her appearances at his crusades. In the people of the Graham organization, she was able to find the love and sense of belonging that she had sought all her life.

At the end of her life, Waters had only a few thousand dollars. She did not believe in purchasing stock or earning interest on bank savings.[13] Almost everything she earned, she gave away to charity. At seventy-six she declared, "In spite of all the money I've made down through the years, I don't have any now. Just a very small nest egg to depend on—what's left from the sale of my home…in Los Angeles, and when it gets down to a certain level—it's like the rain falling—God refills it and the level comes up, just enough. I never know when I'll have to tap that reserve, but I don't worry….You don't need a lot of money when he's in charge of your affairs."[14]

Waters never became a churchgoer. She always remembered the bickering between her Protestant mother and Roman Catholic grandmother and tended to reject the idea of denominations. She called them "fighting denominations." She described herself as "a born-again Christian, nothing more."[15] She refused to sing at denominational gatherings. The Graham Crusades—and Richard Nixon's worship services on Sundays at the White House—were different. In the Graham Crusades, at least, "only Jesus Christ is preached."[16] When someone urged her to join a denomination, she said, "I enjoy what I've got with Jesus….In the Bible it says that if you believe in Jesus Christ, you have Eternal Life. I do, so I plan on going to heaven."[17] Sundays she spent listening to television and radio preachers, and reading the Bible and Oswald Chambers's turn-of-the-century classic book of short meditations, *My Utmost for His Highest.*

Juliann DeKorte, who cared for her in her last year, observed of Waters, "Sometimes right in the middle of a sentence, she would turn her face heavenward and hold private, or sometimes open, chats with her Lord. She would explain: 'The Lord and I have a running conversation. He makes no errors. I do, but he takes me anyway.'"[18]

"What I think most of us don't realize," Waters wrote in old age, "is that turning the other cheek doesn't necessarily mean to receive a physical blow on the other side. It means you can be so right and justified in a situation, but when you're attacked for it, just leave it alone. That's obedience to God. To turn the other cheek even when you know you are right. Let him take the situation in hand. And that isn't easy to do! None of us needs to think we're going to get to the place where this gets easy. Maybe one time we can do it and the next time not….You can get in a rut with Jesus when what he wants is to keep you coming to him constantly, to teach you something new, something fresh. He wants to keep you clinging to him. Because once you think you're stapled to him, you're not good. He wants to keep us humble before him. Over and over I have to say, 'Where did I go wrong?' and cry out, 'Lord, what did I do? Show me. Forgive me—because I looked away.' "[19]

She told a friend, "I can't let myself get down. I have to fight to stay on top of things and not let depression set in, or I would never make it. Satan never wants you to be happy. If I stumble and fall, I just get up and say, 'Devil, you're not gonna get me this time.' "[20] Another time she told another friend, "The devil has never forgiven me for letting him down—we were buddy-buddy for so long. He is constantly trying to trip me up. He comes in so many different ways. He's got guile! If I take my eyes off the Lord, I can feel myself slipping."[21]

Waters continued to perform in public until she was eighty. Toward the end, she was quite infirm. She was physically so frail that she was known to be conveyed to a concert in an ambulance, from which she was removed on a stretcher with an oxygen tank. When the time came for her to perform, she got off the stretcher, and was helped to the stage to sing.[22] During the last year of her life, her health was so bad that she was virtually bedridden and had to be cared for by a friend who was a professional nurse. "I don't know why the Lord doesn't take me home," she said late in life. "I've lived a hard life and now I'm weary. I'm homesick for heaven."[23] Another time she professed, "I'm sitting on the edge of heaven, and his eye is still on me. I'm not afraid to die, in fact I'm kind of looking forward to it. I know the Lord has his arms wrapped around this big fat sparrow."[24]

This longing for heaven increased as numerous infirmities reduced her to painful helplessness. During this time, she said, "No use, complaining....I can't do anything about it, so no use talking about it. Complaining only makes the devil laugh."[25]

She had a horror of being kept alive in the hospital by heroic measures, and begged her nurse-friend Juliann DeKorte, "Don't let anyone hook me up to any machines! When the Lord is ready to take me, don't let anyone try to hold me back."[26] A little later, as she was being moved in bed, she murmured, "Merciful Father—precious Jesus," and never spoke again.[27]

So concluded the pilgrimage of a woman who, during her last twenty years, forsook Hollywood and whose life was so centered in God that she told President Nixon, "When you get to know him, you can't keep from raving about him. Any chance I get to open my mouth and make a loud voice for my Savior, that's my thing."[28]

～

Profile 72
Edward Kennedy (Duke) Ellington

Born: Washington, D.C., April 29, 1899
Died: New York, New York, May 24, 1974

The jazz composer and performer was surrounded by religious influences from his earliest childhood. His father belonged to the John Wesley A.M.E. Zion Church and his mother to the Nineteenth Street Baptist Church in Washington, D.C., and young Edward had to attend services at both each Sunday, as well as one Sunday-school class. It never troubled him that his parents belonged to two different denominations, and, looking back later in life, he was convinced that this did not matter to them. Both churches "preached God, Jesus Christ, and that was the most important thing."[1]

"My mother started telling me about God when I was very young," the composer wrote in his autobiography. "She was mainly interested in knowing and understanding about God, and she painted the most wonderful word pictures of God."[2] Daisy Kennedy Ellington impressed upon her son that he was blessed. "Edward," she told him, "you are blessed. You don't have anything to worry about."[3] Perhaps because of this, he was always an optimist. "I had optimism to the nth degree," he wrote. "Pessimism is...for the sick of mind, for those who have complexes."[4]

The Ellingtons were of African and Irish extraction, but there was little talk about race in their household. "I was quite grown when I first heard about that," Ellington recalled.[5] His younger sister Ruth recalled that when she was four, a cousin told her, "You know dark people and light people don't like each other!" Troubled, the little girl ran to her father, who was reading the paper, and repeated the statement. Without so much as looking up, the elder Ellington growled, "Nonsense, Ruthie!" Both parents believed that "color meant nothing."[6]

Both Ellington parents were musical. "Mother played the piano by [reading] music," Ruth Ellington Boatwright recalled, "But Father played all the European classical music—and couldn't read a note."[7] Duke Ellington's musical genius was largely self-taught as well. As a boy he took music lessons from Marietta Harvey Clinkscales, a devout Baptist who came from a family of musicians. In his autobiography, Duke Ellington recalled that he frequently missed lessons and was unprepared for his recital. In later years, Clinkscales simply recalled that young Ellington was "just an ordinary pupil."[8] Ruth Boatwright surmised that the teacher was unable to teach him anything special because her brother "was not like anything that came before—he was unique."[9]

Even after he became famous, Duke Ellington's family and friends knew him as a kind and affectionate man. "After he made lots of money, he took care of everyone in the family. Everyone who needed help got it," his sister recalled. He persuaded his father to retire from his job in the Navy Yard in Washington and move, with the rest of his immediate family to New York. There he financed the education of his younger sister at Columbia University, and, until she was twenty-five, sent her to school with a chauffeur. So protective of his baby sister was he that when she was at Columbia and had a study period or a break, "the other kids would be on the campus, but the car would pick me up and take me to Riverside Drive to see the boats. I wasn't allowed to socialize."[10]

When he came home from a performance, in the wee hours of the morning, sister Ruth was aware of his presence when he roused her momentarily from sleep by kissing her on the cheeks. "He was always hugging and kissing—even men. He was very affectionate," Boatwright recalled. Ellington's friend of thirty-two years, the Reverend John Garcia Gensel, a pastor at St. Peter's Lutheran Church in Manhattan, wrote, "Edward Kennedy Ellington was always most gracious to me. He always made me feel that it was important for him to greet me. Can you imagine that! And he insisted on kissing my hand. At first, when I attempted to kiss his hand, he resisted, but eventually he let me kiss his hand."[11]

Until the last decade of his life, few people thought of Duke Ellington as a religious man. One biographer found "no hint of religion in anything he said or in his work" during the first part of his life.[12] He usually returned home from a performance around three in the morning, then sat at his piano, composing until noon, when he went to bed and slept until eight. He insisted that such a schedule made it impossible for him to attend church. Even in his last years, Gensel recalled, Ellington went to church "rarely." Even after he began to speak and write about religion, the composer's church attendance was limited to an occasional attendance at the jazz vespers on Sunday afternoon at St. Peter's.[13] Ruth Boatwright affirmed, however, that her brother was active in the Masonic Order, but explained, "I don't know the details. That's a part of his life he didn't want us to see."[14] In fact, before his public funeral services at the Episcopal church of St. John the Divine, there were two private Masonic services.[15]

Ellington's private life contained much that did not obviously reflect his religious commitment. Married early, he spent most of his life separated from his wife, and, according to his sister, was quite a ladies' man. "He had lots of ladies and lovers. My job was to ship this one to Europe, this one to Canada, this one to the Caribbean, where he wasn't. He was trying to get away from them—to some degree—but he liked them."[16]

Like many people in show business, Ellington was superstitious. He thought that green and yellow were unlucky colors, and never wore brown, because he was wearing a brown suit the day his mother died. For him, the color blue had lucky properties. So did the number thirteen. He did not like to receive a knife from anyone, because he believed that this would cut the bonds of friendship. He never gave anyone shoes, socks, or slippers, because this meant that the other person would walk out of his life.[17]

In his mid sixties, Ellington composed the first of three Sacred Concerts. It was performed at Grace Episcopal Cathedral in San Francisco. Many surmised that the composer had recently undergone some sort of conversion experience. His sister, who noted that "he devoted the last ten years of his life writing music to God," did not believe that he underwent a sudden religious conversion. "He was the same all his life. He never talked about his religion. He tried to live it." In fact, Ellington told his sister that throughout his life, "Every time he got to a corner, and did not know which way to go, there was someone to guide him—God."[18] In his autobiography, however, Ellington indicated that at a certain period in his life he "really settled down to read and to think about what I was reading in the Bible" and "found many things that I had been feeling all my life without quite understanding them."[19] As he grew older, Ellington began to read the Bible extensively. After his performances, his musicians frequently saw him studying the Bible in his hotel room. Increasingly, he thought of himself as "God's messenger" who wanted to bring "the devil's music" into the sanctuary. According to Ruth Boatwright, his Sacred Concerts "expressed the *raison d'être*" of his last years.

Ellington wrote both the words and music to his Concerts, and the titles are indicative of what he was trying to say: "Ain't Nobody Nowhere Nothin' Without God," "Praise God and Dance," "Heaven," "Is God a Three Letter Word for Love?" "The Lord's Prayer," "Everyone Prays in His Own Language," "Father, Forgive." Although the composer considered the Sacred Concerts the consummation of his work as a composer—all of which he believed to have been inspired by God—some critics put down his lyrics as "dreadful," and one commentator (a liberal United Methodist minister as well as a musician) criticized Ellington's theology as "time-bound" and "faulty."[20]

John Garcia Gensel, Ellington's minister friend, found the composer "a man of faith" with "deep religious insights," who had read the Bible through at least three times. Although some criticized his lyrics, Gensel believed that many of them conveyed wonderful insights into his "devout and simple faith."[21]

In his autobiography Ellington wrote, "There have been times when I thought I had a glimpse of God. Sometimes, even when my eyes were closed, I saw. Then when I tried to set my eyes—closed or open—back to the same focus, I had no success, of course....Some people who have had the same experience I have had are afraid or ashamed to admit it. They are afraid of being called naïve or square. They are afraid of being called unbrainwashed by the people who brainwash them, or by those they would like to be like, or friendly with. Maybe they just want to be in. Maybe it's a matter of the style, a trend, or whatever one thinks one does to be acceptable in certain circles."[22]

In an interview, late in life, Ellington affirmed that his "best self" wrote and played sacred music and kept him "honest to myself" and also prayed "for the health and survival of others and for the forgiveness of still others."[23] His best habit, he said, was prayer, and, if confined somewhere, all alone, the book he would want with him was the Bible, "because all the other books are in it."[24]

Ellington spoke a great deal about God, but very little about Christ. Gensel, to whom the composer dedicated his song, "Shepherd of the Night Flock," could recall only one song in which Ellington mentioned Christ, and in it he simply mentioned Jesus as one who "violated conformity."[25] Ruth Boatwright, however, was confident that her brother believed in Jesus Christ as Savior.[26] He was, however, tolerant of all religion. "Every man prays in his own language, and there is no language that God does not understand," he insisted.[27] In an interview he declared, "I don't think it's a good idea to play or kid about another man's religion."[28] Not only did he refrain from criticizing or putting down the religion of others (although, as we have seen, he was intolerant of unbelief), he never criticized the actions of other people, and refused to discuss the merits of rival composers or performers. "You have to live the way God wants to you," he said. "You cannot criticize your brother."[29]

He completed the Third Sacred Concert shortly before his death. Asked why it was taking him so long to complete it, he had replied, "You can jive with secular music, but you can't jive with the Almighty."[30] He looked forward to heaven as "a place where you get an opportunity to use all the millions of sensitivities you never knew you had before."[31] He described the world to come as "a very distant future place...where there will be no war, no greed, no unbelievers and no categorization, where love is unconditional and no pronoun is good enough for God."³² During his last illness, Ellington, who suffered from lung cancer, did not speak of religion to Gensel, who visited him faithfully. Although weak and in pain, he talked about recovery. "He didn't expect to die."³³ He spoke for the last time, as far as is known, to his sister Ruth, a few hours before the end. She was convinced that he knew that he was dying, as he pointed in the direction of the window and joyfully exclaimed: "Mother!" Ruth observed, "It was as if she were there, waiting for him."³⁴

～

Profile 73
Gary Cooper

Born: Helena, Montana, May 7, 1901
Died: Los Angeles, California, May 13, 1961

The movie actor, star of many celebrated films, was a nominal Episcopalian for all but the last two years of his life. Then, on April 9, 1959, Cooper, at the Church of the Good Shepherd in Beverly Hills, California, was received into the Roman Catholic Church. Up until that time, Cooper had not impressed those around him as a particularly spiritual, or even moral, man. He had been openly unfaithful to his wife, and, in 1950, they had separated. Two years later she told him that she was willing to divorce him, if he agreed, but they were reconciled, and a year later they were granted an audience with Pope Pius XII. After that, Cooper began to consider seriously the possibility of a religious commitment.[1]

"I saw and began thinking how our family had always done everything together, whether it was traveling around the globe or skin diving, or horseback riding," he told an interviewer shortly after he joined the Church. "So I thought, 'Why am I not sharing a very important part of their life—religion? Why have I been out of it?' I knew then that I didn't want to be any longer."[2]

By his own admission, Cooper was "not a naturally religious man."[3]

Most of his life he had "spent all my waking hours, year after year, doing almost exactly what I, personally, wanted to do, and what I wanted to do wasn't always the most polite thing, either.... I was thinking about...getting myself bigger and better parts and meeting more beautiful and sexier girls. I've had a lot of good things in my life, maybe too many of them: Fame. Success. Money....I've had some moments of swellheadedness, too, moments of horrible conceit. Maybe that's what happens when you make a go of it in this business....People brushing my coat and powdering my face and interviewing me, and nine million otherwise sensible people wanting to know what my favorite dish is. That's apt to make you think you're a pretty remarkable, unique fellow."[4]

Late in 1958, however, Cooper began to think seriously about religion. "I began to dwell a little more on what's been in my mind a long time. I began thinking, 'Coop, old boy, you owe somebody something for all your good fortune.' "[5]

After he made his decision, he felt his life slowly change. "Having a faith...made a big difference to me," he said. "I found out you don't have to get all wound up in religion, but the knowledge that it is there, with its rules and its vast storehouse of experience, gives you an inner security. In any faith, you will find a few cranks who have become bigots, but any person can have faith without the extremes."[6] He found that he was judging others less harshly. Before, "I used to talk about people behind their backs. I never meant any harm. Mine was the kind of gossip we all indulge in, particularly in Hollywood....But the next day I'd think, 'Now what the heck did I say that for?' That's sure a small correction to make in my character, but it's an example of the corrections I'm trying to make." He concluded that "I'll never be anything like a saint, I know. I just haven't got that kind of fortitude. The only thing I can say for me is that I'm trying to be a little better. Maybe I'll succeed."[7]

Cooper was still in reasonably good health when he joined the Church, but, soon after, his health began rapidly to fail rapidly. When, in February 1961, frustrated at his inability to obtain a straight answer from his doctors, he persuaded his wife to admit that he was suffering from advanced cancer, he reacted calmly, telling her, "I'm so glad that you let me know."[8] According to his wife, during his last illness, Cooper's religious faith stood him "in good stead. Every time he'd receive Communion, he said he felt so much better. He was completely unafraid of the future. He really was. No fear whatsoever."[9]

One of Cooper's long-time friends was the writer Ernest Hemingway, a man with many physical and emotional problems who would, shortly after Cooper's death, commit suicide. When Cooper made his decision to join the Church, he expressed his misgivings to Hemingway. Just before he died, however, Cooper, lying in bed of pain, clutching a crucifix, told a mutual friend, "Please give Papa [Hemingway's nickname] a message. It's important and you musn't forget because I'll not be talking to him again. Tell him, that time I wondered if I made the right decision. Tell him it was the best thing I ever did."[10] Shortly before the end, according to one account, the dying man murmured, "It is God's will." And so, surrounded in his last days by his wife and daughter and his pastor, Monsignor Daniel Sullivan, Gary Cooper, departed from the world with the consolations of the faith in which he had found peace.

～

Profile 74
Margaret Mead

Born: Philadelphia, Pennsylvania, December 16, 1901
Died: New York, New York, November 15, 1978

The anthropologist who wrote many books and served for many years as Curator of Ethnology at New York's American Museum of Natural History was described by colleague Ashley Montagu as the only churchgoer he knew of within their discipline. Indeed, some of her associates found it odd that "this highly rational person should be so religious."[1] The fact was that Margaret Mead was a devout high-church Episcopalian who faithfully attended the Church of St. Luke in the Fields on Hudson Street in New York for many years.

Mead's parents were not religious. Her mother was described as a lapsed Unitarian, and both parents have been characterized as atheists or agnostics. But, even as a small child, Margaret was searching for God. By the age of ten, she divided her room into "a pagan half" which contained copies of the *Venus de Milo* and other classical works of art and "a Christian half" which contained paintings of the Madonna, a jar made of clay from the Holy Land, and a kneeler bought at an auction.[2]

When her family was living in Swarthmore, Pennsylvania, Margaret attended a Quaker meeting, but her father mocked her. After going to various religious services with family maids, she went to an Episcopal service with the local pastor and his daughter and decided to join.[3] The day that she was baptized, in Buckingham, Pennsylvania, at the age of eleven, she described at the time as "one of the happiest...of my life."[4] Although she claimed that she never had a "religious experience," she would be a faithful Episcopalian to the end of her long life.

Mead's daughter, Mary Catherine Bateson, in her memoir of her parents, recalled that when she thought about "the ways in which she chose to pass on her own deep commitment to Christianity," she was struck by the fact that her mother rarely talked about doctrine or personal prayer. "We shared the narratives and poetry of religion: the stories of Jesus' life, reading the Nativity narrative aloud each year from the Gospel of Luke, a child's book of psalms that she gave me for my birthday...and mementos from her childhood, like *A Child's Book of Saints and Friendly Beasts*, full of legends, mostly Irish, of saints in friendship with animals." Moreover, Mead bought her daughter "beautiful postcard reproductions of Renaissance paintings of the Gospels" so that she could look at them during the sermons to avoid boredom, and encouraged her to join the children's choir "instead of being bored during Sunday school." Mead's daughter recounted, "The Christian tradition was passed on to me as a great rich mixture, a bouillabaisse of human imagination and wonder brewed from the richness of individual lives, never reduced to a meager and tasteless minimum."[5]

Mead said she went to church, not "for God's sake, but for my own, for the ritual and the repetition and the prayer, though I don't pray at great length."[6] Her daughter recounted that Mead preferred those Episcopal churches where the bent knee of genuflection and the hand moving in the sign of the cross would bridge doubt and separation.[7] Nevertheless, she tended to doze through sermons and usually avoided them by going to the early Mass, where there was no homily.[8] On special church festivals, Mead liked to attend the Church of St. Mary the Virgin, near Times Square, called "Smokey Mary's" because of the quantity of incense that rose in billows heavenward past the great sculpted images of the saints, a church famed for the richness of its traditional worship.

A pastor friend described her as "deeply and instinctively religious" and said that she believed that "objective reality is discoverable, and that people are accountable for the use made of their lives in this world."[9] Once, when an assistant told her that she planned to work on Good Friday, Mead advised her, "I think you need to take stock of your religious days."[10]

In her sixties, Mead became active in the affairs of the Episcopal Church when she was asked to serve on the Committee for the Assembly of the World Council of Churches, to help plan an eight-year program of conventions. She was at first hesitant, because by then she had been married and divorced three times. She was told that it did not matter, and she became a member of the committee.[11] She served on the Commission of Church and Society in the World Council of Churches. During these meetings, she never missed a service of holy Communion. One of her colleagues recounted that she "was very critical if we didn't have high-quality worship. She wanted substance, and she insisted that we not slip in giving the spiritual dimension its due." She really sought, all the time, to deepen her own spiritual life. Once she said, "If you don't provide Communion at this conference, I'm going home."[12]

In 1967, Mead became a consultant to the Subcommittee for the Revision of the *Book of Common Prayer* of the Episcopal Church. She felt that the church could modify and modernize its rituals without sacrificing beauty. She felt that the liturgy had to be old, "otherwise it is not polished.... [O]therwise it cannot reflect the play of many men's imaginations....[O]therwise it will not be fully available to everyone born within the tradition. Yet it must be lively and fresh, open to new vision and changed vision.[13]

Mead proved to be a conservative on her subcommittee. When some of the bishops began to talk about deleting references to Noah's flood and one of them said, "Nobody believes that in this day and age," she retorted, "Bishops may not, but anthropologists do!"[14] She was credited with keeping reference to Satan from being removed from the baptismal rite.[15] When the new liturgy was complete, it is said that Mead preferred the old one.[16]

Margaret Mead believed that religion has two roles. The first, a conservative role, was to form a world-view for the culture and provide a common way of life for members of society. This would involve the fostering of church ritual. The second, dynamic role involved improving conditions in the world.[17] She felt that science and religion needed to work together to solve the world's problems—to feed the hungry, shelter the homeless, clothe the naked, to heal the sick. Speaking at the World Conference on Church and Society in Geneva, Switzerland, in 1966, she confessed that she felt a sense of "frustration and rage that we can now feed people—on a large scale, not just a personal scale— we can carry out the admonitions of Christianity and we're not doing it." The task of Christianity, she contended, is "to learn to combine the command to love our neighbors as ourselves with finding out who our neighbors are, knowing all that is known about them, and knowing all that can be known about carrying out the Christian command."[18]

As a Christian, she advocated a world order, international law, the development of food banks, and the removal of restrictions on the use of contraceptives (so that population growth could be controlled).[19] Though Mead criticized all laws forbidding the practice of abortion, she felt, however, that the practice was "incredibly brutal, lazy, cruel," and was convinced that women were harmed both physically and psychologically by the practice. Moreover, she felt that abortion was "too close to the edge of taking life to fit into a world view in which all life is regarded as valuable."[20] She also wanted a repeal of laws against homosexuals.[21] She also felt that an individual should be able to decide how and when he will die.[22] Yet she believed that there should be a daily period of silent prayer in the public schools "in which each child could pray as his parents had taught him to" and she wanted a constitutional amendment to permit prayer in school.[23]

During her final illness, she consulted a faith healer, the Reverend Carmen di Barazza. When she first met her, she asked, "Do you see more people in this room than we do?" When Di Barazza said she did, Mead questioned her further, "Do you see the tall one and the short one with me?" Then she explained that these were her spirit guides, and that "every tribe I've ever been to has seen them with me."[24] She did not seem to like the hospital chaplain, who was a woman pastor. Mead later chose to take Communion from a male clergyman.[25]

Shortly before she died, Mead told her nurse, "I'm going to die." When she was told, "Yes, we all will some day," she answered, "But this is different."[26]

～

Profile 75
Charles Augustus Lindbergh

Born: Detroit, Michigan, February 4, 1902
Died: Maui, Hawaii, August 26, 1974

The aviator who became an instant celebrity when he became the first person to complete a solo, nonstop flight across the Atlantic in 1927 in the plane named *The Spirit of St. Louis* was interested in religion and the supernatural all his life, but never accepted orthodox Christianity. He dabbled in yoga, and even conducted experiments (which proved unsuccessful) to determine whether the yogi's slow, rhythmic breathing actually controlled the heat-regulation mechanism of the human body.[1] Fascinated with ghosts, at one point in his life he began to search for specters around a "haunted well" in France.[2]

We know most about his thought through his *Autobiography of Values*, on which he worked during his later years and which was published after his death. The son of a congressman from Minnesota, he recounted that he "grew up in a generation torn by the impact of new scientific knowledge on old religious dogma." He described his family was "unbound by religious dogma." His mother read the

Bible to him but explained that "no one knew how much of it was true."[3]

Young Lindbergh was taught about the existence of God, who was "good—all powerful," who had "created life and the earth, the sun, and the stars" and "should therefore be worshiped." However, Lindbergh's elders were so influenced by Darwinism and secular humanism that they conceded that "maybe all our ideas about God were wrong."[4]

As a child, Lindbergh associated God with death. "I wondered, if God is so good, why did he make you die? Why should he not let you live forever? There was nothing good about death; it was terrible.... People got sick or old and went to bed and then life just left them. Their bodies were taken to church where the minister talked about God, and then [they were] buried in a cemetery. Something called 'the Spirit' went on living. That was the way God wanted it to be." But he felt that "even for the good people [God] would take to heaven, death seemed a horrible entrance," and wondered whether it constituted "an inexplicable defect in [God's] character to permit his creations to die."[5]

The parents of Lindbergh were evidently not churchgoers—until the father ran for Congress and decided that it was desirable for a candidate's family to be seen in church. Dressed in "scratchy new clothes" with a felt hat and tight-fitting gloves, he was "taken to church in our home town of Little Falls [Minnesota]." Young Charles hated the experience so much that he "marshaled all the forces at my command against it. I revolted so effectively that I was never taken to church again." He claimed that the incident left him "a skeptic toward religion" and somehow caused him to question "the beneficence of God."[6] From that day forward, he was "never taken to church again," and later, as a young man, looking for a wife, he refused to date women who were churchgoers.[7]

Lindbergh wrote that he lost confidence in the Bible as he gained confidence in science. Lindbergh thought that knowledge was increasing rapidly, that it may be possible that science could achieve a means of eternal life.[8]

But, as he grew older, especially after his oldest child was kidnapped and murdered, he became interested in the mystical. He thought that any branch of science pursued to its conclusion ended in mystery. Humans could neither explain the miracle of creation nor the fact of their awareness, nor conceive the end of space and time. "The miracles of science and technology become trivial in the face of the unknowable," concluded Lindbergh.[9]

Lindbergh felt that there was surely more to life than what could be objectively observed and measured. "We reach a point in observation and analysis where the human intellect stares past frontiers of its evolutionary achievement, toward unreached areas infinitely vast—the mystical realm of God."[10] For him, God was indefinable. "The shape of God we cannot measure, weigh, or clock, but we can conceive of a reality without a form. The growing knowledge of science clarifies man's intuition of the mystical. The farther we penetrate the unknown, the vaster and more marvelous it becomes. Only in the twentieth century, do we realize that space is not empty, that it is packed with energy; it may be existence's source. Then, if space has produced existence and the form of man, can we deduce from it a form of God?"[11]

As Lindbergh aged, he claimed to have "little concern about death." To him it seemed "a desirable phenomenon, part of a cosmic plan that lay above man's wisdom."[12] At the end of his life, he mused: "I think of the forms of man, of myself. I am at once my past, my present, and my future. I am the concentration of millions of ancestors. I will diffuse through millions of descendants and the unforseeable existences they lead....With every generation, I cycle from adult to sperm and ovum to child. I am now male, now female; now knowledge, now innocence. At the same moment I am an individual, I am an organization of billions of living cells, of trillions of atoms—each one itself a cosmos of unknown features, memories, and abilities. I am energy and I am matter, transposed by incomprehensible time."[13]

So Lindbergh concluded his autobiography. Shortly after he wrote those words, realizing that he would soon die, he directed that he be flown from the New York hospital where he was being unsuccessfully treated for cancer to his home on the island of Maui, in Hawaii, and there, without assistance from church or clergy, he peacefully died, commenting to his wife, "It's a natural thing. It's harder on you, watching me die, than it is on me."

～

Profile 76
Clare Boothe Luce

Born: New York, New York, April 10, 1903
Died: Washington, D.C., October 9, 1987

The author, congresswoman, and diplomat, wife of the publisher of *Time* magazine, had little interest in religion until she was in her forties. After she became a Christian, she recalled an extraordinary experience when she was sixteen or seventeen, and described it in these words:

"I no longer remember where it took place, except that it was a summer day on an American beach....

"I remember that it was a cool, clean, fresh, calm, blue, radiant day and that I stood by the shore, my feet not in the waves, and now—as then—I find it difficult to explain what did happen. I expect that the easiest thing is to say that suddenly SOMETHING WAS. My whole soul was cleft clean by it, as a silk veil slit by a shining sword. And I knew....But whatever it was I knew, it was something that made ENORMOUS SENSE.

"I don't know how long this experience lasted....The memory of it possessed me for several months afterward. At first I marveled at it. Then...gradually I forgot it....

"My childhood had been an unusually unhappy and bitter one. I had brooded about it increasingly as I grew older....Until the very day of my conversion, it was a source of deep melancholy and resentment. 'Unless the cup is clean, whatever you pour into it turns sour,' says Plato. A conversion cleans the heart of much of its bitterness. Afterward I seldom remembered my marred childhood, except at one strange moment: at the very beginning of the Mass, during the prayers at the foot of the altar. The priest says: 'I will go unto the altar of God.' And generally a small altar boy responds: 'Unto God, who giveth joy to my youth.' This phrase, unhappily, always awakened faint echoes of bitter youth, and I would think: Why didn't God give joy to my youth?

"One day, long months after I had been a convert, as these words were said, the bitterness did not come. Instead there suddenly flooded into my mind the experience of which I speak, and my heart was gently suffused with an afterglow of that incredible joy. Then I knew that this strange occurrence had had an enormous part in my conversion, although I had seemed to forget it completely. Long ago, in its tremendous purity and simplicity, and now, in its far fainter evocation, I knew it had been, somehow, the most real experience of my whole life."[1]

Luce was, in fact, almost completely without religious resources until she was in her early forties. In her late thirties she became involved in the study of reincarnation, but this brought her no peace. She once told a friend that "I can't understand about you Catholics. You always get up for church. Do you feel you have to?" When the friend told her that they did it because they wanted to, Luce conceded, "It must be a wonderful religion. Someday I'm going to study it."[2]

When Luce's daughter—her only child—was killed in an automobile accident, she went to pieces, and nearly lost her mind. She started seeing things. She saw her dead mother looking at a water lily, saying, "My religion is flowers." She saw her daughter's face and a parade of other faces, and was sure she was going crazy. Wandering aimlessly around her room, contemplating suicide, she noticed an unopened letter on her desk. It was from Edward Wiatrak, a Jesuit priest, whom she knew slightly. She called him and said: "Father, I am not in trouble, but my mind is in trouble." Wiatrak, who knew of her despair, answered, "We know. This is the call we have been praying for."[3]

Father Wiatrak referred Luce to the brilliant priest, Fulton J. Sheen, later an archbishop, then a professor at Catholic University in Washington D.C. Luce invited him to dinner and agreed to take instructions from him with the object of becoming a Roman Catholic. Sheen set some ground rules: "First, we will consider the existence of God. I will talk for fifteen minutes without interruption and at the end of that time you can talk as you like—two, three, or four hours and ask any questions you please."[4]

After Father Sheen talked for just five minutes, Luce jumped up and shook her finger at him and demanded, "If God is good, why did he take my daughter?" Unlike the first priest with whom Luce had spoken, Sheen minced no words: "Perhaps it was in order that you might become a believer. In order that you might be here tonight and to start on the road to wisdom and peace. In order that you might discover God's truth. Maybe your daughter is buying your faith with her life…. Ann's death was the purchase price for your soul."[5]

After that, Luce and Sheen had sessions that frequently lasted for hours. She had, in fact, hundreds of hours of instruction. Sheen later recounted that Luce raised difficulties "the likes of which I never heard before." She refused to accept hell. "I never heard such arguments against hell in my life," Sheen recalled. Then, after about an hour of counterargument about hell, Luce leaped to her feet and cried, "Oh God, what a protagonist you have in this man!"[6] Many years later, Sheen recalled, "No man could go to Clare and argue her into the faith. Heaven had to knock her over. It was about the only way it could get into her."[7]

On February 16, 1946, Clare Boothe Luce was received into the Roman Catholic Church at St. Patrick's Cathedral in New York. Asked why she became a Catholic, she told one interviewer, "It's very simple… to get rid of my sins…to have my sins forgiven. This will not make sense to people who have never sinned."[8] She also said that she had been seeking God through her psychoanalyst and found that psychiatry could not answer the question that concerned her the most: What was the point of striving or keeping alive or fighting, if only an ominous silence reigned throughout all creation when death came?[9] Later she said that becoming a Roman Catholic was "one of the better decisions of my life. It permitted me to love and be loved. Never having had a father, it was a great joy to discover I had the greatest of them all."[10]

Clare Boothe Luce lived for more than forty years after her conversion. Many people did not think she changed very much after she became a Catholic. That was, according to friend, because "there wasn't a trace of sackcloth about her."[11] In the 1950s she became interested in the life and example of Saint Thérèse of Lisieux, the saint of the Little Way. Reading the spiritual autobiography of the short-lived tubercular nineteenth-century French Carmelite nun inspired Luce to try to "sanctify the small things in life and let the big ones go." But she found the Little Way a "pinprick martyrdom." She found that the heaviest cross of all was "getting through the day anonymously and perfectly." After a short time, spiritually and emotionally drained, she decided that the way of Saint Thérèse was "too strenuous."[12]

Henry Robinson Luce for a time accompanied his wife to church. The son of Presbyterian missionaries, he carried his Bible with him, reading it throughout the Mass. Commenting on his wife's desire to convert him to Catholicism, he declared, "That won't happen. I have what has been called 'the Presbyterian's invincible ignorance.'"[13] Despite his Bible-carrying and his churchgoing, Henry Luce was not even a good Presbyterian, as he continued unfaithful to Clare through nearly all their marriage, often reducing her to a near-suicidal state even after her conversion. According to Jesuit priest John C. Murray, a friend of both Luces, "Looking into himself was no habit of his. He said his prayers on his knees every night. He said he'd try to do better. After that he'd sleep soundly, leaving things up to God."[14]

Clare Boothe Luce spoke little about her religion in her later years. Late in life she told her friend Father Murray that she was drifting away from the Church because she resented "its concept that man represented the active brain and the woman a passive heart."[15] Another friend, Wilfred Sheed, said that this particular attitude about the Church and women did not go "very deep."[16] However, he wrote that she complained that most priests were drawn to her fame or her money,[17] and commented about her, in her late seventies, "The hot religious honeymoon cooled into 'dailiness' a good while ago." She told Sheed that Father Murray had told her that he "thought I trusted too much in the goodness of God, and should be a more formally a Catholic."[18] Sheed doubted whether, in later years, Luce went to Mass every Sunday. For one thing she was repelled by what she called "guitar Masses," which had become very popular, especially in Hawaii, where she had a home. But she had no doubts or regrets. Even though she was no longer "terribly active" in the Church, Clare Luce told Sheed that she was glad that she had become a Catholic and felt as if she had been "adopted by a noble family."[19]

~

Profile 77
Vincent Thomas Lombardi

Born: Brooklyn, New York, June 11, 1913
Died: Washington, D. C., September 3, 1970

T he football coach of the Green Bay Packers and later the Washington Redskins, who allegedly said, "Winning is everything," was famous for his explosive temper and aggressive personality. He was a devout Roman Catholic, but some of those who worked with him found it difficult to reconcile his religious commitment with some of the abrasive aspects of his personality. One of his assistant coaches recalled, "It was religion in the morning and the language of the longshoreman in the afternoon."[1] Edward Bennett Williams, who owned the Redskins when Lombardi was the head coach, characterized him as "very, very conservative, very right-wing, and very hard line."[2] Others saw him in a different light. Washington sportswriter Shirley Povich, dismissing the coach's reputation "as an insensitive slave-driver" as "wildly inaccurate," recalled, "An instant after his quick anger, the kindly emotions ran deep with him."[3]

Vince Lombardi was all his life an intensely religious man, whose life centered around the church as much as it did around the football field. The eldest of several children of southern Italian parents, he grew up in St. Mark's Roman Catholic Church in Brooklyn, where he served as an altar boy. Even as an adult, he welcomed the opportunity to serve Mass, because, when he did, he said he felt "closest to God."[4] The family attended Mass every Sunday. Young Vince went to church every day during Lent as his father did throughout the year. The Lombardis were on friendly terms with the parish priest, who often dined with the family and took Vince and other children to ball games and picnics. Lombardi always held the clergy in highest respect, contributing large sums of money to charities run by religious and giving priests and nuns free passes to football games.[5]

In fact, at one time young Lombardi considered entering the priesthood. He was enrolled at the Cathedral College of the Immaculate

Conception, a preparatory seminary for boys who intended to become priests. After three years he left and never discussed his decision.[6] His lifelong devotion to the Roman Catholic Church and the high respect in which he held its clergy makes it unlikely that he had experiences which disillusioned him either with the doctrines of his Church or with the moral character of its clergy. When a young boy from Chicago wrote him to ask his advice on going to seminary, Lombardi, then head coach of the Packers, wrote, "Trust in God. If you have the vocation to be a priest, you will be a very fortunate young man."[7]

Although he decided that the priesthood was not his calling, he remained a faithful Catholic. A teammate of his at Fordham University in New York recalled, "Vinny used to go to Mass every morning, but so did most of us. He wasn't the acolyte, so shiny that the priests fussed over him....Vinny was a decent person, but he wasn't a saint. He enjoyed his occasional beer and he liked a good dice game....[H]e had no holier than thou attitude."[8] Other classmates recalled him as "deeply religious" and pointed out that, while attendance at Mass was compulsory, he did not sit with his friends, as most of the students did, but remained alone, deep in prayer. Whereas most of the students merely "heard" Mass, Lombardi nearly every day actually received Communion.[9]

When he was at Green Bay, Lombardi was active in Resurrection Church, where he belonged to the Holy Name Society and served on the parish planning committee. He attended Mass daily and made his confession face to face with the priest at a time when most Roman Catholics sought the anonymity of the confessional booth. That he did so, in the opinion of his friend, Bishop Aloysius Wycislo of Green Bay, "shows the humility of the man."[10] Whenever he met with Bishop Wycislo, and, presumably, any other bishop, Lombardi knelt down to kiss his ring. When Wycislo tried to dissuade him, the coach insisted, "I still want to do it."[11] One of his assistant coaches at Green Bay recalled that when traveling, Lombardi always took his rosary and never missed Mass.[12] Another assistant coach recounted that he drove to church every morning and kept a Bible next to him on the front seat of the car.[13]

After he became head coach of the Redskins, Lombardi rose at six a.m. each morning to attend either the seven o'clock Mass at Our Lady of Mercy near his home in Potomac, Maryland, or the 7:30 Mass at the Cathedral of St. Matthew, near his office in Washington.[14] When his team was playing out of town, Lombardi made it a point to locate the nearest Roman Catholic Church, where he went to Mass.[15]

Vince Lombardi's piety had a flavor that was distinctly Italian Catholic. Before attending Mass, he prayed each morning to Saint Jude or to the Sacred Heart of Jesus. He clipped a rosary to the steering wheel of his car, and prayed the rosary while he drove. He also said the rosary, kneeling by his bed, after Sunday Mass.[16] Nevertheless, although he urged his players to be religious, he never insisted that they would please God only if they converted to Roman Catholicism.[17] His players prayed together before and after each game. "We don't pray to win," he said. "We pray to play the best we can and to keep us free from injury. And the prayer we say after the game is one of thanksgiving."[18]

Lombardi has never been quoted as speaking of a personal relationship with Christ. That was not a part of his style of religious expression. He spoke, rather, of dependency on God. "I've got a great deal of faith in God, a great deal of dependency on God. I don't think I'd do anything without that dependency."[19] Lombardi's son told a biographer that his father's faith grew out of a need to overcome a painful inner conflict. "I think my father knew he wasn't as great as people made him out to be."[20] Bishop Wycislo recalled, "There was a tension about his faith. I think he wanted to be as perfect a Catholic as he was a coach."[21] Lombardi, asked why he attended Mass every day, answered, "I have such a terrible temper. It's the only way I can keep it under control."[22] He realized that at times he was rude and inconsiderate and lacking in patience. These and other failings he attributed to "original sin."[23] He said this, not in the way of excuse, but because he realized his dependency upon God and his need to commune with him each day at Mass, from which he said, "I derive my strength."[24]

Vince Lombardi's religious faith was deep and it was sincere. "I believe he really understood God," he daughter told a biographer. Although he seldom if ever discussed his deepest religious convictions, he "had an intimate, personal rapport with God. Of everybody on this earth, [God] was his best friend."[25] Although some found Lombardi's relationship with God imperfectly expressed in some aspects of his behavior, there were other aspects of his life where it was quite evident. At the time he was coach of the Packers, there was racial conflict among the players of many of the teams, but Lombardi made sure that his players were free of any outward display of racial hostility. This attitude seemed to be an outgrowth of his religious convictions, for he was known, upon hearing a bigoted remark, to challenge its originator by saying, "How can you, as a good Christian, feel that way?"[26]

A year after taking over the reins of the Redskins, Lombardi became ill with cancer and died two months later. Shortly beforehand, he told his priest, "I'm not afraid to die. I'm not afraid to meet my God now. But what I do regret is that there is so damn much left to be done on earth."[27]

Shortly after his death, President Nixon characterized Lombardi as "a man who in a time when many seem to be turning away from religion was devoutly religious and devoted to his Church; at a time when the moral fabric of the country seems to be coming apart, he was a man who was deeply devoted to his family; at a time when it seems rather square to be patriotic, he was deeply and unashamedly patriotic; at a time when permissiveness is the order of the day in many circles, he was a man who insisted on discipline."[28]

～

Profile 78
Richard Tucker

Born: Brooklyn, New York, August 28, 1913
Died: Kalamazoo, Michigan, January 8, 1975

Richard Tucker, the reigning tenor at the Metropolitan Opera in New York for many years, was born in Brooklyn, New York, to Orthodox Jewish parents who were imigrants from Bessarabia, in Romania. Before he became involved in opera, Tucker, who changed his name from Rubin Ticker, was a cantor, and, throughout his life, his first love was for cantorial music. When he was thirty-one, he auditioned for the Metropolitan Opera. "No one really knows why he chose to go into opera," his son Barry said many years later. "I don't think he had a burning desire to be an opera singer, but it fell into place. Fate worked it out. That's all." Tucker actually lost the audition, but the management of the Met was so impressed by him that, a few months later, they visited the Brooklyn Jewish Center, where he was cantor, for a Friday night service. They returned for the service the following morning, and afterward, begged Tucker to audition again. This time he received a contract to sing the leading role in *La Gioconda*, in which he began his thirty-year tenure at the Met on January 25, 1945.[1]

Barry Tucker characterized his father as a person who was "orthodox in his thinking, conservative in his doing. He said his prayers every day, and he and my mother kept a kosher house, but on the outside he ate shrimp and other things forbidden under our dietary laws. Whenever he got a chance to go to the temple, he would go. He was not a religious man, in the orthodox sense of the word, but he had a very strong sense of his Jewishness. We went to the temple in the mornings and said our prayers, but we did not sit home and pray for the rest of the day. We went out to swim or shop or play ball. He would sing on the Sabbath without any qualms. This is why he had to give up his position as a cantor. After he got his contract to sing with the Metropolitan, he explained that this would obligate him to sing on Friday evenings and Saturday afternoons. However, during the High Holy Days in September and during Passover in the spring, he would not sing in the opera. He passed up many opportunities to sing on opening nights at the Met and also at the Chicago Lyric Opera when the dates of the engagements conflicted with the holidays."[2]

Tucker's religious beliefs had a strong influence on his career. He was extremely devoted to Israel. When the nation was first created in 1948, he sang for free many times, to raise money for Israeli bonds and other charities related to that nation. He did not visit Israel until the late 1950s, when he was the guest of the Israel Philharmonic Orchestra. After that he returned to Israel every other year to donate a month of free performances. Barry Tucker recalled, "He'd be scheduled to sing four or five times, but he would end up singing twenty times for free—all over Israel." Not only that, he and his wife, Sara, purchased numerous instruments for the Israel Philharmonic Orchestra, including the pipe organ for the stage. He gave money for nursing homes, hospitals, and small synagogues. "He never took a penny out of Israel, but left tremendous sums of money there,"[3] the younger Tucker recalled.

Tucker refused to sing in Germany. "I just don't believe in singing for the German people because of what they did in the Holocaust," he said. Even when his son objected, "Even the Israel Philharmonic plays in Germany, and many of the members have numbers on their arms from the concentration camps," the tenor objected, "I don't care. I believe so strongly against these people, I have to refuse. It's not the money. It's the principle."[4]

Around 1950, Tucker recorded two operas—*La Forza del Destino* and *Aida* with soprano Maria Callas and conductor Tullio Serafin. When Callas proposed that they record "every opera that's possible" with Serafin, Tucker enthusiastically agreed. When the contract came from Angel Records, Tucker was dismayed that the conductor was to be not Tullio Serafin but Herbert von Karajan, who had been the conductor of the Berlin Opera and a Hitler supporter. Tucker told Angel Records's representative, "The fact is, this man was associated with a government that murdered six million of my people. The war could be over a hundred years and nothing is going to erase what the Nazis did." When the representative, who was a Christian, reminded Tucker that the essence of religion is forgiveness, Tucker objected, "That's the difference between us as Christians and Jews. I can forgive someone for what he does to me personally, but I'm not God—I don't have the power to forgive what is done to others."[5] And so he turned down the contract.

Tucker was asked many times to sing in the Soviet Union, but never did, because he demanded, "I will sing anywhere, in any opera house they have, if three conditions are met. First, they have to pay me fifty thousand dollars for one month of singing. Second, they have to let me distribute the money in the Jewish communities wherever I sing. And, third, I have to be allowed to sing at services in every synagogue along the way."[6] His conditions were never met, and so he never sang in the USSR. After repeated refusals, the communist government put Tucker on its blacklist.[7] Barry Tucker recalled, "They didn't like him and he didn't like them."

In the opera *La Forza del Destino* by Giuseppe Verdi, Tucker frequently sang the role of Don Alvaro, a Spanish nobleman who, by the last act, has become a friar. His former girlfriend—the soprano—has become, unbeknownst to him, a hermit, in the same convent. At the very end, the soprano is killed by her brother—the baritone—and, as she dies, she and the tenor are blessed by the father superior of the friary—the bass. The first time Tucker sang *La Forza* with basso Jerome Hines, he said to him, "Hey, kid! Whaddya do when she dies?" "Well, I don't know," said Hines. "You don't make the sign of the cross, do you?" asked Tucker. "Oh, yeah, I guess that's it," answered the bass. "Well, don't do it!" insisted Tucker. "I respect your religion, you respect mine. People object!" He explained that his many Jewish fans objected to him even portraying a character who knelt in front of the priest and received a blessing in the form of the sign of the cross. So Hines blessed Tucker with the star of David![8] Tucker also refused to wear a crucifix when he sang the role of Don Alvaro, prompting, on one occasion, criticism from the music critic of the *Christian Science Monitor* that hurt him so deeply that he showed the article to his friend, Francis Cardinal Spellman, Roman Catholic archbishop of New York, who wrote a letter to support the tenor's actions.[9]

Tucker was a tolerant man who respected all religions. Not only was he friendly with Cardinal Spellman and his successor, Terence Cardinal Cooke, he was also a friend of Father Theodore Hesburgh, president of the University of Notre Dame in Indiana. Tucker, who was forced to leave high school after the eleventh grade because of his family's poverty and the necessity of his finding work, was delighted when the university awarded him an honorary doctorate. He was the first Jew so honored. Afterward he personally raised six million dollars for the college, even singing the college song on the television show that Johnny Carson hosted.[10] He also had no difficulty accepting Jacqueline Kennedy's request that he sing the unambiguously Christian hymn, "*Panis Angelicus*," at the funeral of Robert Kennedy in 1968.[11]

Richard Tucker considered his voice a gift from God, but felt it was his responsibility to train and develop it. He never sang at home. Whenever his sons asked him to sing for them, he said, "Come to the opera." Barry Tucker recalled, "His home was home. Singing was business and it was done in New York."[12]

La Juive, a French opera by Jacques Halevy, was perhaps Tucker's favorite. "He liked it because there was a lot of Jewishness in the opera," Barry Tucker said. "There is a Passover scene in which the tenor actually sings the Hebrew prayers."[13] However, the plot revolves around a story of revolting religious intolerance. A bigoted Roman Catholic cardinal has a young Jewish girl boiled in oil—a girl who turns out to be his own illegitimate daughter. The grotesque nature of the plot made many opera companies reluctant to stage the work. Although Tucker sang *La Juive* in concert version in Spain and recorded highlights, he longed to sing it at the Metropolitan Opera. While on a concert tour with baritone Robert Merrill in Kalamazoo, Michigan, in early January 1975, he received the news that the Metropolitan Opera had decided to stage thirteen performances of *La Juive* the next season with a cast in which Tucker would be joined by conductor Leonard Bernstein and three other world-acclaimed singers.[14] He was looking forward to returning to New York the following day to discuss the production, but, within hours of receiving the long-desired news, he suffered a heart attack and died almost instantly.

~

Profile 79
John Fitzgerald Kennedy

Born: Brookline, Massachusetts, May 29, 1917
Died: Dallas, Texas, November 22, 1963

Religion became an issue in the 1960 presidential election because of the religious affiliation of one of the candidates. The identification with the Quaker faith of Republican candidate Richard Nixon caused no stir, but there were some who feared that Democrat John Kennedy might be doomed to defeat because he was a Roman Catholic. Some people actually felt that any Catholic president would be subject to the dictation of the pope.

The issue did come to a head during the primary in West Virginia, a state which was almost totally Protestant. According to Pierre Salinger, who became Kennedy's press secretary: "Kennedy asked a pollster to test the West Virginia polls to see how he would do against [Hubert] Humphrey [a senator from Minnesota who was also seeking the Democratic nomination]. The voters in the poll favored Kennedy to Humphrey, 70 percent to 30 percent. 'Did you mention that I'm Catholic?' Kennedy asked the pollster. He hadn't. [Kennedy] asked him to take another poll after calling attention to the fact that he was Roman Catholic. This time the polls were 60 percent to 40 percent in favor of Humphrey [who was Protestant]."[1] Kennedy's managers brought in Franklin D. Roosevelt, Jr., to campaign for their man. President Roosevelt had been wildly popular in West Virginia, and Kennedy's endorsement by the great man's son and namesake was expected to carry great weight. It did. Kennedy won the primary.

In September, the issue was raised again by the influential Protestant minister Norman Vincent Peale who expressed anxiety as to whether a Roman Catholic president could be loyal to his oath of office and to his Church at the same time.[2] Not long after that, Kennedy was invited to address a group of ministers in Houston, and said: "Because I am a Catholic, and no Catholic has ever been elected president …it is apparently necessary for me to state once again—not what kind of church I believe in…but what kind of America I believe in." He went on to say that he believed in "an America where the separation of church and state is absolute—where no Catholic prelate would tell the president…how to act and no Protestant minister would tell his parishioners for whom to vote." He believed in an America "where no religious body seeks to impose its will directly or indirectly upon the general populace or the public acts of its officials—and where religious liberty is so indivisible that an act against one church is treated as an act against all." Moreover, he contended, "I am not the Catholic candidate for president, I am the Democratic Party's candidate for president, who happens to be a Catholic....I do not intend to disavow either my views or my church in order to win this election. If I should lose on the real issues, I shall return to my seat in the Senate satisfied that I tried my best and was fairly judged. But if this election is decided on the basis that forty million Americans lost their chance of being president on the day they were baptized, then it is the whole nation that will be the loser in the eyes of Catholics and non-Catholics around the world, the eyes of history, and in the eyes of our own people."[3]

With regard to the personal faith of Jack Kennedy, there is some question. His wife, Jacqueline, allegedly said during the campaign that she could not understand the concern of non-Catholics, since Jack is such a "poor Catholic."[4] And when an English writer told one of Kennedy's sisters that someone ought to write a book about her brother's faith, she observed, "It will be an awfully slim volume."[5]

Kennedy's devout mother, Rose, wanted all her children to have a significant part of their education in Catholic schools, but her husband would not permit this in the case of their sons, and as a result, except for a "part of a year" at a Roman Catholic prep school, John Kennedy's education was entirely secular.[6] As early as 1942, when he was twenty-five and in the Navy, he told one of his comrades that he had "lost his religion."[7]

Richard Cardinal Cushing, archbishop of Boston and a close friend of Kennedy and his family, insisted: "He felt his religion profoundly.... [H]e was a man of strong religious commitments."[8] His mother, Rose, while conceding that he was "not demonstrative in his practice of religion...or talkative about his beliefs," noted that he attended church regularly and frequently took Communion.[9] Indeed Kennedy, as senator and then as president, regularly attended Holy Trinity Church in Georgetown and went to Mass even on the campaign trail. His roommate in prep school noted, "Never can I remember Jack not saying his prayers on his knees every night before going to bed."[10] This practice continued to the end of his life, apparently. One of his sisters recalled, "One night when Dad was visiting at the White House, it was late and he started into Jack's bedroom to mention something he had just thought of. Then he stopped short and left without being noticed—because there was the president kneeling by his bed, saying his prayers."[11]

Yet most of those who knew him well did not consider John Kennedy a man of profound spirituality. Press Secretary Pierre Salinger recalled: "He didn't appear to be a religious man. Religion didn't seem to mean a great deal to him."[12] Theodore Sorensen, principal policy advisor and speechwriter, while insisting that the stories of marital infidelity on the part of his boss were "subject to great exaggeration,"[13] declared, "Not once in eleven years, despite all our discussions of church-state affairs—did he ever disclose his personal views on man's relation to God....I never heard him pray aloud in the presence of others."[14] After hearing Billy Graham discuss the Second Coming of Jesus Christ, Kennedy was "amazed and questioned whether the Catholic Church held the same belief,"[15] which in fact it had for two thousand years!

Once Kennedy pointed to a church and asked a friend, "How do you come out on all this?" The friend said that he never had the time to work it all out, but if he did, he would probably have to say, "I don't know." Kennedy told him that this "was about where he stood, too."[16]

Another friend was sure that John Kennedy "found salvation by meeting his own best standards rather than receiving the grace of God." He seemed to feel that life was absurd and its meaning was that which men gave it through the way they lived.[17] A man to whom the president once gave a gift mug inscribed with lines from the Hindu poem *The Ramayana* believed that the verse expressed, as much as anything else, what Kennedy truly believed:

> There are three things which are real:
> God, human folly, and laughter.
> The first two are beyond our comprehension
> So we must do what we can with the third.[18]

~

Profile 80
Leonard Bernstein

Born: Lawrence, Massachusetts, August 25, 1918
Died: New York, New York, October 14, 1990

The conductor and composer was descended from Prussian and
Polish rabbis who claimed descent from the ancient tribe of Benjamin. His grandfather, who immigrated from Russia, was a Hasidic
Jew, who wore a beard and earlocks, a black caftan and a fur hat.[1]
Bernstein's father, a Talmudic scholar, joined a Conservative Congregation (more moderate than the one in which he had spent his early
life) when the boy was nine. Bernstein, who attended Hebrew School
and read the Bible frequently, identified strongly with Judaism, even
though he did not practice most of the rituals.[2]

One way in which the composer complimented friends was to associate them with Jewishness. For instance, one friend declared, "He is
so adamant about music being Jewish. It is important to him that a
composer is a Jew. He told me that...my composition has a Jewish
soul. That is meant as a compliment. I am not a Jew. When Lenny
says, 'You can almost be Jewish,' that is considered by him to be the
most supreme of compliments."[3] Another friend recounted, "Lenny
used to tell me that I had a Yiddish head. That was always meant as
great praise."[4]

Just what did Judaism mean to Bernstein? Perhaps he expressed it
best when he conducted the Second Symphony of Mahler in memory
of his friend, President John Kennedy, who had recently been assassinated. Drawing from a phrase from a speech the president had planned
to deliver in Dallas, "America's leadership must be guided by learning
and reason," Bernstein pointed out that learning and reason were "the
two basic precepts of all Judaistic tradition, the twin sources from
which every Jewish mind from Abraham and Moses to Freud and
Einstein has drawn its living power." He felt that learning and reason,
appropriated by all people, were the key to "the achievement of a
world in which the mind will have triumphed over violence."[5]

357

Although many of those who knew Bernstein felt that he was "touched by God" and endowed by him with extraordinary gifts,[6] the composer seems to have spent much of his life questioning God. Interpreting the theme of his first symphony, which he named for the prophet Jeremiah, he commented, "I wouldn't say that it's God up there watching over me, as much as me down here looking up to find him—I guess you would call that a chief concern of my life."[7] According to one biographer, Bernstein was obsessed with "the difficulty of finding and sustaining faith in God at a time of recurring wars and countless instances of man's inhumanity to his fellow man."[8]

Bernstein titled his third symphony *The Kaddish*, after the prayer glorifying God at the end of the synagogue service. It was dedicated to the memory of John F. Kennedy. The symphony has a spoken monologue, and the speaker, at one point, calls out somewhat peevishly:

> Lord God of Hosts, I call *you* to account.
> And don't shrug me off, as if I were playing
>   Defiant Daughter,
> The teenage rebel, who could do with a slap!...
> And you let this happen, Lord of Hosts?
> You with your Manna, your loaves and your fishes?
> You ask for faith: where is your own?
> Why have you taken away your rainbow,
> The pretty bow tied round your finger,
> To remind you never to forget your promise.
> Shall I quote you your own weighty words?
> "For lo, I do set my bow in the clouds,
> And I will look upon it, that I may remember
> My everlasting covenant...."
> Your covenant! Your bargain with man!
> It crumples in my hand!
> And where is faith now—Yours or mine?[9]

One critic complained, after the first performance of the Kaddish Symphony, that in the monologue Bernstein treated "God as an equal, as one who needs to be comforted for his many mistakes."[10] Another objected to the speaker as a "shrew who thrusts at our Lord without piety or refinement. God is put in the position of the 'heavy' who has failed us completely, lost faith in us, has consigned us to a void of apathy."[11]

In the early 1970s, Bernstein composed a Mass. In writing the libretto he was assisted by lyricist Stephen Schwartz, but later said that "the celebrant" of the Mass was an "extension of my thought."[12] As in the Kaddish Symphony, Bernstein's message seems to be "God, if you're good and all-powerful, why do you permit bad things to happen? Do you really care about us?" During the *Agnus Dei*, the celebrant complains:

> We're fed up with your heavenly silence,
> And we only get action with violence,
> So—if we can't have the world we desire
> Give us peace now and we don't mean later.
> Don't forget you were once our creator.[13]

Bernstein seems to have felt that the evils and disappointments of life contradicted God's love for the human race, as set forth in the Bible. He was never able to reconcile himself to the idea of a loving God who permitted evil. Ultimately, he felt that humankind could find a sort of redemption through "learning and reason."

Bernstein was not given to formal religious observance. One biographer believed that his regular sessions with his psychoanalyst were "more important to him than organized religion as a key to self-knowledge."[14] At the end of his life, he seemed to despair. "When you stop loving life, there's no point and it's all so useless." About ten days before he died, he sadly observed, "I've lost God, and I'm afraid of dying."[15] The end came as his physician tried to give him an injection. In an incredulous tone, Bernstein cried, "What is this?" and died.[16]

~

$\mathcal{P}_{ro}fi\ell e\ 81$
Jack Roosevelt Robinson

Born: Cairo, Georgia, January 31, 1919
Died: North Stamford, Connecticut, October 13, 1972

The man who broke baseball's color line when he took the field for the Brooklyn Dodgers in 1947 has been described as a fierce competitor, outspoken and not infrequently abrasive. In his own autobiography, Robinson quoted a sportswriter friend who wrote of him: "He made enemies. He has a talent for it. He has the tact of [a] child because he has the moral purity of a child."[1]

Robinson has been described by many who knew him well as a very religious man. His mother, the former Mallie McGriff, who worked two jobs to support her five children after her husband deserted her, was a very devout Methodist. "She brought us up believing in God," a niece recalled. Not only did she teach the children that there was a God but also that there was a hell, which she defined as being "shut off from God," and that it was necessary to be "in the will of God."[2]

With his mother frequently out of the home, working day and night, young Jackie, as a teenager, was a member of the "Pepper Street Gang" and might have fallen into bad ways had it not been for the influence of his minister, Karl Downs, pastor of the Scotts Methodist Church of Pasadena, California. Robinson later credited Downs with turning his life around. In his autobiography he recounted: "[The] Reverend Downs set out to win the young members of the congregation who had become church dropouts and reached out to recruit some who had never attended our church or perhaps any church. Those of us who had been indifferent church members began to feel an excitement in belonging. We started planning dances at the church and playing on the new badminton court that the new minister had installed. Many of the youngsters who began coming were finding the church an alternative to hanging out on street corners. Downs," Robinson wrote, had the "ability to communicate with you spiritually, and, at the same time, he was fun to be with. He participated with us in our sports. Most impor-

360

tant, he knew how to listen. Often when I was deeply concerned about personal crises, I went to him."[3] Robinson remained close to his pastor (who performed his wedding) until Downs died just before the start of Robinson's second year with the Dodgers. Robinson's wife, Rachel, would later write, "The religious beliefs that Karl helped stimulate in him would strengthen his ability to cope with all the challenges he would face in life."[4]

After he became a star with the Dodgers, Robinson and his family moved first to New York and then to North Stamford, Connecticut, where they built a home and became associated with the North Stamford Congregational Church. Robinson's daughter wrote that his attendance at church, over the years, was "an occasional activity rather than a regular source of comfort."[5] Nevertheless, according to his wife, he was "religious" and "felt God's presence in the most personal way."[6] One of his most dominant traits, she felt, was humility, which in part "stemmed from religious faith."[7] When asked about his religious faith, she replied: "Oh, it was nothing spectacular. He prayed. He believed that God supported him in his struggles and in his troubles, and he believed that God had given him his talents and abilities."[8] According to his daughter, Robinson, when in difficult circumstances, often insisted "that God was testing him and would not give him more than he could bear."[9]

Robinson said rather little about his religious convictions in his autobiography, which was published the year of his death, but in an interview in the early 1950s, when asked what he believed, he replied that he believed in progress. He insisted that "many of today's dogmas will have vanished by the time [my children] grow into adults....[T]here is nothing static with free people. There is no Middle Ages logic so strong that it can stop the human tide from flowing forward. I...believe ...that what I was able to attain came to be because we put behind us...the dogmas of the past to discover the truth of today, and perhaps find the greatness of tomorrow." Without specifying what dogmas he was rejecting, he affirmed: "I believe in the human race. I believe in the warm heart. I believe in man's integrity. I believe in the goodness of a free society. And I believe that the society can remain good only as long as we are willing to fight for it—and to fight whatever imperfections may exist." Speaking of his fight "against the barriers that kept Negroes out of baseball," he said, "it couldn't be a losing fight—not when it took place in a free society. And, in the largest sense, I believe that what I did was done for me—that it was my faith in God that sustained me in my fight."[10]

∼

Profile 82
Flannery O'Connor

Born: Savannah, Georgia, March 25, 1925
Died: Milledgeville, Georgia, August 3, 1964

I write the way I do because...I am a Catholic,"[1] the novelist and short-story writer confided to a friend. She once told an interviewer, "I see from the standpoint of Christian orthodoxy. For me the meaning of life is centered in our Redemption by Christ and what I see in the world I see in its relation to that."[2]

Mary Flannery O'Connor was born into a prosperous Roman Catholic family in Savannah, Georgia, and remained faithful to her religious heritage throughout her life. As a child she lived in a Roman Catholic neighborhood in Savannah and attended Mass regularly with her parents at the nearby Cathedral of St. John the Baptist. Until the family moved to Milledgeville, she was educated by nuns in Catholic schools, but her high school, college, and graduate education were undertaken at secular institutions.

"When I made my First Communion I was six and it seemed as natural to me and about as startling as brushing my teeth,"[3] she later recounted to a friend. She was not an especially pious little girl. As an adult she recalled that she developed, while going to Catholic schools, "something the Freudians have not named—anti-angel aggression.... From 8 to 12 years it was my habit to seclude myself in a locked room so often with a fierce (and evil) face, whirl around in a circle with my fists knotted, socking the angel. This was the guardian angels which the Sisters assured us we were all equipped. He never left you. My dislike of him was poisonous. I'm sure I even kicked at him and landed on the floor." Eventually, she recounted, "the Lord removed this fixation from me by His Merciful Kindness."[4]

O'Connor, who suffered most of her adult life with a crippling, debilitating illness, lived briefly in New York and Connecticut, but then returned to the South, where she lived, until her comparatively early death, with her mother on a farm called Andalusia near Milledgeville, where she wrote and raised peacocks. She was always a devout Catholic. She went to Mass every day, when her health permitted, and, unlike many Catholics of her generation, was a great reader of the Bible and hoped for a "Biblical revival" within Roman Catholicism.[5]

"I am not a mystic and I do not lead a holy life," she wrote a friend. "Not that I can claim any interesting or pleasurable sins...but I know all about the garden variety, pride, gluttony, envy, and sloth, and, what is more to the point, my virtues are as timid as my vices."[6] Toward the end of her life, she wrote another friend, "I am not good at meditating....If I attempt to keep my mind on the mysteries of the rosary, I am soon thinking about something else, entirely nonreligious in nature. So I read my prayers out of the book, [the office of] prime in the morning and compline at night."[7]

A few months before her death, when the same friend requested her prayers, O'Connor answered, "I do pray for you but in my fashion which is not a very good one. I am not a good pray-er. I don't have a gift for it. My type of spirituality is almost completely shut-mouth."[8] After a pilgrimage to Lourdes she wrote, "I am sure the ceremonies of the convent would get me down. I am a long-standing avoider of May processions and suchlike nun-inspired doings. I am always thankful the Church doesn't teach those things are necessary."[9]

Nevertheless, O'Connor was entirely loyal to the Church. She once said, "I don't find it an infringement of my independence to have the Church tell me what is true and what is not in regard to faith and what is right and what is wrong in regard to morals. Certainly I am no fit judge.... I don't believe Christ left us to chaos."[10]

Her attitude toward the birth control controversy was likewise in keeping with her total commitment to the teaching of the Church.

"The Church's stand on birth control is the most absolutely spiritual of all her stands and with all of us being materialists at heart, there is little wonder that it causes unease," she wrote. "I wish various [priests] would quit trying to defend it by saying that the world can support 40 billion. I will rejoice in the day when they say: This is right, whether we all rot on top of each other or not, dear children, as we certainly may. Either practice restraint or be prepared for crowding...."[11]

O'Connor believed that within the Church, the individual "no matter how worthless himself" was a part of the Body of Christ and a participant in the Redemption. "There is no blueprint that the Church gives for understanding this," she wrote. "It is a matter of faith and the Church can force no one to believe it. When I ask myself how I know I believe, I have no satisfactory answer at all, no assurance at all, no feeling at all. I can only say with Peter, Lord, I believe, help my unbelief. And all I can say about my love of God is, Lord help me in my lack of it."[12]

Explaining her concept of the Roman Catholic Church to a Protestant English professor, she wrote, "I don't believe that if God intends for the world to be spared he'll have to lead a few select people into the wilderness to start things over again. I think that what he began when Moses and the children of Israel left Egypt continues today in the Church....I believe all this is accomplished in the patience of Christ in history and not with select people but with very ordinary ones—as ordinary as the vacillating children of Israel and the fishermen apostles. This comes from a different conception of the Church than yours. For us the Church is the body of Christ, Christ continuing in time, and as such [is] a divine institution. The Protestant considers this idolatry. If the church is not a divine institution, it will turn into an Elks Club."[13]

In her correspondence with this Protestant professor (Ted Spivey of Atlanta), she said that Protestants and Roman Catholics mean "entirely different things" when they say that they believe that the "Church is Divine." Protestants "mean the invisible Church which is somehow related to its many forms," whereas Roman Catholics "mean one and one only visible Church." She did not find it logical "to believe that Christ teaches through many visible forms—all teaching contrary doctrine." Whereas Protestants tended to squabble over such fundamentals of the Christian faith as the Virgin Birth, the Resurrection, and the Divinity of Christ, "for us the one visible Church pronounces on these matters infallibly and we receive her doctrine whether subjectively it fits in with our surmises or not. We believe that Christ left the Church to speak for him, that it speaks with his voice, he the head, and we the members."[14]

O'Connor was extremely uncomfortable with the Protestant idea that the believer can read the Bible on his own and formulate his own personal beliefs. "You can know where I stand, what I believe, because I am a practicing Catholic," she told Spivey, "but I can't know what you believe unless I ask you."[15] The good Catholic receives his beliefs from the Church, and then acts on them "in accordance with his degree of intelligence, his knowledge of what the Church teaches, and the grace, natural and supernatural, that he's been given."[16]

Some of her Protestant friends expressed the concern that religion appeared to be merely mechanical for many Roman Catholics, and, moreover, that many active members of the Church of Rome, both religious and lay, seemed to be truly bad people. O'Connor conceded that she thought of Protestant churches "as being composed of people who are good" and admitted that most of the practicing Protestants she knew were, in fact, "good." However, "the Catholic Church is composed of those who accept what she teaches, whether they are good or bad, and there is a constant struggle through the help of the Sacraments to be good."[17] She conceded that the worship practices of many Catholics "can become mechanical and merely habit." However, she insisted, "It is better to be held to the Church by habit than not to be held at all. The Church is mighty realistic about human nature."[18]

To another friend who was dissatisfied with the Church, O'Connor wrote: "All your dissatisfaction with the Church seems to come from an incomplete understanding of sin....[W]hat you seem actually to demand is that the Church put the kingdom of heaven on earth right here now, that the Holy Ghost be translated at once into all flesh....You are asking that man return at once to the state God created him in, you are leaving out the terrible radical human pride that causes death. Christ was crucified on earth and the Church is crucified in time, and the Church is crucified by all of us, by her members most particularly, because she is a Church of sinners. Christ never said that the Church would be operated in a sinless or intelligent way, but that it would not teach error. This does not mean that each and every priest won't teach error, but that the whole Church, speaking through the Pope, will not teach error in matters of faith. The Church is founded on Peter who denied Christ three times and couldn't walk on water by himself. You are expecting his successors to walk on the water. All human nature vigorously resists grace because grace changes us and the change is painful. Priests resist it as well as others. To have the Church be what you want it to be would require the continuous miraculous meddling of God in human affairs, whereas it is our dignity that we are allowed more or less to get on with those graces that come through faith and the sacraments, and which work through our human nature."[19]

O'Connor saw the Resurrection of Christ as the high point in the law of nature. To someone who suggested that Jesus, while not God in human flesh, might be a "realist," she wrote, "If He was not God, He was no realist, only a liar, and the crucifixion an act of justice."[20] Another time she commented, "If Christ wasn't God, he was merely pathetic, not beautiful."[21] To a woman who rejected the divinity of Jesus, she wrote: "To see Christ as God and man is probably no more difficult today than it has always been....For you it may be a matter of not being able to accept what you call a suspension of the laws of the flesh and the physical, but for my part I think that when I know what the laws of the flesh and the physical really are, then I will know what God is. We know them as we see them, not as God sees them. For me it is the virgin birth, the Incarnation, the resurrection which are the true laws of the flesh and the physical. Death, decay, destruction are the suspension of these laws. I am always astonished at the emphasis the Church puts on the body. It is not the soul she says that will rise, but the body, glorified. I have always thought that purity was the most mysterious of the virtues but it occurs to me that it would never have entered the human consciousness to conceive of purity if we were not to look forward to a resurrection of the body, which will be flesh and spirit united in peace, in the way they were in Christ."[22]

For O'Connor, hell was what God's love became to those who rejected it. "Now, no one has to reject it," she wrote. "God made us to love him. It takes two to love. It takes liberty. It takes the right to reject. If there were no hell, we would be like the animals. No hell, no dignity. And remember the mercy of God. It is easy to put this down as a formula and hard to believe it, but try believing the opposite, and you will find it too easy. Life has no meaning that way."[23]

As we have seen, Flannery O'Connor was not gifted with a constant experience of the presence of God. "Even in the life of a Christian, faith rises and falls like the tides of an invisible sea. It's there, even when he can't see it or feel it,"[24] she told a correspondent. She was sustained, not by her own subjective reactions or experiences, but by her Church and the sacraments. Asked by a Protestant if she believed herself "saved," she replied, "I am quite interested in saving my soul, but I see this as a long developmental, evolutionary process, extending into purgatory, and the only moment of it that concerns me in the least is the instant I am living in."[25] Trust in Christ through his Church was more important than one's own consolations or feelings of assurance. She wrote a friend, "What people don't realize is how much religion costs. They think faith is a big electric blanket, when of course it is the cross. It is much harder to believe than not to believe.... Don't expect faith to clear things up for you. It is trust, not certainty."[26]

O'Connor's writing was very much influenced by her faith. "It seems to me that all good stories are about conversion, about a character's changing....The action of grace changes a character. All my stories are about the action of grace on a character who is not very willing to support it!"[27] Another time she declared, "I can't allow any of my characters, in a novel anyway, to stop in some halfway position. This doubtless comes of a Catholic education and a Catholic sense of history—everything works towards its true end or away from it, everything is ultimately saved or lost."[28]

In all her voluminous correspondence, O'Connor never complained about her deteriorating health. Influenced by the French Jesuit Pierre Teilhard de Chardin, she believed in what has been called passive diminishment, that Christians must accept the fates that befall them. She wrote a friend, "I have never been anywhere but sick. In a sense sickness is a place more instructive than a long trip to Europe, and it's

368 ~ PROFILES OF FAITH

always a place where there's no company, where nobody can follow. Sickness before death is a very appropriate thing and I think those who don't have it missed one of God's mercies."[29] Her response to a friend, less than three months before her death, highlights her attitude toward her illness and toward life in general. When the friend wrote that she caused a Mass to be offered for her intentions—that is, her requests—O'Connor answered, "I don't know what my intentions are but I try to say that whatever suits the Lord suits me."[30]

～

Profile 83
Robert Francis Kennedy

Born: Brookline, Massachusetts, November 20, 1925
Died: Los Angeles, California, June 6, 1968

Attorney General under his brother John and later, for a time, under Lyndon Johnson, he was serving as Democratic senator from New York when he was assassinated while trying to capture his party's nomination for president. He was considered the most religious of the four Kennedy brothers. Pierre Salinger, press secretary to John F. Kennedy, while conceding that religion did not seem to interest J.F.K., recalled that "Bobby was more tied to the Catholic Church," and more than once insisted that he attend Mass with him.[1]

"Bobby" Kennedy served as an altar boy during his youth, and when he was a student at Milton Academy, he rarely missed Mass on Sundays or on holy days of obligation.[2] He read the Bible his mother gave him and said the rosary.[3] As an adult, he continued as a faithful churchgoer. When he was based in Washington, he attended St. Luke's Catholic Church near his home in McLean, Virginia, twice on a Sunday, worshiping at one of the traditional Masses in the morning, then loading his numerous children into a station wagon to participate in the folk Mass in the evening. He was involved enough to take the pastor to task one day for his dull preaching. "My kids are pretty bright, and if they don't get it, other people won't, either," he complained. He told the priest that his sermons should be like his own political speeches— "simple and clear, going directly to the point." When the priest, somewhat put off, suggested that Kennedy might lend him his speechwriter, Kennedy explained, "I didn't mean to be so intense, but religion is so important in life. I want my kids to like it. You all should not be talking about God up there so much. I want to know what God is like down here, how he is concerned with what we do here. I want to know how my life should be lived here now."[4]

A man once, in conversation, suggested that religion was not important, that the only thing important in life was being kind and loving. After asking Kennedy if he believed in an afterlife, the senator answered, "Yes, I do believe in an afterlife. Religion is a salve for confusion and misdirection. It gets people over the hump easier [than a worldly philosophy]."[5]

Despite his devotion to the Church and his belief in the importance of religion, he seemed to have a hard time reconciling the suffering in his life and in the world to the mercies of God. He was a greater admirer of the French philosopher Camus, who, to greatly simplify his ideas, taught that life was meaningless. "I don't know that it makes any difference what I do. Maybe we're all doomed anyway,"[6] Kennedy was once heard to remark in later years. At a dinner in New York the year before his death, he mused, "I don't know why God put us on earth. If I had my choice, I would never have lived. I had no control over it. But why should God put on earth some people who will go to the devil?"[7] Asked if his brother's assassination and other family troubles had undermined his faith, Kennedy, on another occasion, responded, "No, they do not," but that he occasionally thought "that someone up in heaven is out to lunch when he ought to be attending to business."[8]

Once, at table, Kennedy asked all the guests if they believed in God. When they asked if he did, he responded, "Yes, I think. But one question which really shakes me....[I]f God exists, why do poor people exist? Why does a Hitler arise? I can't give an answer for that. Only faith...."[9]

∼

Notes

Profile 1: Benjamin Franklin

1. Norman Foerster, ed., *American Poetry and Prose, Part One*, (Boston: Houghton-Mifflin, 1957), 137.
2. Ibid.
3. Ibid., 138.
4. Ibid.
5. Ronald W. Clark, *Benjamin Franklin: A Biography*, (New York: Random House, 1983), 36–37.
6. Foerster, *American Poetry and Prose*, 139.
7. Carl Van Doren, *Benjamin Franklin*, (New York: The Viking Press, 1938), 124.
8. Foerster, *American Poetry and Prose*, 139.
9. Ibid.
10. Clark, *Benjamin Franklin: A Biography*, 37.
11. Sydney E. Ahlstrom, *A Religious History of the American People*, (New Haven, CT: Yale University Press, 1972), 284.
12. Foerster, *American Poetry and Prose*, 144.
13. Ibid.
14. Ibid., 145.
15. Ibid.
16. Van Doren, *Benjamin Franklin*, 747.
17. Ibid., 642.
18. Foerster, *American Poetry and Prose*, 171.

Profile 2: George Washington

1. Paul F. Boller, Jr., *George Washington and Religion*, (Dallas: Southern Methodist University Press, 1963), 27.
2. Donald Jackson, ed., *Diaries of George Washington*, vol. 3, (Charlottesville, VA: University Press of Virginia, 1978), 285.
3. George Washington Parke Custis, *Recollections and Private Memoirs of Washington*, (New York: Derby and Jackson, 1859), 173.
4. Boller, *George Washington and Religion*, 30.
5. Ibid.
6. Ibid.
7. "Reclaim Our Lady's Land," *Caritas of Birmingham*, May–June 1993, 6.
8. Boller, *George Washington and Religion*, 6.
9. Ibid.
10. Doran Hurley, "Was Washington a Catholic?" *Information*, February 1957, vol. LXXXI, No. 2, p. 4.
11. Boller, *George Washington and Religion*, 52.
12. Ibid., 54.
13. Ibid., 55.
14. Ibid.
15. Ibid., 56.
16. Eighty-Seventh Congress, First Session, *Inaugural Addresses of the Presidents of the United States from George Washington 1789 to John F. Kennedy 1961*, (Washington, D.C.: U.S. Government Printing Office, 1961), 2.
17. Ibid., 4.
18. Boller, *George Washington and Religion*, 57.
19. Ibid., 172.
20. John Frederick Schroeder, ed., *Maxims of George Washington*, (Mount Vernon, VA: The Mt. Vernon Ladies Association, 1989), 179.
21. Ibid., 180.
22. John C. Fitzpatrick, ed., *The Writings of George Washington, from the Original Manuscript Sources*, vol. 4, (Washington, D.C.: U.S. Government Printing Office, 1931), 65.

23. Boller, *Washington and Religion*, 154.
24. Ibid., 89.
25. Ibid., 90.
26. Ibid., 89.
27. Ibid., 71.
28. Ibid., 68.
29. Ibid., 110.
30. James Thomas Flexner, *George Washington and the New Nation (1783–1793)*, (Boston: Little, Brown & Co., 1969), 227.
31. Schroeder, *Maxims of George Washington*, 189, 191.
32. Mason L. Weems, *The Life of Washington*, (Cambridge, MA: The Harvard University Library, 1962), 169.
33. James Thomas Flexner, *George Washington, Anguish and Farewell (1793–1799)*, (Boston: Little, Brown & Co., 1969), 459.
34. Ibid., 460.
35. Ibid., 490.
36. Hurley, "*Was Washington a Catholic?*" 16.
37. Ibid., 4.
38. Ibid., 6.
39. Ibid., 5–6.
40. Douglas Southall Freeman, *George Washington: A Biography*, vol. VI, (New York: Scribners, 1954), 276.
41. Ibid., vol. V, 92.
42. Ibid., 3n.

Profile 3: John Adams
1. Paul C. Nagel, *Descent from Glory: Four Generations of the John Adams Family*, (New York: Oxford University Press, 1983), 81.
2. Lester J. Cappon, ed., *The Adams-Jefferson Letters*, (Chapel Hill, NC: University of North Carolina Press, 1959), 373.
3. Page Smith, *John Adams*, (Garden City, NY: Doubleday, 1967), vol. I, 30.
4. Ibid.
5. Cappon, *Adams-Jefferson Letters*, 373–374.
6. Ibid., 428.
7. Nagel, *Descent from Glory*, 128.
8. Cappon, *Adams-Jefferson Letters*, 374.
9. Ibid.
10. Smith, *John Adams*, vol. II, 1078.
11. Ibid., 896.
12. Cappon, *Adams-Jefferson Letters*, 409.
13. Smith, *John Adams*, vol. II, 896.
14. Ibid., vol. I, 30.
15. Cappon, *Adams-Jefferson Letters*, 395–396.
16. The Adams Family Papers, Massachusetts Historical Society, microfilm in Library of Congress, Washington, D.C., John Adams's Letterbook, Reel 118.
17. Smith, *John Adams*, vol. II, 1017.
18. Ibid., vol. I, 183.
19. Cappon, *Adams-Jefferson Letters*, 494.
20. Smith, *John Adams*, vol. II, 896.
21. Cappon, *Adams-Jefferson Letters*, 494.
22. Adams Family Papers, John Adams's Letterbook, Reel 122.
23. Cappon, *Adams-Jefferson Letters*, 462.
24. Ibid., 515.
25. Ibid., 334.
26. Ibid., 374
27. Ibid., 373.
28. Smith, *John Adams*, vol. I, 30.
29. Ibid.
30. Adams Family Papers, John Adams's Letterbook, Reel 118.
31. Smith, *John Adams*, vol. II, 1078.
32. Cappon, *Adams-Jefferson Letters*, 509.
33. *Adams Family Papers*, John Adams's Letterbook, Reel 118.
34. Fawn M. Brodie, *Thomas Jefferson: An Intimate History*, (New York: Norton, 1974), 353.
35. Ibid., 354.

36. Ibid., 265.
37. Ibid., 353.
38. Cappon, *Adams-Jefferson Letters*, 530.
39. Ibid., 611.
40. Peter Harvey, *Reminiscences and Anecdotes of Daniel Webster.* (Boston: Little, Brown & Co., 1878), 210.
41. Charles Francis Adams, *Memoirs of John Quincy Adams, Comprising Portions of His Diary from 1795 to 1848*, (Philadelphia: Lippincott, 1874–1877), vol. VII, 133.
42. Cappon, *Adams-Jefferson Letters*, 374.

Profile 4: Thomas Paine
1. John Keane, *Tom Paine: A Political Life*, (Boston: Little, Brown & Co., 1995), 17.
2. Ibid., 22–24.
3. Ibid., 390.
4. Norman Foerster, ed., *American Poetry and Prose*, (Boston: Houghton-Mifflin, 1957), vol. I, 202.
5. Ibid., 204.
6. Ibid., 202.
7. David Freeman Hawke, *Paine*, (New York: Harper, 1974), 294.
8. Foerster, *American Poetry and Prose*, 203.
9. Ibid., 206.
10. Ibid.
11. Hawke, *Paine*, 293.
12. Foerster, *American Poetry and Prose*, 205.
13. Samuel Edwards, *Rebel! A Biography of Tom Paine*, (New York: Praeger, 1974), 189.
14. Ibid., 190.
15. Ibid.
16. Ibid.
17. Ibid.
18. Ibid.
19. Ibid.
20. Hawke, *Paine*, 293.
21. Foerster, *American Poetry and Prose*, 202.
22. Edwards, *Rebel*, 266.
23. Ibid.
24. Ibid.
25. Ibid., 220.
26. Ibid.
27. Hawke, *Paine*, 394.
28. Ibid., 340.
29. Ibid., 396.
30. Ibid., 397.

Profile 5: Charles Carroll of Carrollton
1. Ellen Hart Smith, *Charles Carroll of Carrollton*, (Cambridge, MA: Russell and Russell, 1942), 274.
2. Ibid., 275.
3. Ibid., 276.
4. Ibid., 275.
5. Ibid.
6. Kate Mason Rowland, *The Life of Charles Carroll of Carrollton*, (New York: G. P. Putnam's Sons, 1898), vol. I, 82.
7. Ibid., vol. II, 248.
8. Ibid.
9. Ibid., 327–328.
10. Ibid., 355.
11. Ibid., 340.
12. Ibid., 370.
13. Ibid., 369.
14. Ibid., 369–370.

Profile 6: Thomas Jefferson
1. Lester J. Cappon, ed., *The Adams-Jefferson Letters*, (Chapel Hill, NC: University of North Carolina Press, 1959), 506.
2. Ibid., 512.

3. Norman Foerster, ed., *American Poetry and Prose*, vol. I, (Boston: Houghton-Mifflin, 1957), 221.
4. Saul K. Padover, ed., *The Complete Jefferson*, (New York: Duell, Sloan, and Pierce, 1943), 948.
5. Ibid., 949.
6. Ibid., 1036.
7. Ibid., 949–950.
8. Ibid., 1036.
9. Ibid., 949.
10. Foerster, *American Poetry and Prose*, 216.
11. Ibid.
12. Ibid.
13. Andrew A. Lipscomb and Albert E. Bergh, *Jefferson, Writings*, vol. XVI, (Washington, D. C.: Thomas Jefferson Memorial Association, 1903), 101.
14. Padover, *The Complete Jefferson*, 1036.
15. Cappon, *The Adams-Jefferson Letters*, 529.
16. Ibid., 433.
17. Ibid., 368.
18. Foerster, *American Poetry and Prose*, 221.
19. Ibid.
20. Padover, *The Complete Jefferson*, 955.
21. Fawn M. Brodie, *Thomas Jefferson, An Intimate History*, (New York: Norton, 1974), 54.
22. Ibid., 54–55.
23. Cappon, *The Adams-Jefferson Letters*, 368.
24. Dumas Malone, *Jefferson the Virginian*, (Boston: Little, Brown & Co., 1948), 278.
25. Foerster, *American Poetry and Prose*, 211.
26. Ibid., 212.
27. Ibid., 221.
28. Cappon, *The Adams-Jefferson Letters*, 512.
29. Edmund Fuller and David E. Green, *God in the White House: The Faiths of American Presidents*, (New York: Crown, 1968), 29–30.
30. Padover, *The Complete Jefferson*, 95.
31. Dumas Malone, *Jefferson and His Time: The Sage of Monticello*, (Boston: Little, Brown & Co., 1981), 491.
32. Padover, *The Complete Jefferson*, 957.
33. Ibid., 957–958.
34. John Chester Miller, *The Wolf by the Ears: Thomas Jefferson and Slavery*, (New York: Free Press, 1977), 43.
35. Ibid., 53.
36. Ibid., 43.
37. Ibid.
38. Saul K. Padover, *Jefferson*, (New York: Signet, 1942), 184.
39. Ibid., 185.
40. Ibid.
41. Ibid., 184.

Profile 7: Abigail Smith Adams

1. Charles Francis Adams, ed., *Memoirs of John Quincy Adams, Comprising Portions of His Diary from 1795 to 1848*, (Philadelphia: Lippincott, 1874–1877), vol. IV, 157 (indirect quotation).
2. Louis Albert Banks, *The Religious Life of Famous Americans*, (New York: American Tract Society, 1904), 200-201.
3. Ibid., 201–202.
4. Ibid., 202–203.
5. Ibid., 203–204.
6. Ibid., 205–206.
7. Ibid., 206–207.
8. The Adams Family Papers, Massachusetts Historical Society, microfilm, Letters Received and Other Loose Papers, July–December, 1813, Reel 416.
9. Lynn Withey, *Dearest Friend: A Life of Abigail Adams*, (New York: Free Press, 1981), ix–x.
10. Edward T. James, ed., *Notable American Women, 1607–1950*, vol. I, (Cambridge, MA: Belknap Press of Harvard, 1971), 7.
11. The Adams Family Papers, Massachusetts Historical Society, Letter, Abigail Adams to Louisa Catherine Adams, January 3, 1818, Letters Received and Other Loose Papers, Reel 442.

12. Phyllis Lee Levin, *Abigail Adams: A Biography*, (New York: St. Martin's Press, 1987), 180.
13. The Adams Family Papers, Massachusetts Historical Society, Letter, Abigail Adams to John Quincy Adams, October 12, 1815, Letters Received and Other Loose Papers, Reel 427.
14. Ibid., Letter, Abigail Adams to John Quincy Adams, May 5, 1816, Reel 431.
15. Ibid., Letter, Abigail Adams to John Quincy Adams, October 12, 1815, Reel 427.
16. Ibid., Letter, Abigail Adams to John Quincy Adams, May 5, 1816, Reel 431.
17. Ibid.
18. Ibid.
19. Ibid.
20. Charles Francis Adams, *Memoirs of John Quincy Adams*, vol. IV, 157.
21. Ibid., 158.
22. Adams Family Papers, Massachusetts Historical Society, John Quincy Adams' Diary, November 1818, Reel 33.

Profile 8: James Madison

1. John McCollister, *So Help Me, God, The Faith of America's Presidents*, (Louisville, KY: Westminster, 1991), 34.
2. Ralph Ketcham, *James Madison, A Biography*, (New York: Macmillan, 1971), 57.
3. Irving Brant, *James Madison, The Nationalist, 1780–1787*, (Indianapolis: Bobbs-Merrill, 1948), 343.
4. Ibid., 344.
5. Ibid., 351.
6. Ibid., 354.
7. Ibid.
8. Edmund Fuller and David E. Green, *God in the White House, The Faiths of American Presidents*, (New York: Crown, 1968), 44.
9. Irving Brant, *James Madison, The President, 1809–1812*, (Indianapolis: Bobbs-Merrill, 1956), 198.
10. Irving Brant, *James Madison, The Virginia Revolutionist*, (Indianapolis: Bobbs-Merrill, 1941), 113.
11. Irving Brant, *James Madison, Commander-in-Chief, 1812–1836*, (Indianapolis: Bobbs-Merrill, 1961), 364.
12. Ibid., 445.
13. Ketcham, *Madison, A Biography*, 667.
14. Brant, *James Madison, Commander-in-Chief, 1812–1836*, 504.
15. Ketcham, *Madison, A Biography*, 667.
16. Brant, *James Madison, Commander-in-Chief, 1812–1836*, 520.
17. C. Bernard Ruffin, *Last Words, A Dictionary of Deathbed Quotations*, (Jefferson, NC: McFarland, 1995), 127.

Profile 9: Alexander Hamilton

1. Robert Hendrickson, *Hamilton II (1789–1804)*, (New York: Mason/Charter, 1976), 545.
2. Robert Hendrickson, *The Rise and Fall of Alexander Hamilton*, (New York: Dodd, Mead, 1981), 36.
3. Ibid.
4. Hendrickson, *Hamilton II*, 546.
5. Hendrickson, *The Rise and Fall of Alexander Hamilton*, 46.
6. Hendrickson, *Hamilton II*, 545.
7. Ibid.
8. Hendrickson, *Hamilton II*, 546.
9. Ibid.
10. Ibid., 549.
11. Hendrickson, *The Rise and Fall of Alexander Hamilton*, 555.
12. Hendrickson, *Hamilton II*, 545.
13. Ibid., 645.
14. Ibid., 644.
15. Ibid., 645.
16. Ibid., 641.
17. Ibid., 642.
18. Ibid., 643.
19. Ibid.
20. Ibid., 642.

Profile 10: John Marshall

1. Leonard Baker, *John Marshall, A Life in Law*, (New York: Macmillan, 1974), 94–95.
2. Ibid., 752.
3. Ibid., 95.
4. Albert J. Beveridge, *The Life of John Marshall*, vol. IV, (Boston: Houghton-Mifflin, 1974), 70.
5. Ibid., 69.
6. Baker, *A Life in Law*, 752.
7. Beveridge, *Life of John Marshall*, 70.

Profile 11: Andrew Jackson/Rachel Donelson Robards Jackson

1. Arda Walker, "The Religious Views of Andrew Jackson," *East Tennessee History Publication*, No. 17 (1945), 61.
2. Robert V. Remini, *Andrew Jackson and the Course of American Empire (1767–1821)*, (New York: Harper, 1977), 7.
3. Paul F. Boller, Jr., *Presidential Anecdotes*, (New York: Oxford University Press, 1981), 73.
4. Remini, *Andrew Jackson and the Course of American Empire*, 7.
5. Robert V. Remini, *Andrew Jackson and the Course of American Democracy (1833–1845)*, (New York: Harper, 1984), 51.
6. James Parton, *The Life of Andrew Jackson*, vol. II, (Boston: Fields, Aisgood, 1870), 655.
7. Walker, "The Religious Views of Andrew Jackson," 69.
8. Ibid., 61.
9. Ibid., 62.
10. Remini, *Andrew Jackson and the Course of American Empire*, 193.
11. Ibid., 194.
12. Earl Irvin West, *Religion and Politics in the Jacksonian Era*, (Ann Arbor, MI: University Microfilms, Inc., 1968), 164.
13. Ibid., 173.
14. Remini, *Andrew Jackson and the Course of American Empire*, 403.
15. Paul F. Boller, Jr., *Presidential Wives*, (New York: Oxford University Press, 1988), 72.
16. Walker, "The Religious Views of Andrew Jackson," 64.
17. Ibid.
18. Robert V. Remini, *Andrew Jackson and the Course of American Freedom (1822–1832)*, (New York: Harper, 1981), 108.
19. Walker, "The Religious Views of Andrew Jackson," 65.
20. Boller, *Presidential Wives*, 69.
21. Marquis James, *The Life of Andrew Jackson*, (Indianapolis: Bobbs-Merrill, 1938), 479.
22. Ladies Hermitage Association, *Andrew Jackson's Hermitage*, (Hermitage, TN: Ladies Hermitage Association, 1986), 21.
23. Walker, "The Religious Views of Andrew Jackson," 65.
24. Remini, *Andrew Jackson and the Course of American Democracy*, 445.
25. Ibid.
26. Walker, "The Religious Views of Andrew Jackson," 66.
27. Ibid.
28. Ibid., 64.
29. Ibid., 62.
30. West, *Religion and Politics in the Jacksonian Era*, 170.
31. Remini, *Andrew Jackson and the Course of American Democracy*, 91.
32. Walker, "The Religious Views of Andrew Jackson," 68.
33. Ibid.
34. Ibid., 63.
35. Remini, *Andrew Jackson and the Course of American Democracy*, 185.
36. Ibid., 121.
37. Ibid., 51.
38. Ibid., 452–453.
39. Walker, "The Religious Views of Andrew Jackson," 64.
40. Ibid., 62.
41. Remini, *Andrew Jackson and the Course of American Freedom*, 387.
42. Walker, "The Religious Views of Andrew Jackson," 64.
43. Ibid., 64.
44. Remini, *Andrew Jackson and the Course of American Democracy*, 517.
45. Ibid., 519.
46. Ibid.
47. Ibid., 522.

48. Ibid., 524.
49. Walker, "The Religious Views of Andrew Jackson," 64.
50. Remini, *Andrew Jackson and the Course of American Democracy*, 524.

Profile 12: John Quincy Adams
1. Earl Irvin West, *Religion and Politics in the Jacksonian Era*, (Ann Arbor, MI: University Microfilms, 1968), 32.
2. Ibid., 31–32.
3. Charles Francis Adams, *Memoirs of John Quincy Adams, Comprising Portions of His Diary from 1795 to 1848*, (Philadelphia: Lippincott, 1874–1877), vol. VIII, 88.
4. Ibid., vol X, 343.
5. Ibid., vol. XI, 341.
6. Ibid., vol. IX, 340–341.
7. Ibid., vol. VIII, 129.
8. Ibid., n355.
9. The Adams Family Papers, Massachusetts Historical Society, John Quincy Adams to Charles Francis Adams, November 25, 1827.
10. West, *Religion and Politics in the Jacksonian Era*, 38.
11. Adams, *Memoirs of John Quincy Adams*, vol. X, 275.
12. Ibid., 345.
13. Ibid., 350.
14. *Norfolk [VA] Daily Beacon*, November 25, 1840.
15. Adams, *Memoirs of John Quincy Adams*, vol. X, 506–507.
16. Ibid., vol. VIII, 353.
17. Ibid., vol. IX, 438–439.
18. Ibid., 435.
19. Ibid., vol. VII, 147.
20. West, *Religion and Politics in the Jacksonian Era*, 43.
21. Adams, *Memoirs of John Quincy Adams*, vol. IX, 169.
22. Ibid.
23. Ibid., vol. VIII, 214.
24. Ibid., vol. IX, 543.
25. Ibid., 544.
26. Ibid.
27. Ibid., vol. X, 449.
28. West, *Religion and Politics in the Jacksonian Era*, 57.
29. Ibid.
30. Adams, *Memoirs of John Quincy Adams*, vol X, 276.
31. Ibid., vol. XII, 53.
32. Ibid., vol IX, 117.
33. Ibid., vol. VII, 381.
34. Ibid., vol. X, 428.
35. Ibid., vol. VII, 89.
36. Ibid.
37. Ibid., vol. X, 501.
38. The Adams Family Papers, Massachusetts Historical Society, John Quincy Adams Diary, May 3, 1829, Reel 39.
39. *Norfolk [VA] Daily Beacon*, November 25, 1840.
40. Adams, *Memoirs of John Quincy Adams*, vol. XI, 165.
41. The Adams Family Papers, Massachusetts Historical Society, John Quincy Adams Diary, October 23, 1834, Reel 42.
42. Ibid., John Quincy Adams Diary, October 24, 1834, Reel 42.
43. Adams, *Memoirs of John Quincy Adams*, vol. XII, 277.
44. Leonard Falkner, *The President Who Wouldn't Retire*, (New York: Coward and McCann, 1967), 300.
45. West, *Religion and Politics in the Jacksonian Era*, 31–32.

Profile 13: Elizabeth Ann Bayley Seton
1. Joseph I. Dirvin, *Mrs. Seton: Foundress of the American Sisters of Charity*, (New York: Farrar, Straus, & Cudahy, 1962), 25.
2. Ellin Kelly and Annabelle Melville, eds., *Elizabeth Seton: Selected Writings*, (New York: Paulist Press, 1987), 85.
3. Edward T. James, ed., *Notable American Women, 1607–1950*, vol. III, (Cambridge, MA: Belknap Press of Harvard, 1971), 263.
4. Dirvin, *Mrs. Seton*, 150.

5. Ibid., 84.
6. Ibid., 106.
7. Ibid., 148.
8. Ibid., 171.
9. Ibid., 157.
10. Kelly and Melville, *Elizabeth Seton*, 164–165.
11. Dirvin, *Mrs. Seton*, 384–385.
12. Ibid., 386.
13. Ibid.
14. Ibid.
15. Kelly and Melville, *Elizabeth Seton*, 70.
16. James, *Notable American Women*, 265.
17. Kelly and Melville, *Elizabeth Seton*, 44.
18. Ibid.
19. Ibid., 28.
20. Ibid.
21. Ibid., 44.
22. Ibid., 59.
23. Dirvin, *Mrs. Seton,* 337.
24. Ibid.
25. Ibid., 423.
26. Kelly and Melville, *Elizabeth Seton*, 48.
27. Ibid., 51.
28. Dirvin, *Mrs. Seton*, 423.
29. Ibid., 450–451.
30. Ibid., 452.
31. Ibid., 453.
32. Ibid.
33. Ibid., 454.

Profile 14: Roger Brooke Taney

1. Bernard C. Steiner, *Life of Roger Brooke Taney*, (Baltimore: Williams and Wilkins, 1922), 316.
2. Samuel Tyler, *Memoir of Roger Brooke Taney*, (Baltimore: Murphy, 1872), 28.
3. Carl Brent Swisher, *Roger B. Taney*, (New York: Macmillan, 1936), 50.
4. Ibid., 50.
5. Steiner, *Life of Roger Brooke Taney*, 49.
6. Ibid., 50.
7. Ibid., 46.
8. Tyler, *Memoir of Roger Brooke Taney*, 475.
9. Steiner, *Roger B. Taney*, 46.
10. Ibid.
11. Ibid., 47.
12. Ibid., 46.
13. Ibid., 50.
14. Ibid., 51.
15. Ibid., 347.
16. Ibid., 344.
17. Ibid., 347.
18. Ibid., 348.
19. Swisher, *Roger B. Taney*, 94.
20. Ibid., 97.
21. Steiner, *Life of Roger Brooke Taney*, 347.
22. Ibid., 97.
23. Alvin J. Schumaker, *Thunder on Capitol Hill*, (Milwaukee: Bruce Co., 1964), 67.
24. Steiner, *Life of Roger Brooke Taney*, 377–378.
25. Brother Flavius, *The Pride of Our Nation*, (Notre Dame, IN: Dujarie Press, 1961), 17.
26. Swisher, *Roger B. Taney*, 576.

Profile 15: Henry Clay

1. Earl Irvin West, *Religion and Politics in the Jacksonian Era*, (Ann Arbor, MI: University Microfilms, 1968), 120.
2. Calvin Colton, *The Life and Times of Henry Clay*, 2 vols., (New York, 1846), vol. I, 54.
3. Ibid., 56.

4. West, *Religion and Politics in the Jacksonian Era*, 124–125.
5. Ibid., 121.
6. Ibid.
7. Ibid., 125.
8. Robert V. Remini, *Henry Clay, Statesman for the Union*, (New York: Norton, 1991), 481–482.
9. Ibid., 482.
10. West, *Religion and Politics in the Jacksonian Era*, 123.
11. Ibid., 126.
12. Ibid.
13. Colton, *The Life and Times of Henry Clay*, vol. I, 56.
14. Remini, *Henry Clay, Statesman for the Union*, 685.
15. Ibid.
16. Ibid.
17. West, *Religion and Politics in the Jacksonian Era*, 128.
18. Ibid., 129.
19. Ibid.
20. Ibid.

Profile 16: Daniel Webster
1. Earl Irvin West, *Religion and Politics in the Jacksonian Era*, (Ann Arbor, MI: University Microfilms, 1968), 61.
2. Irving H. Bartlett, *Daniel Webster*, (New York: Norton, 1978), 295.
3. West, *Religion and Politics in the Jacksonian Era*, 65.
4. Ibid., 80.
5. Ibid.
6. Ibid., 73.
7. Ibid., 80.
8. Ibid., 69.
9. Ibid., 96.
10. Merrill D. Peterson, *The Great Triumvirate: Webster, Clay, & Calhoun*, (New York: Oxford University Press, 1987), 396.
11. Ibid., 397.
12. Bartlett, *Daniel Webster*, 171.
13. West, *Religion and Politics in the Jacksonian Era*, 88–89.
14. Ibid., 75–77.
15. Peterson, *The Great Triumvirate*, 395.
16. West, *Religion and Politics in the Jacksonian Era*, 98.
17. Peterson, *The Great Triumvirate*, 395.
18. West, *Religion and Politics in the Jacksonian Era*, 98.
19. Ibid., 90.
20. Allan L. Benson, *Daniel Webster*, (New York: Cosmopolitan, 1929), 398–399.
21. Claude M. Fuess, *Daniel Webster, 1830–1852*, vol. III, (Boston: Little, Brown & Co., 1930), 410.

Profile 17: John Caldwell Calhoun
1. Margaret L. Coit, *John C. Calhoun: American Portrait*, (Boston: Houghton-Mifflin, 1950), 22.
2. Ibid., 27.
3. Ibid., 286.
4. Ibid., 397.
5. Ibid., 396.
6. Ibid., 397.
7. Charles M. Wiltse, *John C. Calhoun, Sectionalist, 1840–1850*, (Indianapolis: Bobbs-Merrill, 1951), 117.
8. Ibid.
9. Coit, *John C. Calhoun*, 396.
10. Ibid., 508.
11. Irving H. Bartlett, *John C. Calhoun: A Biography*, (New York: Norton, 1993), 82.
12. Coit, *John C. Calhoun*, 508.
13. Ibid.
14. Ibid.

Profile 18: James Knox Polk/Sarah Childress Polk

1. Earl Irvin West, *Religion and Politics in the Jacksonian Era*, (Ann Arbor, MI: University Microfilms, 1968), 135.
2. Ibid., 141.
3. Ibid., 134.
4. Ibid., 150.
5. Ibid., 153.
6. Ibid.
7. Ibid., 156.
8. Ibid.
9. Ibid., 157.
10. Carl Sferazza Anthony, *First Ladies: The Saga of the Presidents' Wives and Their Power, 1789–1961,* (New York: Morrow, 1990), 13.
11. *In Memoriam, Mrs. James K. Polk* (Nashville, TN: n.p., 1891), 14.
12. Ibid., 15.
13. Ibid.
14. Anson and Fanny Nelson, *Memorials of Sarah Childress Polk*, (New York: A. R. Randolph, 1892), 92.
15. Anthony, *First Ladies*, 138.
16. Jimmie Lou Sparkman Claxton, *88 Years With Sarah Polk*, (New York: Vantage Press, 1972), 189.
17. Ibid., 188.
18. *Nashville Daily American*, August 14, 1891, and Nelson, *Memorials*, 274–275.

Profile 19: Sojourner Truth

1. Carleton Mabee, with Susan Mabee Newhouse, *Sojourner Truth: Slave, Prophet, Legend*, (New York: New York University Press, 1993), 64.
2. Ibid., 18.
3. Ibid., 3.
4. Margaret Washington, ed., *The Narrative of Sojourner Truth*, (New York: Vintage, 1993), 44–47.
5. Mabee, *Sojourner Truth*, 21.
6. Washington, *The Narrative of Sojourner Truth*, 45.
7. Ibid., 52.
8. Ibid., 49.
9. Ibid.
10. Ibid., 50.
11. Ibid.
12. Ibid., 51.
13. Ibid., 52.
14. Mabee, *Sojourner Truth*, 22.
15. Erlene Stetson and Linda David, *Glorying in Tribulation: The Lifework of Sojourner Truth*, (East Lansing, MI: Michigan State University Press, 1994), 5.
16. Mabee, *Sojourner Truth*, 27.
17. Ibid., 29.
18. Ibid., 45.
19. Ibid., 99.
20. Ibid., 241.
21. Ibid., 102.
22. Ibid., 232.
23. Ibid., 236.
24. Ibid., 92.
25. Ibid., 246.
26. Washington, *The Narrative of Sojourner Truth*, 53.
27. Ibid., 5.
28. Mabee, *Sojourner Truth*, 234.
29. Ibid., 233.
30. Ibid.
31. Ibid.
32. Washington, *The Narrative of Sojourner Truth*, 90.
33. Stetson and David, *Glorying in Tribulation*, 90.
34. Ibid.
35. Mabee, *Sojourner Truth*, 237.
36. Ibid., 235.

37. Ibid., 243.
38. Ibid., 244.
39. Ibid., 246.
40. Jacqueline Bernard, *Journey Towards Freedom*, (New York: Norton, 1967), 253.

Profile 20: Nathaniel Hawthorne
   1. Diane Culbertson, ed., *Rose Hawthorne Lathrop: Selected Writings*, (New York: Paulist Press, 1993), 25.
   2. Edward Wagenknecht, *Nathaniel Hawthorne: Man and Writer*, (New York: Oxford University Press, 1961), 176.
   3. Mary V. Hillman, "Hawthorne and Transcendentalism," *Catholic World*, XCIII, May, 1911, as quoted in Kenneth Walter Cameron, *Hawthorne Among His Contemporaries: A Harvest of Estimates, Insights, and Anecdotes from the Victorian Literary World*, (Hartford, CT: Transcendental Press, 1968), 541.
   4. Ibid.
   5. Wagenknecht, *Nathaniel Hawthorne*, 182.
   6. Ibid., 183.
   7. Ibid., 184.
   8. Arlin Turner, *Nathaniel Hawthorne: A Biography*, (New York: Oxford University Press 1980), 331.
   9. Wagenknecht, *Nathaniel Hawthorne*, 186.
  10. Culbertson, *Rose Hawthorne Lathrop*, 24.
  11. Wagenknecht, *Nathaniel Hawthorne*, 177.
  12. Ibid.
  13. Ibid., 187.
  14. Ibid., 188.
  15. Ibid.
  16. Ibid., 189–190.
  17. Ibid., 190.
  18. Hillman "Hawthorne and Transcendentalism," 541.
  19. Wagenknecht, *Nathaniel Hawthorne*, 173.
  20. Julian Hawthorne, *Nathaniel Hawthorne and His Wife: A Biography*, vol. II, (Boston: Houghton-Mifflin, 1884), 179.
  21. Ibid., 178–179.
  22. Hillman "Hawthorne and Transcendentalism," 542.
  23. Ibid.

Profile 21: Robert Edward Lee
   1. Jeffery Warren Scott and Mary Ann Jeffreys, "Fighters of Faith," *Christian History*, 33 (vol. XI, no. 13), p. 35.
   2. Ibid., 34.
   3. James Mellon, ed., *Bullwhip Days: The Slaves Remember, An Oral History*, (New York: Weidenfeld and Nicolson, 1988), 52.
   4. Douglas Southall Freeman, *R. E. Lee: A Biography*, vol. 3, (New York: Scribners, 1934), 249.
   5. Ibid., 331.
   6. Ibid., 198.
   7. Ibid., vol. IV, 297.
   8. Charles Bracelen Flood, *Lee: The Last Years*, (Boston: Houghton-Mifflin, 1981), 213.
   9. T. A. Ashby, M.D., "General R. E. Lee as College President," *The Confederate Veteran*, vol. 13, 1905, 360.
  10. Freeman, *R. E. Lee*, vol. III, 505.
  11. Ibid.
  12. Ibid., vol. IV, 298.
  13. Ibid.
  14. Ibid., vol. I, 424.
  15. Ibid., 475–476.
  16. Ibid., vol. III, 531.
  17. Ibid., 526.
  18. Ibid., 141.
  19. Scott and Jeffreys, "Fighters of Faith," 34–35.
  20. Nigel Hamilton, *Monty: The Final Years*, (New York: McGraw-Hill, 1987), 941.
  21. Robert E. Lee, Jr., *Recollections and Letters of General Robert E. Lee*, (Garden City, NY: Doubleday, 1924), 416.

22. Freeman, *R. E. Lee*, vol. IV, 401.
23. Ibid., vol. I., pp. 372–373
24. Ibid., vol. IV, 400.
25. Mellon, *Bullwhip Days*, 50.
26. Ibid., 50–51.
27. Freeman, *R. E. Lee*, vol. IV, 400.
28. Emory Thomas, *Robert E. Lee: A Biography*, (New York: Norton, 1995), 382.
29. Flood, *Lee: The Last Years*, 214.
30. Lee, *Recollections and Letters*, 299–300.
31. T. A. Ashby, M.D., "General Robert E. Lee as College President," 360.
32. Freeman, *R. E. Lee*, vol. IV, 426.
33. Ibid., 283.
34. Ibid., vol. I, 376.
35. Ibid., vol. III, 217.
36. Flood, *Lee: The Last Years*, 260.
37. Freeman, *R. E. Lee*, vol. IV, 504.
38. Flood, *Lee: The Last Years*, 214.

Profile 22: Henry Wadsworth Longfellow

1. Edward Wagenknecht, *Longfellow: A Full–Length Portrait*, (New York: Longmans, Green, & Co., 1955), 289.
2. Samuel Longfellow, *Life of Henry Wadsworth Longfellow*, (Boston: Houghton-Mifflin, 1896), vol I, 13.
3. Ibid., 54–55.
4. Wagenknecht, *Longfellow*, 290.
5. S. Longfellow, *Life of Henry Wadsworth Longfellow*, vol. I, 14.
6. Ibid., 25.
7. Ibid., vol. II, 64.
8. Wagenknecht, *Longfellow*, 289.
9. Ibid., 291.
10. Ernest Wadsworth Longfellow, *Random Memories*, (Boston: Houghton-Mifflin, 1922), 18.
11. Ibid.
12. Andrew Hilen, ed., *The Letters of Henry Wadsworth Longfellow*, vol. I, (Cambridge, MA: The Belknap Press of Harvard, 1967), 279.
13. Wagenknecht, *Longfellow*, 294.
14. Ibid., 295.
15. E. W. Longfellow, *Random Memories*, 107–108.
16. Hilen, *The Letters of Henry Wadsworth Longfellow*, vol. I, 52.
17. Ibid., 526.
18. Ibid., vol. IV, 241.
19. Ibid., vol. V, 25.
20. E. W. Longfellow, *Random Memories*, 450.
21. Wagenknecht, *Longfellow*, 304.
22. Ibid., 292.

Profile 23: Jefferson Davis

1. Hudson Strode, *Jefferson Davis, Tragic Hero; The Last Hero; The Last Twenty-Five Years, 1864–1889*, (New York: Harcourt, 1964), 75.
2. Clement Eaton, *Jefferson Davis*, (New York: Free Press, 1977), 14.
3. Hudson Strode, ed., *Jefferson Davis: Private Letters, 1823–1889*, (New York: Harcourt, 1966), 42.
4. Hudson Strode, *Jefferson Davis, American Patriot, 1808–1861*, (New York: Harcourt, 1955), 399.
5. Ibid., 393.
6. Ibid., 407.
7. Ishbel Ross, *First Lady of the South: The Life of Mrs. Jefferson Davis*, (New York: Harper, 1959), 147.
8. Hudson Strode, *Jefferson Davis, Confederate President*, (New York: Harcourt, 1959), 147 (from a partially indirect quotation).
9. Ibid.
10. Ibid.
11. Strode, *Tragic Hero*, 77.
12. Ibid., 256.

13. Ibid., 257.
14. Strode, ed., *Jefferson Davis:Private Letters*, 490.
15. Ibid., 493.
16. Ibid., 508.
17. Ibid., 554.

Profile 24: Andrew Johnson
1. Carl Sandburg, *Abraham Lincoln, The War Years*, vol. II, (New York: Scribners, 1959), 552.
2. Hans L. Trefousse, *Andrew Johnson: A Biography*, (New York: Norton, 1989), 41, 49.
3. Edmund Fuller and David E. Green, *God in the White House: The Faiths of American Presidents*, (New York: Crown, 1968), 119.
4. Ibid.
5. *Nashville Union and American*, August 4, 1875.
6. Fuller and Green, *God in the White House*, 123.
7. *Nashville Union and American*, August 4, 1875.
8. Sydney E. Ahlstrom, *A Religious History of the American People*, (New Haven, CT: Yale University Press, 1972), 484.
9. Ibid.
10. Ibid., 485.
11. *Nashville Union and American*, August 4, 1875.

Profile 25: Edgar Allan Poe
1. Edward Wagenknecht, *Edgar Allan Poe: The Man Behind the Legend*, (New York: Oxford University Press, 1963), 206.
2. Kenneth Silverman, *Edgar A. Poe: Mournful and Never-Ending Remembrance*, (New York: HarperCollins, 1991), 333.
3. Ibid., 340.
4. Wagenknecht, *Edgar Allan Poe: The Man Behind the Legend*, 205–206.
5. Ibid., 206.
6. Silverman, *Edgar A. Poe: Mournful and Never-Ending Remembrance*, 333.
7. Ibid.
8. Ibid., 339.
9. Ibid., 340.
10. Hervey Allen, *Israfel: The Life and Times of Edgar Allan Poe*, (New York: George H. Doran, 1927), 846.

Profile 26: Abraham Lincoln
1. John G. Nicolay and John Hay, "Abraham Lincoln: A History," *Century*, vol. 38, August 1889, 567.
2. Eleanor Atkinson, *Lincoln's Boyhood: Reminiscences by His Cousin and Playmate, Dennis Hanks*, (n.y., n.d.), 362.
3. Ibid., 366.
4. Ibid., 362.
5. Ibid.
6. Lloyd Ostendorf and Walter Olesky, ed., *Lincoln's Unknown Private Life: An Oral History by His Black Housekeeper, Mariah Vance, 1850–1860*, (Mamaroneck, NY: Hastings House, 1995), 158.
7. Leo T. Crismon, "The Lincoln Family and the Baptists," *Review and Expositor*, vol. LVII, January 1960, 71–72.
8. Doran Hurley, "Lincoln's Catholic Kinship," *Columbia*, February 1957, 41.
9. Shirley Ness, Corresponding Secretary, Coles County Genealogical Society, letter, July 31, 1995.
10. Carl Sandburg, *Abraham Lincoln: The Prairie Years*, vol. I, (New York: Scribners, 1926), 418.
11. G. Frederick Owen, *Abraham Lincoln: The Man and His Faith*, (Wheaton, IL: Tyndale, 1981), 58.
12. Ostendorf and Olesky, *Lincoln's Unknown Private Life*, 205.
13. Owen, *Abraham Lincoln: The Man and His Faith*, 59.
14. Ibid., 70.
15. Sandburg, *Abraham Lincoln: The Prairie Years*, 418.
16. Ostendorf and Olesky, *Lincoln's Unknown Private Life*, 159.
17. Ibid., 265.
18. Sandburg, *Abraham Lincoln: The Prairie Years*, 415–416.

19. Ibid., vol. II, .372–373.
20. Philip Van Doren Stern, ed., *The Life and Writings of Abraham Lincoln*, (New York: Modern Library, 1940), 635–636.
21. Ostendorf and Olesky, *Lincoln's Unknown Private Life*, 268–269.
22. Carl Sandburg, *Abraham Lincoln: The War Years*, vol. III, (New York: Scribners, 1939), 377.
23. Stern, *The Life and Writings of Abraham Lincoln*, 498.
24. Ibid.
25. Fred Kerner, ed., *A Treasury of Lincoln Quotations*, (Garden City, NY: Doubleday, 1965), 245.
26. Sandburg, *Abraham Lincoln: The War Years*, vol. II, 12.
27. Ibid., vol. I, 570.
28. Ibid., vol. III, 346.
29. Ibid., vol. I, 590.
30. Ibid.
31. Owen, *Abraham Lincoln: The Man and His Faith*, 140–141.
32. Sandburg, *Abraham Lincoln: The War Years*, vol. III, 379–380.
33. Ostendorf and Olesky, *Lincoln's Unknown Private Life*, 160.
34. Peggy Robbins, "The Lincolns and Spiritualism," *Civil War Times Illustrated*, August 1976, 46.
35. Ibid., 5.
36. Stern, *The Life and Writings of Abraham Lincoln*, 752–754.
37. Sandburg, *Abraham Lincoln: The War Years*, vol. II, 359.
38. Olga Jones, *Churches of the Presidents in Washington*, (New York: Exposition Press, 1954), 58.
39. Owen, *Abraham Lincoln: The Man and His Faith*, 163.
40. Stern, *The Life and Writings of Abraham Lincoln*, 841–842.
41. Sandburg, *Abraham Lincoln: The War Years*, vol. II, 558.
42. John McCollister, *So Help Me, God: The Faith of America's Presidents*, (Louisville, KY: Westminster, 1991), 91.
43. Ostendorf and Olesky, *Lincoln's Unknown Private Life*, 268.
44. Justin Turner and Linda Levitt Turner, *Mary Todd Lincoln: Her Life and Letters*, (New York: Alfred A. Knopf, 1972), 567–568.
45. Mark A. Noll, "The Puzzling Faith of Abraham Lincoln," *Christian History*, Issue 33 (Vol. IX, No. 1), 14.

Profile 27: Harriet Beecher Stowe

1. Marie Caskey, *Chariot of Fire: Religion and the Beecher Family*, (New Haven: Yale University Press, 1978), 174.
2. Ibid., 164.
3. Joan D. Hedrick, *Harriet Beecher Stowe: A Life*, (New York: Oxford University Press, 1994), 149.
4. Caskey, *Chariot of Fire*, 180.
5. Ibid., 179.
6. Ibid., 185.
7. Ibid., 180.
8. Edward Wagenknecht, *Harriet Beecher Stowe: The Known and the Unknown*, (New York: Oxford University Press, 1965), 217.
9. Ibid., 218.
10. Ibid., 205.
11. Ibid.
12. Ibid., 219–220.
13. Ibid., 204.
14. Ibid., 197–198.
15. Ibid., 208.
16. Caskey, *Chariot of Fire*, 201.
17. Ibid., 202.
18. Ibid., 204.
19. Milton Rugoff, *The Beechers: An American Family in the Nineteenth Century*, (New York: Harper & Row, 1991), 541–542.
20. Noel B. Gerson, *Harriet Beecher Stowe*, (New York: Praeger, 1976), 65.
21. Ibid., 7.
22. Ibid., 162.
23. Caskey, *Chariot of Fire*, 175.

24. Ibid., 195–196.
25. Ibid., 173.
26. Ibid., 196.
27. Wagenknecht, *Harriet Beecher Stowe*, 209.
28. Caskey, *Chariot of Fire*, 207.
29. Wagenknecht, *Harriet Beecher Stowe*, 210.
30. Caskey, *Chariot of Fire*, 207.
31. Gerson, *Harriet Beecher Stowe*, 209–210.

Profile 28: Henry David Thoreau

1. Walter Harding, *The Days of Henry Thoreau*, (New York: Knopf, 1966), 322.
2. Ibid., 3.
3. Edward Wagenknecht, *Henry David Thoreau: What Manner of Man?* (New York: Oxford University Press, 1981), 156.
4. Ibid.
5. Ibid., 158.
6. Ibid., 159.
7. Ibid.
8. Ibid., 161.
9. Ibid., 160.
10. Robert D. Richardson, Jr., *Henry David Thoreau: A Life of the Mind*, (Berkeley: University of California Press, 1986), 193.
11. William Ellery Channing, *Thoreau: The Poet-Naturalist*, (New York: Biblo and Tannen, 1966), 89.
12. Richardson, *Henry David Thoreau: A Life of the Mind*, 286.
13. Ibid.
14. Wagenknecht, *Henry David Thoreau: What Manner of Man?* 171.
15. Ibid., 168.
16. Ibid., 170.
17. Ibid., 163.
18. Ibid., 166.
19. Ibid.
20. Walter Harding, "This is a Beautiful World; But I Shall See A Fairer," *American Heritage*, December 1962, XIV, no. 1, 110.
21. Ibid.
22. Ibid., 109.
23. Ibid., 107.
24. Ibid.
25. Ibid., 110.
26. Ibid., 107.
27. Ibid., 111.
28. Ibid., 109.
29. Ibid.
30. Ibid., 111–112.
31. Ibid., 112.

Profile 29: Frederick Douglass

1. John W. Blassingame, ed., *The Frederick Douglass Papers*, Series One, vol. 2, (New Haven: Yale University Press, 1982), 175.
2. Ibid.
3. Ibid.
4. William S. McFeely, *Frederick Douglass*, (New York: Norton, 1991), 38.
5. Ibid.
6. Frederick Douglass, *Narrative of the Life of Frederick Douglass*, (New York: Signet, 1968), 87.
7. McFeely, *Frederick Douglass*, 82.
8. Blassingame, *The Frederick Douglass Papers*, vol. 2, 100.
9. Ibid., 284.
10. Philip S. Foner, *Frederick Douglass: A Biography*, (New York: The Citadel Press, 1964), 272.
11. Waldo E. Martin, *The Mind of Frederick Douglass*, (Chapel Hill, NC: University of North Carolina Press, 1984), 177.
12. Douglass, *Narrative of the Life of Frederick Douglass*, 120.
13. Foner, *Frederick Douglass: A Biography*, 269.

14. John W. Blassingame and John R. McKivigan, eds., *The Frederick Douglass Papers*, Series One, vol. 5 (New Haven: Yale University Press, 1992), 137.
15. Ibid., 524.
16. Ibid., 556.
17. Ibid., 130.
18. Ibid., 129.
19. Ibid., 131.
20. Ibid., 136.
21. Ibid., 137.
22. Letitia W. Brown and Elsie M. Lewis, *Washington in the New Era, 1870–1970*, (Washington: Smithsonian Institution, 1972), 14.
23. Blassingame and McKivigan, *The Frederick Douglass Papers*, vol. 5, 555.
24. Foner, *Frederick Douglass: A Biography*, 270.
25. Ibid., 271.
26. Ibid.
27. Blassingame and McKivigan, *The Frederick Douglass Papers*, 302
28. Ibid.
29. Carter G. Woodson, ed., *The Works of Francis J. Grimké*, (Washington: Associated Publishers, 1942), 69.

Profile 30: Mary Ann Todd Lincoln

1. John W. Blassingame and John R. McKivigan, eds., *The Frederick Douglass Papers*, Series One, vol. 5 (New Haven, CT: Yale University Press, 1992), 343.
2. Carl Sferazza Anthony, *First Ladies: the Saga of the Presidents' Wives and Their Power, 1789–1861*, (New York: Morrow, 1990), 187.
3. Ibid., 185.
4. Justin G. Turner and Linda Levitt Turner, *Mary Todd Lincoln: Her Life and Letters*, (New York: Alfred A. Knopf, 1972), 15.
5. Ibid., 460.
6. Ibid., 189.
7. Ibid., 131.
8. Ibid., 128.
9. Ibid., 242.
10. Ibid.
11. Ibid., 400.
12. Ibid., 525.
13. Lloyd Ostendorf and Walter Olensky, eds., *Lincoln's Unknown Private Life: An Oral History by His Black Housekeeper, Mariah Vance, 1850–1860*, (Mamaroneck, NY: Hastings House, 1995), 159.
14. Turner and Turner, *Mary Todd Lincoln: Her Life and Letters*, 124.
15. Ibid., 526.
16. Ibid., 597–598.
17. Ibid., 633.
18. Ibid., 688.
19. Ibid., 682.
20. Ibid., 627.
21. Ibid., 354.
22. Ibid., 545.
23. Ibid., 633.
24. Ibid., 704.

Profile 31: Susan Brownell Anthony

1. Mary D. Pellauer, *Toward a Tradition of Feminist Theology: The Religious, Social Thought of Elizabeth Cady Stanton, Susan B. Anthony, and Anna Howard Shaw*, (Brooklyn, NY: Carlson, 1991), 196.
2. Ibid., 199.
3. Ibid., 198.
4. Ibid., 199.
5. Ibid.
6. Ibid., 214.
7. Ibid., 205.
8. Ibid., 199.
9. Ibid., 205.
10. Ibid., 201.

11. Ibid.
12. Ibid., 201.
13. Ibid.
14. Ibid., 194.
15. Ibid.
16. Kathleen Barry, *Susan B. Anthony: A Biography of a Singular Feminist*, (New York: New York University Press, 1988), 95–96.
17. Ibid., 96.
18. Pellauer, *Toward a Tradition of Feminist Theology*, 197.
19. Barry, *Susan B. Anthony*, 355–356.
20. Pellauer, *Toward a Tradition of Feminist Theology*, 211.
21. Ibid., 194.

Profile 32: Frances Jane (Fanny) Crosby
1. C. Bernard Ruffin, *Fanny Crosby*, (Philadelphia, Pilgrim Press, 1976), 224.
2. Ibid., 69–70.
3. Scrapbook, New York Public Library. (This large album, composed of letters, clippings, and manuscripts, both loose and fixed to unnumbered pages, was compiled by Dr. H. Adelbert White, a professor of English at the University of Nebraska, who served as Crosby's secretary and amanuensis for several years.)
4. Ibid.
5. S. Trevena Jackson, *Fanny Crosby's Story of Ninety-Four Years*, (New York: Revell, 1915), 118.
6. Scrapbook, New York Public Library.
7. Ibid.
8. Ibid.
9. Ibid.
10. Ibid.
11. Florence Booth Paine, interview, Waterbury, CT, August, 1971.
12. Scrapbook, New York Public Library.
13. Ibid.
14. Ibid.
15. Ibid.
16. Rev. Clarice Bray Griffins, interview, Long Hills, CT, 1971.
17. Basil Miller, *Fanny Crosby: Singing I Go*, (Grand Rapids, MI: Zondervan, 1950), 92.
18. Scrapbook, New York Public Library.
19. Ibid.
20. Ibid.
21. Florence Booth Paine, interview.

Profile 33: Ulysses Simpson Grant
1. Richard Goldhurst, *Many Are the Hearts: The Agony and Triumph of Ulysses S. Grant*, (New York: Readers Digest Press, 1975), 188.
2. Ibid., 189.
3. Ibid.
4. Ibid., 190.
5. Ibid., 191.
6. Ibid.
7. Stefan Lorant, "The Baptism of U.S. Grant," *Life*, March 26, 1951, 92.
8. Ibid., 94.
9. Ibid., 102.
10. Goldhurst, *Many Are the Hearts*, 192.

Profile 34: Thomas Jonathan (Stonewall) Jackson
1. James I. Robertson, Jr., "Stonewall Jackson: Molding the Man and Making a General," *Blue and Gray Magazine*, June 1992, 8.
2. Ibid.
3. R. L. Dabney, *The Life and Campaigns of Lieut.-Gen. Thomas J. Jackson*, (New York: Blelock & Co., 1866), 641.
4. Ibid., 37.
5. Ibid., 56.
6. Ibid., 57.
7. Ibid., 90.
8. Robertson, "Stonewall Jackson: Molding the Man," 13.

9. Dabney, *Life and Campaigns*, 647–648.
10. Byron Farwell, *Stonewall: A Biography of General Thomas J. Jackson*, (New York: Norton, 1992), 14.
11. Ibid., 134.
12. Ibid., 118.
13. Ibid.
14. Dabney, *Life and Campaigns*, 121.
15. Ibid., 106.
16. Ibid., 104.
17. Ibid., 103.
18. Ibid., 714–715.
19. Ibid., 89.
20. Ibid., 654.
21. Ibid., 111.
22. Ibid.
23. Ibid., 120–121.
24. Ibid., 112.
25. Ibid., 124.
26. Robertson, "Stonewall Jackson: Molding the Man," 17.
27. Dabney, *The Life and Campaigns*, 635.
28. Ibid., 641.
29. Ibid., 644.
30. Robertson, "Stonewall Jackson: Molding the Man," 17.
31. Ibid., 8.
32. Ibid., 17.
33. Dabney, *The Life and Campaigns*, 643.
34. Ibid., 229.
35. Robertson, "Stonewall Jackson: Molding the Man," 54.
36. Ibid.
37. Farwell, *Stonewall: A Biography*, 200.
38. Dabney, *The Life and Campaigns*, 107.
39. Ibid., 708.
40. Ibid., 722–723.
41. Ibid., 723.

Profile 35: Andrew Carnegie

1. Joseph Frazier Wall, ed., *The Andrew Carnegie Reader*, (Pittsburgh: The University of Pittsburgh Press, 1992), 171.
2. Ibid.
3. Burton J. Hendrick, *The Life of Andrew Carnegie*, vol. II, (New York: Doubleday, 1932), 294.
4. Joseph Frazier Wall, *Andrew Carnegie*, (Pittsburgh: The University of Pittsburgh Press, 1970), 368.
5. Ibid., 368–369.
6. Ibid., 369.
7. Ibid.
8. Hendrick, *The Life of Andrew Carnegie*, 295.
9. Ibid.
10. Wall, *The Andrew Carnegie Reader*, 1009.
11. Ibid.

Profile 36: Samuel Langhorne Clemens (Mark Twain)

1. Caroline Thomas Harnsberger, *Mark Twain's Views on Religion*, (Evanston, IL: Schori Press, 1961), 2.
2. Ibid., 8.
3. Edward Wagenknecht, *Mark Twain: The Man and His Work*, (Norman, OK: University of Oklahoma Press, 1961), 175.
4. Harnsberger, *Twain's Views on Religion*, 11.
5. Ibid., 10.
6. Wagenknecht, *Twain: The Man and His Work*, 178.
7. Ibid.
8. Harnsberger, *Twain's Views on Religion*, 18.
9. Ibid., 15.
10. Wagneknecht, *Twain: The Man and His Work*, 195.

11. Ibid., 178.
12. Justin Kaplan, *Mr. Clemens and Mark Twain*, (New York: Simon and Schuster, 1966), 400.
13. Wagenknecht, *Twain: The Man and His Work*, 199.
14. Harnsberger, *Twain's Views on Religion*, 33–34.
15. Wagenknecht, *Twain: The Man and His Work*, 192.
16. Harnsberger, *Twain's Views on Religion*, 22.
17. Ibid., 42.
18. Ibid., 44–45.
19. Ibid., 41–42.
20. Ibid., 43.
21. Wagenknecht, *Twain: The Man and His Work*, 191.
22. Harnsberger, *Twain's Views on Religion*, 35.
23. Ibid., 30.
24. Wagenknecht, *Twain: The Man and His Work*, 196.
25. Ibid.
26. Ibid., 195.
27. Ibid., 196.
28. Ibid., 188.
29. Hamlin Hill, *Mark Twain: God's Fool*, (New York: Harper & Row, 1973), 266.
30. Harnsberger, *Twain's Views on Religion*, 39.
31. Ibid.

Profile 37: Dwight Lyman Moody

1. Martin E. Marty, *Pilgrims in Their Own Land: 500 Years of Religion in America*, (Boston: Little, Brown, & Co, 1984), 314.
2. Ibid.
3. Carter G. Woodson, ed.; *The Works of Francis J. Grimké*, vol. III, (Washington, D.C.: Associated Publishers, 1942), 420.
4. William R. Moody, *The Life of Dwight L. Moody*, (New York: Revell, 1900), 21.
5. Ibid., 23.
6. Ibid., 40.
7. Ibid., 26.
8. Ibid., 42.
9. Turnbull, *Best of Dwight Moody*, 11–12.
10. James F. Findlay, Jr., *Dwight L. Moody, American Evangelist, 1837–1899*, (Chicago: University of Chicago Press, 1969), 132.
11. William R.. Moody, *Life of Dwight Moody*, 82.
12. Ibid., 93.
13. Albert Gould Hopkins, in a conversation with C. Bernard Ruffin, around 1967.
14. Findlay, *Dwight Moody, American Evangelist*, 265–266, 271.
15. Ibid., 227–228.
16. William R. Moody, *Life of Dwight Moody*, 139.
17. Turnbull, *Best of Dwight Moody*, 9.
18. Findlay, *Dwight L. Moody*, 222.
19. Ibid.
20. Ibid., 233.
21. Ibid., 237–239.
22. Ibid., 240.
23. Ibid., 244.
24. Ibid., 248.
25. Catherine Owens Pearce, *Mary McLeod Bethune*, (New York: Vanguard Press, 1951), 66–67.
26. Ibid., 279.
27. Ibid.
28. Ibid., 276.
29. Ibid., 283.
30. Marty, *Pilgrims in Their Own Land*, 315.
31. Findlay, *Dwight Moody: American Evangelist*, 250.
32. Ibid, 257.
33. Ibid., 258.
34. Paul D. Moody, *My Father: An Intimate Portrait of Dwight Moody*, (Boston: Little, Brown & Co., 1938), 191.
35. Ibid.
36. Findlay, *Dwight Moody: American Evangelist*, 410.

37. Paul D. Moody, *My Father*, 44.
38. Findlay, *Dwight Moody: American Evangelist*, 65.
39. Findlay, *Dwight Moody: American Evangelist*, 248.
40. W. H. Daniels, ed., *Moody: His Works, His Work and Workers*, (New York: Nelson & Phillips, 1877), 28–29.
41. William R. Moody, *Life of Dwight Moody*, 150.
42. Ibid., 441.
43. Fanny Crosby Scrapbook, New York Public Library, New York.
44. William R. Moody, *Life of Dwight Moody*, 477.
45. Ibid., 431.
46. Ibid., 547.
47. Ibid., 552–554.
48. Ibid., 554.
49. Ibid., 554–555.

Profile 38: Stephen Grover Cleveland
1. William Seale, *The President's House: A History*, (Washington: White House Historical Association, 1986), 554.
2. William Judson Hampton, *The Religion of the Presidents*, (Somerville, NJ: Press of Unionist-Gazette Association, 1925), 71.
3. John McCollister, *So Help Me, God: The Faith of America's Presidents*, (Louisville: Westminster, 1991), 114.
4. George F. Parker, *Recollections of Grover Cleveland*, (New York: The Century Co., 1909), 382.
5. Ibid.
6. Ibid., 383.
7. Ibid., 383–384.
8. Ibid., 384.
9. Robert McElroy, *Grover Cleveland: The Man and the Statesman*, (New York: Harper Brothers, 1923), 328.
10. Ibid., 385.
11. Ibid.
12. Bridgeport, Connecticut, Public Library: Fanny Crosby Scrapbook.

Profile 39: John Pierpont Morgan, Sr.
1. Stanley Jackson, *J. P. Morgan: A Biography*, (New York: Stein & Day, 1983), 194.
2. Ibid., 115.
3. Ibid., 296.
4. Andrew Sinclair, *Corsair: The Life of J. Pierpont Morgan*, (Boston: Little, Brown & Co., 1981), 47.
5. Ibid.
6. Ron Chernow, *The House of Morgan: An American Banking Dynasty and the Rise of Modern Finance*, (New York: Atlantic Monthly Press, 1990), 51.
7. Jackson, *J. P. Morgan: A Biography*, 296.
8. Chernow, *The House of Morgan*, 51.
9. Jackson, *J. P. Morgan: A Biography*, 295.
10. Ibid., 133.
11. Sinclair, *Corsair*, 67.
12. Chernow, *The House of Morgan*, 52.
13. Ibid.
14. Sinclair, *Corsair*, 69.
15. Chernow, *The House of Morgan*, 52.
16. Jackson, *J. P. Morgan: A Biography*, 133.
17. Ibid., 295.
18. Sinclair, *Corsair*, 217.

Profile 40: John Davison Rockefeller, Sr.
1. William Manchester, "The Founding Grandfather," *American History*, vol. II, (Guilford, CT: The Dushkin Publishing Group, 1987), 68.
2. Ibid.
3. Ibid.
4. Peter Collier and David Horowitz, *The Rockefellers: An American Dynasty*, (New York: Holt, Rinehart, and Winston, 1976), 11.
5. Ibid., 19.
6. Ibid., 35.

7. Ibid., 69.
8. Manchester, "The Founding Grandfather," 72.
9. Allan Nevins, *John D. Rockefeller: The Heroic Age of American Experience*, (New York: Scribners, 1940), vol. I, 121.
10. Ibid., vol. II, 455.
11. Ibid.
12. Manchester, "The Founding Grandfather," 72.
13. Nevins, *John D. Rockefeller*, vol. II, 175.
14. Ibid., 457.
15. Ibid., vol. I, 120.
16. Ibid., 121.
17. Manchester, "The Founding Grandfather," 72.
18. Ibid., 70.
19. Collier and Horowitz, *The Rockefellers*, 48.
20. Ibid., 45.
21. Manchester, "The Founding Grandfather," 72.
22. Collier and Horowitz, *The Rockefellers*, 48.
23. Ibid., 11.
24. Nevins, *John D. Rockefeller*, vol. I, 120.
25. Manchester, "The Founding Grandfather," 70.
26. Collier and Horowitz, *The Rockefellers*, 61.
27. Ibid.
28. Ibid., 71.
29. Manchester, "The Founding Grandfather," 67.
30. Ibid., 72.

Profile 41: William McKinley

1. Edward Leight Pell, et. al., *McKinley and Men of Our Times*, (Washington: Historical Society of America, 1901), 83.
2. Ibid.
3. Paul F. Boller, *Presidential Anecdotes*, (New York: Oxford University Press, 1989), 189.
4. Frederick Barton, "A Christian Gentleman: William McKinley," *The Chautauquan*, November 1901, 136.
5. Louis A. Banks, *The Religious Life of Famous Americans*, (New York: American Tract Society, 1904), 68–69.
6. Margaret Leech, *In the Days of McKinley*, (New York: Harper, 1959), 462.
7. Barton, "A Christian Gentleman: William McKinley," 134.
8. Ibid., 136.
9. Ibid., 134.
10. Ibid.
11. Ibid., 136.
12. Ibid.
13. Ibid., 135.
14. Ibid., 134.
15. John McCollister, *So Help Me, God: The Faith of America's Presidents*, (Louisville, KY: Westminster, 1991), 122.
16. Leech, *In the Days of McKinley*, 12.
17. Charles S. Olcott, *The Life of William McKinley*, vol. II, (Boston: Houghton-Mifflin, 1916), 110–111.

Profile 42: Thomas Alva Edison

1. Robert Conot, *Thomas A. Edison: A Streak of Luck*, (New York: Da Capo, 1979), 6.
2. Ibid.
3. Ibid.
4. Ibid., 427.
5. Ibid.
6. Ibid.
7. Edward Marshall, "No Immortality of the Soul," *New York Times*, October 2, 1910.
8. Ibid.
9. Ibid.
10. Ibid.
11. Wyn Wachhorst, *Thomas Alva Edison: An American Myth*, (Cambridge, MA: The MIT Press, 1981), 126.
12. Marshall, "No Immortality of the Soul," *New York Times*.

13. Thomas A. Edison, "Has Man an Immortal Soul," *The Forum*, November 26, 1926, 641.
14. Ibid., 644–645.
15. Ibid., 645.
16. Ibid.
17. Ibid.
18. Wachhorst, *Thomas Alva Edison: An American Myth*, 139.
19. Edison, "Has Man an Immortal Soul," 646.
20. Ibid., 647.
21. Ibid.
22. Ibid., 648.
23. Ibid., 650.
24. *Scientific American*, October 30, 1920, 446.
25. Neil Baldwin, *Edison: Inventing the Century*, (New York: Hyperion, 1995), 407.

Profile 43: Booker Taliaferro Washington
1. *New York Times*, March 14, 1898.
2. Louis R. Harlan, *Booker T. Washington: The Making of a Black Leader, 1856–1901*, (New York: Oxford University Press, 1972).
3. Louis R. Harlan, ed., *The Booker T. Washington Papers*, vol. 3, (Urbana, IL: University of Illinois Press, 1974), 72–73.
4. Ibid., 72.
5. Ibid., 73.
6. Ibid.
7. Ibid. p.74
8. Basil Matthews, *Booker T. Washington: Educator*, (College Park, MD: University of Maryland Press, 1969), 126.
9. Ibid. 127.
10. Ibid., 190.
11. Ibid., 160.
12. Louis R. Harlan and Raymond W. Smock, ed., *The Booker T. Washington Papers*, vol. 2, (Urbana, IL: University of Illinois Press, 1981), 528.

Profile 44: Louis Dembitts Brandeis
1. Philippe Strum, *Louis D. Brandeis: Justice for the People*, (Cambridge, MA: Harvard University Press, 1984), 9–10.
2. Ibid., 44.
3. Ibid., 247.
4. Ibid., 257.
5. Leonard Baker, *Brandeis and Frankfurter: A Dual Biography*, (New York: Harper and Row, 1984), 71.
6. Lewis J. Paper, *Brandeis: An Intimate Biography*, (Englewood Cliffs, NJ: Prentice-Hall, 1983), 4.
7. Ibid., 200.
8. Ibid., 200–201.

Profile 45: Thomas Woodrow Wilson
1. Arthur S. Link, ed., *The Papers of Woodrow Wilson*, (Princeton, NJ: Princeton University Press, 1978), vol. 28, 104.
2. Ibid., vol. 61, 1989, 65.
3. Ibid., vol. 33, 1980, 8–9.
4. Ibid., vol. 23, 1977, 15.
5. Ibid., 495.
6. Ibid., vol. 35, 1980, 330.
7. Ibid., 334.
8. Ibid., vol. 24, 1977, 209.
9. Ibid., vol. 23, 1977, 13.
10. Ibid., vol. 27, 1981, 576.
11. Ibid., vol. 36, 1981, 630.
12. Ibid., vol. 30, 1979, 90.
13. Ibid., vol. 32, 1979, 430.
14. Ibid., vol. 23, 1977, 20.
15. Ibid., 20.
16. Ibid., 377.
17. Ibid., 20.

18. Ibid., vol. 31, 1979, 11.
19. Ibid., vol. 24, 1977, 443.
20. Ibid., vol. 42, 1983, 452.
21. Edmund Fuller and David E. Green, *God in the White House: The Faiths of American Presidents*, (New York: Crown, 1968), 178.
22. Link, *The Papers of Woodrow Wilson*, vol. 65, 1991, 109n.
23. Walter Lord, *The Good Years*, (New York: Harper, 1960), 292.
24. Charles W. Thompson, *Presidents I've Known*, (Indianapolis: Bobbs-Merrill, 1929), 253.
25. Wyn Craig Wade, *The Fiery Cross: The Ku Klux Klan in America*, (New York: Simon and Schuster, 1987), 125.
26. Link, *The Papers of Woodrow Wilson*, vol. 31, 1979, 301–302.
27. Ibid., 303.
28. John McCollister, *So Help Me, God: The Faith of America's Presidents*, (Louisville, KY: Westminster, 1991), 136.
29. Link, *The Papers of Woodrow Wilson*, vol. 35, 1980, 172.
30. Ibid., vol. 36, 1981, 630–631.
31. Ibid., vol. 30, 1979, 357.
32. Ibid., vol. 31, 1979, 3.
33. Ibid., vol. 42, 1983, 452.
34. Ibid., vol. 68, 1993, 370.
35. Ibid., 555.
36. Ibid., 556.
37. Ibid., vol. 33, 1980, 125.

Profile 46: William Howard Taft
1. Charles W. Thompson, *Presidents I've Known and Two Near Presidents*, (Indianapolis: Bobbs-Merrill, 1929), 228.
2. Henry F. Pringle, *The Life and Times of William Howard Taft*, vol. I, (New York: Farrar and Rinehart, 1939), 25.
3. Ibid.
4. Ibid., 45.
5. Ibid., 374.
6. Judith Icke Anderson, *William Howard Taft: An Intimate History*, (New York: Norton, 1981), 261.
7. Olga Jones, *Churches of the Presidents in Washington*, (New York: Exposition, 1954), 70.

Profile 47: Theodore Roosevelt
1. Albert Bushnell Hart and Herbert Ronald Ferleger, *Theodore Roosevelt Cyclopedia*, (Westport, CT: Theodore Roosevelt Association and Meckler Corporation, 1989), 517.
2. Christian F. Reisner, *Roosevelt's Religion*, (New York: Abingdon Press, 1922), 229.
3. Hart and Ferleger, *Theodore Roosevelt Cyclopedia*, 517.
4. Ibid.
5. Ibid., 76.
6. Reisner, *Roosevelt's Religion*, 233.
7. Hart and Ferleger, *Theodore Roosevelt Cyclopedia*, 77.
8. Ibid.
9. Reisner, *Roosevelt's Religion*, 271, 273.
10. Ibid., 231.
11. "Mr. Roosevelt's Religion," *Literary Digest*, October 18, 1919, 30.
12. Oscar S. Straus, "The Religion of Roosevelt," *The Forum*, February, 1923, 1195.
13. Ibid.
14. Hart and Ferleger, *Theodore Roosevelt Cyclopedia*, 519.
15. Ibid., 518.
16. Reisner, *Roosevelt's Religion*, 249.
17. Hart and Ferleger, *Theodore Roosevelt Cyclopedia*, 42.
18. Reisner, *Roosevelt's Religion*, 255.
19. Ibid., 241.
20. Ibid., 235.
21. Ibid., 261.
22. Peter Collier with David Horowitz, *The Roosevelts: An American Saga*, (New York: Simon and Schuster, 1994), 73.
23. G.J.A. O'Toole, *The Spanish War*, (New York: Norton, 1984), 162.
24. Hart and Ferleger, *Theodore Roosevelt Cyclopedia*, 131.
25. Ibid.

26. Ibid.
27. Ibid., 517.

Profile 48: William Jennings Bryan

1. Louis W. Koenig, *Bryan: A Political Biography of William Jennings Bryan*, (New York: Putnam, 1971), 21.
2. Robert W. Cherny, *A Righteous Cause: The Life of William Jennings Bryan*, (Norman, OK: University of Oklahoma Press, 1994), 9.
3. Lawrence W. Levine, *Defender of the Faith: William Jennings Bryan, The Last Decade, 1915–1925*, (New York: Oxford University Press, 1965), 258.
4. Cherny, *A Righteous Cause*, 10.
5. Koenig, *Bryan: A Political Biography*, 607.
6. Ibid.
7. Cherny, *A Righteous Cause*, 72.
8. Paolo E. Coletta, *William Jennings Bryan: Political Puritan, 1915–1925*, (Lincoln, NE: University of Nebraska Press, 1969), 29.
9. Ibid.
10. Levine, *Defender of the Faith*, 251.
11. Cherny, *A Righteous Cause*, 113.
12. Ibid., 136.
13. Levine, *Defender of the Faith*, 84–85.
14. Ibid., 92.
15. Coletta, *Political Puritan*, 206.
16. Ibid.
17. Levine, *Defender of the Faith*, 248.
18. Coletta, *Political Puritan*, 206.
19. Ibid., 205.
20. Ibid., 229.
21. Ibid.
22. Ibid., 281.
23. Ibid., 265.
24. Ibid., 272
25. Levine, *Defender of the Faith*, 262.
26. Coletta, *Political Puritan*, 272.
27. Ibid., 208.
28. Levine, *Defender of the Faith*, 262.
29. Ibid., 251.
30. Ibid.
31. Cherny, *A Righteous Cause*, 175.
32. Coletta, *Political Puritan*, 251.
33. Ibid., 261.
34. Ibid.
35. Koenig, *Bryan: A Political Biography*, 651.
36. Cherny, *A Righteous Cause*, 188.
37. Charles Morrow Wilson, *The Commoner: William Jennings Bryan*, (Garden City, NY: Doubleday, 1970), 437.

Profile 49: Jane Addams

1. Jane Addams, *Twenty Years at Hull-House*, (New York: Macmillan, 1910), 14–15.
2. Ibid., 3.
3. Ibid., 49–50.
4. Ibid., 51.
5. Allen F. Davis, *American Heroine: The Life and Legend of Jane Addams*, (New York: Oxford University Press, 1973), 17.
6. John C. Farrel, *Beloved Lady: A History of Jane Addams' Ideas on Reform and Peace*, (Baltimore: Johns Hopkins Press, 1967), 35.
7. Ibid.
8. Ibid., 41.
9. Addams, *Twenty Years at Hull-House*, 78–79.
10. Farrel, *Beloved Lady*, 35.
11. Ibid., 200.
12. Daniel Levine, *Jane Addams and the Liberal Tradition*, (Madison: State Historical Society of Wisconsin, 1971), 20.
13. Davis, *American Heroine*, 15.
14. Farrel, *Beloved Lady*, 41.

15. Levine, *Jane Addams and the Liberal Tradition*, 74.
16. Addams, *Twenty Years at Hull-House*, 122–123.
17. Ibid., 124.
18. Ibid., 187.

Profile 50: Henry Ford

1. Robert Lacey, *Ford: The Men and the Machine*, (Boston: Little, Brown & Co., 1986), 7.
2. Ibid., 57.
3. Ibid., 234.
4. Ibid.
5. Peter Collier and David Horowitz, *The Fords: An American Epic*, (New York: Summit Books, 1987), 132.
6. Harry Bennett, *Ford: We Never Called Him Henry*, (New York: Tom Doherty Associates, 1987), 83.
7. Lacey, *Ford: The Men and the Machine*, 57.
8. James Brough, *The Ford Dynasty: An American Story*, (Garden City, NY: Doubleday, 1977), 180.
9. Brough, *The Ford Dynasty*, 180.
10. Lacey, *Ford: The Men and the Machine*, 235.
11. Ibid.
12. Collier and Horowitz, *The Fords: An American Epic*, 37–38.
13. Bennett, *Ford: We Never Called Him Henry*, 232–234.
14. Ibid., 96.
15. Ibid., 82.
16. Ibid., 83.
17. Ibid., 220.
18. Ibid., 219.
19. Ibid., 284.
20. Ibid., 283.

Profile 51: George Washington Carver

1. Linda O. McMurry, *George Washington Carver: Scientist and Symbol*, (New York: Oxford University press, 1981), 17.
2. George Kremer, ed., *George Washington Carver in His Own Words*, (Columbia, MO: University of Missouri Press, 1987), 128.
3. Ibid., 130.
4. Ibid., 127.
5. Ibid., 131.
6. Ibid., 136.
7. Ibid., 137.
8. *New York Times*, November 19, 1924.
9. Kremer, *Carver in His Own Words*, 130.
10. Rackham Holt, *George Washington Carver: An American Biography*, (Garden City, NY: Doubleday, 1943), 220.
11. Ibid., 227.
12. McMurry, *Carver: Scientist and Symbol*, 269.
13. Kremer, *Carver in His Own Words*, 128.
14. Basil W. Miller, *George Washington Carver: God's Ebony Scientist*, (Grand Rapids, MI: Zondervan, 1943), 122.
15. Ibid., 188.
16. Kremer, *Carver in His Own Words*, 143.
17. Ibid., 135.
18. Lawrence Elliott, *George Washington Carver: The Man Who Overcame*, (Englewood Cliffs, NJ: Prentice-Hall, 1966), 196.
19. Ibid., 192.
20. Kremer, *Carver in His Own Words*, 133.
21. Holt, *Carver: An American Biography*, 198.
22. Miller, *Carver: God's Scientist*, 151.
23. McMurry, *Carver: Scientist and Symbol*, 269–270.
24. Holt, *Carver: An American Biography*, 181.
25. Kremer, *Carver in His Own Words*, 141.
26. Miller, *Carver: God's Scientist*, 144.
27. Kremer, *Carver in His Own Words*, 139.
28. Ibid., 178.

29. Barry Mackintosh, "George Washington Carver and the Peanut: New Light on a Much-Loved Myth," *American Heritage*, August 1977, 71.
30. Ibid., 70.
31. Elliott, *Carver: The Man Who Overcame*, 207.
32. Ibid.
33. Holt, *Carver: An American Biography*, 282.
34. Kremer, *Carver in His Own Words*, 173.
35. Ibid., 192.
36. Miller, *Carver: God's Scientist*, 165.
37. Ibid.

Profile 52: Warren Gamaliel Harding
1. William Judson Hampton, *The Religion of the Presidents*, (Somerville, NJ: Press of the Unionist-Gazette Association, 1925), 91.
2. Francis Russell, *The Shadow of Blooming Grove: Warren G. Harding and His Times*, (New York: McGraw-Hill, 1968), 46.
3. Ibid., 168–169.
4. Ibid., 202.
5. Bliss Isely, *The Presidents: Men of Faith*, (Boston: Little, Brown, & Co., 1953), 224.
6. Ibid.
7. Hampton, *Religion of the Presidents*, 93.
8. *Washington Post*, March 7, 1921.
9. Hampton, *Religion of the Presidents*, 94.
10. Ibid., 95.
11. Ibid., 96.
12. Ibid., 97.

Profile 53: William Edward Burghardt Du Bois
1. David Levering Lewis, *W.E.B. Du Bois, A Biography of a Race*, (New York: Holt, 1993), 49.
2. Ibid., 66.
3. Ibid., 65.
4. Ibid., 66.
5. Herbert Aptheker, *The Correspondence of W. E. B. Du Bois*, vol. III, (Amherst, MA: University of Massachusetts Press, 1978), 395–396.
6. Lewis, *Du Bois, A Biography of a Race*, 198.
7. Ibid., 66.
8. Ibid., 216.
9. Ibid., 312–313.
10. Ibid., 335–336.
11. Aptheker, *Correspondence of W. E. B. Du Bois*, vol. III, 27.
12. Ibid., 223.
13. Ibid., 414.
14. Shirley Graham Du Bois, *Dubois: A Pictorial Biography*, (Chicago: Johnson Publishing Company, 1978), 148.
15. Shirley Graham Du Bois, *His Day Is Marching On: A Memoir of W. E. B. Du Bois*. (Philadelphia: Lippincott, 1971), 364.
16. Ibid., 366.

Profile 54: John Calvin Coolidge
1. William Allen White, *A Puritan in Babylon: The Story of Calvin Coolidge*, (New York: Macmillan, 1938), 14.
2. Ibid.
3. Claude M. Fuess, *Calvin Coolidge: The Man from Vermont*, (Boston: Little, Brown, & Co., 1940), 316–317.
4. Ibid., 316.
5. Ibid.
6. Albert Menendez, *Religion and the U.S. Presidency, A Bibliography*, (New York: Garland, 1986), 20.
7. Fuess, *The Man from Vermont*, 27.
8. *Literary Digest*, May 7, 1927, 32.
9. Ibid., November 7, 1925, 29.
10. Donald R. McCoy, *Calvin Coolidge, The Quiet President: A New Assessment*, (Lawrence, KS: University of Kansas Press, 1988), 396.

11. Fuess, *The Man from Vermont*, 351–352.
12. Ibid., 351.
13. McCoy, *The Quiet President*, 414.
14. Fuess, *The Man from Vermont*, 316.

Profile 55: Herbert Clark Hoover

1. George H. Nash, *The Life of Herbert Hoover: The Engineer, 1874–1914*, (New York: Norton, 1983), 500.
2. Ibid., 8.
3. Ibid.
4. Herbert Hoover, *The Memoirs of Herbert Hoover: Years of Adventure, 1874–1920* (New York: Macmillan, 1951), 8.
5. Ibid., 7.
6. Nash, *The Life of Herbert Hoover: The Engineer*, 15.
7. Ibid.
8. Hoover, *Memoirs: Years of Adventure*, 20–21.
9. Nash, *The Life of Herbert Hoover: The Engineer*, 573.
10. George H. Nash, *The Life of Herbert Hoover: The Humanitarian, 1914–1917*, (New York: Norton, 1988), 255.
11. Richard Norton Smith, *An Uncommon Man: The Triumph of Herbert Hoover*, (New York: Simon and Schuster, 1984), 96.
12. Ibid., 121.
13. Edmund Fuller and David E. Green, *God in the White House*, (New York: Crown, 1969), 199.
14. Herbert Hoover, *The Memoirs of Herbert Hoover: The Cabinet and The Presidency, 1920–1933*, (New York: Macmillan, 1952), 207.
15. Ibid., 208.
16. John R. M. Wilson, "The Quaker and the Sword: Herbert Hoover's Relations with the Military," *Military Affairs*, vol. 38, April 1974, 41.
17. Hoover, *Memoirs: Years of Adventure*, 12.
18. Wilson, "The Quaker and the Sword," 41
19. Ibid., 42.
20. Ibid., 46.
21. Smith, *An Uncommon Man*, 350.
22. Ibid., 23
23. Ibid., 355
24. Edward P. Morgan, ed., *This I Believe*, (New York: Simon and Schuster, 1952), 75–76.

Profile 56: Albert Einstein

1. Abraham Pais, *Einstein Lived Here*, (Oxford: Clarendon Press, 1994), 114–115.
2. Ibid., 115.
3. Ibid.
4. Jamie Sayen, *Einstein in America: The Scientist's Conscience in the Age of Hitler and Hiroshima*, (New York: Crown, 1985), 158.
5. Ibid.
6. Pais, *Einstein Lived Here*, 118.
7. Ibid., 117.
8. Ibid., 121.
9. Ibid., 119–120.
10. Ibid., 120.
11. Ibid.
12. Ibid., 117.
13. Ibid., 120.
14. Ibid., 119.
15. Ibid., 118.
16. Ibid., 120.
17. Ibid., 117.
18. Ibid., 118.
19. Sayen, *Einstein in America*, 156.
20. Ibid.
21. Ibid.
22. Ibid., 159.
23. Ibid., 159–160.
24. Pais, *Einstein Lived Here*, 119.

25. Sayen, *Einstein in America*, 160–161.
26. Pais, *Einstein Lived Here*, 118.
27. Ibid., 155.
28. Ibid., 118.
29. Sayen, *Einstein in America*, 163.

Profile 57: Douglas MacArthur
1. William Manchester, *American Caesar: Douglas MacArthur 1880–1964*, (Boston: Little, Brown, & Co., 1978), 517.
2. Joseph Choate, *Douglas MacArthur As I Knew Him*, (Los Angeles: Joseph Choate, 1986), 94.
3. D. Clayton James, *The Years of MacArthur: Triumph and Disaster*, (Boston: Houghton-Mifflin, 1985), 290.
4. Ibid.
5. Ibid.
6. James, *The Years of MacArthur*, 288.
7. Douglas MacArthur, *Reminiscences*, (New York: McGraw-Hill, 1964), 310.
8. James, *The Years of MacArthur*, 289.
9. Ibid., 288.
10. MacArthur, *Reminiscences*, 310–311.
11. James, *The Years of MacArthur*, 292.
12. Ibid.
13. Ibid.
14. Michael Schaller, *Douglas MacArthur: The Far Eastern General*, (New York: Oxford University Press, 1989), 126.
15. MacArthur, *Reminiscences*, 310.
16. James, *The Years of MacArthur*, 291.
17. Manchester, *American Caesar*, 3.

Profile 58: Franklin Delano Roosevelt
1. Frances Perkins, *The Roosevelt I Knew*, (New York: Viking, 1946), 141.
2. Ibid.
3. Edmund Fuller and David E. Green, *God in the White House: The Faiths of American Presidents*, (New York: Crown, 1968), 203.
4. Ibid., 205.
5. Perkins, *The Roosevelt I Knew*, 144.
6. Ibid., 142.
7. Ibid., 145.
8. Ibid., 143.
9. Ibid., 148.
10. Fuller and Green, *God in the White House*, 206.
11. Ibid.
12. Ibid.

Profile 59: Felix Frankfurter
1. Felix Frankfurter, *Felix Frankfurter Reminisces, Recorded in Talks with Dr. Harlan D. Phillips*, (New York: Reynal & Co, 1960), 289.
2. Leonard Baker, *Brandeis and Frankfurter: A Dual Biography*, (New York: Harper and Row, 1984), 76.
3. Frankfurter, *Frankfurter Reminisces*, 290.
4. Ibid.
5. Ibid., 291.
6. Ibid.
7. Baker, *Brandeis and Frankfurter*, 492.

Profile 60: Harry S. Truman
1. Alonzo L. Hamby, *Man of the People: A Life of Harry S. Truman*, (New York: Oxford University Press, 1995), 475.
2. Charles Robbins, *Last of His Kind*, (New York: William Morrow, 1979), 48.
3. Margaret Truman, *Bess W. Truman*, (New York: Macmillan, 1986), 36–37.
4. Robbins, *Last of His Kind*, 49.
5. Hamby, *Man of the People*, 386.
6. Truman, *Bess W. Truman*, 163.
7. Ibid., 36–37.

8. Robbins, *Last of His Kind*, 49.
9. David McCullough, *Truman*, (New York: Simon and Schuster, 1992), 117.
10. Ibid., 185.
11. Ibid., 181.
12. Ibid., 113.
13. Ibid., 186.
14. Ibid., 353.
15. Ibid., 360.
16. Ibid., 597.
17. John McCollister, *So Help Me God: The Faith of America's Presidents*, (Louisville: Westminster, 1991), 159.
18. Marshall Frady, *Billy Graham: A Parable of American Righteousness*, (Boston: Little, Brown, & Co., 1979), 252–253.
19. Ibid., 253.
20. Merle Miller, *Plain Speaking: An Oral Biography of Harry S. Truman*, (New York: Berkley Publishing, 1973), 363.
21. McCullough, *Truman*, 728.
22. William J. Murray, *Let Us Pray: A Plea for Prayer in Our Schools*, (New York: William Morrow, 1995), 29.
23. Edmund Fuller and David E. Green, *God in the White House*, (New York: Crown, 1968), 209.
24. McCullough, *Truman*, 55.

Profile 61: Anna Eleanor Roosevelt

1. Edward P. Morgan, ed., *This I Believe*, (New York: Simon & Schuster, 1952), 155.
2. Joseph P. Lash, *Eleanor and Franklin*, (New York: Norton, 1971), 48.
3. Ibid.
4. Ibid., 49.
5. Ibid., 241.
6. Blanche Wiesen Cook, *Eleanor Roosevelt: 1884–1933*, vol. 1, (New York: Viking, 1992), 94.
7. Morgan, *This I Believe*, 155.
8. Ibid.
9. Ibid.
10. James Roosevelt with Bill Libby, *My Parents: A Differing View*, (London: W. H. Allen, 1977), 49.
11. Jess Flemion and Coleen M. O'Connor, *Eleanor Roosevelt: An American Journey*, (San Diego, CA: San Diego State University Press, 1987), 342.
12. Ibid.
13. Joseph P. Lash, *Eleanor Roosevelt: A Friend's Memoir*, (Garden City, NY: Doubleday, 1964), 150.
14. Ibid., 321.
15. Ibid.
16. Ibid., 150.
17. Ibid., 47.
18. Ibid., 198.
19. Ibid., 80.
20. Ibid., 287.
21. Ibid., 291.
22. Morgan, *This I Believe*, 155–156.
23. Peter Collier with David Horowitz, *The Roosevelts: An American Saga*, (New York: Simon & Schuster Trade, 1995), 469.
24. Elliott Roosevelt and James Brough, *Mother R.: Eleanor Roosevelt's Untold Story*, (New York: Putnam, 1977), 197.
25. Morgan, *This I Believe*, 155–156.
26. Joseph P. Lash, *Eleanor: The Years Alone*, (New York: Norton, 1972), 327.

Profile 62: Hugo Lafayette Black

1. Hugo L. Black and Elizabeth Black, *Mr. Justice and Mrs. Black*, (New York: Random House, 1986), 21.
2. Roger Newman, *Hugo Black: A Biography*, (New York: Pantheon, 1994), 68.
3. Black, *Mr. Justice and Mrs. Black*, 70.
4. Ibid.
5. Newman, *Hugo Black*, 521.

6. Black, *Mr. Justice and Mrs. Black*, 143.
7. Ibid.
8. Newman, *Hugo Black*, 521.
9. Ibid.
10. Ibid., 362.
11. Ibid.
12. Ibid., 522.
13. Ibid.
14. Ibid.
15. Ibid.
16. Ibid., 521.
17. Black, *Mr. Justice and Mrs. Black*, 95.

Profile 63: Marcus Moziah Garvey
1. Rupert Lewis, *Marcus Garvey: Anti-Colonial Champion*, (Trenton, NJ: Africa World Press, 1988), 17, 20.
2. Robert A. Hill, ed., *Marcus Garvey: Life and Lessons*, (Berkeley: University of California Press, 1987), 167.
3. Ibid., 221.
4. Ibid., 221–222.
5. Ibid., 222.
6. Ibid., 229.
7. Ibid., 226.
8. Ibid., 226–227.
9. Ibid., 231.
10. Ibid., 229–230.
11. Ibid., 231.
12. Lewis, *Marcus Garvey: Anti-Colonial Champion*, 7.
13. Hill, *Marcus Garvey: Life and Lessons*, 230.

Profile 64: Walter Perry Johnson
1. Letter, Carolyn Johnson Thomas to C. Bernard Ruffin, November 21, 1995.
2. Henry W. Thomas, *Walter Johnson: Baseball's Big Train*, (Washington: Phenom Press, 1995), 4.
3. Carolyn Johnson Thomas, Letter to C. Bernard Ruffin.
4. Ibid.
5. Ibid.
6. Ibid.
7. Henry W. Thomas, *Walter Johnson*, 348.
8. Carolyn Johnson Thomas, Letter to C. Bernard Ruffin.

Profile 65: Knute Kenneth Rockne
1. Jerry Brondfield, *Rockne: The Coach, the Man, the Legend*, (New York: Random House, 1976), 172.
2. Ibid., 177.
3. Ibid., 173.
4. Ibid., 174–175.
5. Ibid., 176.
6. Ibid., 17.

Profile 66: Irving Berlin
1. Mary Ellin Barrett, *Irving Berlin: A Daughter's Memoir*, (New York: S & S Trade, 1994), 72.
2. Ibid., 123.
3. Ibid., 124.
4. Ibid., 123.
5. Ibid., 72.
6. Ibid., 293.
7. Ibid., 213.
8. Ibid., 217.
9. Ibid., 218.

Profile 67: Rose Fitzgerald Kennedy

1. Rose Fitzgerald Kennedy, *Times to Remember*, (New York: Doubleday, 1995), 12.
2. Ibid.
3. Ibid., 140.
4. Ibid., 141.
5. Ibid., 424.
6. Ibid., 140.
7. Ibid., 445.
8. Ibid.
9. Ibid.
10. Ibid.
11. Ibid., 411
12. Ibid., 446

Profile 68: Earl Warren

1. Jack Harrison Pollac, *Earl Warren: The Judge Who Changed America*, (Englewood Cliffs, NJ: Prentice-Hall, 1979), 351.
2. John D. Weaver, *Warren: The Man, The Court, The Era*, (Boston: Little, Brown, & Co., 1967), 268.
3. Pollac, *Earl Warren*, 212.
4. Earl Warren, *The Memoirs of Earl Warren*, (Garden City, NY: Doubleday, 1977), 122.
5. Ibid., 316.
6. Pollac, *Earl Warren*, 212.

Profile 69: George Herman (Babe) Ruth, Sr.

1. Telephone interview, the Rev. Thomas H. Kaufman, O.P., October, 1995.
2. Babe Ruth and Bob Considine, *The Babe Ruth Story*, (New York: Dutton, 1948), 233.
3. Marshall Smelser, *The Life that Ruth Built: A Biography*, (New York: Quadrangle, 1975), 540.
4. Ruth and Considine, *The Babe Ruth Story*, 233.
5. *New York World -Telegram*, August 17, 1948.
6. Kaufman interview.
7. Ibid.
8. Ibid. (In response to the question, "Did Babe Ruth trust Jesus Christ as his Lord and Savior?")
9. *New York World-Telegram*, August 17, 1948.
10. Ibid.

Profile 70: Oscar Hammerstein II

1. Raymond Swing, ed., *This I Believe: 2*, (New York: Simon & Schuster, 1954), 68–69.
2. Hugh Fordin, *Getting to Know Him: A Biography of Oscar Hammerstein II*, (New York: Da Capo, 1977), 349.
3. Ibid., 16.
4. Ibid.
5. Ibid., 357–359.

Profile 71: Ethel Waters

1. Twila Knaack, *Ethel Waters: I Touched a Sparrow*, (Waco, TX: Word Books, 1978), 100.
2. Ibid., 102.
3. Ibid., 108.
4. Hugh T. Kerr and John M. Mulder, ed., *Conversions: The Christian Experience*, (Grand Rapids, MI: Zondervan, 1983), 220.
5. Ibid.
6. Ethel Waters, *To Me, It's Wonderful*, (New York: Harper, 1972), 14.
7. Kerr and Mulder, *Conversions*, 222.
8. Waters, *To Me, It's Wonderful*, 15.
9. Ibid., 135–136.
10. Ibid., 28.
11. Ibid., 32.
12. Ibid., 81.
13. Juliann DeKorte, *Ethel Waters: Finally Home*, (Old Tappan, NJ: Fleming Revell, 1978), 27.
14. Waters, *To Me, It's Wonderful*, 142.
15. Ibid., 137.
16. Ibid., 138.

17. Ibid.
18. Ibid., 78.
19. Ibid., 49–50.
20. Knaack, *Ethel Waters: I Touched a Sparrow*, 111.
21. DeKorte, *Ethel Waters: Finally Home*, 79.
22. Ibid., 104.
23. Ibid., 110.
24. Ibid., 111.
25. Ibid., 108.
26. Ibid., 114.
27. Ibid., 120.
28. Ibid., 79.

Profile 72: Edward Kennedy (Duke) Ellington
1. Edward Kennedy Ellington, *Music Is My Mistress*, (Garden City, NY: Doubleday, 1973), 15.
2. Ibid., 12.
3. Ibid., 15
4. Ibid., 259
5. Ibid., 12.
6. Ruth Ellington Boatwright, interview, July 1, 1996.
7. Ibid.
8. Rosina Harvey Corrothers-Tucker, interview, early 1970s. She was a sister of Marietta Harvey Clinkscales.
9. Boatwright, interview.
10. Ibid.
11. John García Gensel, letter, January 19, 1996.
12. James Lincoln Collier, *Duke Ellington*, (New York: Oxford University Press, 1987), 291.
13. Gensel, letter.
14. Boatwright, interview.
15. Even Stwertka, *Duke Ellington: A Life of Music*, (New York: Impact Biographies, 1994), 120.
16. Boatwright, interview.
17. Stwertka, *Duke Ellington*, 106.
18. Boatwright, interview.
19. Ellington, *Music Is My Mistress*, 259.
20. Text of a 1989 lecture by Dr. Mark S. Harvey, entitled "New World A'Comin: Religious Perspective on the Legacy of Duke Ellington," quoted in letter from John García Gensel, January 19, 1996.
21. Gensel, letter.
22. Ellington, *Music Is My Mistress*, 260.
23. Ibid., 452.
24. Ibid., 468.
25. Gensel, letter.
26. Boatwright, interview.
27. John Edward Hasse, *Beyond Category: The Life and Genius of Duke Ellington*, (New York: Simon and Schuster, 1993), 357.
28. Ellington, *Music Is My Mistress*, 469.
29. Boatwright, interview.
30. Hasse, *Beyond Category*, 383.
31. Ellington, *Music Is My Mistress*, 468.
32. Gensel, letter.
33. Ibid.
34. Boatwright, interview.

Profile 73: Gary Cooper
1. George Carpozi, *The Gary Cooper Story*, (New Rochelle, NY: Arlington House, 1970), 208.
2. Ibid.
3. Ibid., 206.
4. Ibid., 206–207.
5. Ibid., 207.
6. Ibid., 209.
7. Ibid., 210

8. Ibid., 215.
9. Ibid.
10. Hector Arce, *Gary Cooper, An Intimate Biography*, (New York: Morton, 1979), 279.

Profile 74: Margaret Mead

1. Jane Howard, *Margaret Mead: A Life*, (New York: Simon and Schuster, 1984), 341.
2. Ibid., 32.
3. Robert Cassidy, *Margaret Mead: A Voice for the Century*, (New York: Universe Books, 1982), 139.
4. Howard, *Margaret Mead*, 31.
5. Mary Catherine Bateson, *With a Daughter's Eye: A Memoir of Margaret Mead and Gregory Bateson*, (New York: HarperPerennial, 1994), 100.
6. Howard, *Margaret Mead*, 340.
7. Bateson, *With a Daughter's Eye*, 101.
8. Ibid.
9. Howard, *Margaret Mead*, 341.
10. Ibid., 340.
11. Ibid., 343.
12. Ibid., 349.
13. Ibid., 350.
14. Ibid., 347.
15. Ibid., 348.
16. Ibid., 352.
17. Cassidy, *Margaret Mead*, 142.
18. Ibid., 140.
19. Ibid.
20. Ibid., 146.
21. Ibid.
22. Ibid., 147.
23. Ibid., 150.
24. Howard, *Margaret Mead: A Life*, 412.
25. Ibid., 422.
26. Ibid., 424.

Profile 75: Charles Augustus Lindbergh

1. Dorothy Herrmann, *Anne Morrow Lindbergh: A Gift for Life*, (New York: Ticknor & Fields, 1992), 204.
2. Ibid.
3. Charles A. Lindbergh, *Autobiography of Values*, (New York: Harcourt, Brace, 1978), 384.
4. Ibid., 5.
5. Ibid., 384.
6. Ibid., 308.
7. Ibid., 119.
8. Ibid., 6.
9. Ibid., 331–332.
10. Ibid., 383.
11. Ibid., 384.
12. Ibid., 331
13. Ibid., 385.

Profile 76: Clare Boothe Luce

1. Hugh T. Kerr and John M. Mulder, eds., *Conversions*, (Grand Rapids, MI: Eerdmans, 1983), 248–250.
2. Ralph G. Martin, *Henry and Clare: An Intimate Portrait of the Luces*, (New York: G. P. Putnam's Sons, 1991), 236.
3. Ibid., 257.
4. Ibid., 231.
5. Ibid., 258.
6. Ibid.
7. Ibid., 259.
8. Stephen Shadegg, *Clare Boothe Luce: A Biography*, (New York: Simon and Schuster, 1970), 210–211.
9. Ibid., 21.
10. Martin, *Henry and Clare*, 260.
11. Wilfred Sheed, *Clare Boothe Luce*, (New York: E. P. Dutton, 1982), 110.

12. Ibid., 8.
13. Martin, *Henry and Clare*, 288.
14. Ibid., 348.
15. Ibid., 404.
16. Telephone conversation with Wilfred Sheed, December 12, 1996.
17. Sheed, *Clare Boothe Luce*, 8.
18. Ibid., 160.
19. Telephone conversation with Wilfred Sheed.

Profile 77: Vincent Thomas Lombardi

1. Michael O'Brien, *Vince: A Personal Biography of Vince Lombardi*, (New York: Morrow, 1987), 186.
2. Ibid., 368.
3. Ibid., 375.
4. Ibid., 187.
5. Ibid., 25.
6. Ibid., 26.
7. Ibid., 28.
8. Jerry Kramer, ed., *Lombardi: Winning Is the Only Thing*, (New York: Thomas Crowell, 1976), 33.
9. O'Brien, *Vince*, 36.
10. Ibid., 188.
11. Ibid.
12. Kramer, *Lombardi*, 65
13. Ibid., 143.
14. O'Brien, *Vince*, 360.
15. Ibid., 186.
16. Ibid.
17. Ibid., 187.
18. Ibid.
19. Ibid., 26.
20. Ibid., 189.
21. Ibid., 188.
22. Ibid., 189.
23. Ibid., 186.
24. Ibid., 189.
25. Ibid.
26. Ibid., 265.
27. Ibid., 373.
28. Ibid., 375.

Profile 78: Richard Tucker

1. Telephone interview with Barry Tucker, June 19, 1995.
2. Ibid.
3. Ibid.
4. Ibid.
5. James A. Drake, *Richard Tucker, A Biography*, (New York: Dutton, 1984), 137.
6. Ibid., 220.
7. Barry Tucker, telephone interview.
8. F. Paul Driscoll, "The Tucker Review," *Opera News*, January 21, 1995, 20.
9. Barry Tucker, telephone interview.
10. Ibid.
11. Ibid.
12. Ibid.
13. Ibid.
14. Ibid.

Profile 79: John Fitzgerald Kennedy

1. Telephone conversation with Pierre Salinger, February 22, 1996.
2. Edmund Fuller and David E. Green, *God in the White House: The Faiths of America's Presidents*, (New York: Crown, 1968), 221.
3. Ibid., 222.
4. Albert J. Menendez, *John F. Kennedy: Catholic and Humanist,* (Buffalo, NY: Prometeus Books, 1979), 2.

5. Arthur M. Schlesinger, Jr., *Robert F. Kennedy and His Times,* (Boston: Houghton-Mifflin, 1978), 60.
6. Rose Fitzgerald Kennedy, *Times to Remember,* (New York: Doubleday, 1995), 141.
7. Menendez, *John F. Kennedy: Catholic and Humanist,* 66.
8. Ibid., 2.
9. Ibid.
10. Kennedy, *Times to Remember,* 144.
11. Ibid.
12. Salinger, telephone conversation.
13. Theodore Sorensen, telephone conversation, March 8, 1996.
14. Menendez, *John F. Kennedy,* 66–67.
15. Ibid., 67.
16. Schlesinger, *Robert F. Kennedy and His Times,* 17.
17. Ibid., 602.
18. Ibid.

Profile 80: Leonard Bernstein
1. Meryle Secrest, *Leonard Bernstein: A Life,* (New York: Alfred A. Knopf, 1994), 16.
2. Ibid.
3. Joan Peyser, *Bernstein: A Biography,* (New York: Beech Tree Books, 1987), 437.
4. Ibid.
5. Humphrey Burton, *Leonard Bernstein,* (New York: Doubleday, 1994), 338.
6. Peyser, *Bernstein,* 175.
7. Secrest, *Leonard Bernstein: A Life,* 107.
8. Burton, *Leonard Bernstein,* 403.
9. Leoard Bernstein, *Symphony No. 3 (Kaddish),* (New York: Circle Blue Printing Co., 1963), 31–32.
10. Peyser, *Bernstein,* 328–329.
11. Secrest, *Leonard Bernstein: A Life,* 290.
12. Burton, *Leonard Bernstein,* 408.
13. Leonard Bernstein, *Mass,* (New York: Circle Blue Printing Co., 1971), 22–23.
14. Ibid., 31
15. Burton, *Leonard Bernstein,* 527.
16. Ibid., 528.

Profile 81: Jack Roosevelt Robinson
1. Jackie Robinson, *I Never Had It Made: An Autobiography,* (New York: Putnam, 1972), 143.
2. David Falkner, *Great Time Coming: The Life of Jackie Robinson, from Baseball to Birmingham,* (New York: Simon and Schuster, 1995), 25.
3. J. Robinson, *I Never Had It Made,* 7–8.
4. Rachel Robinson, *Jackie Robinson: An Intimate Portrait,* (New York: Harry N. Abrams, 1996), 18.
5. Sharon Robinson, *Stealing Home: An Intimate Family Portrait by the Daughter of Jackie Robinson,* (New York: HarperCollins, 1996), 153.
6. R. Robinson, *Jackie Robinson,* 18.
7. Ibid., 167.
8. Brief conversation with Rachel Robinson, Washington, D.C., September 23, 1996.
9. S. Robinson, *Stealing Home,* 153.
10. Edward P. Morgan, ed., *This I Believe,* (New York: Simon and Schuster, 1952), 151–152.

Profile 82: Flannery O'Connor
1. Sally Fitzgerald, ed. *Flannery O'Connor: The Habit of Being,* (New York: Farrar, Straus, Giroux, 1979), 90.
2. Rosemary M. Magee, ed., *Conversations with Flannery O'Connor,* (Jackson: University of Mississippi Press, 1987), 10.
3. Fitzgerald, *Flannery O'Connor,* 164.
4. Ibid., 131–132.
5. Magee, *Conversations with Flannery O'Connor,* 87.
6. Fitzgerald, *Flannery O'Connor,* 92.
7. Ibid., 521.
8. Ibid., 572.
9. Ibid., 286.
10. Ibid., 489.

11. Ibid., 338.
12. Ibid., 92–93.
13. Ibid., 337.
14. Ibid., 341.
15. Ibid.
16. Ibid., 345.
17. Ibid., 346.
18. Ibid.
19. Ibid., 307.
20. Ibid., 100.
21. Ibid., 460.
22. Ibid., 92.
23. Ibid., 354.
24. Ibid., 477–478.
25. Ibid., 361.
26. Ibid., 354.
27. Susan Balee, *Flannery O'Connor: Literary Prophet of the South*, (New York: Chelsea House, 1995), 88.
28. Ibid., 91.
29. Balee, *Flannery O'Connor: Literary Prophet*, 97.
30. Fitzgerald, *Flannery O'Connor*, 577.

Profile 83: Robert Francis Kennedy
1. Telephone interview, Pierre Salinger, February 22, 1996.
2. Warren Rogers, *When I Think of Bobby*, (New York: HarperCollins, 1993), 26.
3. Lester and Irene David, *Bobby Kennedy: The Making of a Folk Hero*, (New York: Dodd, Mead, 1986), 24.
4. Ibid., 223.
5. Arthur M. Schlesinger, Jr., *Robert F. Kennedy and His Times*, (Boston: Houghton-Mifflin, 1978), 814.
6. David, *Bobby Kennedy*, 223.
7. Schlesinger, *Robert F. Kennedy*, 814.
8. Ibid., 655.
9. Ibid., 814.